AF361347

FASHIONING SPANISH CINEMA

Costume, Identity, and Stardom

Fashioning Spanish Cinema

Costume, Identity, and Stardom

JORGE PÉREZ

UNIVERSITY OF TORONTO PRESS

Toronto Buffalo London

ISBN 978-1-4875-0911-8 (cloth)
ISBN 978-1-4875-3974-0 (EPUB)
ISBN 978-1-4875-3973-3 (PDF)

Toronto Iberic

Library and Archives Canada Cataloguing in Publication

Title: Fashioning Spanish cinema : costume, identity, and stardom /
Jorge Pérez.
Names: Pérez, Jorge, 1976– author.
Series: Toronto Iberic ; 61.
Description: Series statement: Toronto Iberic series ; 61 |
Includes bibliographical references and index.
Identifiers: Canadiana (print) 20210228342 | Canadiana (ebook) 20210228377 |
ISBN 9781487509118 (hardcover) | ISBN 9781487539740 (EPUB) |
ISBN 9781487539733 (PDF)
Subjects: LCSH: Costume design – Spain. | LCSH: Motion pictures – Spain –
History. | LCSH: Fashion design – Spain.
Classification: LCC PN1995.9.C56 P47 2021 | DDC 791.4302/60946–dc23

This book has been supported by the Peter T. Flawn Centennial Professorship
at the University of Texas at Austin.

University of Toronto Press acknowledges the financial assistance to its
publishing program of the Canada Council for the Arts and the Ontario Arts
Council, an agency of the Government of Ontario.

Canada Council   Conseil des Arts
for the Arts   du Canada

ONTARIO ARTS COUNCIL
CONSEIL DES ARTS DE L'ONTARIO
an Ontario government agency
un organisme du gouvernement de l'Ontario

Funded by the   Financé par le
Government gouvernement
of Canada   du Canada

Canada

Contents

Illustrations

Acknowledgments

I would like to acknowledge the amazing support I have received from my current institution, the University of Texas at Austin, to complete this book expeditiously. A Tomás Rivera Regents Professorship put at my disposal generous funds to purchase materials and to attend professional conferences to present content from the manuscript. A Research Travel Grant from the Center for European Studies made possible an extended period of archival research in Spain in the summer 2018 that was crucial to the development of this project. Last but certainly not least, a semester leave in spring 2019 released me from all teaching and administrative responsibilities, thus allowing me the time and peaceful state of mind to write the last portion of the manuscript and craft a book proposal.

One section of chapter 1 originally appeared as an article entitled "The Noir Side of Couture: Balenciaga and Luis Marquina's *Alta costura* (1954)," in *Film, Fashion and Consumption* vol. 8, issue 2 (2019), and another section will appear in the volume *Fashioning Spain* (forthcoming from Bloomsbury). A reduced version of chapter 2 appeared as an article entitled "Significant Outfits: Almodóvar Wears Chanel," in *Modern Language Notes*, vol. 133, no. 2, 2018. I wish to express my gratitude to the publishers for their permission to use material here. I presented material from the manuscript at invited talks at University of Alabama, Tuscaloosa, Durham University, and University of California, Santa Barbara. The feedback I received in those venues helped me refine my arguments and ideas.

I want to express deep gratitude to my editor at the University of Toronto Press, Mark Thompson, for his efficiency and guidance throughout the publication process. I also want to thank the editor of the Toronto Iberic series, Robert Davidson, for his strong support of this project. The two anonymous readers selected by the press were very helpful with their suggestions on the first draft of the manuscript. I also want to thank Joanna Zuckerman Bernstein and Robin Myers for their excellent work editing parts of the manuscript.

I am beholden to the staff of the Filmoteca Española, the Biblioteca Nacional, and the Museo del Traje in Madrid for their help granting me access to archives and materials over the years. At the Filmoteca, special thanks go to José Luis Estarrona and Trinidad del Río for their continued help identifying films and facilitating film stills for publication. At the Museo del Traje, I want to thank curator Juan Gutiérrez for his kindness in making available the resources of the museum. Christian Mieves deserves a special mention for his help converting film stills into high resolution images.

A number of colleagues at the University of Texas have been extremely supportive of this project. Jossianna Arroyo-Martínez and Héctor Domínguez Ruvalcaba have always offered their friendship and support. Jossianna has also inspired me with her own colourful fashion choices. Luis Cárcamo-Huechante has been my writing partner in crime, as we have set up camp at many coffee shops of East Austin. Sam Vong, now gone to pursue bigger and better endeavours at the Smithsonian Museum, hosted wonderful dinner parties along with Luis. Occasionally, he was also a great clubbing buddy. I wrote a significant chunk of the manuscript while serving as chair of my department. I wish to thank the staff members in Spanish and Portuguese, especially Lisa Mailloux, for making my life easy during that period with their efficiency and also for helping me as top-notch fashion consultants.

I need to recognize colleagues and friends from other institutions who have helped me during the writing of this book. Silvia Bermúdez, Ana Corbalán, Santiago Fouz-Hernández, Roberta Johnson, Alfredo Martínez-Expósito, Yajaira Padilla, and Parisa Tadrissi deserve my gratitude for sharing words of advice and bibliographical references, for reading portions of the manuscript, or simply for their comforting words.

Two other people deserve special thanks. As always, my mother has been the best research assistant I could ever have. As a major fashionista, she has deep knowledge of styles, fabric choices, and cuts. Since I don't have formal training in fashion studies, her insights have been super helpful. Our daily Skype chats during lunch break often turned into costume analysis sessions. My partner, Matthew Henderson, was extremely patient with my being perpetually missing in action and in front of the computer. He gave up holding me accountable for my broken promises. I always promise him this will be the last research book I write, and I always change my mind. Books are gone to press, new book projects appear, but he always sticks around. Thank you, *pelirrojo*.

A Note on Translations

English translations of film dialogues and quotes from written sources are my own, unless otherwise indicated.

FASHIONING SPANISH CINEMA

Costume, Identity, and Stardom

Fashion, Costume, and Spanish Cinema

About half an hour into Pedro Almodóvar's *Volver* (2006), we see Raimunda (Penélope Cruz) pushing a shopping cart that is crammed with groceries for a catered lunch. Critical responses to the film have noted that this sequence engages in an intertextual dialogue with Italian neorealism through the camerawork and editing (a long take in deep focus without editing cuts), as well as through a particular detail of the costume: the enhancement of Raimunda's skirt with padding at the back, which is reminiscent of Anna Magnani's working-class maternal femininity. Much praise has focused on Penélope Cruz's performance as she walks with her artificial butt extension, which Steven Marsh calls "a spectral supplement to her own 'natural' body, one that links the physical body to *Volver*'s filmic legacy" ("Missing" 351). When I first watched the film, I was captivated by Cruz's masterful hip-swaying. For full disclosure, though, I was mesmerized by the look as a whole: the riveting combination of her clothes, accessories, hairstyle, and make-up. Raimunda is wearing a simple yet close-fitting pencil skirt and a lacy shirt (see fig. I.1) an outfit created for her by costume designer Sabine Daigeler, who was much celebrated (and Goya-nominated) for combining original designs with clothes she found at flea markets. The black outfit gives her an air of severity. Black, after all, is the national colour of mourning, and she has just stored her dead husband in a pantry refrigerator until she has the time and means to dispose of the body properly. The austere black also evokes an anti-hedonist mindset. It suggests that she has business to take care of – finding enough produce to cook a meal for thirty people and making her husband disappear so that her daughter is not incriminated – and no time for earthly pleasures.

Still, there is something undeniably magnetic about this outfit, especially in combination with other components of her look. Raimunda's hair, arranged in a perfectly loose but flattering updo; her gold hoop

Fig. I.1. Raimunda's iconic grocery shopping outfit in *Volver*

Fig. I.2. Raimunda's trendsetting wedge espadrille sandals in *Volver*

earrings; her dark look "strengthened by a liberal use of black eye-liner" (Smith, "Women" 16); and, above all, the shoes, Castañer wedge espadrilles laced up her ankles, complement this sober yet fashionable ensemble, one that delivers a sense of ordinary elegance for working women with flair but little time for grooming (see fig. I.2). In contrast to Almodóvar's previous homage to the female stars of Italian neorealism via the character of Gloria (Carmen Maura) in *¿Qué he hecho yo para merecer esto?* (1984), Raimunda radiates both sensuality and a casually polished sense of style that beautifies working-class femininity. I was not alone in my fervent reaction to Raimunda's grocery shopping out-fit. It became an iconic look – it even appeared as the cover image for

Alberto Mira's *Historical Dictionary of Spanish Cinema* (2010) – that set trends among Spanish women and even increased the sales of wedge espadrilles that season (Castillo and Prats 141; Smith, "Women" 16).

The fuss over the shoes was not entirely surprising. First of all, they are not the generic wedge espadrille sandals a working-class woman would buy at her neighbourhood discount store. The original design, especially the creative entwining of the laces around each other and up the ankles as well as the high-quality natural fabric of the shoes' back support, indicates an artisanal production process for this particular pair of Castañer's (the final credits confirm the use of this brand). The shoes are highlighted later in the film as well. Raimunda pays a surprise visit to her sister Sole (Lola Dueñas), where their supposedly dead mother, Irene (Carmen Maura), is hiding. Two close-ups of the shoes, both POV shots from Irene's perspective as she hides under the bed, allow us to contemplate the unique details of the shoes' design and materials. As in other Almodóvar films that prominently feature high-heeled shoes, such as *Mujeres al borde de un ataque de nervios* (1988), *Tacones lejanos* (1991), and *La flor de mi secreto* (1995), Raimunda's wedge espadrilles serve as a metaphor for the significance of temporality in the film's overall conversation. As the first part of her daughter that Irene sees from the floor, they physically and metaphorically link past and present, connecting ghosts and the dead with the living. Raimunda paces the room while Irene watches her shoes in motion, their back-and-forth thus emphasizing the chronological progression. The image functions almost as a reality check for Irene: she is suddenly forced to deal with the passing of time, reminded that she will have to face her daughter and address past traumas. At one point, Raimunda stands right in front of the bed, so close that Irene can almost touch the shoes, which represent the return of a vintage style as much as of what this family had repressed – unfinished business between mother and daughter.

Given all of the above, the choice of Castañer wedge espadrilles is brilliant, as these shoes connote the reconciliation of time frames and the fusion of popular forms of footwear and high fashion. Espadrille sandals have been traditional footwear for peasants and soldiers on the Mediterranean cost of Spain and France since at least the fourteenth century; they are mentioned in a document written in Catalan that dates from 1322. However, more primitive forms can be traced back as far as ancient Egypt, before their later adoption by the Romans (Garrudo). The Catalan brand Castañer first created the wedge espadrilles for Yves Saint-Laurent in the 1970s.[1] Castañer was able to translate Saint-Laurent's vision into the new design, which became a major hit that went on to inspire other designers; for example, they created a leather version for Jean Paul Gaultier in the late 1980s. Since then, these shoes have become a summer fashion classic, and, in *Volver*, they evoke something closer to their humble origins.[2] Interestingly, the "Penélope Cruz effect" had a decisive impact on the resurgence of this classic in 2006. However, no such effect was noticeable fourteen years earlier: Cruz had already rocked a pair of black wedge espadrilles in a similar sequence in *Jamón, jamón* (Bigas Luna, 1992), her big-screen debut. In that film, a very young Cruz plays Silvia, a teenager of lowly origins who works in an underwear factory and has to help her mother with the daily household chores. In one sequence, Silvia walks home carrying a heavy bag of groceries and wearing a pair of wedge espadrilles. Silvia's shoes had a simpler design than Raimunda's, which meant they were similar to the affordable models that young Spanish women could find in stores, but they did not set a new trend. At that point, Cruz was a debut actor. By 2006, however, she was a global star, and a measure of her status was the swirling speculation about what she wore both onscreen and off (more about this in chapter 5).

I have commented in depth on this costume because it encapsulates the overarching concerns of this book. The costume serves to construct the character in a credible way, thus imbuing the story with narrative purpose. Simultaneously, it calls attention to itself as a discourse beyond the "mandatory bridesmaid status afforded to costume" in film (Bruzzi, *Undressing* xv); that is, as a compelling signifying element, a "costume idiolect" (Gaines, "Costume" 205), not entirely contingent on narrative or characterization for its meaning. Raimunda's clothes in *Volver* work in tandem with make-up and hair to create an entire look that foregrounds issues of class and gender; together, they articulate a unique and widely imitated image of working-class femininity. Throughout this book, I will analyse a wide array of outfits in Spanish cinema, all of which hold paramount importance to the films' engagement with questions of identity – identity as related to gender, sexuality, race, ethnicity, class, nationhood, and so on. Costume thus evokes broader issues beyond the cinematic text. It constitutes a form of non-verbal communication, delivering visual representations that express and create both individual and social identities, even if these identities seem to be multiple, fluid, mutable, unstable – rather than merely reflecting them. Clothes, as Diana Crane observes, are a key tool in the construction of identity (171). In acknowledging this point, we must also consider the possibility that costume might have a social impact, sometimes even influencing fashion trends beyond the film – as was the case with the wedge espadrilles worn by Penélope Cruz in

Volver. This possibility leads me to an additional concern I will explore in this book: how the intersections between costume and fashion are relevant to understanding and theorizing film stardom.

Fashioning Spanish Cinema is a timely book because Spanish film studies have paid only limited attention to costume and fashion. Apart from several contributions to a volume edited by David Arranz, the work of Kathleen Vernon and Eva Woods on the early periods of Spanish cinema, and three essays in a recent issue of the journal *Film, Fashion and Consumption* (number 8, issue 2, 2019), only Pedro Almodóvar's films have prompted analyses that explicitly focus on the function of costumes and their relationship with fashion (Dapena; Pérez, "Significant"; Smith, *Vision* 37–55, and fragments of *Desire*). I do not mean to suggest that no one else has addressed costume in relation to other visual components of the film image in the context of Spanish cinema, but rather that costume analysis has not been the exclusive or even primary focus of such studies. To my knowledge, no monographs in English (or Spanish, or any other language, for that matter) have been devoted to costume design in Spanish film, which makes this book the first of its kind. However, there are signs of growing interest in fashion and clothing within the broader field of Iberian cultural studies, suggesting that further consideration of this topic is on its way.[3]

I must also clarify what I do not attempt to deliver. This book offers the first sustained analysis of the importance of costume in Spanish cinema, an analysis that encompasses examples from different periods and genres. However, readers should expect neither a comprehensive history of costume design in Spain nor a painstaking account of fashion movements. Informative histories of fashion's role in Spanish society and culture can be found, for instance, in the work of Josefina Figueras and Margarita Rivière. By contrast, *Fashioning Spanish Cinema* is a piece of film studies scholarship. It centres on representations of clothing and fashion as costumes within Spanish cinema, and particularly on the significance of those costumes in relation to the visual styles and the narratives of the films selected for study. Moreover, this book also explores examples in which costumes have discursive autonomy, especially when it comes to the relationship between high fashion and cinema; in which costumes are essential to shaping the public image of film stars; in which costumes engage with broader issues of identity; and, relatedly, in which costumes impact everyday practices and fashion trends beyond the cinematic text. In so doing, the book explores the links between costume analysis and other fields and theoretical frameworks, for example, fashion studies, the history of dress, and gender and feminist studies, among others. My aim with this book is to contribute a

Spanish perspective – as Eugenia Paulicelli and Ginette Vincendeau have done in focusing on the Italian and French film industries, respectively – to the expanding interdisciplinary work on the intersections between film and fashion. This junction includes their connections to other related (sub-)fields, such as star studies and celebrity studies, that are developing with a marked Anglo-American slant.

As is true in other parts of the world, interdisciplinary crossings in the Spanish film context are not exempt from tensions among scholars and practitioners. Costume designers typically resent their work being affiliated with the fashion world, as they feel that the fashion industry generally misunderstands and co-opts their craft. In the ensuing sections of this introduction, I trace the contours of these tensions and debates. First, I discuss the historically marginal position of costume designers within film crews and their precarious status in the Spanish film industry. Next, I unpack the reasons why the association with fashion has been detrimental to costume design – and why, in turn, fashion has been subject to a number of biased cultural assumptions that dismiss it as frivolous, trivial, commodifying, and exploitative. While acknowledging the need to recognize the individuality of costume designers, I also argue that their preoccupation with distancing themselves from fashion designers has the equally adverse consequence of reinforcing their ancillary role within the film industry; in other words, they inadvertently incite descriptions of costume as a mere narrative prop. Towards the end of the introduction, I suggest that embracing the multifaceted intersections between film and fashion (both onscreen and off) can bring more benefits than downsides to the legitimacy of costume analysis within film studies, as it draws attention to clothing as utterly essential to cinema.

The Ugly Duckling of the Industry

The art of costume design in cinema has been something of a thankless job. Although it has a crucial role in a film's visual look, in making characters believable, and in the narrative coherence of the story, it goes largely unnoticed. Costume is a key signifying system within "the great sense-making machine of cinema," often more critical than other elements of a motion picture's mise en scène (Calefato, *The Clothed* 91), but is not always consciously received as such. In the words of Elizabeth Leese, as "the art that conceals art" (5), costume design has frequently been taken for granted or ignored altogether. This disregard is especially conspicuous in the context of realist cinema, when the symbiotic relationship between costume and character becomes so naturalized that costume ceases to be seen as costume at all. This is when the viewer perceives, according to Jane Gaines, one of the first scholars to deliver sustained and rigorous analyses of film costume, "a character as merely wearing clothes" ("Costume" 192). When endowed with extra substance and even signifying independence, costumes allegedly become superfluous distractions with the potential to break the "illusion and the spell of realism" (193). This view of costume has extended beyond realist cinema, with the regrettable outcome of reinforcing industry-related prejudices against the work of costume designers.

To begin with, they are ominously underpaid in relation to other film crew members. Deborah Nadoolman, who served two terms as president of the Costume Designers Guild, points out that in Hollywood "the base salary for the costume designer is nearly one third less than an entering production designer" (*Costume* 2012, 11). Moreover, given that they "do not own their sketches, or the costumes, and jewelry they design," costume designers "receive no credit or compensation for copies made from their designs for action figures and dolls, Halloween costumes, or fashion lines" (12). For a long time, the Academy of Motion Pictures did not even acknowledge the profession. Today, even though costume design has been recognized with its own Oscar category since 1948 (two of them, initially: one for black and white and another for colour films, until the categories were unified in 1967), "designers usually sit at the back of the credit bus" (Munich 2). It takes considerable work to locate them in online databases (on IMDb, you need an extra click before scrolling down), if they are even listed at all. For instance, Film Affinity, a movie recommendations website with three million users in Spain, does not provide any costume design information.

The Spanish film industry is a compelling case in point. Prior to the Spanish Civil War, the costume designer (*figurinista*) rarely appeared in Spanish film credits (one exception was Santiago Ortañón for his work in *La verbena de la paloma* [1935, Benito Perojo]). Designers' names were listed more frequently after the war, but the practice was still far from constant. Famous dressmakers of the early Francoist period, such as Pedro Rodríguez, Asunción Bastida, and Cristóbal Balenciaga, were sometimes publicized as the designers of the clothes worn by film stars, even when they weren't responsible for the entire wardrobe of a movie. Juan Bayo, Álex Navarro, and Roberto Olcina have noted that, exacerbating the struggle for individual recognition of design work, there was great confusion around the term "ambientación" at the time: a label that included costume, props, set design, and cinematography. Since some *figurinistas* also worked as set designers, the *sastrerías* Peris and Cornejo (two historic Spanish tailor shops devoted to film and theatre costume) were often credited as the costume designers of films (11). In the late 1940s and early 1950s, *figurinistas* such as Manuel Comba and José Caballero achieved significant recognition, including in film magazines like *Primer Plano* (more about this in chapter 1), especially for their work on major CIFESA productions. Such acknowledgments helped dignify the profession a bit; well into the 1960s, however, Spanish films continued to credit Peris or Cornejo for the costume design.

It is then no wonder that Yvonne Blake (1940–2018), perhaps the most celebrated costume designer in the Spanish industry, described her profession as "el patito feo del cine" (the ugly duckling of cinema) (Bayo, Navarro, and Olcina 85).[4] The 2016 appointment of the British-born but Spain-based Blake as president of the Spanish Academy of Cinematographic Arts and Sciences meant a great deal in terms of expanding recognition for costume design within the industry. Unfortunately, her unexpected death due to stroke-related complications curtailed her term in 2018. Blake asserted that a major handicap for the profession in Spain – as compared to national industries with stronger traditions, like Italy and the United Kingdom – is the lack of a formal system to train new generations of costume designers: "En España hay muy poca escuela y cero tradición en aprender el oficio. Diseñar vestuario es arte, pero también oficio" (In Spain, there is little instruction and zero tradition in learning the trade. Costume design is an art, but it is also a trade) (84). Tellingly, some of the costume designers interviewed by Bayo et al. could not pinpoint when or why they had become *figurinistas* (Eduardo de la Torre in 23; Javier Artiñano in 97; Pedro Moreno in 155), while others confessed that they arrived at costume design by accident (Gumersindo Andrés in 59; Yvonne Blake in 75; José María de Cossío in 119). Becoming a costume designer in Spain appears to be more a twist of fate than a vocation per se.

While Blake acknowledged recent progress in the appreciation of costume art (85), the number of professionals drawn to this sector of filmmaking seems unlikely to undergo a radical increase, especially given the inadequate resources at their disposal. As pioneering *figurinista* Eduardo Torre de la Fuente (1919–2009) noted: "los figurinistas siempre hemos sido el pariente pobre de los equipos cinematográficos" (costume designers have always been the poor relatives of film crews) (26). With this statement, he addresses not only how poorly remunerated costume designers have always been for their work, but also the limited funds made available to them in the average budget of a Spanish film production. Humberto Cornejo, a third-generation member of the Cornejo tailor house founded in 1920, points out that a typical Spanish film allocates between 1.5 and 2 per cent of its budget to costume design; in international films, the amount rises at least to 5 per cent (202). The only exception to this customary shortage of resources for costume design in the Spanish industry may be Pedro Almodóvar; after all, costume consistently plays a central role in his work, a priority reflected in more generous budgets. José María de Cossío, the costume designer for all of Almodóvar's films throughout the 1980s and 1990s with the exception of *La flor de mi secreto* (1995) – a history that earned him the nickname of "el chico Almodóvar" – has admitted that working with Almodóvar was a privilege because he had abundant resources at his fingertips (119). Moreover, he worked with a director who understood and valued his art (Bayo, Navarro, and Olcina 117–29). While more money does not necessarily translate into higher quality, it does give designers more options in terms of, say, fabric choices, and professionals they can hire to work on their design teams.

Costume designers working in the Anglo-American context often cite two external impediments that partially explain their field's struggle for recognition. One such obstacle is the word "costume," which connotes something vulgar rather than a refined art form; it "is invariably associated with Halloween, fancy dress, parade, theme park, Mardi Gras, carnival, and the clothes in fantasy and period films" (Nadoolman, *Costume* 2012, 8). Nadoolman's point is well taken: on several occasions, I myself have had to answer questions about the validity of my object of study, based on terminology that audience members have learned to associate with something ludicrous and thus lacking epistemic value. However, this factor alone cannot account for the hurdles facing costume design, particularly because the confusing nomenclature is not applicable to other languages and film industries in which this trade has confronted equal precariousness. In Spanish, for example, the technical term for costume design is "diseño de vestuario," or simply "vestuario," which does not carry the same negative connotations as the word "costume" in English.

The other oft-cited stumbling block for costume design is a more complex and controversial one: its association with fashion and, in particular, with what Deborah Nadoolman calls "the mellifluous but mistaken moniker 'fashion in film'" (*Dressed* xvi). This affiliation apparently complicates the conception of costume design and its status as a serious topic of academic enquiry. Costume is certainly not synonymous with fashion. Nadoolman defines it as among the signifying elements that a director can use to tell a story in film, so its effectiveness depends on how it is absorbed into the narrative, helps to sell a character, and supports actors in their work. By contrast, "disappearing is bad business for fashion designers," who aspire "to create a look that is recognizable enough that it can be copied, reproduced, and sold successfully at every marketable price point" (*Dressed* xxi). Moreover, audiences perceive film costumes two-dimensionally: their judgment is mediated by a distorting lens and photographed under a particular lighting. By contrast, the look created by a fashion designer is worn by a real person and can be seen in three dimensions and under diverse conditions depending on when and who wears it. For Nadoolman, costumes fulfil their role exclusively within the context of a movie, which means that they cannot be assessed beyond that context of enunciation; in other words, they have no dealings with real life (*Costume* 2003, 81). While I very much agree that the automatic conflation is simplistic and unfair, I would also insist that clear-cut distinctions or boundaries between fashion and costume can, in some cases, be hard to define. What's more, such boundaries do not necessarily help the cause: they generate their own problematic set of assumptions, including some avoidable anti-fashion biases that I will address in more detail below.

The argument that a costume designer's only concern should be to "telegraph information" about characters – an argument used to make the point that fashion and costume are antithetical endeavours because they have "directly opposing and contradictory purposes" (Nadoolman, *Costume* 2003, 9, 7) – warrants further discussion. For one thing, a costume designer's bread and butter is certainly to help actors create their characters and enhance the story. When this primary function is ineffectively fulfilled, the negative results are evident. In *Lobo* (Miguel Courtois, 2004), Eduardo Noriega is José María "Txema," a Basque construction worker who infiltrates the ETA terrorist group as a mole working for Franco's secret services in the last years of the regime. Most of the narrative takes place during 1973 and 1974, but Txema wears baggy jeans with a loose cut and faded colour in parts of the back – a style typical of the late 1990s and early 2000s – instead of the bell-bottoms that young folks used to wear in the early to mid-1970s. This is an example of a costume that calls attention to itself for the wrong reasons: it distracts from the narrative and makes it difficult for viewers to suspend their disbelief. But does this mean that costumes must categorically and universally vanish into the narrative? I wonder, as does Stella Bruzzi, how we should interpret the many instances when costumes make "spectacular interventions that interfere with the scenes in which they appear and impose themselves onto the character they adorn" (*Undressing* xv). In chapter 2, I analyse the knock-off Chanel suit worn by Agrado in *Todo sobre mi madre* (Pedro Almodóvar, 1999) as an example of a costume with narrative purpose, since it introduces one of the film's major themes: the concept of authenticity in relation to a performative understanding of identity. At the same time, the costume suggests other messages – for instance, it evokes a multifaceted discussion about the (anti)feminist legacy of Chanel's style – that do not wholly rely on narrative structure for signification.

Relatedly, another plausible question arises: what role do we ascribe to costume design in non-narrative films, where costume is part of a visual aesthetic that may not have an easily decoded representational value? Or in a film like Tarsem Singh's *The Fall* (2006), which is self-reflective about the concept of storytelling, and where Eiko Ishioka's spectacular costumes make radical interjections that trigger a narrative discontinuity between how one character tells the story and how another imagines it? In fact, Ishioka (1938–2012) was among the few costume designers to admit that she liked "designs that are innovative and monumental, not ones that simply explain the story or roles to the audience and end there" (Nadoolman, *Costume* 2003, 55). Her stimulating, out-of-the-ordinary costume aesthetic was certainly not everyone's cup of tea. For instance, renowned British costume designer James Acheson openly stated that he had little respect for the "'look at me' school – where the costumes are wearing the actors, rather than the actors wearing the costumes" (Nadoolman, *Costume* 2003, 21). But it is one thing to express personal distaste for a type of costuming that invigorates the visual lexicon of a film and quite another to negate that it should be considered costume design at all. This stance amounts to refuting the validity of avant-garde cinema just because it does not follow mainstream narrative conventions.

Furthermore, claiming that costume's sole raison d'être is character development at the service of storytelling denies viewers a host of other possible pleasures – some of which may exceed the purview of the costume designers themselves – when watching a film. These include, for example, the desires associated with the fetishistic relationships some people develop with clothes. Such desires may or may not have anything to do with sex. While eroticism is the most commonly recognized form of fetishism (and it is especially linked to specific types of apparel, such as underwear, leather garments, and high-heeled shoes), fetishism is not just about sexuality. As fashion historian Valerie Steele has shown, it is also about power and perception (*Fetish* 5). For Pam Cook, fetishistic obsessions with clothes can potentially be transgressive in how they play with identity and identification; they can easily undermine ingrained assumptions about social identities (*Fashioning* 46). Besides, costumes may stimulate the tactile sensorial experience that Laura Marks calls "haptic visuality," which evokes the sensation of touching the clothes with our eyes (xi). The tactile perspective is essential to chapter 3 of this book. There, I explore how the softness and pristine whiteness of the underwear worn by the juvenile delinquents of Eloy de la Iglesia's films seek not only to spark an erotic response in viewers, but also to inspire their sympathy for the vulnerability of the criminal yet morally honourable characters.

Another glitch in the argument that costume design is merely a directorial storytelling tool is that it treats the director as the sole author of a film, and thus as the creative force behind every technical aspect and signifying element within it. This is an old-fashioned view of film authorship – associated with the tradition of auteur criticism – that has been revised in favour of a more pluralist model that views a film not as the outcome of a single person's creative agency, but rather as a collaborative endeavour to which many agents contribute with their artistic and technical expertise (Jordan and Allinson 72–3). The director-centric stance contains an additional drawback when posed by Spanish costume designers. Since Spanish is not an inclusive, gender-neutral language, when *figurinistas* state that they see their job as supporting a filmmaker's creative vision, they are assuming, unconsciously or otherwise, a masculine identity for that director. For example, Javier Artiñano states: "De nada sirve hacer un vestuario maravilloso si no responde a las necesidades del director para contar su historia" (There is no point in creating fabulous costumes if they don't meet the director's needs in telling his story) (Bayo, Navarro, and Olcina 109). This is hardly an isolated example. The book *Vestir los sueños* interviews eleven distinguished *figurinistas* of the Spanish film industry – including three female designers, Yvonne Blake, Laia Huete, and Sonia Grande – yet none tries to address both genders, which makes one wonder whether they could even imagine working for a female filmmaker. In this context, their call for their work to be recognized creates another – gender-related – layer in the notorious imbalance among film crew members. Indeed, describing themselves as having a subservient role to an almighty male director does not help their cause.

Along these lines, costume designers' overemphasis on their dependent status with respect to other components of a film gratuitously creates, in my view, what we might call a "dependency fallacy." If we take a strict functionalist approach, no signifying element of a motion picture, regardless of its importance, is fully independent; each makes sense only in relation to the other elements that work together to produce the multidimensional form of communication that we experience as a film. For example, a screenplay is arguably one of the most crucial components of a movie (no script = no film). A screenplay, then, is the bedrock of what appears onscreen, but it is not in itself a film. Neither is the cast, however famous and outstanding the stars may be, or even the director, who often receives most of the credit for a film's success. My point is that costume designers need not contribute to the disproportionate acclamation and neglect that are typically projected onto certain aspects of film crews by belittling their own role – by depicting it as subordinate to what are conventionally seen as more important pieces of the product.

Fashion and Film, Fashion in Film, and the Fashion Film

Undoubtedly, the confusion over fashion has been detrimental to the status of costume analysis in film studies: it has exposed costume design to the same suspicions that fashion raises in academic circles. Pamela Church Gibson has succinctly described the likely causes of this neglect. One motive is the deep-rooted assumption that fashion is a frivolous endeavour, easily dismissed as lacking in substance. As Gilles Lipovetsky says in the opening line of his influential *The Empire of Fashion*, "[t]he question of fashion is not a fashionable one among intellectuals" (3).[5] Regrettably, leftist intellectuals (namely Frankfurt School thinkers such as Theodor Adorno and Max Horkheimer) have underpinned this inimical view of fashion. Applying a Marxist-based perspective, such thinkers have seen it as nothing but a quintessential expression of capitalist commodity fetishism.[6] Equally influential, and equally damaging to the legitimacy of fashion and costume studies, has been the belief, upheld in certain feminist currents, that fashion is among the major ways in which women exhibit themselves to indulge the male gaze (Church Gibson, "Film Costume" 36). This view originated in Simone de Beauvoir's conviction, vehemently expressed in *The Second Sex* (1949), that women's eroticization through clothes exists in direct proportion to their subjugation to masculine control. Drawing on de Beauvoir, prominent feminists such as Susan Brownmilller, Naomi Wolf, and Sheila Jeffreys have further developed these attacks on fashion, rejecting it as demeaning to women and alleging that it reinforces oppressive standards of female beauty as dictated by capitalism and the patriarchy.

Consciously or not, these feminist stances concurred with male fashion historians, psychologists, and sociologists who had posed problematic ideas on the subject of gender, fashion, and clothes. For instance, sociologist Georg Simmel, whose theories have been influential in fashion studies, claimed that women's emancipation could only be achieved through "indifference to fashion" (551). From a psychoanalytic perspective, psychologist John P. Flügel theorized clothes as an extension of the body with an ambivalent function: clothing could serve as protection for the body (for purposes of modesty, to hide its vulnerability), but it could also be used to display that body (as associated with sexual exhibitionism). His observations essentially portrayed women as more narcissistic than men – a conclusion that historian James Laver took a step further in asserting that women primarily used clothes to attract male attention (*Modesty* 14). At the core of this contention was what Flügel famously called "the Great Masculine Renunciation" (111). He coined this term to describe a tectonic shift in the history of clothing: men began to relinquish the flashy, elaborate styles they had used in the past (typically as a mark of distinction and wealth) and became exclusively concerned with practical dress.[7] Men, who became "excluded from the glitter of artifice" (Lipovetsky 74), left decorative attire and the quest for beauty to women, and men's self-imposed sartorial austerity led to the adoption of the black business suit as a kind of universal uniform, a symbol of cultural hegemony (Harvey). This notion reinforced the perception of women as increasingly passive, decorative objects who existed for male contemplation – and the perception of men's garb and appearance as important only insofar as it enhanced "their active roles"; that is, if it bolstered their occupation and social status (Craik 176). This provision also explains why "the history of men's fashion is perhaps principally, though not exclusively, a story of business attire" (R. Martin 3), and, furthermore, why "male fashions have played such a modest role in the history of fashion" (Svendsen 43).[8] Indeed, the masculinity of men who express interest in other types of clothing has long been called into question (Crane 179; Reilly and Cosbey xii). Although the male renunciation narrative has been criticized as somewhat reductionist (Breward 25; Edwards, *Men* 19; Entwistle 160–1),[9] and academic interest in men's fashion has increased significantly in recent years, these traditional gender-related assumptions about fashion and dress – and, above all, about the perception that male fashion is bound up in a series of denials (Craik 176) – still retain some power over us.[10]

These views have had a tangible impact on the study (or lack thereof) of film costuming. With respect to the context of classical Hollywood cinema, feminist film theory has placed considerable weight on establishing a correlation between female costume and the objectification of women. Among the implications of Laura Mulvey's influential article "Visual Pleasure and Narrative Cinema" was that costume has served as one of Hollywood's key technical devices: a device employed to offer spectacular displays of women's sexualized bodies for the erotic contemplation of the male protagonist's controlling look, as well as the spectator's, who invariably identifies with this voyeuristic male gaze.

For instance, commenting on the female character played by Grace Kelly in *Rear Window* (Alfred Hitchcock, 1954), Mulvey claims that "Lisa's exhibitionism has already been established by her obsessive interest in dress and style, in being a passive image of visual perfection" (45). As is widely known, ensuing feminist scholarship has questioned Mulvey's depiction of the film gaze as inherently male (Stacey; Kaplan) and – a crucial point for the purposes of my study – of fashion as an intrinsically frivolous concern (Wilson, *Adorned*). While not specifically about film, Elizabeth Wilson's *Adorned in Dreams* has been essential to the feminist reclaiming of fashion. Wilson argues that fashion emerged intertwined with capitalist modernity and its fragmentation of stable, traditional identities, and that it developed in association with the idea of continuous social change. Rejecting the simplistic assumption that "fashionable dress and the beautification of the self" are mere "expressions of subordination," Wilson goes on to affirm the possibility that fashion may also be used as a tool to enact agency, emancipation, and even countercultural opposition (13). The key, of course, is that this remains a possibility. As a complex signifier of gender and sexuality, fashion can be both liberating and oppressive, "for fashion, the child of capitalism, has, like capitalism, a double face" (13).

In understanding fashion as a two-faced phenomenon, we find the seed of another crucial argument for fashion studies and its related disciplines: the impossibility of defining fashion according to just one theoretical approach or explicative interpretation (10). This is why Malcolm Barnard claims that we should talk about "fashion theories," plural, as there are many theories that "explain the different objects, practices, institutions and personnel that make up the fashion system" (*Fashion* 19).[11] Both arguments have been crucial to the development of film costume studies, such as the influential volume *Fabrications* (1990), edited by Jane Gaines and Charlotte Herzog, which developed Wilson's ideas in the context of film. As important as this collection proved to be in opening up new avenues of research, most of the essays were still marked by two significant limitations. First, they analysed costumes in relation to the female body, so the enquiry was based on the body, not on an interest in the costumes per se. Second, the essays maintained an exclusive emphasis on classical narrative cinema, particularly in Hollywood, and on the subservient role of costumes in relation to narrative and characterization. The implication of this perspective is that, when cinema employs lavish, intricate costumes that become entangled in their own system of signification, a "fabrication" or "cinematic illusionism" ensues that "takes its toll on the body of the actresses" (Gaines and Herzog 19): a visual spectacle perceived as a bothersome disruption. The detrimental outcome is supposedly the obscuring of the female body as it takes on a merely decorative role, thus bringing us back to the argument that costumes are merely a form of female objectification.

Stella Bruzzi addressed and convincingly overcame these limitations in *Undressing Cinema* (1997), where she proposed, as I have mentioned above, that costumes could interfere in film narratives and impose meaning. These "spectacular interventions" are especially conspicuous when films commission the work of couture designers, who typically create grand authorial statements for the spectatorial gaze – among her key examples is Jean Paul Gaultier's vamp and robot costumes for Victoria Abril in Pedro Almodóvar's *Kika* (1993) (10–13). By examining the significant use of couture as spectacle, Bruzzi extended the scope of film costume analysis beyond its typical constraints as a subsidiary of narrative and characterization. Contrary to the traditional fixation of scholars and costume designers on extricating costume from fashion, Bruzzi showed us the value of studying *fashion in film*. She also expanded the boundaries of the field by including chapters on male film costuming – a serious oversight in costume analysis, due to the aforementioned gender assumptions derived from the masculine renunciation narrative – and by paying attention to the relationship between race and costume.

In my view, Bruzzi's model has been vital to the development of film costume analysis. She encouraged crossovers with other disciplines – especially the history and theory of fashion – and spurred further investigations that examined varied facets of the costume-fashion interface. These comprise the relevance of costume in broader debates about form in cinema, the role of the mise en scène in a film's visual aesthetics, and the impact of costumes on audiences in their everyday lives, including fashion trends and identity construction. Since then, a solid corpus of books has emerged, focusing on diverse aspects of costume in popular film (Berry, Cook, *Fashioning*; Harper; Jeffers McDonald; Street), the relationship between costume and star studies (Belluscio; Moseley; Stacey), and the multifaceted synergies between film and fashion (Arranz; Bruzzi and Church Gibson; Calefato, *Moda y cine*; Church Gibson, *Fashion and Celebrity Culture*; Lannes; Laverty; Munich). The creation of the journal *Film, Fashion, and Consumption* has further contributed to the expansion of this field, especially in seeking out interdisciplinary research that broadens the scope of costume analysis.

Although it falls outside of my focus on fiction film, another noteworthy layer of the multidimensional intersections between fashion and cinema is the growing significance of digital fashion films. They bear some relation to but should not be mistaken for narrative films about the fashion world (for example, Robert Altman's *Ready to Wear* [1994]); films depicting fashion shows (i.e., the Spanish film *Alta Costura* [Luis Marquina, 1954], which I discuss in chapter 1); or filmed catwalk shows (Paul Poiret had already done this by the early twentieth century, taking the films on the road for promotion). Rather, I am referring to the digital fashion film as a new genre in its own right, one that has emerged and flourished thanks to the new possibilities for moving image production as enabled by digital technologies since the early 2000s.[12] Typically under ten minutes long, they comprise a diversity of formats, such as "Promotional videos for seasonal collections, substitutes for conventional catwalk display, electronic look-books, experimental films used to advertise brands (clothing, accessories, and perfume), 'promos' for the digital platform versions of print magazines, e-stores, and brand-funded artists' videos" (Needham 105). These films amplify the prospects of fashion advertising by shifting their focus from the still image – the fashion photograph, which appeals to viewers as consumers – to a moving image that also entices them as spectators (Khan 253). While she acknowledges the more active kind of spectatorship that digital fashion films have stimulated, Marketa Uhlirova argues that they should not be conflated with fashion advertising. Fashion houses, initially reluctant to harness the promotional potential of digital films, started to develop projects driven mostly by the artistic directors' creative ambitions: a means to regain control over the perception and dissemination of their work amid escalating industry-imposed restrictions ("One Hundred Years" 150). The swift and unexpected interest in digital fashion films – some of which have replaced traditional catwalk shows – prompted many major fashion houses (such as Dior, Prada, Chanel) to allocate bigger budgets to increasingly polished films, which were sometimes made according to the visual conventions of narrative film (Khan 252).[13] The extraordinary development of this genre has quickly made it a robust presence in the media landscape, spawning its own circuit of film festivals around the world. One of these international festivals, the Madrid Fashion Film Festival (MFFF), has been held annually in Spain since 2014. In its first year, organizers received three hundred film submissions to the competition; for the second, the number increased to five hundred. Apart from the film contest, the festival also includes lectures, panels, round-table discussions, presentations, installations, and exhibits, in a multimedia event that promotes the ties between fashion and film – as well as their bonds with other forms of art and media.

Fashion beyond the Film

Fashion and film also interact in a meaningful way outside the cinematic text. Until the 1990s, fans venerated and imitated stars' on-screen attire. Since then, things have changed: although film stars continue to be idolized as fashion icons, "when fans admire a star's style, they will usually be talking of the clothes that he or she wears *off* screen" (Church Gibson, *Fashion* 66, emphasis in the original). What film stars wear on the red carpet of international film festivals and major award ceremonies (the Oscars, the Golden Globes, the Goyas in the Spanish context) is particularly relevant. Commenting specifically on the magnitude of the fashion parade that opens the Oscars, Adrienne Munich points out that the fashion show spills over into other media, producing plenty of "reverential or snippy commentary, reviews, and photographs" to the extent that it might "assume a life of its own, a life that many follow more avidly than the Oscars themselves" (1). A red carpet look can launch aspirants into the A-list of stardom as much as their acting does; conversely, the wrong look can instantly convert a star into a has-been. Global film audiences might not remember that Penélope Cruz received her first Academy Award nomination in 2007 for her leading role in *Volver*. However, the stunning blush-coloured Versace gown she donned for the ceremony – with a silk chiffon bodice and a spectacular, floor-sweeping feather train made of silk chiffon, organza, and tulle – is already part of the cinema history books, and countless celebrity-centred media and fashion blogs feature it on their lists of "best red carpet looks ever."

The red carpet also plays a decisive role for the other player in this game: the fashion industry. As "the new catwalk of the twenty-first century," it can have more impact and provide more visibility for designers than their own shows (Church Gibson, *Fashion* 54), and a successful red carpet look can be a bigger publicity boost than expensive advertising campaigns. Armani was the first fashion house to truly capitalize on this state of affairs. The 1991 Academy Awards ceremony was popularly nicknamed "the Armani Awards," because "anybody who was anybody was wearing Armani" (Agins 37). Valued as celebrities, fashion designers now compete to sign film stars who will wear their garments on red carpets. Indeed, today's designers strive to attain celebrity status (Tom Ford and the recently deceased Karl Lagerfeld have probably been the most successful at this), and some film stars, such as Penélope Cruz, have crossed over and become designers (more on this in chapter 5). In this new scenario, fame and celebrity take centre stage over the actual clothes and the designers, who are "reduced to a mere footnote" (Agins 37).

Of course, in the #MeToo era, the red carpet is also relevant for reasons beyond the flashy (and profitable) spectacle that celebrates the partnership between the film and fashion industries. Since 2014, the campaign #AskHerMore has been calling attention to sexism on the red carpet. After all, the media tends to ask only actresses about their choice of outfit, while male actors are fielded more substantive questions about their work – a trend indicative of a larger culture that diminishes women's professional accomplishments and fixates on their looks. The campaign gained traction when major industry players such as Reese Witherspoon and Shonda Rhimes joined the cause. It expanded even further amid the headlines on the Harvey Weinstein case – and subsequent scandals related to power abuse and sexual harassment in Hollywood. The fashion blackout at the 2018 Golden Globes – where almost all female attendees wore black to express their solidarity with the #MeToo movement against sexual harassment – was a supreme example of how the red carpet can also be a platform where the political meets the sartorial.

Some might argue that none of this has much to do with Spanish cinema, a national industry in which the very existence of a star system has often been questioned or mentioned with restraint (Perriam, *Stars* 1–2). Until recently, in fact, words such as "stardom," "glamour," and "Spanish cinema" rarely appeared in the same sentence. The image of the glamorous actor was perceived as foreign to an industry in which the real stars were internationally distinguished directors such as Luis Buñuel, Carlos Saura, and Pedro Almodóvar (Jordan and Allinson 123). Spanish actors have tended to view themselves "as workers doing a job" (Walsh 92), not particularly allured by the siren song of stardom. Far from mythical figures with a coveted lifestyle, actors in Spain have traditionally been undervalued and subjected to fierce criticism, sometimes for "engaging in excessive left-wing political involvement" (Pavlović, Perriam, and Triana Toribio 326–7). The few actors who have cultivated a glamour-steeped public persona are those who went abroad to work in industries with a more established star system tradition, such as Hollywood and France (Antonio Banderas and Penélope Cruz are probably the foremost contemporary examples, while Raquel Meller and Sara Montiel stand out in previous eras of Spanish cinema). Barry Jordan and Mark Allinson note that homegrown Spanish stars were not historically tied to glitz and style, but rather "rooted in the theatre and particularly the music hall, in the folkloric musical" (123). This was the case of child stars such as Joselito and Marisol, created for the domestic market in the 1950s and 1960s. However, recent enquiries have begun to amend this long-entrenched view of the Spanish panorama. Notably, Kathleen Vernon and Eva Woods Peiró have shown that Spain already housed an incipient star system by the 1920s, one that created "star consciousness through the linkage of stars to fashion," and was best epitomized by the case of Raquel Meller (295). My discussion of Conchita Montenegro's return to Spain in the early 1940s (chapter 1) serves as another example of how glamour and fashion have been wielded to renegotiate a star's position in the Spanish film industry.

Writing seventeen years ago, Chris Perriam had already noted the existence of "a matrix of production and consumption" with enough media platforms to promote and market stars in Spain (*Stars* 2). Over the past decade, the apparatus has only expanded. Setting aside the cases of Antonio Banderas, Penélope Cruz, and Javier Bardem, who have achieved transnational celebrity prestige and are globally perceived as "Spanish-born stars of world cinema status rather than just Spanish stars" (Pavlović, Perriam, and Triana Toribio 339), Spanish cinema now regularly produces stars who are reliable vehicles for box-office returns. Prominent examples include celebrity power couples such as Clara Lago and Dani Rovira, as well as María Valverde and Mario Casas. Although these couples may be no longer together in real life (Lago and Rovira have been dating on and off; Valverde and Casas broke up a long time ago), their chemistry on and off screen has definitely played a role in the massive success of two different sagas. The former involved the stars in *Ocho apellidos vascos* (Emilio Martínez Lázaro, 2014) – at US$77 million the highest-grossing film in the history of Spanish cinema – and its sequel, *Ocho apellidos catalanes* (2015). Valverde and Casas head the cast of the teen romance *Tres metros sobre el cielo* (Fernando González Molina, 2010) – the highest-grossing Spanish film that year – and its sequel *Tengo ganas de ti* (2012). These and other young actors (of various talents and aptitudes) now have commercially profitable star personae, thanks to their acting skills and fans' curiosity about their lifestyles and personal affairs. These public roles are possible due to strong public interest in stars' images and lives through a wide-ranging network of gossip and lifestyle magazines, daily and weekly press, and, above all, online and social media.

Even the Spanish Film Academy (Academia de las Artes y las Ciencias Cinematográficas de España) is making great strides at highlighting the spectacular side of Spanish film cultures; in so doing, it has sought to facilitate a bourgeoning star system. Over the last decade or so, for instance, it has revamped the annual Goya Awards ceremony. In the early 2000s, the event was in the headlines mostly because it became a platform for political activism – i.e., the anti-Iraq war protests in 2003 and the controversy over freedom of speech apropos of Julio Medem's *La pelota vasca* (2003) at the 2004 Goyas. Over the years, the ceremony has retained its activist edge – for example, Candela Peña's and Maribel Verdú's polemical speeches in 2013 against the government's neo-liberal austerity policies and lack of support for the film industry. Yet it has also successfully stimulated emphasis on professional matters – the films and the awards – and on becoming an increasingly popular televisual spectacle. Instead of merely wondering which political issues (and politicians) will be the target of the annual speeches, film audiences now get excited about "the attendant build-up in the press and other media, the corporate sponsors, and the red carpet moments with couture frocks and celebrity gossip" (Triana-Toribio, *Spanish Film Cultures* 36). Though not nearly as glitzy and impactful as its Hollywood counterpart – which is always a point of tension and criticism (54–5) – the red carpet matters to the Spanish film industry, too.

A fine illustration of this phenomenon appeared in an article by Marta Alameda for Spain's online version of *Elle* magazine in mid-January 2019. The article reported on the "cena de nominados" for the 2019 Goyas, the dinner organized by the Spanish film academy following the official announcement of the award nominations to generate interest among fans and the media in advance of the actual ceremony that would take place a few weeks later. The main promotional hook was not the information about the actual ceremony. In fact, readers had to scroll way down to find out that comedian couple Andreu Buenafuente and Silvia Abril would be hosting the event, and that there would be a historic change of location from Madrid to Seville – just the second time in thirty-three years that the ceremony took place outside the capital. Instead, the article focused on describing the outfits chosen by some of the female nominees (Anna Castillo, Natalia de Molina, and Najwa Nimri). Predictably, images of male nominees (Javier Bardem and Antonio de la Torre) lacked commentary about their clothes and looks.

Besides the disappointingly persistent gender asymmetries, what I find noteworthy about the *Elle* article is the media buzz around the stars' pre-ceremony clothing styles – symptomatic of the escalating importance of the red carpet event for the Spanish film industry.[14] In recent years, celebrity looks for the Gala de los Goya have even attracted attention with respect to feminist advocacy. On the occasion of the 2017 Gala, actress Cuca Escribano arrived on the red carpet draped in a silk shawl embroidered with the message "Más personajes femeninos" (more female characters). In her subsequent comments to the media, she pointed out that only 20 per cent of the roles in Spanish cinema are female ones. A year later, many attendees held red fans with the hashtag

#MÁSMUJERES to advocate for more opportunities for women in the still largely male-dominated film industry. The campaign, evidently mirroring the fashion blackout of the Golden Globes a few weeks before, was espoused by CIMA (Asociación de Mujeres Cineastas y de Medios Audiovisuales) and had a positive media aftermath, acting as a warm-up event to the feminist strike held over Spain on 8 March 2018. At the 2019 Gala, CIMA also distributed red fans, this time stamped with the hashtag #NIUNAMENOS, to protest against gender violence. All of these examples urge us to consider the promotional, spectacular, and political relevance of the red carpet event, along with other fashion performances, for the Spanish film industry. I undertake this task in the final chapter by examining how various Spanish actors have used the red carpet as a platform to take control of their star image and shape their professional paths.

About This Book

In the ensuing chapters, I will present a series of case studies that illustrate the uniquely Spanish contribution to the growing interdisciplinary dialogue between cinema and fashion, two industries with a crucial role in the construction and representation of identities. The first two chapters tackle these multidimensional synergies by analysing two prominent examples of high fashion's engagement with the Spanish film industry. Beyond the material gains of these collaborations for both parties (publicity, product placement, etc.), and in addition to the spectacular effects of costumes that call attention to themselves beyond simply dressing characters, the two cases provide us with discursive vehicles for addressing issues of identity that are central to the film texts and their reception. Chapter 1, "Fashioning National Stars: Balenciaga and Spanish Cinema," focuses on the use of Cristóbal Balenciaga's designs in Spanish cinema. Analysing examples that span over three decades, I contend that these collaborations were beneficial to the couture brand, the film producers, and the stars who donned the garments. For the Balenciaga fashion house, dressing stars such as Conchita Montenegro in the early 1940s and Sara Montiel in the early 1960s – the eras when they were the biggest stars in Spanish film – was a valuable form of product placement. However, as I show in the last part of the chapter, perhaps the most productive commissions came in the 1960s, when Balenciaga dressed Isabel Garcés, a second-tier yet very popular actress in her sixties, and Rocío Dúrcal, a rising teenage star. These examples displayed Balenciaga's remarkable range as a dressmaker: he was able to make flattering designs for women of different generations and body types. Meanwhile, for the film producers, there was an effective promotional strategy at work in the media hype around the fact that the actors were to be the dressed by Spain's top couturier. For Conchita Montenegro and Sara Montiel, both global stars with an erotic image, their association with the House of Balenciaga helped to "Hispanize" them and also to sanitize their star image when they returned to the Spanish film industry. As the fashion brand favoured by the Spanish upper classes, including several generations of the Franco family, Balenciaga costumes were the perfect conduit for dressing the lead roles in stories of moral redemption and making them perfectly credible.

In chapter 2, "Almodóvar and Chanel: High Fashion, Desire, and Identity," I explore the most ostensive example of how costumes can be used as spectacle and thus presented as apparently independent of character and narrative. I analyse the function of Chanel clothes and accessories in three of Pedro Almodóvar's films: *Tacones lejanos* (1991), *Todo sobre mi madre* (1999), and *Los abrazos rotos* (2009). A close reading of scenes in which the Chanel clothes make spectacular interventions into the narrative enriches our perception of the films' unique visual styles and ethical propositions about non-normative gender and sexual identities. In *Tacones*, Chanel couture complicates the presumed association of fashion with sexual display. Although Rebeca (Victoria Abril) does not wear a number of elegant Chanel suits with the goal of looking sexually attractive, they paradoxically become an instrument of queer incestuous seduction, as they give her an air of maturity and sophistication that appeals to her object of desire: her own mother. In *Todo sobre mi madre*, the fake Chanel suit worn by Agrado (Antonia San Juan) in a short sequence at the beginning of the film condenses and even insinuates one of the film's key themes and critical conversations: the concept of authenticity in relation to a performative notion of gender and identity, and a critique of traditional gender roles and sexual identities. The Chanel outfits donned by Lena (Penélope Cruz) in *Los abrazos rotos* serve as an entryway for reflecting on the feminist debate over whether fashion is an empowering tool or a form of enslavement for women. Initially suggesting her situation as the mistress of a finance magnate, they gradually begin to express a progression in Lena's ability to enact agency and, eventually, to liberate herself from the domineering male figure altogether.

The relationship between costume and social and cultural assumptions about gender and sexuality is also the topic of chapter 3, "Men in Underwear in Spanish Cinema." In particular, this chapter re-evaluates the notion that men and fashion do not belong in the same sentence: a notion that explains the relative dearth of studies on men's costume and clothing. This ingrained view originates in Flügel's influential concept of the Great Masculine Renunciation, which posits, applying Freud's ideas to the context of clothes, that men self-imposed a complete sartorial austerity as of the late eighteenth century, leaving exhibitionism and sexual display through clothes to increasingly passive and ornamental women. If we narrow the discussion to the ambit of underwear, the renunciation narrative gains even more traction, since men's underwear could not be conceived for any purposes beyond cleanliness and protection until recently. Drawing from emergent studies on men's underwear styles (Shaun Cole; Daniel Delis Hill) and how they have been marketed (Paul Jobling), I propose a journey through key representations of men's underwear in Spanish cinema. I focus on men in this chapter to try to mitigate the gender imbalance of costume analysis and fashion studies. I show that these images have oscillated between two modes: on the one hand, provoking laughter; on the other, prompting erotic stimulation, which has also provided ways to visualize changing models of masculinity, developments in male sexuality, and new trends in consumer society. The sex comedies of the 1960s and 1970s recurrently deployed the humorous image of an average Spaniard in boxers to ridicule the male body as an object of sexual desire. This image revealed social anxiety over the stability of normative patterns of masculinity and virility, fear of feminization, and a homophobic unease associated with the eroticized masculine subject. In the late 1970s, Eloy de la Iglesia's *quinqui* films pioneered a shift towards the overt sexualization of men's underwear and the male body, paving the way for the contemporary display of underwear designed to arouse a range of spectatorial pleasures and identifications. In the last section of the chapter, I show how contemporary Spanish cinema exposes the underwear-clad images of stars such as Miguel Ángel Silvestre, Álex González, and Maxi Iglesias not only for sexual titillation, but also to entertain the possibility of male narcissism and to cater to male viewers as consumers of masculine clothing styles. Spanish film profits from exhibiting men's underwear as fashion and from furnishing alluring images of global consumerist trends that spectators (irrespective of their sexual orientation) might want to adopt.

Chapter 4, "Dressing the Immigrant Other," also engages the role of costuming in the production of cinematic identities; here, however, I shift my focus from gender and sexuality to race and ethnicity. I examine immigration films that visualize the experiences of first-generation immigrants as they try to integrate into Spanish society, paying particular attention to the portrayals of three specific migrant groups: sub-Saharan males, Caribbean women, and Central and Eastern Europeans.

Spanish film critics have remarked that immigration films are typically conceived to raise awareness about the xenophobia endured by migrants on reaching Spain. Critics have also noted, though, that these films constitute an ambivalent form of social cinema, because their representational practices often reinforce the stereotypical treatment of immigrants in public discourse and sometimes reproduce the same power asymmetries that evoke colonial scenarios. I seek to contribute to these critical debates by analysing the essential role that costume has played in Spanish cinema's racialization of immigration. Turning to the work of Stuart Hall, Richard Dyer, and Maxime Cervulle, who theorize how cinema produces racialized images of ethnic alterity, I show that costume patterns in immigration films deliver a sartorial hypervisibility of non-white characters of African and Caribbean origin. Such films render this visibility either by stripping characters to their bare bones – as in *Las cartas de Alou* (Montzo Armendáriz, 1990), *Bwana* (Imanol Uribe, 1996), and *El Dios de madera* (Vicente Molina Foix, 2010) – or by dressing them in gaudy colours and body-revealing designs that visualize them as exotic and oversexualized – as in *Flores de otro mundo* (Icíar Bollaín, 1999), *I Love You, Baby* (Alfonso Albacete and David Menkes, 2001), and *Forasters* (Ventura Pons, 2008). By contrast, Spanish characters dress with inconspicuous restraint (subdued colours and loose-fitting shapes) to convey their neutral position: the hegemonic norm from which the racial other diverges. Proving the racialized hierarchical dynamics at work in Spanish immigration films, Caucasian-featured migrants from Central and Eastern European countries are depicted with comparable clothes-related restraint – e.g., in *Hola, ¿estás sola?* (Icíar Bollaín, 1996), *Menos que cero* (Ernesto Tellería, 1996), *El sudor de los ruiseñores* (Juan Manuel Cotelo, 1998), and *A mi madre le gustan las mujeres* (Inés París and Daniela Fejerman, 2002) – even if some of the films deploy other mechanisms to visualize them as inadequately white.

My critique of racialized costume patterns also highlights counterexamples that illustrate how meaning can never be categorically fixed by representation. Films like *Sobreviviré* (Alfonso Albacete and David Menkes, 1999), *El traje* (Alberto Rodríguez, 2002), *Princesas* (Fernando León de Aranoa, 2005), and *Agua con sal* (Pedro Pérez Rosado, 2005) deploy costume to enact what Arjun Appadurai conceptualizes as an "ethics of possibility": by sharing clothes and fashion secrets, the main characters of these films develop non-sexual transnational alliances and interracial kinships. The films envision the possibility of migrants' integration into the Spanish social fabric beyond the trope of heteronormative romance, and they allow viewers to dream of a society that might alter the prevalent structures of inequity – draconian immigration policies, surveillance mechanisms, and ruthless media coverage of migratory displacements – into something better.

In chapter 5, "Self-Fashioning Stardom: The Red Carpet Matters," I focus on the mounting importance of film stars' off-screen attire for contemporary film cultures. Departing from Richard Dyer's pioneering theoretical work on stars, which maintains that the meaning of film celebrities is not defined by their film roles alone, I explore how the growing fields of fashion studies and celebrity studies are cross-pollinating and revitalizing star studies. I take issue with discussions of costume, fashion, and stars that dismiss stars as mere products of corporate control – as commodities manufactured by a range of media industries – and thus diminish their own contributions to their stardom. I examine how four Spanish actors of different generations (Victoria Abril, Penélope Cruz, Eduardo Casanova, and Brays Efe) deploy their red carpet looks, along with other fashion performances, as a discourse to articulate or modify previous versions of their star images. I contend, along with Pam Cook, that their fashion sense is part of their "portfolio of performance expertise," and could therefore be theorized as a form of performed agency: a means by which they display considerable control over the images circulating in secondary texts. I analyse a variety of fashion-related materials about these stars that appear in entertainment and fashion journalism (magazine articles, interviews, fashion blogs, etc.), the actors' personal websites, and content from their social media accounts. Victoria Abril and Penélope Cruz, for instance, have effectively adopted fashion to enhance their international profiles. Abril has done so by carving out an eccentric image that extends to her roles in European film productions and has helped her secure a respected standing in the transnational cinema circuits without being subjected to typecasting. Cruz has linked her star image to old Hollywood glamour – which, I argue, has contributed to the critical recognition of her skill as an actress. Cult stars Eduardo Casanova and Brays Efe employ fashion as a communicative mechanism to express their unique individuality. Casanova's genderqueer red carpet looks have drawn attention for performing gender identity beyond binaries, thus enhancing his reputation as a cult auteur of films that sidestep the mainstream circuits of cinema. For Brays Efe, the red carpet has been an opportunity to increase his cult star image, one associated with excess and non-adherence to narrow codes of gender presentation. Additionally, it has allowed him to perform body positivity and raise questions about fat phobia in society, interrogating the lack of opportunities for non-normative bodies in the film, fashion, and entertainment industries.

It bears repeating that this book is not an all-encompassing study. Indeed, it could have included many other examples of how film costume and fashion intersect in the context of Spanish cinema. Each of the five analytical chapters is intended to function as a stand-alone discussion of particular topics; they do not follow any particular chronology, adhere to a given arrangement, or lead to a specific destination. Having said that, certain themes and theoretical questions stretch across multiple chapters: for instance, how film costume and fashion help us reassess assumptions about gender and sexuality in Spanish society. I hope, then, that reading the book in sequence will provide a multilayered examination of such issues. Let us now turn to my first case study and explore the fascinating uses of Cristóbal Balenciaga's designs in Spanish films.

Chapter One

Fashioning National Stars: Balenciaga and Spanish Cinema

The purpose of this chapter is to examine the multifaceted relationship between motion pictures and fashion through Spanish cinema's use of clothes from the House of Balenciaga. In the early 1910s, Parisian couturier Paul Poiret started to film his fashion shows to promote his collections (Leese 9), ushering in a period of fruitful collaboration between the fashion and the film industries that has been described as symbiotic (Regine and Peter Engelmeier 8) and codependent (Butchart 8). While mutually beneficial, this partnership has not been tension-free. When collaborating on a film, couturiers somehow have to adapt their métier to the demands of the industry, since their one-of-a-kind garments become costumes within the film. Couture houses have endured these production constraints because of the publicity generated by dressing major stars in big films. As fashion historian Marylèene Delbourg-Delphis argues, cinema became the main arbiter of styles in the 1930s, possibly earlier (161–70). This is why many couture houses have taken on film commissions, even though some of them have notoriously failed.[1]

The alliance with the film industry opened up the hermetic world of couture, until then a select club only enjoyed by the elite, to a wider audience. This partial democratization of couture meant that while the majority of film viewers could not afford to purchase the costumes on display, they could at least enjoy them as a visual spectacle, and even produce imitations with more modest fabrics. At times, fashion houses have done what Angelika Berg and Regine Engelmeier call "promo costuming," providing the whole costume collection for a movie as a form of advertisement (20). Of course, the gains have been reciprocal. Films, especially in the mid-twentieth century, also profited from selling stardom with the allure of a couture brand. In some cases, fashion proved fundamental to moulding the image of a star. This was the case with Audrey Hepburn, who perhaps would not have risen to such heights if not for her long-lasting professional relationship and friendship with French couturier Hubert de Givenchy. Today this synergetic union continues, although it is perhaps more apparent on the red carpet of major award ceremonies such as the Academy Awards and high-profile international film festivals, such as Cannes and Venice.

In the context of critical discussions on the couture-cinema relationship, the case of Cristóbal Balenciaga demands attention, on historical as well as aesthetic grounds. He was one of the greatest couturiers of his time. Even Christian Dior, his main rival in the post-war years, referred to Balenciaga as "the master of us all" (Blume 3). Moreover, Balenciaga had a steady number of commissions for film costumes (spanning three decades). Since Balenciaga was so deeply committed to perfecting his métier and despised having to deal with the marketing of his brand, it is generally assumed that he did not entertain collaborations with the film industry (Miller 120). This is a common misconception about his career; in fact, Balenciaga designed clothes for an extensive list of renowned film stars. Within Spanish cinema, he dressed Blanca de Silos, Conchita Montenegro, Isabel Garcés, María Martín, Sara Montiel, and Rocío Dúrcal. Abroad, he made his debut in French cinema when he dressed Marie Déa in *Pièges* (Robert Siodmak, 1939). After that, he dressed global stars such as Ingrid Bergman in *Anastasia* (Anatole Litvak, 1956), Eva Marie Saint in *North by Northwest* (Alfred Hitchcock, 1959), María Félix in *La estrella vacía* (Emilio Gómez Muriel, 1960), Francine Weiswieller in *Testament of Orpheus* (Jean Cocteau, 1960), Ava Gardner in *The Angel Wore Red* (Nunnally Johnson, 1960), and Marlene Dietrich in *Paris When It Sizzles* (Richard Quine, 1964).[2] Yet the growing scholarship on the relationship between couture and cinema has thus far overlooked Balenciaga's contributions. Notably, in *Fashion in Film*, Christopher Laverty conducted a wide-ranging study of forty-eight designers' work for motion pictures, from the early 1920s to the present. The extensive list of designers selected for brief commentary includes Balenciaga's contemporaries such as Chanel, Dior, and Givenchy – yet there is no mention of the Basque couturier.

I aim to elucidate how the collaboration between the House of Balenciaga and the film industry in Spain was mutually enriching for both material and aesthetic reasons. For Balenciaga, dressing major stars with an international pedigree like Conchita Montenegro and Sara Montiel – at the peak of their careers – was a convenient way to promote his brand in Spain. However, as my analysis will reveal, perhaps his greatest publicity boost came from furnishing costumes for the second-tier star Isabel Garcés, and for Rocío Dúrcal when she was emerging in the early 1960s, because they highlighted Balenciaga's ability to dress women of different generations. Spanish cinema was the ideal platform for flaunting the couturier's range as a dressmaker as well as the evolution of his métier across time. For the producers of the films at hand (all mainstream films seeking to appeal to massive audiences), the designer stamp helped increase the allure of the leading stars. In the case of Conchita Montenegro and Sara Montiel, the Balenciaga costumes also contributed to "Hispanizing" their image. This was crucial to incorporating them into the star system of Spanish cinema and, above all, to enabling the actresses – whose star personae were quite sensual – to comply with the moral strictures of film censorship in Spain under Franco.

There were also times when Balenciaga's costumes performed a spectacular visual role on screen in Spanish cinema. In these moments, the garments take centre stage and become independently significant, defying the secondary role typically afforded to them in academic discussions of cinema. In particular, my analyses of *Lola Montes* (Antonio Román, 1944) and *Alta costura* (Luis Marquina, 1954) will illustrate how the use of Balenciaga garments becomes what Jonathan Faiers calls "cinematic dysfunctional dress": clothes and accessories that, instead of "acting as vestimentary indicators of character," develop agency "beyond the parameters determined by the film's narrative" (6–7). Here, dysfunctionality does not refer to an absence of function but rather to an excess, a "disproportionate or unexpected emphasis placed" on the clothes, which generates a "surplus" of meaning and can trigger a variety of affective responses in viewers, including negative ones (8). In these two films the costumes play a disruptive, intrusive role in the narrative to the extent that they turn into what Faiers calls a "negative cinematic wardrobe" (9), because they adopt a function that is contrary to their expected positive image and become associated with unregulated, even criminal behaviour. *Alta costura* is an especially disturbing example of a negative cinematic wardrobe, for the display of an entire collection of Balenciaga serves not only to show the couturier's groundbreaking innovations in the female silhouette but also to make a strong anti-fashion statement. The director, Luis Marquina, equates fashion with death and destruction, and makes a case for the conservative notions of gender roles that prevailed in the mid-1950s in Francoist Spain. *Alta costura* demonstrates that the relationship between fashion and film is multidimensional and contains layers of meaning – commercial, theoretical, aesthetic, even patriotic and political – that merit our critical attention.

Dressing a Star Closer to Culver City than to Chamartín

In the early 1940s, Balenciaga rose to prominence in Spanish cinema by dressing Blanca de Silos (1914–2002) in *La casa de la lluvia* (Antonio

Román, 1943) and, more importantly, Conchita Montenegro (1911–2007), the biggest – and most unusual – star of the national industry at the time. Montenegro became an international celebrity before Spanish audiences even knew who she was. After brief roles in two Spanish films (*Sortilegio* [Agustín de Figueroa, 1927] and *Rosa de Madrid* [Eusebio Fernández Ardavín, 1927]), Montenegro moved to Paris to study dance. Her career took a dramatic turn when she was chosen for the role of an exotic Andalusian dancer in *Le femme et le pantin* (Jacques de Baroncelli, 1929), where she performed naked in front of a tavern audience in a key scene of the film. Her full-frontal nude – reflected on a bottle of champagne – caught the attention of some Metro-Goldwyn-Mayer executives, who immediately offered her a contract. Initially, she was hired for the Spanish versions of Hollywood blockbusters, but her prompt adaptation to the ways of the American industry and her quick mastery of English helped her secure star roles in English-language films such as *Never the Twain Shall Meet* (W.S. Van Dyke, 1931). From 1930 to 1935, she made a total of seventeen films in Hollywood (under contract with MGM and Fox), working with high-calibre male stars like Ramón Novarro, Buster Keaton, and Leslie Howard (with whom she had a well-publicized affair) (Bou and Pérez 43). When Fox Studios did not renew her contract, she continued to pursue an international career, appearing in films in France, Brazil, and Argentina.

In 1940, the foremost film production company in Spain, CIFESA, hired Conchita Montenegro as part of an ambitious attempt to create a star system similar to the Hollywood studio model – adapted to the idiosyncrasies of the national industry and the political context.[3] Montenegro was sent to Italy, where she starred in several co-productions directed by Luis Marquina (she made a total of six films in her Italian period). The idea was to use her as the star vehicle to sell the CIFESA brand abroad, but these co-productions failed because of their low quality (Fanés 104). Therefore, producer Vicente Casanova brought Montenegro back to Spain, where she acted in five films between 1942 and 1944: *Rojo y negro* (Carlos Arévalo, 1942), *Boda en el infierno* (Antonio Román, 1942), *Ídolos* (Florián Rey, 1943), *Aventura* (Jerónimo Mihura, 1944), and her very last film, *Lola Montes* (Antonio Román, 1944). However, Montenegro did not even partake in the post-production promotion of *Lola Montes*, because she decided to retire after marrying Ricardo Giménez Arnau, a diplomat and prominent member of the Falangist Party. She never attended an industry-related event again, and refused to give any interviews except for the brief chat she had before her death with José Rey-Ximena for his book *El vuelo del Ibis* (2008). She did not even attend an homage to her at the San Sebastián Film Festival, and declined to accept the Medalla de Oro al Mérito Artístico that Spain's Ministry of Culture awarded to her in the 1990s (Moro 366; Ro 513–14). For all intents and purposes, Conchita Montenegro tried to disappear from the history of Spanish cinema, and she was quite successful for a long time. She only appeared in descriptive accounts of the contingent of Spanish actors who landed in Hollywood to make the foreign-language versions of American films in the late 1920s and early 1930s (Armero; García de Dueñas).

Fortunately, the recent mounting interest in the reconfiguration of the star system in the 1940s has brought her back into academic discussions of Spanish cinema (Bou and Pérez; Comas; Rodríguez Fuentes; Vernon and Woods Peiró). In addition, Montenegro has received attention even beyond the academic sphere in two recent novels (*Mientras tú no estabas* [Carmen Ro, 2017] and *Mi pecado* [Javier Moro, 2018, Premio Primavera de Novela]), which fictionalize her life story. My contribution to these discussions about Montenegro's place in Spain's star system of the 1940s will centre on assessing the importance of fashion in reshaping her star image. In particular, I will highlight how she became some sort of muse of Balenciaga in Spanish cinema – as the cover jacket of Carmen Ro's novel describes her – and how this played a significant part in the adaptation of her image, associated with the glamorous yet dangerous vamp type, to the rigid moral codes of Francoist cinema in the early 1940s. I will employ three types of material. First, I will analyse the importance of the Balenciaga garments that Montenegro wears in *Ídolos* and *Lola Montes* as narrative devices that contribute to her performance and star image. Second, I will call attention to the function that promotion (magazine ads and articles about her starring role in these films) and publicity (what she disclosed about herself in interviews) had in the reshaping of Conchita Montenegro as a fashionable star who had an international pedigree yet did not show signs of moral excess in her private life. A third important source will be the impact that commentaries and criticism in film magazines had on this adaptation of her image through fashion.[4]

Ídolos is particularly apt for reflecting upon the refashioning of Montenegro's stardom, since Florián Rey was a director who specialized in films about stars' trials and tribulations, whether they were actors, singers, dancers, or football players. A variant of a popular subgenre of the 1930s and 1940s that "focused on the making or furthering of a star's career" (Vernon and Woods Peiró 302), *Ídolos* zooms in on the harmful side of stardom, which it portrays as incompatible with a decent life. In fact, it tells a story that echoes Montenegro's own trajectory. She plays the role of Clara Bell, a famous Parisian actor who goes on a tour of southern Spain to prepare for her next film role. During her trip, she meets an attractive matador, Juan Luis Gallardo (Ismael Merlo),

Fig. 1.1. Clara (Conchita Montenegro) performing a song in *Ídolos*

but a jealous producer who ruins Clara's career thwarts their romance. Back in Paris, she cannot find any acting roles and has to earn a living by modelling for a fashion house. Luckily, Juan Luis tracks her down and saves her from her professional demotion by proposing to her.

In one of the first sequences of the film, Clara performs a song-and-dance routine during a film shoot in Paris (see fig. 1.1). An extreme long shot taken from the back of the room shows the diva making her grand entrance onto the stage wearing an evening gown that radiates sophistication. It is a Balenciaga black dress with inventive shoulder lines: each sleeve in the form of a ruffle – one white, the other one black – is stitched to the dress.[5] This symmetrical combination of black and white is a typical element of Balenciaga's style throughout his career. For Véronique Belloir, this association in his work "brings to mind the lace-trimmed ruffs illuminating the severe costumes of Spanish monarchs, synonymous with both luxury and renunciation," and, more broadly, "the tension between light and darkness that so characterized Spanish cultural expression" (17). This contrasting effect is reinforced by the beaded and embroidered ensemble of rich, multilayered arabesques that adorns the front part, while the lower part is made of black tulle and decorated with black fringe tassels (*madroños*). Clara completes her look with a spectacular hat also made of black tulle and ornamented with tiny black tassels that match the lower part of her dress. While performing the song "Amour, amour" – the film credits specify that Montenegro wrote the lyrics – Clara walks around the room seducing the audience with sensual gestures. A tracking shot follows her, but surprisingly for a performance intended to emphasize the star's sex appeal, there are no close-ups of the flirtatious looks she directs at the intra- and extra-diegetic audience. This is a noteworthy technical decision, given that close-ups play a key role in star image-making – they are the moments seen only by us and not by other characters, "thus disclosing for us the star's face, the intimate, transparent window to the soul" (Dyer, *Heavenly* 10). With so little information available about Montenegro, close-ups could have functioned for the audience as unmediated gateways into the star's inner self – the illusion of getting a glimpse of who she really is. Instead, all shots of Clara are either medium-long or long shots, so her charm has to be conveyed through other aspects of the mise en scène, such as the elegant Balenciaga dress and the plasticity of the composition.[6]

The inclusion of geometrical motifs framing the foreground, often in elaborate compositions that resemble a static painting or an altarpiece, is common in Florián Rey's films (Benet 203). In this case, the geometrical pattern underscores the seductress's agency. As Clara walks around the room, she disappears and reappears behind thick columns, which adds a touch of mystery to her alluring performance.[7] Along with the absence of close-ups, this visual element intensifies the glamorous effect of Clara's performance. Virginia Postrel has theorized glamour as "a form of nonverbal rhetoric" that generates a subjective response in the audience, typically a sense of yearning (48). In this case, it triggers a desire for Clara's wealth, beauty, and sex appeal. While her outfit is an emblem of glamour, it is not glamour itself, as glamour does not simply exist inside a dress or any other object (44). Glamour is something more elusive, a mechanism of persuasion that requires mystery, which Postrel considers its "defining perceptual quality," because it inspires projection (110). This is why the technical decisions about the scene's camerawork and visual composition, while initially unexpected because they partially hide the star from sight, contribute to heightening the audience's desire for her, because they compel viewers to fill in the gaps with their longings.

The scene that follows Clara's performance further underscores the significance of the dress, beyond its important role in this ceremony of glamorous persuasion. As Clara is walking towards the dressing room, the film's producer stops her in the hallway to remind her about the upcoming shoot for her next film, set in Spain. She expresses her disgust at having to participate in this film – "Pues yo no hago españoladas" (I don't act in *españoladas*). The daughter of a Spanish woman, Clara says that her mother always voiced her indignation at the hackneyed image of "una España de pandereta" (the Spain of the tambourine), a reference to how the country was depicted (and misrepresented) on screen with cheap commercial folklore in order to attract tourists. This is why Clara announces that she is going to Spain to learn about its authentic culture, and the visual motifs of her dress highlight this verbal vindication of genuine Spanish culture. The decorative *madroños* (tassels) of the hat and the lower part of the dress show the influence of Spain's regional dresses on Balenciaga's designs; fashion historians have pointed out that these dresses inspired him throughout his career. Ana Balda writes that in the archives of the House of Balenciaga in Paris, there is a copy of the book *El traje regional de España* (Isabel de Palencia, 1925), which the couturier might have referred to when creating his designs (59). There is also evidence that before moving to Paris, Balenciaga travelled around Spain and learned about popular vestimentary traditions (Bowles 187). In particular, the lower part of Clara's dress evokes the *basquiñas*, the black skirts that Spanish women wore in the nineteenth century when they went to town for shopping or social events. As Helena López de Hierro has noted, the most sophisticated versions of the *basquiñas* "were made of net embroidered and embellished with black pompons" (23), like the *madroños* that decorate Clara's dress and hat. Balenciaga also drew inspiration from the paintings of Goya, especially those that depicted the dresses of the Spanish *majas* (Arzalluz, *Cristóbal* 203), which also resonate in the *madroños* of Clara's dress and hat.

We must frame Clara's fervent position on the (mis)representation of "Spanishness" in cinema within the context of a crusade initiated in the pages of *Primer Plano*, a film magazine that channeled the Falangist views of the new regime and its attempt to appropriate cinema as a vehicle for political propaganda. Núria Triana-Toribio has noted that the early issues of *Primer Plano* included several articles calling for the elimination of the *españolada* from the Spanish film industry (*Spanish National Cinema* 43–4). The strongest one, which appeared in issue 137 in 1943 under the headline "Alerta contra la españolada," aggressively described the *españoladas* as a despicable form of cinema that delivered a mistaken representation of Spanish culture. The producers of *Ídolos* had to take the vitriolic views of *Primer Plano* very seriously, because this influential magazine held sway over the critical and commercial fate of the film. It is thus fitting that Florián Rey had Montenegro conveniently give a speech against the *españolada*; after all, *Primer Plano* had made Montenegro the flag-bearer of cinema in the "New Spain" by putting her on the cover of its first issue in 1940. Besides, in the early fall of 1943, several issues of the magazine contained promotional information about the upcoming premiere of *Ídolos* that consistently made use of Montenegro's stylish star image. She appeared, for example, on the cover of issue 160 wearing a spectacular white mink coat, a deliberate attempt to sell the star and the film using fashion. The cover also notes that the film would be screened "bajo el patrocinio simbólico de *Primer Plano*" (with the symbolic patronage of *Primer Plano*). This refers to the film producers' clever promotional decision – already announced in issue 154 of September 1943 – to donate all the earnings from the premiere to the Asociación de la Prensa with an honourable mention for *Primer Plano*. This ensured plenty of promotional coverage and, just as importantly, a favourable review after the premiere. Indeed, José Luis Gómez Tello's review of the film that appeared in issue 161 (November 1943) lauded the filmmaker for making a modern, versatile film with a European flair. Conchita Montenegro, with her aura of chic international celebrity, embodied that sense of European modernity.

In effect, there was a lot at stake for the producers of the film as well as for Montenegro. *Ídolos* was an expensive film with a budget of around 2.5 million pesetas, which was above average for a Spanish film at the time. Moreover, it was the first film made in the new studios of the production company Sevilla Films, an additional reason to make sure it had a lucrative commercial run (Sánchez Vidal 284). For Montenegro, it was important to succeed in the box office if she wanted to preserve her privileged position in the star system of Spanish cinema. This was especially true after *Rojo y negro*, where she arguably delivered her best performance in a Spanish film, flopped: it was banned by the regime's authorities for political reasons and disappeared from the theatres after only three weeks.[8] Carmen Rodríguez Fuentes provides evidence that Conchita Montenegro was the highest-paid Spanish actress in the early 1940s thanks to her Hollywood pedigree. She made around 150,000 pesetas per film – and some sources estimate it was 200,000 for *Lola Montes* – while her female contemporaries (such as Conchita Montes, Amparo Rivelles, Maruchi Fresno, and Ana Mariscal) were making below 100,000 (168). Montenegro was an expensive bet and the return on the investment was far from guaranteed. She was not popular among Spanish audiences, because neither her Hollywood films nor her European productions had been seen in Spain; her celebrity was based on what film magazines had reported about her success abroad.

This is why it was vital that popular and influential film magazines continued to portray her in a glamorous fashion. Montenegro kept up her side of the bargain by playing the publicity game. In an interview with Juan Ares for issue 24 of *Cámara* (September 1943), she was photographed in her home performing summer leisure activities such as horse riding, reading, and petting her dog. The interview also contained information about her impeccably decorated house. It was imperative to create an image of mysterious glamour but also to reveal something personal that would make her seem approachable to film audiences. Virginia Postrel notes that the mystery that is essential to glamour cannot lead to "complete inscrutability" (112). This type of publicity interview with Montenegro effectively galvanized the mechanisms of glamour by conjuring a sense of translucence. As Postrel further argues, "glamour is neither transparent nor opaque. It is *translucent*. It invites just enough familiarity to engage the imagination, allowing scope for the viewer's own fantasies" (20, emphasis in the original). The interview delivered the perfect combination of accessibility to, and detachment from, the star – inviting desire in the form of distanced identification. It offered a glimpse of Conchita Montenegro performing quotidian activities without revealing too much, without breaking the glamour spell.

Promotional pressures and Florián Rey's own commitment to making films that would contribute to the creation of a robust national cinema, a deep-rooted concern throughout his career (García Carrión 95), explain why providing an "authentic" depiction of Spanish cultural traditions – bullfighting, flamenco, popular religiosity, and monumental architecture – is a central preoccupation in *Ídolos*.[9] In this sense, the elegant Balenciaga dress that Montenegro wears in this film, with its combination of sophistication and traditional elements of the regional Spanish dress (the *madroños*), is perfect for transmitting the film's counter-image of Spanish culture. One could speculate that Montenegro – who donned Balenciaga in almost all of her late films and who had the power to make costume decisions – probably chose to wear this dress, and that it was not a conscious selection by the costume designer of the film, Julio Laffitte. Whatever the circumstances, this Balenciaga dress is an ideal narrative vehicle and visual spectacle – dramatically coloured by *Radiocinema* in its promotional display for its issue 90 in July 1943 – for attempting to add a touch of European modernity to Spanish folk traditions. Conversely, it also functions effectively as an element of the mise en scène to suggest the "Hispanization" of the female star, both the intra-diegetic Clara Bell and Conchita Montenegro. Hispanizing Montenegro entailed taming her sensual image, which in the resolution of the film is clinched through marriage. Juan Luis proposes while Clara is modelling the bridal dress in the fashion house where she works. Far from the confident and flirtatious diva she was at the onset of the film, Clara appears docile in this white bridal dress. She is barely able to look her soon-to-be husband in the eyes to accept his marriage proposal and her future as a submissive Spanish wife. The diva has turned into a virtuous spouse.

After *Ídolos*, fashion continued to be key to adapting Montenegro's star image to the sui generis Spanish film industry. In *Aventura* (Jerónimo Mihura, 1944) she is Ana Luna, a libertine actor who, while shooting a film set in a rural village, begins to seduce Andrés (José Nieto), a local married man. When she realizes how much Andrés means to his wife, she changes her mind and leaves the village without breaking up the marriage. The film pivots both thematically and ideologically between rural vs. urban and tradition vs. modernity. Radical costume differences – between Ana's lavish gowns and the local women's regional dresses – visually convey those oppositions. Montenegro's over-the-top outfits became a topic of critical discussion when *Aventura* was released in the summer of 1944, as some reviewers deemed her costumes incongruous with the rural setting of the story. On the other hand, Manuel Tovar Rodríguez defended Montenegro in the pages of *Radiocinema* ("Rápidos," issue 103, August 1944) by contending that negative reactions to her costume choices came from a misunderstanding of her star image, which "está más cerca de Culver City que de Chamartín" (is closer to Culver City [California] than to Chamartín [Madrid]). Although Montenegro's outfits in *Aventura* do border on ridiculous (especially a white chiffon gown she wears for a hike and picnic in the woods), Tovar had a point in the sense that Montenegro occupied a unique niche in the Spanish star system (Comas 85; Rey-Ximena 141; Rodríguez Fuentes 386). She embodied like no other the international type of the glamorous vamp, which was "the antitype of the folklórica, who wore her heart on her sleeve" (Woods Peiró 78–9). Modelling herself after her idols Marlene Dietrich and Greta Garbo, Montenegro convincingly played heartless, manipulative, and extremely intelligent women. However, to comply with the rigid moral codes of early-Francoist cinema and to get approved by the censors, those vamps had to be somewhat redeemed, or else they were punished with a tragic ending.

The extravagant costumes of a dangerous yet ultimately well-intentioned vamp were also the main attraction of *Lola Montes* (Antonio Román, 1944), a biopic that centred on a personality whose fame (or better yet, her notoriety) belongs to a previous era. Montenegro plays the role of Lola Montes, an Irish-born dancer who adopted a fake Spanish identity, even passing as the daughter of a bullfighter, and became an international celebrity through her performances and affairs with distinguished noblemen and kings in the mid-nineteenth century.[10] While Lola gallivants across Europe, she is being used without her knowledge by a mysterious agent of an international revolutionary movement to destabilize political regimes. Lola seduces King Ludwig I of Bavaria and provokes a serious political crisis and a popular revolt against the monarchic institution. But Carlos Benjumea (Luis Prendes), a Spanish military officer who is in love with her, rescues Lola when she is about to be put to death, and the film ends with her on a church altar, atoning for her extravagant life.

When *Lola Montes* was in the pipeline, the promotional weight shifted from director Antonio Román, one of the sacrosanct pro-regime directors of the early 1940s (Coira xiv), to the costume designers commissioned for the film. In issue 186 of *Primer Plano* (May 1944), the critic Alfonso Sánchez drummed up excitement for the film's imminent premiere by writing about how costume designers Pepe Caballero and Juan Antonio Morales created "figurines que por sí solos constituyen ya un maravilloso espectáculo" (fashion sketches that are a marvellous spectacle in themselves). What the article does not reveal is that Balenciaga created many of these garments. In fact, Balenciaga received screen credit and critical praise for this collaboration. For example, a few decades later Jesús García de Dueñas cited this film to make the case that impressive acting and costumes can make up for a bad script: "la presencia de Conchita, maravillosamente vestida por Balenciaga, nos redime de esa infección literaria" (the presence of Conchita [Montenegro], splendidly dressed by Balenciaga, can save us from literary pretension) (191).

Remarkably, recent accounts offer a different interpretation of the function of costume in *Lola Montes*. In the most in-depth scholarly account thus far of Montenegro's acting career, Núria Bou and Xavier Pérez assert that the clothes she wears in this film serve to neutralize the erotic potential upon which she had built her star image. They claim that the film features a "vestuario abigarrado" (motley array of costumes), with a focus on the dresses themselves and not "en el cuerpo que los sostiene" (on the body that wears them) (50). The body is covered with "vestidos suntuosos que dificultan la identificación de sus líneas" (with sumptuous dresses that make it hard to see the body's shape), which leads to the unfortunate obliteration of Montenegro's sex appeal altogether (52). For Bou and Pérez, *Lola Montes* was the pinnacle of the moral rectification of Montenegro's trajectory since her return to Spain, and it signposted her subsequent disappearance from the cinema (53). It is true that, as I have been arguing in this section, the specific circumstances of the early 1940s in Spain and, especially, the strict censorship over cinema, compelled Montenegro to tweak her star image. The challenge was to "Hispanize" her persona, which involved somewhat mitigating her erotic appeal, while retaining the glamour that made her suitable for roles in films set abroad. However, it is one thing to say that her erotic potential was softened, and another to claim that it was destroyed, as the title of their essay suggests.

In my view, Bou and Pérez's assessment of the function of costume in *Lola Montes* is somewhat problematic because it oversimplifies its importance with a blanket statement, neglects fashion history, and thereby exposes an anachronistic bias. Their analysis overlooks the fact that costume plays a central role in historical dramas, since it lends crucial historical authenticity to the overall look of the film. Lola wears a number of outfits with a wide and full-length skirt supported by a *miriñaque* (crinoline), that is, a frame of hoops of metal that functions as a petticoat to hold a woman's skirt in place. These bell-shaped dresses were bulky and covered Lola's body from head to toes, but they were not mere pretexts for concealing her body. Rather, they were common in the period in which the film takes place. The film is set sometime in the mid-nineteenth century (the real Lola Montes was born in 1821 and died in 1861), an epoch in which the crinoline was in fashion. Therefore, it seems only fitting that Lola Montes, a courtesan who had influence over noblemen and kings across Europe, would sport those styles.

Besides, those dresses resonated with film audiences because of the historicist fad in the fashion scene of the late 1930s and early 1940s. Balenciaga led the pack with his 1939 collection of *Infanta* dresses, inspired by Velázquez's seventeenth-century portraits of the Spanish royal family, which catered to "the Parisian public's fascination with the masters of Spanish painting" (Arzálluz, *Cristóbal* 201).[11] In his first few years in Paris, Balenciaga stood out for his technical perfection and the flawless cut of his suits, but it was because of his clever allusions to Spanish art and culture, imaginatively incorporated into his evening gowns, that he quickly earned recognition. Some of Lola Montes's spectacular gowns bear resemblance to those *Infanta* dresses. When she pays a visit to the King of Bavaria to defend herself against her enemies, the top part of her gown is heavily ornamented, including a white lace frill that falls from the neckline to the waistline, and decorative bows stitched to the sleeves and shoulders. One can detect in those decorative bows the influence, for instance, of the *Infanta* dress designed by Balenciaga in red velvet for Madame Bemberg in 1939 (image found in Arzalluz, *Cristóbal* 201).[12]

Audiences responded well to seeing Montenegro in those lavish costumes because nineteenth-century silhouettes were trendy in the 1940s. In fact, Amber Butchart claims that costumes in period films "often reveal more about the fashions of the present day than they do about those of the past" (68). In the aforementioned satin gown, Lola Montes is clearly dressed to impress, and, seduced by her stunning looks, the king asks her to dance for him at the opera house. One could even draw a direct connection between Lola's most elaborate clothing and her tempting manoeuvres with men. Her obsession with chocolate, paired with her flashy gowns, underscores the image of her as a calculating vamp: she is both playful and seductive. What I am suggesting here is that costume plays a dysfunctional role in the sense suggested by Jonathan Faiers, as a form of negative wardrobe associated with subversive, unregulated behaviour – including sexuality – that causes conflict and political turmoil. Throughout most of the film, she is a femme fatale with a *miriñaque*, using sartorial seduction to make things happen.

When Bou and Pérez state that Montenegro's clothes erase her star image as a sex symbol, the assumption is that sex appeal is only expressed through the body. They also take for granted that those clothes are signifiers and their only function is to help the audience understand the body that wears them – in this case, to obliterate its erotic potential by concealing it. Bou and Pérez's point of departure for grasping the function of costume is therefore the body and not clothing. This is a limited view of film costume that neglects the diverse ways costume can generate desire independent of the body it dresses. One cannot avoid, for instance, considering the potential of clothing fetishism. The textures, colours, and designs of film costumes can prompt a tactile and visual desire in the viewers that may lead to a compulsion to possess those clothes and/or erotic arousal (I will explore a prominent example of tactile desire in chapter 3, illustrated by the underclothes in Eloy de la Iglesia's *quinqui* films).

For Bou and Pérez, Montenegro's body disappears underneath the costumes, which leads to the eradication of the star's erotic appeal and ultimately of her own star image – since they one-dimensionally conflate it with her capacity to sexually arouse viewers with her body. I disagree with that categorical assessment. My analysis has shown that Montenegro's costumes in *Lola Montes* call attention to themselves and produce a surplus of meaning that takes the story in new directions. They are intra- and extra-diegetic instruments of the vamp's agency and sex appeal. Within the film's narrative, they become weapons to provoke seismic changes to power structures, and even a political revolution; in terms of the promotional tactics to sell the film, they serve as a strategic way to generate viewing expectations through stardom. It is true that at the end of the film her seductive energy is mitigated: Lola has an epiphany, rejects her previous life choices, and ends up in front of a church altar praying for forgiveness. But this is depicted as the felicitous outcome of Carlos's positive influence, the Spanish officer who shows her the path to redemption.[13] Ultimately, the key to Lola's moral conversion lies, much like in the case of Clara Bell in *Ídolos*, in her "Hispanization," and not so much in how much flesh she shows or conceals.

Although Montenegro's sex appeal had to be tamed, it was not destroyed altogether. As Richard Dyer argued, star images "have a temporal dimension," which means that they can change or develop over time (*Stars* 64). Thus, certain features of a star's image can prevail in certain periods of her or his career, and wane in others (*Heavenly* 3). In the early 1940s, it was important to de-emphasize Montenegro's sex appeal, or better yet to sublimate it through fashion and glamour, in order to make her look more "Spanish." Balenciaga was an ideal fit to promote this renationalization of her star image, because his creations always exuded an air of "Spanishness." Although he perfected his craft and ascended to the top of the couture world in Paris, the culture and traditions of his native Spain never ceased to inspire his work. Audrey Hepburn, one of the most fashion-conscious film stars, once stated – borrowing from a popular phrase attributed to Mark Twain – that "if clothes maketh man, then costumes certainly make actors and actresses" (11). Montenegro was already "made" when she returned to Spain, but Balenciaga garments definitely contributed to reshaping her image for the cultural context of Francoist Spain in the early 1940s.

The Noir Side of Couture

Scholarly accounts of the fashion-film interface have noted that fashion shows and cinema emerged around the same time, since at the turn of the nineteenth century "designers were sending models to horse shows and to other public functions to show off their creations in order to set fashion trends and promote sales" (Herzog 134). Besides their synchronous emergence, they shared several key features. Caroline Evans explains that both early cinema and fashion shows "were presentational rather than narrative" and their female leads "appeared as 'attractions,' rather than as personalities with character and individuality." Just as early films delivered their action "in a series of homogeneous spaces, or tableaux," models showcased outfits for clients and fashion journalists gathered in a salon. Moreover, the point of view of the audience in a salon "mirrors the single, unified viewpoint of the camera" in early cinema (118–19). Given these commonalities, it was only a matter of time until both spectacles joined forces. As early as 1910, according to fashion historian Elizabeth Leese, there is evidence of the existence of fashion films, short pieces featuring mannequins parading garments (9). Nevertheless, cinema and fashion shows soon took divergent paths, for cinema quickly adopted a narrative style while fashion shows "settled into a relatively static format" (C. Evans 110), with mannequins modelling each new collection in identical or analogous ways. Writing about Weimar-era popular cinema in Germany (1919–33), Mila Ganeva says that the fashion sequences in these films provided "a brief, interruptive moment of pure visual pleasure within the narrative" that contributed little to the development of the plot (141). This is why fiction films about fashion, or in which fashion plays a significant role in the plot, have increasingly eschewed modelling scenes; they are seen as disruptive and inconsequential from a narrative standpoint.

Luis Marquina's *Alta costura* (1954), based on Darío Fernández Florez's homonymous novel, offers a fascinating counter-example to this customary configuration. The majority of the film takes place in the couture house of Amaro López (Manolo Díaz), and centres on a noir plot involving the investigation of a homicide during a show for private clients and fashion magazine experts. The costumes shown in the parade (all created by Balenciaga) become a key narrative instrument: changes in the psychological condition of the leading characters as well as in the surrounding, and often sordid, circumstances of their lives are communicated through their garments. The fashion show thus becomes a structural pillar providing a framework for characterization and plot development, instead of a mere narrative digression. Furthermore, some garments of the fashion show – as well as other costumes in the film – adopt the function of what Jonathan Faiers conceptualizes as a "negative cinematic wardrobe" (9), in the sense that they become linked to illicit, even criminal behaviour. I will show how this negative cinematic wardrobe in fact encapsulates the film's ethical message that is coded negatively: fashion becomes associated with a number of deplorable character traits, such as vanity, selfishness, fakeness, and ultimately (self-)destruction.

Cinema has had a peculiar inclination to connect fashion with crime, violence, and death. In the preface to a volume on this topic, Marketa Uhlirova asserted that films tend "to portray criminality and evil as lethally stylish," since they turn to fashion to render the crime "more captivating, in its intensity, cruelty, even brutality" ("Preface" 12). In addition, clothing and accessories (hats, gloves, jewellery, shoes, and so on) conventionally function in crime films as forensic clues (Faiers 12; Wilson, "Introduction" 14). In this section, I would like to draw attention to *Alta costura* as a film that places the fashion industry at the centre of a crime narrative. *Alta costura* merits consideration if only because the main attraction of the film is not the investigation of the murder or the murderer's point of view, but a catwalk show with all garments designed by Cristóbal Balenciaga.

Notably, while the entire collection displayed in *Alta costura* is a Balenciaga creation, the fashion show in the film could not be more different from a real Balenciaga show. For starters, Balenciaga shows always took place in absolute silence, with an air of reverence and austerity (Figueras, *Moda Española* 44; Healy 12; Join-Diéterle 143; Mears 193; Miller 70; Walker 114). A Balenciaga show "was the closest fashion gets to a religious experience" (Irvine 48), to such an extent that it resembled "a nunnery or a monastery, and his workers were sometimes referred to as the 'monks of couture'" (Healy 9). By contrast, the Amaro López show in this film takes place in a noisy salon where clients comment aloud on the garments presented. Amaro walks around soliciting client feedback on his work and even begging for praise from the editors in chief of *Vogue* and *Harper's Bazaar*, who are both in attendance. This would never have happened at a real Balenciaga show. The couturier watched his shows from behind a curtain (Figueras, *Moda* 44) and never came out to greet the audience, not even after the five-minute ovation he received when presenting his 1950 winter collection (Blume 82). Another stark difference is that Balenciaga forbade any interaction, smile, or even eye contact with clients, and asked models to keep their "heads held high, gazing into the distance, waist and hips thrust forward" (Jouve 10). This was part of the "signature loping walk" that Balenciaga demanded of his models (Blume 34). His shows' severe austerity is completely at odds with the *Alta costura* models' flirtatiousness with the male clients in the audience, as if they were engaging in a dual form of business: parading their bodies to increase garment sales as well as to sign a good deal for themselves.[14] In the dressing room, they ferociously compete for who is receiving the most attention, with Lina (Margarita Lozano) winning the contest because she was doted on by an aristocrat, who they refer to as the duke.

Besides the absence of human interaction at Balenciaga's shows, each mannequin carried a number, which is how clients kept track of their preferences. No other staging effects (such as titles or music) were ever used, given that the emphasis was solely on the clothes (Miller 114). In contrast, in the *Alta costura* show, each model walks out to suggestive music – sometimes dramatic, sometimes romantic – and is presented with a mysterious title that is supposed to evoke some kind of symbolic meaning about the garment (i.e., "Niebla," "Tulipán," "Capricho"). The Amaro López show was closer to the theatricalization of the fashion presentation mastered by Poiret and Dior, Balenciaga's precursor and contemporary, respectively, in the couture scene in Paris. Poiret crafted evocative titles with narrative subtexts for his fashion parties. As Nancy Troy documents, Poiret "even filmed his fashion shows in the gardens of his House so that he could take them with him on the road for publicity (films now lost)" (99).[15] Similarly, Dior delivered full entertainment shows that went beyond mere fashion parades for selected clients. Each design received a sophisticated and original name, and the mannequins often sped up or

Fig. 1.2. Tona (Lyla Rocco) donning the garment "Drama" in *Alta costura*

slowed down in dramatic fashion (Collado 54). Creating a spectacle was more important than making sure clients had a good view of the garments.

The disparity between the collection on display and the mechanics and aesthetics of the fashion show should be interpreted as a conscious choice for narrative and dramatic purposes. The austerity and sacredness of a Balenciaga show would not translate well as the setting of a film (unless, perhaps, it was a religious horror film). Take the "Drama" model that Tona (Lyla Rocco) wears (see fig. 1.2). It is a black evening dress gathered at the waist, with a ruffled overskirt in black tulle. A voluminous shawl made in the same black tulle adorns the outfit, which becomes the biggest hit of the collection. It also makes Tona the show's main attraction and, eventually, earns her the honour of modelling the last look of the collection. Following the couture runway tradition, the last look is a bridal dress. This garment is typically the most virtuosic and hardest to produce, and it gets a special visual treatment in the film. While long and medium shots frame the parade of all the other clothes, viewers get plenty of close-ups of several parts of Tona's bridal look, such as the lower part of the dress, the bridal cape, and the shoes. Still, the most gripping presentation is the "Drama" look, which makes a big impact on the audience. Tona's fierce catwalk and the dramatic music that accompanies her presentation beget an intensity that changes the mood of the show – and of the film.

Catwalk modelling is an individual performance for an audience in which the model asserts her or his creativity in an exhibition of style that also involves a component of storytelling, and sometimes even a certain politics and/or poetics of the self narrated through facial expressions, movement, posture, and attitude. Tona walks around the salon exuding distress, selling the air of poetic anguish that Amaro intended for this look. The film's viewers, unlike the diegetic audience of the fashion show, know that Tona's strong runway walk here is not the outcome of a perfectly rehearsed performance designed to sell the garment. Instead, it is the walk of someone who is affected by the events that took place earlier that afternoon. She went to visit her secret lover, Paco, only to find him dead on the floor of his apartment in the Residencia Fortuny – another reference to fashion.[16] With no time to digest the shocking news, she has to run to the fashion house for the show, and the implications of Paco's death – she fears being a murder suspect – start to sink in. Her inner drama serves to convey the "drama" of the garment, thus resulting in a remarkable catwalk performance that garners accolades from both the audience and the couture designer. Conversely, Tona's inner drama is further amplified by the effects that the catwalk – and the outfit itself – has on her. As she walks, the camera follows her in a medium tracking shot in which the viewer can appreciate how her grief escalates. It is as if the dramatic music, the show announcer's nagging repetition of the title of the look, and the emotional weight of the smooth, glossy black glacé silk dress and the over-the-top black tulle were asphyxiating her. When Tona reaches the end of the catwalk and has to turn around, the perspective changes to a point-of-view shot, and we feel how her gaze is lightheadedly spinning around the salon. This is the climax of the performance, when her intensity rockets and the drama of the look is especially exposed.

The spectator is also reeled into the drama of the performance by strategically unconventional camerawork. Instead of a front row point-of-view shot perspective, which would have the viewer identify with the on-screen internal audience of the fashion show, a typical viewing position for a fashion show embedded in a narrative film (Herzog 144), during most of Tona's walk viewers get a moving camera offering a point of view of the walk that does not correspond to that of anyone in the diegetic space. Moreover, it leads to the bouncy handheld shooting that projects Tona's dizzy gaze at the end of her walk. Unlike the typical fashion show scenes in early feature-length films, which tend to be static and digressive (C. Evans 128), and the predictable routines that emphasize the promotional aspects of the fashion show in popular 1930s Hollywood films such as *Roberta* (William Seiter, 1935), *Stolen Holiday* (Michael Curtiz, 1937), and *The Women* (George Cukor 1939) (Herzog 139), the fashion show in *Alta costura* is key to shaping the narrative rhythm of the film. In this case, it heightens the intensity of the drama and enhances the feeling of suspense that is common currency in a thriller. As we can see, the show needed to have a theatrical component that could only be achieved by drawing inspiration from Dior's spectacular shows, not from Balenciaga's austere parades. This theatrical dimension extends to the non-public areas of the Amaro López headquarters, which could not resemble the monastic severity one would find in the House of Balenciaga. That would have neutralized the narrative and dramatic potential of these spaces and, as a result, curtailed the development of the plot. During the fashion show, the dressing room becomes a multifaceted stage, in which the movement of models heading to the catwalk in the salon and returning to put on their next outfits steers the narrative rhythm of the film, as it shapes the models' friendships, alliances, and rivalries. During these backstage interactions, the main narrative conflict of the film is exposed, developed, and finally solved – they figure out the identity of Paco's murderer and, thereby, Tona gets exonerated.

Upon the film's release, the industry press did not care for this unique use of the non-public areas of the fashion house as a theatrical stage, nor for the inclusion of a crime plot within the elongated fashion show. For example, the review of *Alta costura* in the magazine *Cine Asesor* criticized the detective story: "no es sino el pretexto para presentar una colección de trajes femeninos creados por el famoso modisto Balenciaga, vestidos por un escogido plantel de jóvenes y fotogénicas intérpretes que hacen los papeles de las distintas modelos" (it's only a pretext for presenting a collection of women's dresses created by the famous couturier Balenciaga, worn by a select pool of young, photogenic actresses who play the fashion models) (no. 675, 1954). A careful viewing of the film, especially if one is familiar with the trajectory of Balenciaga's style and the innovations of the female silhouette that he introduced in the 1950s, would reveal that this interpretation is somewhat simplistic. The Balenciaga clothes are not merely displayed to advertise the greatness of the Basque designer, even though *Alta costura*, a CIFESA production directed by the once major-league player Luis Marquina, may have been an effective marketing platform for the fashion house in Spain.[17] Likewise, the fashion show in *Alta costura* is not only a visual extravaganza that complements a spectacular mise en scène. Besides its aforementioned role in the characters' psychological development, couture clothing provides a significant visual channel to convey narrative conflicts among the characters.

Midway through the film, there is a scene that perfectly illustrates this point. Sole (Laura Valenzuela) and Kiki (María Martín) engage in a dialectic battle over their views on Tona. Kiki, whom the voice-over narrator introduces as the most famous model in Madrid at the onset of the film, fears losing her privileged position as Amaro López's leading model, and starts trashing Tona's reputation in the dressing room. Sole steps up and defends Tona. The visual composition of this scene is meticulously planned to highlight their rivalry. A deep-focus shot shows Kiki's backside in the foreground and a frontal view of Sole in the background. Both are in focus thanks to the adept combination of several technical devices: 1) a wide-angle lens; 2) a high-key lighting treatment, whereby several sources of light are arranged so that all elements within the frame appear evenly well lit; and 3) a balanced composition with Sole on the left side of the frame, Kiki on the right, and a strategic pillar in the middle that visually emphasizes their separation. Both women appear with their arms akimbo, a stance that suggests defiance. And so does their attire. Sole wears a balloon-style dress, constructed in a single length of silk satin – flat, without any patterns – that runs from the shoulders to the hem. Balenciaga first showed balloon skirts in his 1950 collection (Miller 68), but it was in 1952–3 when they became a staple in his silhouette palette. The narrow waistline divides the evening dress into two contrasting parts. From the waist up, the satin fabric hugs the body, with a low rounded neckline, and a three-quarter sleeve, one of Balenciaga's signature sleeves. From the waist down, the puckered and puffed skirt creates a sense of great volume. Kiki, on the other hand, wears a more traditional silhouette – a sleeveless cocktail dress, with a V-neck on both the front and back, and an accentuated waist that is fitted with a belt in the same fabric as the dress. The contrast between the silhouettes – traditional versus innovative – fittingly parallels the dialectic rivalry between the two women.

Upon closer inspection, one can detect a silhouette-related logic throughout the fashion show. The younger models (Sole and Tona) tend to don the most innovative silhouettes, which display Balenciaga's relentless exploration of alternative relations between garments and the body. After the balloon dress, Sole wears a kimono-inspired jacket that exhibits Balenciaga's interpretation of Asian cultural influences (see fig. 1.3). Following up on the *tonneau* (barrel) line of coats that he initially presented in 1947, this jacket features a barrel-like curve at the back that forms an arc so that the jacket is detached from the waist. Slightly different from the barrel line, which included a more fitted look in the front, this jacket is detached from the waist in both the back and the front. Miren Arzalluz has noted that Balenciaga's exploration of options

Fig. 1.3. Sole (Laura Valenzuela) with the Balenciaga kimono jacket in *Alta costura*

for a looser waistline, a daring move at a time when the wasp waist came back into fashion with Dior's New Look, should be regarded as an example of Asian influences on his work. In particular, Balenciaga appears to have been influenced by "Japonism," the impact of Japanese artistic elements on European fashion and art since the 1850s, when Japan opened up to the rest of the world (*Cristóbal* 236). The cocoon shape of the back of this jacket evokes the way Japanese women arranged their outer kimono over their *obi* to form a stylish arc (249). But it also reveals other Asian influences. For example, it is made of a luxurious ivory silk with polychrome floral embroidery that evokes the *mantones de Manila* (Manila shawls) that were imported to Spain from the Philippines.[18] Balenciaga's own interpretation of these Asian influences marked his escalating tendency towards abstraction – which would lead to some of his most radical avant-garde designs in the 1960s. The loose style of the jacket, which hides Sole's waist and breast (the two traditional focal points of Western women's fashion), illustrates Balenciaga's ongoing experimentation with the female silhouette. Fashion historians agree that this experimentation became his signature element in the fifties to the point that "clothes that we think of as typical of that decade are, in fact, mostly dilutions of Balenciaga" (Irvine 9). The kimono-style jacket that Sole models in the fashion show pushes the envelope in terms of the artistic autonomy of the garment with respect to the body it dresses, as if the proportions and shape of that body had no role in the affair.

To understand the impelling cause of this life-long enquiry into the possibilities of the female silhouette, one should, according to Miren Arzalluz, bear in mind that "Balenciaga's formative years and early development coincided with the explosion of Modernism," which is a cultural movement "driven by an energetic desire to make a deliberate break with the past" ("Iconoclastic Visions" 55). Although this modernist mantra is evident in all stages of his career, it became more noticeable from the 1950s onwards. In the 1950s, Balenciaga presented a number of innovative silhouettes, which were almost always considered too radical at the time, but would eventually transform the couture world, such as the aforementioned "balloon dress"; the unfitted middy blouse (winter 1951); the semi-fitted suit (summer 1952); the tunic dress (summer 1955); the sack dress (1957); and the A-line baby-doll dress (summer 1958). Although they don't reach the level of abstraction of his late 1960s designs – which featured architectural qualities that produced a unique degree of autonomy from the body – Balenciaga's collections in the 1950s do offer an experimentation with structure and form that "became ever more audacious, innovative, and abstract" (Bowles 19).

The fashion show that provides the structural framework for *Alta costura* thus succeeds in conjuring up Balenciaga's iconoclastic aesthetics by presenting some of his most innovative silhouettes of the 1950s. Ironically, though, avant-garde fashion is employed in this film to make an anti-fashion statement. Luis Marquina reactivates the conventional tension between the fashionable, adorned woman versus the unadorned and ordinary woman who in the end finds happiness (cyphered in her marrying a man). Marquina, a director well known for his conservative viewpoints and Catholic convictions (Pérez Perucha 8), retrieves from Darío Fernández Florez's novel the association of high fashion with female moral looseness, and bareness with moral rectitude, which is ultimately rewarded. The masculine voice-over taxonomizes the female characters according to their sartorial style. As the workers of the house of Amaro López exit the building for their lunch break, the models are introduced as pretty yet unhappy, while the seamstresses are not as well dressed but much more self-confident. Also, the film opens and closes with two unsophisticated yet ultimately content characters who serve as the exemplars of the film's moral message. In the first sequence of the film, Carlos (Mario Berriatúa) gets off work and goes to pick up his fiancé Pituca (Mónica Pastrana). He tells his friends that he is excited to marry her, as she is a great person and deserves to be saved from her current job. Pituca is the youngest model of the house of Amaro López, and the one they all ridicule for being gullible and unsophisticated. She idolizes all the other models because of their beauty and refinement, and wishes to marry in the spectacular bridal dress that Tona models during the fashion show. At the end of the film, when the crime mystery is solved while Tona is still wearing the bridal dress, Pituca throws herself at Carlos in tears and tells him she no longer wants to walk down the aisle in that dress – she will wear a cheap one, instead. Although Tona is not guilty, her affair with Paco was the catalyst of the homicide, perpetrated by her fiancé Ramón (Alfredo Mayo). The message is clear: high fashion is associated with false appearances, meaningless vanity, a lack of integrity and, ultimately, deadly destruction.

This negative view of fashion has to do with a broader standpoint on modernization and its pernicious effects. The male voice-over at the onset of the film frames his presentation of the characters working in the fashion house by linking them to the vibrant, changing city, which is emerging from the harsh, hungry years after the civil war. Fashion is presented in *Alta costura* as a paradigmatic constituent of modernity, inextricably connected to the conditions of urban life and to the first signs of the accelerating development of the capitalist economic system in post-war Spain. But modernity and fashion are associated with death here. This is not a brand-new idea. Rather, it evokes an influential school of thought, primarily espoused by Walter Benjamin. In *The Arcades Project*, Benjamin argues that fashion plays an important role in modernity and in everyday life by embodying both a rupture with the immediate past and an anticipation of the future. This temporal nature of fashion, and especially its ephemeral quality, leads him to link fashion with death:

Here fashion opened the business of dialectical exchange between woman and ware – between carnal pleasure and the corpse. The clerk, death, tall and loutish, measures the century by the yard, serves as mannequin himself to save costs, and manages single-handedly the liquidation that in French is called revolution. For fashion was never anything other than the parody of the motley cadaver, provocation of death through the woman, and bitter colloquy with decay whispered between shrill bursts of mechanical laughter. That is fashion. And that is why she changes so quickly;

she titillates death and is already something different, something new, as
he casts about to crush her. (63)

For Benjamin, fashion "titillates death" because it converts clothes into a
fetish in which women's bodies are sexualized, turned into a commodity
that constantly renders obsolete anything that comes prior to it. Fashion,
he further asserts, "couples the living body with the inorganic world"
and, therefore, "defends the rights of the corpse" (79). In Benjamin's view,
fashion is an agent of capitalism's false consciousness, because it lures the
modern consumer, the bourgeois subject, into a game of deception and
death. This is what fashion scholar Elizabeth Wilson, when examining the
contradictions underpinning fashion as a cultural product that emerges
from capitalist modernity, refers to as the double face of fashion (*Adorned*
13). In this sense, it fosters a yearning for things "that remain just beyond
our reach" (14). The fashionable garment is an object of desire that will
forever be replaced by another object that people will seek to purchase.

Although Luis Marquina most likely did not have this Marxist framework of historical analysis in mind when presenting the kinship between
fashion, sex, and death, *Alta costura* still functions as a cautionary tale
against the excesses of modernity. For him, as for the novelist Darío
Fernández Flórez, who provides the raw narrative material for the story,
the deadly hazard of fashion, and of modern life in general, seems to
be the erasure of the core values underpinning the stable social fabric.
This is visualized in gendered terms, by showing how fashion is a threat
to the integrity of women, who are the repositories of society's moral
standards. Tellingly, fashion in this film informs viewers about the female characters' sexuality. It lines up the virgins – those on the right path
to becoming happy wives – on one side of the clothing divide, and the
post-virgins – those condemned to remain alone and unhappy – on the
other. A skilful edit starkly juxtaposes two scenes. The soon-to-be-married
Pituca and Carlos take a romantic walk in a park and are therefore associated with the natural world. By contrast, the fashionable Tona gets in a
taxi to go see her secret lover, who is lying dead on the floor – so fashion
is associated with the inorganic world, to recall Benjamin's words.

To reinforce the link between fashion and death, the film cleverly
plays with traditional narrative conventions of the crime stories. As
Jonathan Faiers examines in-depth in *Dressing Dangerously*, the use of
"clothing and personal possessions as constituting clues" and "wit-
nesses to a crime" is a solidly established notion in crime films (12).
This means that items of clothing and accessories can play noteworthy
roles in solving criminal activity, as they have the potential to implicate
someone, yet also to deceive. Both functions resurface in *Alta costura*.

When Tona discovers Paco's dead body on the floor of his apartment, she immediately starts walking towards the entrance to disappear, but remembers that her black gloves are still on the coffee table. An editing cut leads to a close-up of the gloves, which could have implicated her at the crime scene. Gloves are, of course, usual suspects in crime films, a device typically used by perpetrators to avoid leaving incriminating fingerprints at the crime scene. Aware of that, Tona retraces her steps to go pick up her gloves, but when she leans into the coffee table, she is interrupted by the sound of the phone ringing – another convention of cinematic crime scenes. The shocking sound of the phone makes her drop her purse, and all her belongings slip out onto the floor. She picks them up nervously, and the insistent ringing makes her visibly anxious – as shown in a close-up of her anguished face – to the extent that she ponders answering the phone. Again, when she is about to pick it up, she sees the smoke coming from a cigarette butt in the ashtray on the side table where the phone is situated, another crime film convention to suggest that someone else is hiding in the apartment, probably the murderer. She quickly changes her mind, and proceeds to move towards the front door, but remembers, yet again, that she forgot her gloves. This time she is not interrupted: she grabs her gloves, and leaves. However, in her rush, she does not realize that she is leaving one incriminating clue: the cigarette case that fell out of her purse.

It is not gratuitous that Tona almost forgets her gloves twice. The gloves could have incriminated Tona but do not in the end, mainly because the audience knows that she is not the perpetrator of the crime. But Marquina consciously flirts with cinematic conventions to deliver the anti-fashion message of the film. The guessing game of whether or not she will forget the gloves suggests that she is somehow guilty of the crime because of her infidelity. Ultimately, she does leave a trace behind, a silver cigarette case, which points to the real culprit, her fiancé, Ramón, who gave it to her as a gift with an engraved note of affection. With its sophisticated-looking stainless steel finish, the cigarette case is a superfluous accessory (reduplicating the function of the cigarette box) that epitomizes the wasteful essence of fashion here and its link to criminal behaviour and death. The methodically dressed and accessorized Tona is depicted as a transgressive subject who, though innocent of the actual crime, triggers the deadly fight between Paco and Ramón. In contrast, the fact that the unsophisticated Pituca does not have a good taste in clothing is an indicator of her moral integrity. In a semantic reversal of the appropriation of the juridical discourse that fashion journalists are so keen on, Tona is a "fashion victim" not of the "crimes against fashion," but of the crimes instigated by the shallow and fruitless pursuit of fashion.

It is hard to know if Balenciaga was aware that this film would co-opt his designs to promote a conservative moral fable. One could certainly see him being in accordance with the gender ideology of this film, which followed the strict gender codes of 1950s Francoist Spain, given that Balenciaga was a profoundly religious person with a traditional mindset towards life and society (Bowles 107; Walker 15). He was also a favourite among the Francoist upper classes, including three generations of the Franco family. Besides dressing Franco's wife, Carmen Polo, Balenciaga came out from his retirement to design his very last garment for them: the bridal dress that Carmen Martínez-Bordiú, Franco's granddaughter, wore for her first wedding in 1972.[19] Despite these business connections with the Franco elite, no one is absolutely certain of Balenciaga's political alliances, for he never made any public pronouncements about his political views. As Leslie Ellis Miller observes, he was a Spaniard working in Paris for a clientele that was mostly American, British, and French. Given that Franco's Spain remained neutral yet favoured the Axis powers during the Second World War, overt sympathy for the Spanish government would not have helped him cement his reputation in Paris. For the same reason, he could not openly oppose the regime, because he "also owned three dressmaking houses in different parts of Spain, which supported a large number of his family" (24). But even if we were to assume that Balenciaga supported the Franco government, one thing is to share the conservative gender values of the regime upheld by *Alta costura*, and another one is to accept that his couture clothes would symbolize evil.

It would be fascinating to know if the couturier saw the film and, if so, what he thought about it. But one thing is for sure: no other fiction film highlights a designer's innovations and contributions to fashion history as well as this one, while also propagating such a negative, anti-fashion message. Four decades later, Robert Altman's *Ready to Wear* (1994), released in Europe as *Prêt-à-Porter*, also features fashion shows and a murder. In this "hate letter to the fashion industry" (Ebert), Altman exposes the preposterous side of couture, its unwearability and "total lack of functionalism" (Bruzzi, *Undressing* 31), though it is packaged in a comedic form, with plenty of moments of slapstick humour that entertain the audience and never really target anyone in the fashion world in particular. *Alta costura* is different; it is all Balenciaga, and all dark. The unfashionable Pituca and Carlos, two simpletons who embody Francoism's cult of marriage and family values, provide the only beam of light. They are portrayed as the moral victors of this film, the ones who have learned Benjamin's anti-fashion lesson, here recodified to deliver a Franco-era morality tale where fashion is superficial, profligate, and in the end unfulfilling.

Dressing Multigenerational Stars

In the early 1960s, Balenciaga had risen to the very top of the fashion world pyramid. Dior's tragic death in 1957 meant that Balenciaga was the only king of couture left standing. Coco Chanel had come back in 1954, and had quickly reclaimed a prominent position in the industry, but with adaptations of her classic designs and cuts, and not with the type of trailblazing innovations of the female silhouette that Balenciaga was introducing. Accordingly, it seems only fitting that his occasional collaborations with the movie industry would entail dressing the most famous stars, the ones who were larger than life and could therefore add allure and pedigree to his brand. At that time, no star of Spanish cinema was bigger than Sara Montiel. After a few years of cementing her global celebrity in Mexico and Hollywood, she came back to Spain and starred in blockbusters such as *El último cuplé* (Juan de Orduña, 1957), *La violetera* (Luis César Amadori, 1958), *Carmen la de Ronda* (Tulio Demichelli, 1959), *Mi último tango* (Luis César Amadori, 1960), and *Pecado de amor* (Luis César Amadori, 1961). The plots of these films were rather inconsequential, because what the massive audiences that rushed to the theatres wanted to see was Montiel's unique repertoire: her melodramatic songs, her affected performance, and her extravagant gowns.

Among those over-the-top dresses – we are talking about several dozen in these films at the peak of her career – two Balenciaga gowns stand out. After all, Montiel was hardly the model of discreet elegance associated with the Balenciaga style. She made a career of personifying simultaneously "la obscenidad barata y el *glamour* más deslumbrante" (cheap obscenity and the most dazzling glamour) (Mira, *Para entendernos* 533). She overused her autobiography to enhance the provocative side of her star image, which chafed against the gender ideology of the Franco regime. Upon her return to Spain, Montiel carried the stigma of the fallen woman, the mistress of an American celebrity – her civil marriage to filmmaker Anthony Mann was never considered legitimate in Spain. This scandalous aura and her radiant beauty made her an erotic myth and a camp icon for several generations of queers (Perriam, "Sara Montiel"). Montiel became virtually a household name associated with sex, and this was at odds with the female model Balenciaga had in mind for his clothes. According to fashion editor Diana Vreeland, the Basque couturier "often said that women did not have to be perfect or beautiful to wear his clothes. When they wore his clothes, they became beautiful" (Healy 9). Granted, there was some room within Balenciaga's evening styles for Montiel's sensual exuberance. His couture philosophy entailed restrained simplicity and comfort for daywear, but did not shy away from sheer extravagance and boldness for the evening wear (Healy 28; Jouve 7; Miller 53). Interestingly, the Balenciaga gowns that Montiel wore were not among her most extravagant, and one could even make the case that the costumes in these occasions had some kind of taming effect on her voluptuous eroticism. They played an important role in the redemption subtext of some of her melodramatic musicals – she was a fallen yet ultimately decent woman granted a chance to redeem herself.

In *Pecado de amor*, she plays the role of Magda Beltrán, a Madrid nightclub performer with a dark past who becomes a global superstar. She embarks on a worldwide tour not because she wants to become an international icon, but because she is running away from the deleterious consequences of her tormented love for a married man. The tour, which almost seems like a convenient pretext for showcasing that Montiel's stardom stretched well beyond Spain, starts in Paris, where Magda performs the classic "Sous les toits de Paris" – the song which inspired the title of the celebrated 1930 film by René Clair. She is dressed in a Balenciaga black gown that exudes an inhibited air of elegance. The gown features an original asymmetrical neckline – which visually parallels Magda's unbalanced psychological state – and she wears two red roses tucked in her hair, meant to evoke the accessories of flamenco dancers. Balenciaga experts have deemed the recurring use of black throughout his career to be synonymous with Spanish elegance and style. "Every collection up until his retirement," Robyn Healy notes, "featured a 'little black dress' made entirely by Balenciaga himself" (18). For a brief moment, Sara Montiel appears as ideal an ambassador for the Balenciaga brand as any. Like the couturier, whose work was "enthusiastically received by a Parisian audience historically fascinated with the displays of Iberian exoticism" (Arzalluz, "Iconoclastic" 37), she personifies a touch of exotic "Spanishness" in this little black dress. But there is an additional undertone attached to this stylish costume: the "Spanish" black of Magda's gown symbolizes her impending atonement for her sinful life, as she will eventually become a nun.

Mi último tango offers an even more sanitized image of Montiel. As usual, she plays the role of a show business star. Marta is the disgraced daughter of a theatre company owner, and she claws her way out of poverty by passing as the major international star Luisa Marival (Laura Granados). Marta's lie is uncovered and, on top of that, she falls out of favour again because she becomes temporarily blind. Yet, unlike Montiel's other blockbusters, in this case there is no need to expiate any previous moral depravity. Montiel plays the role of a virgin for a change, or at least a young woman with no evidence of a carnal relationship with a man until she meets the male lead of the film, Darío Ledesma (Maurice Ronet). Midway through the film, there is a sequence in which costume plays a crucial role in sealing this unusually virtuous image of Montiel. Sailing on a boat that takes her to Buenos Aires, Marta, with all the costumes of the diva Luisa at her disposal, chooses to wear a dazzling gown to a ball where she unexpectedly reunites with Darío. The gown is made of gold lamé, a luxurious yet delicate fabric – easily susceptible to seam slippage – typically used in evening wear for special occasions. It is definitely a statement piece, and Marta becomes the centre of attention in the ballroom, reigniting Darío's love for her. The gown – appropriately accessorized by elegant gloves and jewellery (a collar and earrings), all in a similar gilded tonality – produces an opulent visual spectacle that delivers a textbook effect of cinematic glamour (see fig. 1.4): the talents of the star and the designer are on display, and provoke aspirational desire and jealousy both in the diegetic audience and in the actual cinema viewers.

As is emblematic of many Balenciaga evening gowns, the emphasis is on the back of the dress and the exposed neckline (Miller 78). The dress strips on the back of the shoulders are golden chains that add a touch of luxury. There is a train, also made of gold lamé, which runs from the waist down and further emphasizes the back of the dress as the centre of gravity of the look. Recognizing the fundamental importance of the back of the dress, and therefore showing an impressive fashion sense here, Amadori – probably advised by the costume designer, Joaquín Esparza – includes a long take in which we get to contemplate the back of the gown in all its glory. Marta and Darío leave the ballroom to have a moment alone. They stop at a window to get some fresh air and chat, but they hear some singing voices coming from the deck and decide to head over there. The camera remains on a stationary support, and the abundant lighting of the room allows us to admire all the details of the back of the gown as Marta and Darío walk towards the deck of the boat.

Touched by the poor Galician migrants singing about their longing for their homeland, Marta decides to join them. A close-up, followed by a medium shot of her and Darío while she is singing in Galician, effectively employs lighting to offer an idealized image of Marta. This is achieved through a high-key treatment throughout the whole scene. The various sources of light are measured so that there is enough fill and back light to neutralize the intensity of the primary source of light and, as a result, eliminate any shadows that this key light might produce on Marta's face. This contributes to making her look beatific, and downplaying her sex appeal. As Richard Dyer argues in his study of lighting effects as an aesthetic technology to accentuate gender differentiation, this a conventional lighting treatment in classical cinema to depict female leads as idealized representations of righteousness (*White* 127). For this lighting convention to work, the virtuous woman needs to glow

Fig. 1.4. The angelic glow of Sara Montiel in *Mi último tango*

instead of shine. "Shine," as Dyer notes, "is the mirror effect of sweat, itself connoting physicality, the emissions of the body and unladylike labour" (122). Shine, due to its visual link to bodily secretions, could hint at a sexual activity that would be unsuitable for the image of decency and integrity sought here. Thus, the lighting treatment works in tandem with the proper make-up to ensure that Marta's face does not look shiny. This image of Montiel as angelically glowing is heightened by the comparatively dim lighting on her male counterpart in their two-shot on the deck. Darío appears perceptibly darker and some shadows are cast on his face. Casting more light on female stars than male ones is a widespread convention in mainstream cinema's portrayals of heterosexual relationships, as it tends to convey "the connotations of dark desire for the light" (Dyer, *White* 134). In romantic scenes, when the male character gets close to the virtuous female, the light seems to grow progressively stronger on him. The same pattern appears in the closing scene, when Marta and Darío reunite and passionately kiss while vowing that they will always love each other. Marta's body is rimmed with light, which she seems to radiate onto him. The visual effect is that she brightens him with her light and, subliminally, with her purity.

Additionally, there is a hard back light that makes Marta's (dyed) light brown hair look blonde, which further highlights her angelic glow – and makes her hair perfectly match the gold lamé gown. Marina Warner, writing about fairy tales, delineated an enduring tradition linking blondeness to lightness, with chaste, virtuous, and good undertones (366). Marta's blondeness makes her skin look paler, suggesting a lack of exposure to the sun, which, from a sexual point of view, suggests a lack of exposure to the desiring male gaze. This combined effect of lighting, costume, and make-up on female leads to give them an angelic appearance was common in Spanish cinema in the early 1960s. For example, it was widely used in hagiographic films that tried to fashion idealized images of female sainthood (Pérez, *Confessional* 43–50). While film audiences were conversant in the use of this technical convention, what is important here is that it was adopted to construct a sanitized image of Montiel, arguably the biggest erotic myth of the Franco era. Dressed in Balenciaga, and lit like a pious woman, Montiel glows in *Mi último tango* like a model of moral rectitude.

While portraying Montiel as angelic may have required audiences to suspend their disbelief, the most startling fantasy in *Mi último tango* has to do with the costumes worn by Isabel Garcés. She plays the role of Clarisa, Marta's aunt, who works in her brother's theatre company and is always by Marta's side. While Marta has access to Luisa Marival's expensive wardrobe, it is not clear how Clarisa, an assistant at an insolvent theatre company, can afford to wear lavish Balenciaga outfits. One particular look is striking. As they are boarding the boat that will take them to Buenos Aires – still working as Luisa Marival's helpers – Clarisa tells one of the boat's errand boys where Marival's suitcases should go. She is wearing a complete Balenciaga look that includes an elegant semi-fitted brown suit (the revolutionary 1950s silhouette that evolved from the barrel line introduced in the late 1940s), luxuriously accessorized with a fox fur scarf, a pillbox hat, and a classy-looking brown leather bag.

Clarisa's outfit is entirely uncoupled from the narrative and the construction of her character, and it is a confusing signifier of class. It only makes sense if one considers Garcés's career holistically, including both her on- and off-screen activity. Garcés was an atypical actress in that her debut in Spanish cinema did not come until she was fifty-nine years old – *Mi último tango* was only her second film. Prior to that, she had a distinguished career in theatre: she was the headliner of the Teatro Infanta Isabel – and was married to its owner, theatre entrepreneur Arturo Serrano – for three decades. In the 1960s, she found her niche in Spanish cinema in supporting roles alongside rising young stars such as Marisol (in six films) and Rocío Dúrcal (in three films). In these films, all big blockbusters, she plays an ingenuous aunt, a house cleaner, and an assistant who looks after the young stars and, simultaneously, serves as a comic contrast to them. Garcés's characters are mostly flat with no psychological development: it is her physical appearance and her characters' naivety that are supposed to amuse the audience. However, she tends to be impeccably dressed, often in Balenciaga clothes.

For viewers who were familiar with Garcés's distinguished theatre career, her luxurious outfits might not seem odd, even though they are so illogically out of character. It is safe to speculate that these incongruous costumes were chosen by the actress. Pedro Usabiaga documents that Garcés was frequently dressed by Balenciaga in her film roles because of the friendship she had with the dressmaker; Usabiaga provides photographic evidence of Garcés looking glamorous in Balenciaga garments at film premieres and social events (139). The dysfunctionality – in the sense conceptualized by Jonathan Faiers – of her costume choices on screen made them all the more likely to be noticed and, therefore, susceptible to trigger some kind of affective response in the viewer, including the desire to purchase the garments or imitate her style. Furthermore, Garcés was an appropriate cinematic model for Balenciaga because of her age; his loose styles, which diverged from the traditional accent on the waist, were both comfortable and charming for mature women. While Dior remained attached to uncomfortable and unnatural nineteenth-century silhouettes, and to designing clothes only for beautiful women, always displayed by gorgeous models (Join-Diéterle 144), Balenciaga was committed to exploring wider silhouettes that could be worn by modern women of several generations (Balda 67; Healy 27). It is well known that no particular height or size was required to become a Balenciaga model, because he liked to have "a representative spread of different types of woman, able to reflect the diverse clientele" (Golbin 18). Balenciaga's lines suited several types of female figures and were "flattering both to the extremely slim and to those with curves and stomach, since they ignored the waist" (Miller 60). In fact, some "of his favorite clients were older women with matronly physiques [like Isabel Garcés] who inspired his grand silhouettes, and who, in turn, were enhanced by his innovations" (Mears 193). In her films, Garcés showcased the practicality of these lines; this is especially conspicuous in several films in which she had more prominent roles. In *Las hijas de Helena* (Mariano Ozores, 1963), for example, Garcés wears fabulous evening gowns, perfectly fitting cocktail dresses, and colourful daywear suits – outshining the three young stars who play her daughters (Laura Valenzuela, María Mahor, and Soledad Miranda).

In *Prohibido enamorarse* (José Antonio Nieves Conde, 1961), Garcés played her first leading role: her name preceded the film's title in the opening credits. Although commissioned director José Antonio Nieves

Conde resented making this film, which he deemed a "simpática comedieta blanca, sin mayor relevancia" (an entertaining light comedy, completely irrelevant) (Llinás 117), it is actually pioneering in its positive representation of aging. The two main characters, played by Garcés and Ángel Garasa, challenge the narratives of decline that typically circulate in mainstream cinema about aging. Physically deteriorating and sick at the beginning of the film, they are able to transform and become active and dynamic subjects who fall in love. The drastic change in Elena's costumes – from sombre black dresses at the beginning of the film to outfits with innovative silhouettes – visually depicts this positive transformation. Two coats she wears throughout the film are particularly prominent in this regard: they have puffed volume on the sleeves and back – the kimono-style Japanese influence on Balenciaga at its best – and do not have a waist, representing his increasing experimentation with enveloping volumes that embrace but do not confine the body.[20]

Como dos gotas de agua (Luis César Amadori, 1963) is perhaps the film where Garcés's expensive wardrobe makes the most sense from a narrative point of view, since she plays the role of Angela Goñi, a successful, if disorganized, lawyer. Throughout the film, she wears several suits that have the signature ease of Balenciaga – made in flexible fabrics (wool or tweed), with slimline skirts that are easy at the waist, and jackets that are loose in cut, have straight lines at the waist, and feature three-quarter sleeves that do not obstruct the wrists. These day suits cater to Ángela's needs as a professional woman while still making her look elegant. In genuine Balenciaga fashion, she complements these outfits with attention-grabbing accessories, such as hats that create a sophisticated counterbalance to the understated suits. In one scene, Ángela, clad in a simple day suit, dons a spectacular pillbox hat decorated with white silk flowers. Balenciaga first introduced the pillbox hat (*sombrero casquete*) in 1955, and it instantly became a big hit in the fashion world and one of his trademarks: it was a "small, round, brimless hat which could be quite plain or decorated with a sculptural curl, or ornately beaded for night" (Healy 35). In embodying the Balenciaga look from head to toe, Garcés served as a visual record of fashion history in the 1960s. This is rather remarkable considering that she was a late bloomer in cinema, mostly known for secondary and clichéd roles. Although Conchita Montenegro and Sara Montiel were the perfect star vehicles for the promotion of the couture brand on the global stage, one could make the case that Isabel Garcés, albeit unexpectedly, was Balenciaga's true muse in Spanish cinema. She capitalized on every opportunity – both on screen and off – to highlight the designer's commitment to dressing women of diverse generations and body types.

As if proving that he was truly a designer for women of all ages, Balenciaga accepted another film collaboration in the early 1960s that is worth discussing briefly. I am referring to his much-publicized work for *Rocío de la Mancha* (Luis Lucia, 1963), where he dressed the rising star Rocío Dúrcal. In this film, Dúrcal plays an orphan teenager who ekes out a living for herself and her four young siblings by convincing tourists that an old windmill in her village is the one that Don Quijote fought in Cervantes's novel. Then, an opportunity presents itself to put her lying and performing skills to better use: she has to pass as the daughter of a famous composer to help a couple going through a rough patch. She shows up at the composer's mansion dressed in a Balenciaga day suit. Similar to the ones worn by Isabel Garcés, the jacket is unfitted, with three-quarter sleeves, straight lines at the waist, and an opening in the back that allows for extra mobility. Dúrcal's hair is mostly down – only partially pinned up with a simple clip – which gives her a youthful appearance that mitigates the seriousness of the below-knee-length skirt. Later in the film, Dúrcal wears several variations of the chemise dress (first introduced by Balenciaga in 1957, to great controversy), accessorized with casual pieces such as a raffia bag and comfortable flat shoes. In these juvenile outfits designed by Balenciaga, Dúrcal exudes an air of enthusiasm, freshness, and self-confidence that resonated with the hopeful Spanish viewers of the *desarrollismo* years, eager to leave behind the harsh decades of the 1940s and 1950s. As I have explored more in-depth elsewhere, Dúrcal, when she first started acting, embodied a specific type of Cinderella of the development years: modern yet decent, usually of low-class origins, a girl who can move up in society – generally through marriage – if she proves herself, especially if she proves that she is pure ("Vestida" 82–3). In this modern yet decent look, the knee was the boundary of exhibition of the body, hence explaining the length of Rocío's day suit in this film, as well as in her subsequent blockbusters *Más bonita que ninguna* (1965) and *Acompáñame* (1966), both directed by Luis César Amadori.[21]

Fashion and clothes were central to the marketing of Dúrcal's star image. Commissioning Balenciaga for her wardrobe in *Rocío de la Mancha* was an attempt to promote a chic look that would differentiate her from Marisol. Rocío Dúrcal was four years older, and she was supposed to appeal to a slightly different audience so that the two emerging stars would not compete with each other. Marisol was a child star cultivated in the model of Shirley Temple, while Rocío Dúrcal was more of a teenage star à la Deanna Durbin (Aguilar 25). And it worked. In her second film role, dressed by Balenciaga, Rocío became a huge icon not only in the domestic market but also in Mexico.[22] Audiences were not at all bothered by the incongruous use of couture in *Rocío de la Mancha* – indeed, it was a stretch to believe that an almost indigent young woman could own those perfectly tailored garments. Inspired by the Cinderella motif that was so central in her films, Dúrcal's fans tried to emulate her, hoping that this look would help them undergo a similarly transformative experience. The star's fabulous clothes and style thus created an inspirational and aspirational spectacle that disguised the actual distance between the privileged star and the audiences enticed by her look. As Guy Debord asserted in his influential *The Society of the Spectacle*, the spectacle needs to remain eminently positive, irrefutable, and out of reach to ensure maximum results (15). The abiding fascination with the spectacle hinges on its unattainability: it must be an aspiration that one can dream of and even come close to, but never fully have. Dúrcal's look in this film was simple enough that young women who admired her could adapt the patterns, even if they knew that they could never afford the flawless and expensive tailoring of those dresses.

Conclusion: Fashion, Publicity, and Agency

The case of Rocío Dúrcal in the early 1960s, much like that of Isabel Garcés, demonstrates that both the fashion and film industries, especially when working in tandem, propagated fantasies of inaccessible glamour that also had the potential to positively impact female agency. Their films displayed costumes that could be adjusted for Spanish women to wear in their everyday lives. These films offered spectacles beyond reach – in the sense theorized by Debord – but were also a source of hands-on stylistic tips for women of several generations. This was particularly relevant at a time of substantial changes for women in Spanish society, as the regime's newly appointed technocratic government approved some measures to enhance the incorporation of women into the public life. In the 1958 revision of the Civil Code, some – though certainly not all – legal provisions that limited women's rights were removed. In addition, the 1961 Women's Political, Professional, and Employment Rights Law created opportunities for women in the work environment. The increasing number of women in the labour force meant that they had some money to spend and also that they needed clothes suitable for their active lifestyles – like the practical suits that the lawyer played by Garcés wears in *Como dos gotas de agua*. It also meant that women were not a passive consumer group shaped by the external forces of a changing Spanish society, but instead were actively involved in the creation of their own modern image.

Given the massive success of Dúrcal's image as a modern yet decent young woman, Balenciaga could have continued to pursue these kinds of collaborations reaping profits and staying ahead of the curve in the fashion industry. Amid the rapidly unfolding "youth-quake" revolution, that is, the dramatic influence of youth culture on fashion in the 1960s, adapting his métier to the demands of young clients would have been a clever business decision. Youth were a progressively influential consumer class that required a more casual approach and the development of ready-to-wear collections.[23] Instead, Balenciaga decided to stay true to himself and continued to innovate in design and technique, refining lines and silhouettes he had introduced throughout his career. In the 1960s, his style evolved towards shapes with fewer seams, sometimes with only one seam, which gave the dress an unparalleled degree of autonomy by further separating it from the female body (Arzalluz, "Iconoclastic" 33; Balda 68). The pinnacle of this abstract minimalism came in 1967, when Balenciaga presented three celebrated garments that were sculptural pieces: the four-sided envelope dress, made in black silk gazar and "shaped like an inverted pyramid" (Mears 187), the bridal gown with a coal-scuttle headdress, and the so-called "chou" dress, "with its deep black ruffle around the face that could be lowered to the shoulders" (Blume 180). With these avant-garde pieces, Balenciaga paradoxically hit a creative dead end. By maximizing the sculpturing potential of clothing in these garments – now considered icons of twentieth-century fashion history – Balenciaga achieved what we can term, borrowing from what Roland Barthes conceptualized in the context of writing, some sort of degree zero of fashion: a clothing style that seemed to function completely autonomously from its historical matrix, from social currents, and even from the body it is supposed to dress. Balenciaga had achieved the perfection he had sought throughout his entire career, but this landed him in a closed universe without any ostensible link to everyday life. As Mary Blume aptly put it, it seemed impossible, "even for him, to go further than those three outfits, and he closed his house the following year" (180). Just like that. He retired without any prior notice, leaving many faithful clients and film audiences bereft of his extraordinary designs. Let us now turn to analysing how the garments of another paramount couture house, Chanel, have been employed in the films of the most internationally acclaimed Spanish filmmaker, Pedro Almodóvar.

Chapter Two

Almodóvar and Chanel: High Fashion, Desire, and Identity

Fashion has consistently made an appearance in the films of Pedro Almodóvar, and seldom at the mercy of narrative or characterization. In an insightful study focusing on Almodóvar's early films, Gerard Dapena writes that he is "the most fashion-conscious European director of his generation," since couture has played a "meaningful part in both the look of his films and the construction of Almodóvar's public persona" (495). Repeatedly employed by Almodóvar to make what Stella Bruzzi calls "spectacular interventions" in his films, couture garments play a disruptive role in "the scenes in which they appear and impose themselves onto the character they adorn" (*Undressing* xv). Remarkably, Jean Paul Gautier designed a number of extravagant outfits for Andrea (Victoria Abril) in *Kika* (1993) and Zahara (Gael García Bernal) in *La mala educación* (2004) that have been duly analysed by prominent scholars (Allinson 178–81; Bruzzi, *Undressing* 10–13; Dapena 515–17; D'Lugo, *Pedro* 82–4; Smith, *Vision Machines* 37–55; and Acevedo-Muñoz 266). Much less critical attention has been paid to the products of the House of Chanel, even though it is the couture brand that the "chicas Almodóvar" most frequently wear, and its beauty products are also essential in the bathroom of Leo (played by Marisa Paredes) in *La flor de mi secreto* (1995). Except for Dapena's substantial comments about *Tacones lejanos* (511–15), the Chanel-Almodóvar collaboration has been mentioned only in passing, and usually to point out the costumes' ancillary role in underscoring the characters' social status, as Mark Allinson writes about *Tacones* (181).

The purpose of this chapter is precisely to examine the compelling presence of Chanel outfits and accessories in three of Almodóvar's films, *Tacones lejanos* (1991), *Todo sobre mi madre* (1999), and *Los abrazos rotos* (2009). Interestingly, he works with a different *figurinista* in each of these films (José María de Cossío, Sabine Daigeler, and Sonia Grande), so this is not simply evidence of a particular costume designer's predilection for the Chanel brand. Given that the Chanel clothes and accessories periodically appear in Almodóvar's films, I believe they merit more than a quick appraisal as a status symbol. That explanation is unsatisfactory because it reduces the work of one of the most acclaimed and groundbreaking designers of the twentieth century to its material value, detached from any aesthetic quality or cultural impact. Identifying a fixed pattern of meaning for the Chanel outfits in all of these films – which have different diegetic and extra-diegetic contexts – proves to be rather difficult. Yet a close reading of the scenes in which Chanel couture makes a spectacular intervention in the narrative enhances our understanding of the films' unique visual styles and thought-provoking ethical implications. Additionally, this chapter argues that it is more fruitful to think of the Chanel-Almodóvar connection not as a one-way street – only in terms of what Chanel garments bring to the narratives and characterization in Almodóvar's films – but rather as a mutually enriching collaboration in which both branded products infuse each other with meaning. My point here is that the Chanel outfits take on a unique significance in the specific context of each film, and appreciating them via Almodóvar's cinematic universe stimulates original nuances in their sartorial vernacular. Cinema influences fashion too.

Unexpected Affinities

Before analysing the specific functions of Chanel couture in Almodóvar's films, I want to draw attention to some broad-spectrum, and perhaps unexpected, kinships between both artists in terms of their biographies, career trajectories, and the reception of their unique oeuvres. The comparison between Coco Chanel and Pedro Almodóvar is both preposterous and fitting. At first glance, it might be hard to find a more far-fetched analogy between artists. Chanel represents the triumph of functional simplicity, while Almodóvar has been discussed as a paradigm of a contemporary neobaroque aesthetic that is keen on visual and narrative artifice and exaggeration (Egginton 107–26; Varderi). Chanel exudes classic, ageless elegance; Almodóvar made a name for himself by embodying, performing, and presenting iconoclast modernity. A long list of traits makes their artistic approach seem mutually exclusive. And yet, strikingly similar aspects of their respective biographies and career paths make them ripe for comparative enquiry. Both came from humble origins to become internationally acclaimed in their respective industries, and the line between reality and fiction is a bit fuzzy when it comes to certain details of their life stories. Traumatized by her childhood years (she was a maternal orphan who grew up in an orphanage after her father abandoned her), Coco Chanel was notorious for inventing and embellishing her past (Urrea 38–9). Thomas Sotinel has also noted multiple (self-fashioned) versions of Almodóvar's biography: "Up until the early 1990s, Pedro Almodóvar was said to have been born in Calzada de Calatrava, in La Mancha, on 25 September 1949. Later, the calendar shed a couple of years […] That perhaps suggests a touch of the flirt, but it should also ring an initial warning bell: Almodóvar's real life is beyond our grasp" (7).[1]

Admittedly, these biographical parallels are anecdotal. However, they serve to set the stage for more relevant creative and authorial similarities. Both are lauded as trendsetters whose influence exceeds the contours of their corresponding trajectories. The imprint of Chanel in the fashion world is beyond dispute. Chanel is credited with the liberation of women's fashion and with creating key design strategies that had an enduring effect throughout the twentieth century and were endlessly copied (Evans and Thornton 132; Steele, *Women* 11). Regarding her place in fashion history, Elizabeth Wilson categorically deems Chanel's style "the paradigm of the twentieth-century style" (*Adorned* 40). Similarly, Marvin D'Lugo and Kathleen Vernon consider Almodóvar alongside a select group of auteurs such as Hitchcock, Chaplin, and Buñuel who might be categorized as "matrix figures" of cinema. With that term, they are referring to Almodóvar's authorial status as a director with a recognizable visual style that other filmmakers have tried to copy, since "the adjective 'Almodovarian' is not only applied to his own work but also to the style of others who appear to be emulating him" (4).

This reputation as originators of creative trends goes in tandem with what is probably the single most important similarity between them: their authorial standing transcends classical models of couturier and film auteur. Both are known to be consummate perfectionists, very demanding of their collaborators, and in complete control of every aspect of the design, production, and distribution of their products. What set Chanel apart from previous designers was that she went beyond just creating a distinctive style (this is required of all couturiers) and was able to offer a revolutionary approach to fashion. While other designers had tried to expand their reach to jewellery and accessories (i.e., Paul Poiret), only Chanel achieved what became known as the "Total Look." She was able to fashion a "totality of vision" that was composed not only of clothes, jewels, and accessories, but also other intangible and, therefore, unpurchaseable components that oozed the Chanel look. These included, for example, an androgynous hairstyle and "the Chanel body," which was moulded on Coco's own youthful

and athletic body. This totality of vision raised fashion to an unprece-
dented "status of an all-encompassing worldview, a *Weltanschauung*"
(Garelick 289–90). Moreover, Coco was behind more than just the creative dimensions of her fashion house. She was also a hands-on entrepreneur who supervised the commercialization of her products. Likewise,
Almodóvar distinguished himself from most film auteurs by creating
his own production company, El Deseo, in 1987, which allowed him to
exercise control over every facet of the production process. Almodóvar
is a master in using publicity and marketing strategies to shape his
authorial persona and to promote his films. As a matter of fact, he is
transforming "the image of the filmmaker into a multimedia figure"
(D'Lugo and Vernon 7), since he has expanded the scope of his professional endeavours to become a prosperous entrepreneur who experiments with other forms of media (for example, the commercialization
of his films' signature songs in 1997).

Despite these comparable pioneering accomplishments, Chanel and
Almodóvar's paths to global stardom were both fraught with trials and
tribulations, especially in their homelands. Chanel grew to be considered "the essence of French chic" (Vaughan 3), and Almodóvar became
"the embodiment of post-Franco Spain, the representative of the new
nation" (Smith, *Desire* 2). Nevertheless, they were grudgingly praised
at home. For example, the American market first discovered Chanel
when the women's fashion magazine *Harper's Bazaar* featured one of her
garments in 1916, which was baptized as "Chanel's charming chemise
dress," and later became widely celebrated (Charles-Roux 238). One
cannot find a mention to this dress or to anything else by Chanel in the
French press until 1920. America rediscovered Chanel again in 1954 (this
time from an extensive piece in *Vogue* that multiplied store sales), while
the initial reception to her comeback in France was glacial, if not overtly
hostile (Gautier 233; Koda and Bolton 12; Richards 94; Urrea 139). Similarly, Almodóvar's evolution from underground enfant terrible to European art cinema star is indebted, as Marvin D'Lugo and Kathleen Vernon
noted, to "the 'Frenchness' of the international Almodóvar" in combination with "his critical and commercial success in the U.S. market" (6).
Almodóvar conquered the French and American markets and critics, but
he continues to have a tense relationship with the Spanish Film Academy, which controls who and what becomes canonized in the national
industry. He has often been considered an outsider to Spanish cinema –
he has described himself that way, too – because he departed from the
more respected tradition of politically engaged *cine social* to make films
that were visibly influenced by Hollywood comedies and melodramas
as well as by popular genres and culture in Spain (Triana-Toribio, *Spanish*

National Cinema 132–42, *Spanish Film Cultures* 56–71). Almodóvar's relationship with the Spanish film press has been equally troubled, including infamous polemics with prominent film critics such as Carlos Boyero (Smith, "Almodóvar's Self-Fashioning" 34–6), *El País*'s cinema pundit, who is notoriously unenthusiastic about Almodóvar's films.[2]

Besides their debatable status as national icons, both of them have been in the spotlight for gender-related controversies. Although they are regarded as pioneers in probing gender assumptions of their particular historical eras, they have simultaneously had a rocky relationship with feminism. As revolutionary as Chanel's style was in providing comfort, mobility, and independence to women, her rigid ideas about how women should or should not dress were not always taken as progressive gender statements. For instance, Chanel liberated the female figure and polemically shortened skirts in the second decade of the twentieth century, but then never took the skirt above the knee for aesthetic reasons. When the miniskirt revolution happened in the 1960s, Chanel was its most adamant enemy, claiming it was indecent and unappealing to men (Madsen 323). This resistance to new fashion ideas for women was especially bizarre given that Chanel had been such a trailblazer herself; for example, her introduction of jersey in the second decade of the twentieth century was just as provocative as the miniskirt revolution, if not even more so (Gautier 37). Her disreputable statements about how women were losing their femininity with the stylistic innovations of the 1960s brought to the fore the complex and often contradictory ties between fashion and feminism. Chanel's self-assigned role as the guardian of femininity clashed with the emerging views of the second wave of feminism, which considered ideals of feminine beauty such as the ones dictated by the Chanel "Total Look" to be mechanisms of women's oppression, since fashion turned women into victims who needed to look good in order to attract the male gaze. Likewise, Almodóvar's women-centred films have been celebrated for questioning traditional configurations of gender and sexuality, but he has also been accused of misogyny and legitimizing patriarchal structures. One major feminist concern with his films is a certain glorification of a submissive role for women, often involving self-abnegating maternity. The other problematic area is, undoubtedly, the recurrent and disturbing representations of rape in many of his films, which have led prominent critics to assert that Almodóvar's films might not be the most fertile terrain to explore the creation of a feminist consciousness in Spanish cinema (Martin-Márquez, *Feminist* 40).[3]

Apart from the surprising similarities between the two, there is another fact that may help explain why the outfits and accessories of the

House of Chanel make periodic and noteworthy appearances in Almodóvar's films. We know that Pedro is an admirer of the Chanel brand,
as he is a familiar presence in the front row of some of the House's
flashy runway shows. For example, in the video of the Cruise 2017/2018
Collection show, available on the Chanel official website (www.chanel.
com), one can see Almodóvar sharing the front row with other celebrities, including one of the newest members of the "chicas Almodóvar"
club, Adriana Ugarte, legendary French actress Isabelle Huppert, and
the fashion guru and the editor-in-chief of *Vogue*, Anna Wintour. In
what follows, I examine how Almodóvar's passion for the French couture brand has translated into a number of fruitful collaborations for his
films, illustrating the fascinating aesthetic possibilities of the interface
between cinema and fashion.

The (Sex) Appeal of a *Tailleur*: *Tacones lejanos*

Right after the opening credits of *Tacones lejanos*, there is a skylight shot.
The camera then tilts downward until we see, through the glass window of an airport lounge, an Iberia plane approaching its gate. On the
right side of the glass window (and of the frame), we see the reflection
of a woman sitting in the airport lounge. She is wearing a white collar-
less suit jacket adorned with a luxurious broach, gold buttons, and a
necklace of pearls. Two other items complete the look: red sunglasses
and a red purse. The combination of the white and red of her outfit
matches the colours of the Iberia plane on the left side of the frame,
thus conferring on the shot the symmetrical plasticity that so delights
Almodóvar. While the image is a bit too blurry to make any conclusions about the concrete brand and condition of the outfit (if the jacket
is couture or ready-to-wear, if the pearls are real or fakes), one thing
is instantly recognizable: this is a classic Chanel-inspired look (see fig.
2.1). After an editing cut, we see a high-angle close-up of the lady's
face in profile. Again, the visual plasticity of the shot was meticulously
pondered, combining variations of red (of the frame of the glasses and
the airport lounge seats) and white (the jacket and pearls as well as the
very light grey, almost white, tile floors). A detail of this shot confirms
what an attentive viewer might have already guessed: the frame of the
glasses displays the famous self-designed Chanel logo with the interlocking double C's.

The lady, who will soon be identified as Rebeca (Victoria Abril), the
female lead of the film, gets up and walks around the lounge, checks
the monitor for arrivals and departures, and then sits again. A frontal shot of Rebeca again emphasizes the symmetrical plasticity by

Fig. 2.1. Rebeca (Victoria Abril) in a classic Chanel *tailleur* in *Tacones lejanos*

accumulating objects with red colours (Rebeca's purse and the lounge seats) on the lower part of the frame versus objects in white (Rebeca's suit and the horizontal white lines of a pedestrian crossing behind her, which we can see through the window glass). Rebeca nervously fidgets in her seat and tugs at the hem of her Chanel skirt to pull it down. The camera tracks forward to the medium close-up position, which allows the viewer to more fully appreciate the details of her outfit. The hand-stitched trims and the stunning gold buttons reveal that the suit is unmistakably a Chanel. And so do the quilted handbag and the colourful broach that complete the "Chanel look" – they are inventive accessories that complement the austere garment.[4]

While she is waiting, Rebeca remembers episodes from her childhood with her mother, such as a trip to Isla Margarita, where she bought a pair of white earrings for Rebeca. After the flashback, Rebeca opens her handbag to fish out the same earrings, which she is going to wear to reunite with her mother. A detail shot of the handbag reveals its splendid finishing as well as the brand name "Chanel." In this protracted yet visually fascinating prelude, two things immediately stand out. One is the extraordinary – even for an Almodóvar film – attention to costume to such an extent that the costume design seems, in this first sequence, to be the protagonist of the film itself. The second is, on a similar note, the immediate emphasis on product branding (Chanel, Iberia). This focus on costume design and accessories was indeed the subject of many harsh critiques of the film upon its release. As Gerard Dapena documents, the importance of fashion was considered, especially by English-language press reviews, to be merely trivial and decorative

(513). Spanish film scholars have further understood this as evidence of the rise of rampant consumerism in post-Franco Spain (Smith, *Desire* 124) and the associated formation of a wealthy and materialistic bourgeoisie within a complacent Spanish society under the socialist administration of the early 1990s (Bellos Caballero 148). Correspondingly, some Almodóvar scholars have interpreted *Tacones lejanos* as part of a progression in his films towards portraying ever wealthier characters (with the financial resources to wear couture clothes) that seems to parallel the director's own trajectory from provocative underground artist to profitable international auteur (Varderi 164).

In particular, the overt strategy of product branding of Chanel garments and accessories at the beginning of the film has been regarded as a marketing tactic. *Tacones lejanos* was El Deseo's first co-production with the French company Ciby 2000, which later also participated in the production of *Kika* (1993) and *La flor de mi secreto* (1995). For Gerard Dapena, the French funds played a big role in Almodóvar's unexpected "preference for haute couture clothes 'made in Europe' by foreign celebrity fashion designers" (497). This marks a noticeable change from his earlier films, in which he collaborated with Spanish designers (for instance, Francis Montesinos in *Matador* [1986]). One might plausibly connect the insistence on displaying the Chanel logo and brand to a need to appeal to a French audience. This explanation is not particularly convincing, however, as there is an equally overstated presence of Italian Armani products, which appear as soon as Becky (Marisa Paredes) arrives at the airport. An interest in reaching French audiences may explain, though, the casting of veteran French actor Féodor Atkine in the role of Manuel, Rebeca's husband and Becky's former lover. The tactic worked well, since Almodóvar collected a prestigious César award for *Tacones lejanos* and, most importantly, the loyalty of the elusive French market.

Dapena is also right when he mentions that beyond conquering the French box office, the use of couture in this film is part of a broader strategy to galvanize fashion as another vehicle for shaping and underlining Almodóvar's authorial persona on the global stage. The celebrity status of the international couturiers with whom he collaborates further reinforces his own status as a star auteur and imbues his films with an aura of glamour that sells well in international markets (500). To expand on Dapena's point, it may be useful to reflect briefly on the meaning of the Chanel logo that emerges prominently in the first sequence of the film. This logo, which endures as the company's emblem almost half a century after Mademoiselle's death, first appeared on the Chanel No. 5 perfume, in order to make a clear connection between the famous perfume and its creator. The logo "represented the first use of a designer's own initials as an aesthetic motif in its own right" (Garelick 130). The two interlocking *C*'s subsequently appeared on just about every accessory and garment designed by Chanel, to the extent that they became inseparable from the brand itself. In *Tacones lejanos* Almodóvar invokes the global appeal of this brand as a means of strengthening the global projection of his own brand in the making. *Tacones* is only the second film marketed as "un film de Almodóvar" (the 1989 film *Átame* was the first before that the credits used to introduce "un film de Pedro Almodóvar"), which as Vicente Rodríguez Ortega suitably notes, became a way of selling the brand "Almodóvar" as a recognizable label of European art cinema (45). Like Chanel with her instantly recognizable logo, Almodóvar created his own kind of initials, his own sign system that enabled him to sell his products globally. Audiences around the world saw the logo "Almodóvar" and they would show up at the theatre. Following in the footsteps of Chanel, and benefitting from her aura of global glamour, Pedro invented the cult of Almodóvar.

At the narrative level, critics have viewed the use of the Chanel and Armani clothes in *Tacones lejanos* as a symbol of the characters' social status (Allinson 181), and a tool to highlight the rivalry between the two female leads, whose fidelity to opposing couture brands suggests that they have a tense relationship (Dapena 511; Varderi 205). The symmetrical plasticity of the opening sequence balancing red and white is maintained in the composition of the very first shot in which both female characters appear together. Becky (Marisa Paredes) wears a magnificent red Armani suit, a red Pamela hat, and a red handbag with a white blouse that matches the white and red of Rebeca's Chanel suit and accessories. Alejandro Varderi criticizes Rebeca's repeated use of Chanel garments as an overstated and, for him, ineffective fashion dialogue with the Armani choices of her rival, her own mother (played by Marisa Paredes) (205). The Chanel-Armani contrast is indeed exaggerated, but what is not in an Almodóvar film? As Paul Julian Smith aptly put it, Almodóvar offers a "cinema of saturation" in which costumes, vibrant colours, and other visual aspects that typically take on a supporting role in cinema "compete for attention with outrageous narratives and dialogue" (*Desire* 3). To pay no heed to the costume choices because they are excessive seems like missing half the point.

In *Tacones lejanos*, couture clothes are certainly excessive and disruptive in the sense that they make meaningful interventions in the narrative and characterization. Couture costumes are signifying elements that are key to understanding the complexity of the tense mother-daughter relationship. Rebeca's and Becky's clothes perform "the proclamatory function" that Stella Bruzzi assigns, borrowing from Roland Barthes, to "iconic clothes": they have a prior, independent meaning that is "not necessarily subservient to or even compatible with that of the dominant narrative" (*Undressing* 17). For Gerard Dapena, the extratextual meanings imprinted on the film through the inclusion of Chanel and Armani garments help display the tense rivalry between the two female leads, something that "would resonate with spectators attuned to the discourses of haute couture fashion and the meaningfulness of choosing one designer over another" (511). Yet like Varderi, his emphasis on the Armani-Chanel dialogue in *Tacones lejanos* is misplaced, because this dialogue does not take the form of a rivalry. A more logical fashion rival for Armani would have been Gianni Versace, Armani's contemporary (both surged into the fashion world in the 1970s), and whose flamboyant and provocative designs "were generally perceived as Armani's polar opposite in terms of taste" (Polan and Tredre 167). Versace was the rebel who constantly pushed the envelope of sexiness in fashion, sometimes even bordering on vulgar, which was diametrically opposed to Armani's search for simple and sophisticated elegance that followed a sense of decorum. Beyond their radically different notion of aesthetics in fashion and a personal aversion to each other (inflated by the media), the rivalry between Armani and Versace was about who was the best ambassador of Italian fashion (Potvin 31–2). On a more profound level, the Armani-Versace rivalry tells the story of "the contradictory outlook of a country deeply divided by class" (Laurino 55). Conversely, if Almodóvar wanted to pit Chanel against a rival for the pleasures of spectators conversant in the couture vernacular, he would have probably gone for someone like Christian Dior or André Courrèges – her contemporaries in her comeback years – instead of someone she predated, like Armani. Dior's whimsical yet nostalgic "New Look" created an "hourglass silhouette predicated on waist cinchers, padded brassieres, and boned corsets" that was antithetical to Chanel's approach to fashion based on practical simplicity (Koda and Bolton 12).[5] And Courrèges, who incorporated the miniskirt into French fashion (and was for that reason loathed by Chanel), was described by Roland Barthes in a famous 1967 article published in *Marie Claire* as embodying youthful and modern fashion, the extreme opposite to Chanel's classicism (*Language* 99–103).[6]

Fashion history, therefore, does not support the interpretation of the narrative conflict of *Tacones lejanos* as a story of sexual rivalry over a man. By wearing Chanel, Rebeca is not seeking a clothing confrontation with her mother for the attention of her husband Manuel. Instead, it is Rebeca's incestuous and homoerotic desires for her mother that are at the core of their tense relationship (Acevedo-Muñoz 140; Kinder,

Blood Cinema 250–62; Williams 171–82). As Marsha Kinder and Linda Williams argue, Rebeca's obsession with her mother is not Oedipal desire or a regression to pre-Oedipal non-differentiation or fusion, but rather, an example of what Kaja Silverman, borrowing from Freud, calls a "negative Oedipal complex," one that is post-Oedipal, incestuous, and homosexual. In this scenario, the girl (Rebeca) needs to dispense with father figures (or with any patriarchal figure that becomes an obstacle) in order to secure her mother's undivided attention and love. This is why Rebeca gets rid of her stepfather and later of her own husband (who was her mother's lover), and in the end is comfortable staying with Eduardo/Letal (Miguel Bosé), the father of her soon-to-be-born child. Eduardo reminds her of her mother, as he literally impersonates her, dressing up as Becky and singing her pop songs in a nightclub. In fact, Rebeca gets pregnant in a sexual encounter in Letal's dressing room immediately after his performance of one of Becky's songs, when he is still not completely out of the drag outfit. Sexual intimacy with Letal only interests Rebeca insofar as it makes her feel as if she were being intimate with her true object of desire: her mother.

Almodóvar thus transforms the traditional melodrama of mother-daughter rivalry into a much more provocative taboo queer romance. Crucially for the purposes of my discussion here, costume design plays a central role in this presentation. The elongated first sequence with emphasis on the details of Rebeca's Chanel outfit now achieves its full signification. Rebeca wears Chanel to conquer her mother even on her mother's deathbed. Yet she does not use couture to appear sexually attractive. A Chanel *tailleur*, a tailor-made suit (even considering Lagerfeld's version, where the skirt is significantly shortened), is barely the epitome of sexual appeal. Rebeca looks attractive in the sense that she radiates distinction and sophistication. Knowing her mother's taste for classic fashion, she seeks to impress her with the timeless elegance of her Chanel suit. And it works. A fashion connoisseur, Becky immediately notices and admires her look: "Estás reguapa con ese Chanel, hasta te hace cintura" (You look pretty in that Chanel, it highlights your waist). Most importantly, she notices that it makes Rebeca look like "toda una mujer" (a real woman). Rebeca wears couture to perform adulthood and let her object of desire know she is no longer a girl. Therefore, couture here makes a spectacular intervention, to the degree that it has an independent, prior meaning (the Chanel *tailleur* as a fashion signifier loaded with meaning) imposed onto the characters and narrative, and not the other way. Apart from questioning the secondary role assigned to costume design in cinema, this disruptive use of fashion also complicates the almost predictable association of fashion with sexual display.

In my view, Rebeca's Chanel outfit is a prominent fashion intrusion in the film narrative, glamourizing the character without necessarily sexualizing her. The emphasis is not on the sexual display of the body wearing the suit, but on the aura of maturity and sophistication that the outfit confers on Rebeca. Just like we will shortly see in *Todo sobre mi madre*, the Chanel suit's appearance in a leading role serves to incorporate a long-standing tradition of meanings and overtones into the narrative. In the process, it becomes imbued with Almodóvar's signature proposition of non-normative desires. The non-sensual Chanel suit paradoxically becomes an instrument of queer incestuous seduction on the Almodóvar runway.

The Private Life of a *Tailleur*: *Todo sobre mi madre*

Long shot of a public square in the Barcelona historic city centre. Manuela (Cecilia Roth) and Agrado (Antonia San Juan) walk past the camera, which remains in a stationary position on a low angle to show the gait of both women dressed in bright-looking outfits as if they were walking down the runway. Agrado sways her hips disproportionately, flaunting over-the-top femininity and self-confidence in a flattering knock-off Chanel suit that Manuela cannot help but notice: "You look fabulous" ("Estás estupenda"). In the reverse medium close-up, the camera travels with both women as Manuela asks, "Is this Chanel authentic?" ("¿Y el Chanel este es auténtico?"). In campy fashion, Agrado responds: "How could I spend half a million pesetas on a Chanel outfit given that there is famine all over the world? The only real things I have are my feelings and the litres of silicone that weigh tons."[7] Previous enquiries into *Todo sobre mi madre* have noted that this brief and seemingly inconsequential scene functions as an overture to a major theme of the movie: the concept of authenticity in relation to a performative understanding of gender and identity. In fact, Marvin D'Lugo points out that this is the first time this theme "is explicitly introduced in dialogue," and serves to prepare the spectator for Agrado's monologue when entertaining the theatre audience after the cancellation of the performance of *A Streetcar Named Desire* (*Pedro Almodóvar* 104). In her speech, Agrado comically explains her "authentic femininity" ("Yo soy muy auténtica") by outlining in full detail all the surgical procedures that she has gone through to become a woman. As in some of his previous films such as *La ley del deseo* (1987) and *Tacones lejanos*, Almodóvar explores in *Todo sobre mi madre* the notion that (gender) identity is not innate, or something you are necessarily born with, but rather something you can make and remake. And so are family and motherhood.

Fig 2.2. Agrado (Antonia San Juan) in a knock-off Chanel suit in *Todo sobre mi madre*

While acknowledging the significance of this scene's dialogue within the thematic macrostructure of the film, critics have largely overlooked its visual elements, which in my view are just as crucial to evaluating its weight in the broader film narrative. For example, the setting of the scene is significant. Agrado and Manuela are walking through some of the iconic streets of Barcelona's city centre. In the travelling medium close-up of Agrado and Manuela, the viewer can observe on the left side of the frame some exterior parts of the concert hall, Palau de la Música, one of the crown jewels of Catalan modernist style that was built by architect Lluis Doménech i Montaner. Concretely, we see thick columns decorated in glazed ceramic with floral motifs and vivid colours. The vivid colours of the columns go well with the colours of the costumes that Agrado and Manuela are wearing: Agrado's pink suit, Manuela's gaudy and tight dress that combines bright pink, orange, and green, and especially the jacket with brown prints. The purpose of that jarring colour combination is to pretend that Manuela is a sex worker trying to get off the street, since they are heading to meet Sister Rosa (Penélope Cruz) to ask for her help with finding a job. The visual matching of the costumes and the columns is underscored even more if we take into consideration another detail: the columns have oval-shaped mouths that function as the ticket offices to pay for entrance into the palace, just as a financial transaction is necessary to pay for the services of these "street girls." As if putting into effect some sort of comic reversal, the "real" sex worker wears a fake suit that gives her a respectable feminine look that she was not born with, and which she exaggerates through her posture and gait (see fig. 2.2); the fake sex worker wears a hooker-looking outfit that enables her to pass as a genuine one.

As we can see, the combined work of dialogue and visual elements serves to highlight at least three aspects of the theme of authenticity, as it relates to the costumes, femininity, and professions of these two women. This is why it is rather surprising that critical approaches to this film have not paid attention to the meaning of the costumes. Does it matter that Agrado is wearing a knock-off Chanel suit instead of a Versace, a Dior, or any other couture brand? For starters, it matters because this is not the first or the last time that a Chanel suit takes centre stage in an Almodóvar film. And it does so to a great degree, as Agrado points out to Manuela: "There is nothing like wearing a Chanel suit to feel respectable" ("no hay nada como un Chanel para sentirse respetable").

One might think that Agrado in *Todo sobre mi madre* degrades the meaning and aura that a real Chanel outfit carries because she is wearing a fake version of one of her signature pieces, the *tailleur*. To the contrary, I believe that the Chanel legacy might be even more honoured precisely because it is a knock-off suit, and not a real one. How is that possible? As many of the biographers and specialists of Chanel document, for Chanel fashion did not exist until it went out into the streets. Coco did not want fashion to be solely a privilege of the wealthy and was therefore happy to see her designs copied (Balmaceda 97; Bond 45; Charles-Roux 540; Marquand 115). Two factors made this very feasible. First, the austere shapes of her outfits required a small quantity of fabric compared to other couture designers; and second, Chanel's use of inexpensive textiles such as jersey made imitations of her pieces more manageable (de la Haye 53). In fact, the relationship between original and copy is an essential ingredient of her innovation and, as a consequence, of the mythology surrounding her work. Take the most (in)famous Chanel suit, the pink wool suit that Jackie Kennedy was wearing with a pillbox hat the day her husband was assassinated in Dallas on 22 November 1963. This emblematic piece "was itself a copy – albeit, according to recent versions of the story, an authorized New York-made copy – of a Chanel original" (Bruzzi, "Pink" 235). Authorized or not, the key point is that the piece that put Chanel in the history books as "the ultimate fetish object of the JFK assassination" (247), and which is still preserved – in an area not accessible to the public – in the National Archives of the U.S. government, was not an original.

Chanel was also the first couture designer to use fake pearls and costume jewellery as a fashion statement (Charles-Roux 426; Koda and Bolton 20; Madsen 197; Urrea 94). Coco valued jewels as objects of adornment, since they complemented her simple designs, but she never used them as symbols of wealth. Chanel's use of accessories was excessive, especially given how austere her actual clothes were, and they often served to make a parodic statement about the intrinsic distinctiveness of couture fashion. At any rate, jewellery should be for decoration and amusement, never to look rich. This is why, even though Chanel owned some expensive pieces of jewellery, she was rarely seen with those in public (de la Haye 50). This "studied nonchalance" (Richards 25) offered women the possibility of accessorizing their look with abundant, bold, even over-the-top jewellery without breaking the rules of decorum, which banned wearing jewels by day. She made a name for herself by mixing high and low, authentic and fake, by proudly admitting that her designs thrived in the crossroads between the unique couture design and the mechanical reproduction intended for the masses (Koda and Bolton 20). But contrary to Walter Benjamin's famous contention, Chanel did not believe that the aura of her work withered with mechanical reproduction; rather, she celebrated imitations and replicas of her work because, as Rhonda Garelick observes, "the more simulacra of herself she created, the more original *she* would seem" (281, emphasis in the original). Chanel persuaded women to purchase her designs (original or mass-produced) by convincing them that individual sophistication and taste could be maintained despite mass standardization. A famous editorial in the October 1926 issue of *Vogue* compared the design of Chanel's "little black dress" (*la petite robe noire*) to the mass-produced model-T Ford automobile. The suggestion was that the simple dress, which was made in black crêpe de Chine ending below the knee, would be unanimously adopted by the masses. The *Vogue* editorial anticipated that the "Chanel Ford" would be "the frock that all the world will wear" (quoted in de la Haye 44). And it could not have been more accurate in its prediction.

Taking all of this into consideration, far from cheapening the Chanel brand, Agrado's fake *tailleur* is a testament to the far-reaching manufacturing that Coco treasured. In addition, Agrado's homage is all the more relevant because she invokes the gender-bending attributes of Chanel's trademark designs. The appeal of her style rested upon comfort and simplicity, traits that had been traditionally associated with menswear. Chanel turned the world of fashion upside down by breaking away from the baroque opulence that had characterized women's clothing towards the end of the belle époque. As Janet Wallach puts it, her brilliance "lay not in the fanciful but in the functional" (3). This entailed incorporating masculine items like cardigans, pullovers, sweaters, and blazers into the female wardrobe as well as making outfits using fabrics associated with male suits, such as wool and tweed. These flexible and comfortable materials liberated women's fashion from the rigid designs, shapes, and fabrics that had hindered female mobility. With the so-called jersey revolution, Chanel unfettered the female body and invented a new silhouette with no waistline, no superfluous embellishments such as lace or embroidery, and no tailored curves (Leymarie 60). Besides, she added pockets and functional buttons to the top pieces of her suits, which until that point had only been seen in men's wear (Balmaceda 89). She made functionality and comfort, which were erroneously regarded as the opposite of elegance when she surged into the industry, the main pillars of the "Chanel look." This is why details such as jacket pockets were added not for ornamental reasons, but rather for a practical purpose: they offered women the possibility of doing away with handbags by providing a place to store their belongings. She completed her revolutionary vision by shortening skirt lengths and by introducing the short haircut as an option for women.

Chanel was not the first designer to flirt with the androgynous look, but she was the one who made it fashionable and desirable for a large audience.[8] This *garçonne* look, which she embodied herself, was truly revolutionary for modern, independent, and sexually liberated women who wanted to look elegant without sacrificing their advancement and independence in the professional arena. All this was epitomized by her famous *tailleur*, the woman's suit, which Roland Barthes called "Chanel's own invention" and deemed "very close to men's clothing" because it shared the ideal of "distinction" that men's suits historically carried (*Language* 101). The *tailleur*, made in 1913, best represents the Chanel style because it was created at a time "when a minority of women went out to work and had social independence and therefore it had to transpose into clothing something of men's values" (*Language* 101). The masculine "distinction" was the subtle way men were allowed to distinguish themselves – after the drastic changes to men's clothing in the aftermath of the French Revolution – with a "discreet detail," a "next-to-nothing" element that encapsulated their social value (61). Chanel was able to grasp this historical legacy of men's clothing and incorporate it into her style for women. This is key to understanding her philosophy of the *luxe caché* (hidden luxury), which she put into effect, for example, "by sewing gilt chains inside hems, hiding luxurious fur inside simple trench coats, or inserting glossy, printed silk linings into basic wool jackets" (Garelick 195). By translating "masculine" garments, fabrics, details, and social values for women, Chanel reinvented them, which contributed to blurring the strict gender boundaries underpinning the universe of clothing. Nevertheless, she was not trying to make women pass as men; instead, she was appropriating "masculine" elements and values that made them a privileged social group and including them in her vision of modern womanhood.[9]

These values resonate with Agrado's outfit, since she exudes that modern, gender-bending, and sexually liberated womanhood associated with the Chanel look. Agrado is a transgender subject who modifies her body with "female" physical traits (listed in full detail in her monologue), yet decides to retain her penis for professional reasons because her clients prefer their women well hung ("bien dotadas"). The key is that while Agrado spends her life performing womanhood, she does not try to pass as a biological woman or to offer herself as the poster child of a gender-change success story. By flamboyantly impersonating Chanel femininity against the backdrop of the unique Barcelona modernist architecture, Agrado is performing gender identity as "authentic" artificiality, which makes a case for the instability of gender and sexual identity. But her performance (both while walking down Barcelona's "runway" in her fake Chanel and later in her life-story monologue in front of the theatre audience) has less to do with making a case for the understanding of gender as a sociocultural construction than with embracing what Patrick Garlinger aptly calls "authenticity of sentiment" (123). Agrado's performance canonizes sincerity as the only thing that matters when it comes to gender and identity, thereby shifting the focus "to the realm of sentiment as a form of epistemology" (123). She rejects drag queens, whom she calls "mamarrachas" (ridiculous clowns), because they use gender deception and lack sincerity. Thus, one should not see Agrado as the embodiment of the figure of the chameleon, suggested earlier in the narrative through the Capote book that Manuela gives to Esteban, and which Marvin D'Lugo sees as "the central structural-artistic motif of the film" (*Pedro Almodóvar* 103). Unlike the chameleon, unlike the drag queens, she is not simulating authenticity; rather, she *is* "very authentic" because her feelings and her dreams are genuine.

This is why it does not matter that the Chanel suit is a copy. Agrado does not really aspire to own a "real" Chanel and does not mind revealing that hers is fake, just as she does not hide that she still has a penis. The important thing is that she feels like a very authentic (and respectable) woman wearing it, and that this authenticity is perceived by others (such as Manuela). In tune with the legacy of the "Chanel look," in which how clothes are worn is much more important than what is worn (Baudot 9), Agrado radiates that professional "distinction" that Chanel translated so well from the sartorial vocabulary of men's clothing. After all, she is on her way to try to find a job that would allow her to retire from the streets, and the Chanel suit was a core garment in the wardrobes of successful professional women. Agrado shows here a great awareness of fashion history, in the sense that she interprets and embodies the Chanel tradition, while also adding her own two cents. It is not a coincidence that she chooses to wear the knock-off *tailleur* in this particular context – and not, for example, to go out at night – in order to show that she *is* a professionally reputable woman because she *feels* like one.

In contrast to the Chanel philosophy, of course, the "distinction" Agrado seeks does not pertain to a fantasy of social mobility but to her gender "authenticity," to her ability to embody respectable femininity. This is especially clear in the monologue scene when she offers exhaustive details of her artificially tailored feminine body. Medium shots and medium close-ups of Agrado with the red curtain of the theatre in the background underscore the performative nature of her identity, and of gender identity in a broader sense. When Agrado states that "the more a woman resembles what she has dreamed for herself, the more authentic she is," she is proclaiming the collapse of the boundaries between "artificiality" and "naturalness." The use of a telephoto lens gives these shots a narrow field of view, thus emphasizing Agrado's fusion with the red curtain and, hence, her "theatrical," artificially manufactured yet "very authentic" identity. Agrado's pink cardigan and red hair also suggest this fusion by establishing a chromatic continuity with the red curtain, as if painting her into the theatrical background. This flattening of the image obliterates any depth of field by blurring the line between foreground and background, which creates an egalitarian surface that eliminates differences. A prominent feature of *Todo sobre mi madre* and, as Emmanuel Vincenot remarks, of Almodóvar's visual style in general (246–9), this flatness of the image further accentuates the ethical conversation of this film regarding gender identity. The democratization suggested by the flat image (by eliminating spatial differences within the frame) can be linked on the thematic level to the questioning of rigid and essentialist gender and sexual identities, which Agrado embodies. Therefore, we should interpret the meaning of Agrado's "Chanel look" in relation to this democratization suggested by the visual style of the film and, above all, by the emphasis on superficiality and the elimination of differences. What I am suggesting is that instead of making her look distinguished, the "Chanel look" helps Agrado fit in by proving her "authentic" womanhood.

This certainly diverges from the effect Chanel intended with her *tailleurs*. Although the French couturier was happy to see all kinds of women wearing her designs – or imitations of them – the point was to make women feel exclusive and unique doing so, not to help them blend in. Agrado's diverse bearing of the "fashion classic" makes an additional and provocative point regarding fashion theory and history. Influential fashion theorists have unveiled the ideological manoeuvres through which a particular garment, such as the Chanel *tailleur*, achieves the pedigree of a "classic." Malcom Barnard contends that the quality and design of a garment have little to do with its canonization as a classic. Instead, the key is that the garment "represents one dominant group's taste at one time and place," which is subsequently "presented by that group and accepted by the majority as good or fashionable taste at every time and place" (*Fashion Theory* 71). From this perspective, it follows that the fashion classic has a significant ideological role in legitimizing social and cultural hierarchies. The fashion classic functions as a powerful instrument of class dominance by way of becoming a social myth in the sense described by Roland Barthes. The ideological operation at stake here makes "contingency appear eternal," for it gives something that is profoundly historical "a natural and eternal justification" (*Mythologies* 143). Therefore, a piece becomes a fashion classic by being taken out of history, by being naturalized as an innocently timeless garment when in reality it epitomizes the values of a social group imposing its taste over the rest of society. The insidious outcome of this process is that if a particular group's taste is accepted as natural, and as naturally superior, then that group's position at the top of the social hierarchy becomes equally regarded as natural and, thereby, indisputable. In "rocking" a fake Chanel *tailleur*, Agrado denaturalizes this process of cultural hegemony. She appropriates certain "natural" values associated with this fashion classic (such as respectable femininity) but has no qualms about calling attention to the social injustice involved in possessing an "authentic" – and dreadfully overpriced – piece of this timeless classic garment.

Agrado's gesture is obviously not enough to confront the entire structure of unequal social relations that come with elitist cultural forms such as haute couture, but it does contribute to calling critical attention to the ideological functions behind the process of the naturalization of fashion classics. Put bluntly, Agrado brings the classic Chanel *tailleur* back to history by exposing the power dynamics involved in making it a timeless classic. Agrado's historization – and politicization – of the fashion classic goes hand in hand with her destabilization of the boundaries between "naturalness" and "artificiality" in relation to gender and sexual identities. Agrado shifts our attention from what is seen as "natural" or has been socially naturalized – be it related to class, gender, or sexuality – to the contingent, the provisional, and the historical; from essentialist notions of identities and subjectivities to a performative understanding of those; from a sense of eternal, immutable social order to social mobility. In doing so, Agrado endorses a democratization of society by performing the possibility that certain social differences can cease to be so visible.

All of these compelling ideas sparked by Agrado's knock-off Chanel prove that theories that understand fashion as a closed structure detached from historical change are inadequate. This is a deeply post-Barthesian understanding of fashion. In most of his writings about fashion, but especially in his monumental *The Fashion System*, Barthes contended that fashion was a rigid social system that followed purely formal rules. Like a language, fashion possesses a grammar and a vocabulary, and scholars should study it as long as they articulate their conclusions within that strongly coded structure; that is, what Barthes called a "written system" of signification rather than actual clothes being worn (x). His radically formalist view of fashion and clothing has been remarkably influential in elevating the study of fashion to the category of a cultural form capable of producing important social meanings. Yet the downside is that his proposed methodology detached fashion and clothing from the contingency of historical change and, as a result, from the enriching perspective of ideological critiques of clothing. A semiological analysis of fashion such as the one proposed by Barthes ignores that there are several competing fashion systems (and not just one) and, as Jennifer Craik notes, "elite fashion design does not constitute all fashion behaviour, nor uniformly determine other sets of arrangements" (225). This leads us to a crucial point that Agrado makes by wearing that knock-off Chanel suit. Her performance can be conceptualized as what Joanne Entwistle calls "situated bodily practice," that is, the practice of translating fashion into everyday dress (4). Fashion shapes Agrado's body not as an a priori structuring determinant, but through her empowering bodily practice that activates certain cogent historical meanings of the Chanel suit in a particular social context that, in turn, infuses the classic outfit with original connotations. Bridging the gap between fashion and dress, Agrado demonstrates that making a fashion statement entails, contrary to what Barthes thought, a balance between structuring influence and active agency.

Granted, what Agrado embodies is the contemporary Chanel look fashioned by Karl Lagerfeld, the last artistic director of the House of Chanel, and not the original style crafted by Coco Chanel. This adds another layer to the conversation about authenticity. The knock-off suit copies Lagerfeld's own interpretation (or shall we venture to say imitation?) of the Chanel look. Yet Chanel's legacy is not lost in this chain of imitations – instead, it is reinvigorated. Lagerfeld succeeded in strengthening the Chanel brand while challenging some of Coco's untouchable ideas. For example, he shortened skirt lengths above the knee (even to micro-mini proportions), liberated tweeds from the limiting palette of soft pastels (Richards 123), and played with multicolour combinations that are trendily eccentric. He transformed the traditional features of Chanel into a style that works in the present day. This has entailed a parallel process of recognizing her legacy while simultaneously proposing a parody or caricature of it (Garelick 427). Like the German designer, Almodóvar is a master in interpreting cinematic and cultural references, in incorporating elements from unlikely cultural phenomena, past and present, in an eclectic blend that emanates modernity. Two prominent examples from *Todo sobre mi madre* illustrate this point. Joseph Mankiewicz's *All About Eve* (1950), which inspired the title and certain themes and characters' relationships in Almodóvar's film (when Manuela substitutes Nina in the play, Nina accuses her of being just like Eve Harrington), and Tennessee Williams's *A Streetcar Named Desire* (1947) are key references in the film. However, as others have noted, Almodóvar does not merely cite them with reverence; rather, he reinterprets these intertexts, adding new meanings and adapting them to the circumstances of his film narrative (Ballesteros, "Performing Identities" 80; Davies, *Pedro Almodóvar* 93–5). In *Todo sobre mi madre*, Almodóvar rewrites *All About Eve*'s "conservative portrayal of women's work as pure ambition" to instead emphasize solidarity among women (Garlinger 119). And in Almodóvar's version of *A Streetcar Named Desire*, which is represented at different moments in the film, Stella is not submissive to Stanley, as she moves on at the end and promises to never return. Stephen Maddison contends that the Spanish filmmaker's reworking of Williams's play shows that "women have choices outside of their relations with men" (267), which is best exemplified by Manuela's newfound bonds with other women (and her new maternal roles with Rosa and then Esteban III) that help her move past her troubles with men.

Not all influences Almodóvar appropriates are as canonical as these two. In fact, he has become famous (and controversial among some film critics) for carrying out what Andy Medhurst calls "cultural cross-stitching" (127), that is, for recycling lowbrow and popular culture elements, often with a camp sensibility (Mira, *De Sodoma* 553–9, *Miradas* 418–19; Yarza) along with art cinema components, into his unique style.[10] Again, this echoes Lagerfeld's postmodern eclecticism, which entailed incorporating popular elements into his haute couture vision. Working "with the skill of a *bricoleur*," Lagerfeld introduced blue-collar materials such as denim to the glamorous world of couture, and overtly borrowed from the vocabulary of street styles including punk, surfer culture, and hip-hop (Koda and Bolton 37, 35). Both Lager-feld and Almodóvar thrive in the art of recycling, combining, and re-combining those references and, especially, in mixing elite and popular elements. And both have contributed to making Chanel's style eternal.

At the same time, Agrado's knock-off Chanel also revives notable feminist concerns about Chanel style and, more broadly, about the abil-ity of fashion to promote progressive gender roles. Almodóvar's films, and *Todo sobre mi madre* in particular, has elicited similar scepticism, even outright rejection, from feminist scholarship. For example, Bar-bara Zecchi has taken Almodóvar to task for presenting womanhood and motherhood as synonymous in *Todo sobre mi madre*, which she says obliterates the prospect of liberating female identity from mater-nity ("All about Mothers" 154). In another piece, Zecchi and Jacque-line Cruz assert that the maternal drive overshadows any possibility of female sexual desire in the film, since the only desire depicted in the narrative is the desire to be a mother, or the desire to become a woman to be able to be a mother, in the case of Agrado ("Maternidad" 155). While the option of maternity in this film is open to a range of subjects (not only to biological women), destabilizing the hegemonic concept of the traditional heteronormative family, it reestablishes other patriar-chal structures such as the confinement of female identity to maternal instincts. For these critics, *All About My Mother* implies that all a woman can be is a mother.

These sharp critiques point to one of the hardest issues to grapple with from a feminist point of view in Almodóvar's films: the para-doxical coexistence in his narratives of radically queer – in the vari-ous senses of fluid, unstable, and performative – gender and sexual identities along with essentialist notions of womanhood repeatedly tied to self-abnegating maternity. As Susan Martin-Márquez observes, "few filmmakers have presented so many competing examples of 'naturally' self-sacrificial, and 'unnaturally' selfish, mothers" ("Pedro Almodóvar's" 498). *Todo sobre mi madre* certainly draws on this ances-try of "good" and "bad" Almodóvar mothers, presenting Manuela and Rosa's mother (Rosa María Sardá) as textbook cases of each model. Nevertheless, as Susan Martin-Márquez additionally argued, it is rea-sonable to give Almodóvar credit for going beyond these essentialist archetypes in *Todo sobre mi madre* by presenting motherhood as the in-terest in the well-being of the self and others that should "become the ethical standard for all human relationships," instead of something that pertains strictly to women. In so doing, Almodóvar might be deliver-ing his biggest feminist statement yet, by redefining what have been traditionally considered female-specific concerns as universal concerns

("Pedro Almodóvar's" 508). Along these lines, Julián Daniel Gutiérrez-Albilla contends that *Todo sobre mi madre* proposes a form of queer maternity: "an ethical gesture that is associated with a capacity to hold the other, beyond normative conceptions of the family" (575). This ethical mode of relationality is, in this film, "adopted by women, transgendered subjects, and men of all possible sexual orientations," and entails renouncing selfishness in order to offer opportunities to someone else (575). Seen through the critical lenses suggested by Martin-Márquez and Gutiérrez-Albilla, maternity in *Todo sobre mi madre* is not intrinsically bound to a patriarchal and heteronormative structure.

Given this multifaceted representation of motherhood in *Todo sobre mi madre*, mixed reactions are to be expected, and even celebrated, for prompting a productive scholarly debate about all the nuances and implications, all the achievements and shortcomings, of this complex film for feminist discourse in Spanish culture. Other feminist controversies around this film that are more closely related to the topic of my discussion are, however, less comprehensible and indeed appear to be extremely misguided. In particular, I am troubled by Maria Donapetry's assertion that the character of Agrado comes close to a "ginocidio" (gynocide). The emphasis on the performative nature of gender identity erases female difference, what she calls "lo específicamente femenino" (the intrinsically feminine) (383), which can apparently only be embodied by biological women. Donapetry goes even further by stating that Agrado cannot be called a woman because "la cirugía estética no produce a una mujer, ni la ropa, ni siquiera un tono de voz o unos movimientos" (surgery does not make a woman, and neither does clothing, the voice, or body movements), even in the postmodern era in which "la réplica sustituye al modelo y vale lo mismo que el modelo" (the replica replaces the model and has the same value as the model) (382). What bothers Donapetry about the character of Agrado is that she embodies an "artificial" gender identity that copies with excess certain aspects of womanhood (the less important ones – the superficial look, the clothes), but she cannot get close to the "natural" essence of a woman (whatever that means). Leaving aside the problematic understanding of gender as an essence and the blatant transphobia behind her words, Donapetry's disapproval of Agrado's concern with expressing her gender identity through clothing draws on a common misconception about fashion that Janet Radcliffe Richards identified among certain strands of feminism: a misperception around the notion of "the natural" that confuses it with "authenticity" (239). The implication is that only "natural" women are authentic, and that clothing and fashion are masks, trivial and deceptive, that hide the real body underneath and only serve to attract the male gaze. This view ignores the pleasures that some women find in dressing to the nines as well as the practices of female spectatorship that may generate potentially empowering scenarios of fantasy and identification (not to mention erotic arousal) with fashion images.

When Agrado walks through Barcelona in her fake Chanel flaunting excessive femininity, she is of course calling attention to her body, not to reinstate the supremacy of the natural but on the contrary, to celebrate the blurring of the boundaries between artificiality and naturalness and, furthermore, to equate authenticity with sincerity. This encapsulates the broader ethical conversation Almodóvar explores in *Todo sobre mi madre* in relation to a critique of traditional gender roles and sexual identities in favour of a performative notion of sex and gender identity. As we can see, rather than a flat symbol of status, or of aspiration to status in this case, the Chanel knock-off suit exhibited by Agrado, who is presenting feminine "realness," is invested with multiple layers of meaning within this Almodóvar film, as if there were no better habitat for it to flourish. In the specific case of *Todo sobre mi madre*, Almodóvar contributes to the Chanel legacy by overhauling Chanel's rigid, essentialist, and heterocentric vision of femininity – especially after her comeback in 1954 – by having a character who would not typically be considered in the prevailing heterosocial order embody the "Chanel look." The transgender character revitalizes the Chanel style while benefitting from the undertones of the modern yet respectable femininity that this style contributes to her gender presentation. Both global brands (Chanel and Almodóvar) imbue each other with their own cultural legacy, which includes their own complex and sometimes-tense relationship with feminism.

Variations on a Familiar Outfit: *Los abrazos rotos*

Early in the narrative of *Los abrazos rotos*, there is a medium close-up of Lena (Penélope Cruz) curling her eyelashes in front of a mirror. She appears impeccably groomed with her hair in a sophisticated low bun and low-key make up that draws attention to her eyes: dark eyeshadow that complements Lena's dark eyes, her black dress, and her naturally black hair. The high-key lighting treatment of the shot underlines Lena's beauty, as there is a balanced combination of different light sources, with sufficient fill light to offset the intensity of the key light and, therefore, to eliminate any unflattering shadows on her face. To top it off, a hard backlight creates a halo effect over her head by lightening her hair. The background appears completely out of focus, ensuring that the spectator's undivided attention is on Lena's radiant face. The glowing beauty of this shot (almost a textbook example of the use of lighting and make-up for a female lead in commercial cinema), is further accentuated by the editing, since it comes right after the dark screen of a fade-out that marks a temporal shift from 2008 to 1994.

A backward tracking shot opens the frame to display Lena's spectacular outfit: a tight, black Chanel sheath evening dress dramatically ornamented with gilded jewellery that covers the upper part of the dress, from the hips all the way up to the shoulders. Lena completes the look with a large gilded necklace and gold button earrings. As noted before, pairing simple dresses with theatrical jewelry was a trademark of the Chanel style. Yet for Chanel the bold jewellery was always a form of ornamentation and never a medium for projecting a woman's wealth. Jewellery was helpful to make women look beautiful, not rich. In Lena's case, the ostentatious gilded necklace and earrings are redundant at best, since the dress is already covered with gilded chains (see fig. 2.3). As Almodóvar suggests in the script of the film, this outfit is like a double-edged sword of signification: it makes Lena look splendid while simultaneously chaining her to luxury and affluence ("la encadena al lujo y bienestar") (*Los abrazos* 40). The fact that her wealthy lover, Ernesto Martel (José Luis Gómez), has to help her tie the knot of the necklace further emphasizes the high price she has to pay for being his mistress, as she has replaced freedom with wealth.

In contrast to the multilayered use of the Chanel (fake) garment in *Todo sobre mi madre*, in *Los abrazos rotos* it seems like a clear symbol of Lena's social climbing from corporate secretary to mistress of a financial magnate. However, given how much nuance Almodóvar had extracted from the products of the House of Chanel in previous films, one could hardly expect that he would include this reference to suggest only a straightforward interpretation. Later in the film, Ernesto is waiting for Lena, and he is visibly jealous because it is late at night and she is still not home. Lena walks into the living room with a radiant smile, dressed in a red-and-blue checkered Chanel wool bouclé cardigan worn with tight jeans and a tank top. The cardigan has gold chains stitched on the sides, back, shoulders, and arms, as well as luxurious gold buttons. Lena also wears a quilted 2.55 handbag, another signature piece of the Chanel fashion lexicon. The gilt chain that functions as a shoulder strap in tandem with the golden motifs of the cardigan inevitably makes the viewer associate this outfit with the previous evening dress that Lena ornamented with heavy gilded chains. Nevertheless, the context is significantly different. Lena arrives home tired but happy after a long day of work, shooting the film *Chicas y maletas* (Girls and suitcases) and

Fig. 2.3. Wealth and affluence chaining Lena (Penélope Cruz) in *Los abrazos rotos*

passionately making love with Mateo (Lluís Homar), who is also the director of the film. Moreover, this time she is not in front of a mirror, which, according to John Sanderson, in Almodóvar's films tends to "reflect the expectations society has of a female character and, as a consequence, what she has become before realizing that it is not what she really wanted" (482). Instead, she has made her dream come true – acting in a film – and has found the love of her life. Still, the gilt chains seem to reactivate, at least in her unconscious, the sense that she is trapped by the "sugar daddy" who pays for her lifestyle as well as for the film they are making. To her disgust, Ernesto suggests that they go away for the weekend to his Ibiza house, and Lena instinctively takes off her cardigan, as if all of a sudden the garment was asphyxiating her because it was paid for by Ernesto. The gesture is subtle but perceptible, signposting her impending rebellion in a third instance in which she is dressed in a Chanel outfit.

Lena is walking out of Mateo's house after another passionate encounter with her lover. Ernesto Jr. (Rubén Ochandiano) is waiting for her in the street with a camera on a tripod ready to shoot evidence of their affair. Like L.B. Jefferies (James Stewart) in Hitchcock's *Rear Window* (1954), he has previously recorded their silhouettes through the window. He is Ernesto Martel's grief-stricken gay son, who develops his own crush on Mateo, and is filming a "making-of" documentary of

Fig. 2.4. Lena's Chanel nautical look in *Los abrazos rotos*

Chicas y maletas. In reality, though, he is being used by his dad to spy on Lena. Ernesto then watches the footage provided by his son with the aid of a professional lip-reader he hires to complete the missing audio. When Lena notices that Ernesto Jr. is filming her in an intimate moment, she becomes furious and runs towards him to try to prevent him from filming her. She is wearing a Chanel navy blue knitted suit with white braid trims (see fig. 2.4). The pleated ending of the dress above the knee facilitates Lena's frantic movement, as does the elasticity of the jacket and its length, with sleeves ending just below the elbow for a three-quarter-length sleeve that allows ease of movement. This nautical look, reminiscent of the stripped jersey sweaters that Chanel designed in her early days and that she later translated into the vocabulary of suits, is inspired by military garb – hence the navy blue – which makes it all the more appropriate for a scene in which she physically attacks Ernesto Jr.

As we can see, there is a gradation in the degree of signifying complexity expressed through the garments of the Chanel brand in relation to the agency afforded to the female lead. The Chanel looks reveal a noticeable progression in the plot, from stultifying symbol of Lena's status as "trophy mistress" to military-inspired outfit that she wears when expressing her intention to unshackle herself from the domineering magnate. This is an important nuance that challenges one-dimensional interpretations of the use of costumes in this film. The mostly negative reviews of *Los abrazos rotos* rushed to lambast Almodóvar for over-fixating on matters of surface and style at the cost of psychological characterization, especially of its female lead. Although "visual pyrotechnics" and "rich saturated colors" (Byrne) are usual suspects that one is almost assured to find in the visual lexicon of an Almodóvar film, the critical consensus about this film seemed to endorse Nick Schager's view that "the actress is largely relegated to being a ravishing mannequin whose true thoughts and feelings remain a mystery" (*Slant Magazine*). Spanish film scholars, for the most part, also subscribed to this take, which was articulated in press reviews. In a feminist-informed analysis of the film, Samuel Amago contends that *Los abrazos rotos* presents "an aggressive masculine gaze" that concentrates so much on its female lead's exterior looks that it erases her subjectivity. Even though the spectator sees "everything of Lena's body, her face, her hair adorned with a variety of wigs, her body dressed in an array of dresses, and even X-rays of her bones," according to this critic, "at the film's conclusion we are left with very little sense as to who she really is" (27). The epitome of this focus on appearance comes when Lena poses for still shots in the pre-shooting rehearsals and Mateo has her try on a variety of costumes and wigs dolling her up as Audrey Hepburn and engineering a platinum-blonde Marilyn Monroe look.

While these critics and scholars are right in pointing out that the focus on female physical beauty – costumes included – is remarkably high, my issue with their critiques is twofold. First, these negative reactions to the importance of costume in this film are so categorical that they seem to echo the almost routine rejection of dress and fashion in elitist academic circles as a superficial aspect of culture that does not merit meaningful scholarly attention. As Jennifer Craik aptly puts it, clothing and fashion are "often thought of as a kind of mask disguising the 'true' nature of the body or person," or of a film character in this case, seen "as a superficial gloss" (1). Taking into consideration the reception of previous Almodóvar films that give costume design a prominent role, especially *Tacones lejanos*, these critiques certainly evoke a bit of déjà vu. In addition, they seem to overlook or play down the multifaceted reflexivity involved in this overload of cinematic surfaces. This shortcoming is especially noteworthy in Amago's case, since reflexivity is precisely the fulcrum of his study.

Los abrazos rotos is an ode to film and filmmaking, "a masterful celebration of cinema's power of resilience" in the age of digital video (Kinder, "Restoring Broken" 28), and also a thoughtful reflection on the artifice of cinema, including the expectations that the film industry imposes on its female stars (Sanderson 485). So when "Almodóvar's camera goes into a kind of swooning trance" to portray Penélope Cruz "in a state of almost hyperreal gorgeousness," as Peter Bradshaw vividly put it in his review of *Los abrazos rotos* after its screening at Cannes, we need to go beyond merely rejoicing over the stunning visual rendition of the star or condemning it for sheer lack of substance. An important detail of these instances of ecstatic fixation on Cruz's beauty is that they encapsulate a deep awareness of the fabricated nature of that female beauty – as part of the artifice and illusion created by cinema – and, most importantly, of the hard work that goes into it. As Ann Davies notes, in the much-criticized scene in the dressing room, it appears that the actress merely "becomes the canvas on which the director tries out his artistic experiments," but the montage sequence of poses also suggests that "beauty itself is a performance that needs time, thought and staff to maintain" (*Penélope* 118). Being a muse is not just about being a passive object of desire; it is an elaborate construction that requires the performance and expertise of a variety of crew members (the costume designer, make-up artists, hair stylists, artistic directors, camera technicians, the director, and so on).

When Lena is getting ready to wear the Chanel evening dress, we see Cruz's stunning beauty reflected in the mirror. The same scenario of mirror reflection appears in the pre-shooting photo session in the studio dressing room, although this time her image is also mediated by Mateo's photo camera and Ernesto Jr.'s digital camera. In fact, Lena's entire life appears mediated by camera lenses, since her developing romance with the film director is captured by Ernesto Jr.'s "making-of" documentary. Ensnared by visual technologies, Lena is, as Almodóvar noted in the press book of *Los abrazos rotos*, a woman predestined to fatality rather than "femme fatale" ("Lena no es una mujer fatal, sino condenada a la fatalidad"). In a prominent intertextual nod to Hitchcock's *Vertigo* (1958), Lena appears as a victim of the male construction of femininity through visual mechanisms of control. Her tragic fate, for she ends up dying in a car accident that her male lover survives – which does not escape the controlling gaze of Ernesto Jr.'s camera – further reinforces her connection to Hitchcock's female leads. However, Almodóvar also affords his character a partial way out of this visual trap. Marvin D'Lugo has compellingly argued that the emphasis on the power of voice and speech in this film serves as a strategy to counteract "the force of self-consuming cinematic illusion" ("*Los abrazos*" 213). The female voice works "as a subversive narrative strategy, challenging the patriarchy that owns the airwaves" (214), as exemplified by the long monologues of Judit (Blanca Portillo), Mateo's former lover and current production director, and Chon (Carmen Machi), the fictitious character in *Chicas y maletas*. These two speeches privilege the verbal dimension of film over the visual one and, furthermore, "provide a symmetrical structure with two scenes in which male characters seek to control the telling (Mateo, Martel)" (220).[11]

Most decisively, Lena gets her own, albeit shorter, speech. In the scene in which she attacks Ernesto Jr. while wearing the navy blue Chanel outfit, Lena demands that Ernesto focus the camera on her while she gives a speech for Martel. She dubs her own voice when she enters Martel's viewing room and interrupts the projection, to the magnate's astonishment. This repetition of the verbal act functions as an empowering mechanism by which Lena "threatens the privilege of what up to this point had been the naturalised and unchallenged assertion of male mastery over story" (D'Lugo, "*Los abrazos*" 222). I would like to add to D'Lugo's fitting assessment that this sequence also affords Lena the opportunity to threaten the visual male mastery over her story. When she attacks Ernesto Jr., she grabs his camera tripod and traps him against the wall. She starts hitting the camera hard to try to knock it down and, thereby, to prevent Ernesto from further intruding on her life, which in the broader conversation of the film signifies an attempt to dismantle the aggressive visual technology that has held her captive. Yet she immediately changes her strategy and appropriates the medium to fashion her own image and message directed towards the master exploiter of that technological medium, Ernesto Martel. Samuel Amago claims that Lena is "the object of all visual technologies in the film," but is at the end of the day relegated to "an absent and obscure object of male desire" (25), and to being "all surface and no depth" (27). My analysis of this sequence has demonstrated that Almodóvar displays a more intricate and reflexive use of the aesthetic technologies of visual and aural representation – including a sophisticated use of costume choices – that allows for the assertion of female agency and subjectivity.

Ultimately, Lena is more than a gorgeous, empty figurine shaped and reshaped – through costume, accessories, and makeup – by the male gaze and the camera lenses controlled by that gaze. At several points in the narrative, she takes charge of the grooming and performative skills to sculpt the most convenient image of herself, which serves as a survival mechanism. Most prominently, during the weekend retreat in Ibiza, she adeptly employs make-up and hair styling to hide from Ernesto's view of her pale appearance caused by nausea and vomit. This sequence emphasizes how Lena brilliantly performs her best acting role in her private life – and thus without the instructions of the male director, or anyone else for that matter – where she uses her dexterous grooming skills to hide her disgust. Later, when she decides to stop hiding her feelings, she appropriates those visual technologies that seemed to imprison her in order to put her inner desires and aversions on display. The digital camera – with her own post-dubbed voice – is the witness of her most intimate reality, and the medium of communication through which Ernesto finds out about her repulsion for him and love for Mateo. In the end, the visual technology reveals her genuine self, below the surface. As in *Todo sobre mi madre*, performance (cinematic in Lena's case, theatrical in Agrado's) and costume play a crucial role in enacting female subjectivity and identity. Dressed in Chanel – fake or otherwise – both female characters unveil their most authentic selves. Thus, fashion in these two films cannot be conceptualized and considered separate from the bodies that wear its products, since it is tied to the individuals and their self-fabricated identities. Agrado and Lena embody the fluctuating tension in feminist critiques between considering fashion to be either an empowering expression or a limiting form of oppression, but in the larger ethical conversation of the films, both seem more like fashion soldiers than victims.

Conclusion

It is no accident that Almodóvar resorts to Hitchcock and Chanel as points of reference for his intricately (self-)referential homage to the art of filmmaking in *Los abrazos rotos*. Chanel's influence on Almodóvar is obviously not as weighty and extensive as Hitchcock's, whom Dona Kercher aptly deems "Almodóvar's primary textbook and industrial model" (63), yet she is certainly not a minor presence in his films. Chanel garments resurface in films in which Almodóvar worked with three different costume designers, which points to the fact that, even though he is an auteur with valuable collaborators, Almodóvar is ultimately behind the decision to revert to Chanel. As with the references to Hitchcock, Almodóvar adopts those outfits for making his own statements on the politics of gender and sexual identity.[12] As I have shown in my detailed analyses of key scenes in these films, the garments retain some recognized meanings from the aesthetic legacy of the House of Chanel, but they are reactivated with new significance and ideological implications in each of the films. The Chanel garments become "Almodovarized," so to speak.

The Chanel outfits have become, like certain narrative situations, plot twists, and visual elements (i.e., his fascination with the colour red), a customary ingredient of the Almodovarian grammar and vocabulary. This might be the ultimate commonality with the French couturier whom he so adores. François Baudot argues that what gave Chanel her identifiable global image was the repetition of a number of elements of her unique style that belonged to her alone (12). Chanel did not design completely different garments every season. Occasionally, she introduced a new piece into her operational lexicon, but she typically worked on variations of the same classic pieces. Yet the key to her prolonged success was that she never presented the same exact model twice. That is, Chanel did not plagiarize herself, but rather delivered recreations of garments that included a new detail or manner of constructing and sewing, however subtle, that kept generating interest and, most importantly, massive sales.

Almodóvar's cinema also follows a similar logic of repetition with adjustments. Among other stylistic features, Almodóvar is known for constantly evoking and borrowing elements from his previous films, which become recreated in new narrative scenarios. Marsha Kinder fittingly terms this trademark "retroseriality," which she asserts is not only a feature of Almodóvar's films, since they offer "variations of the same genetic material," but also a way of reading them ("All About the Brothers" 268). *Los abrazos rotos* lends itself perhaps to the ultimate retroserial reading, as it earned Almodóvar a fair share of criticism (Garcés; Smith, "Los abrazos rotos") for reverting to too many of his signature elements such as his fascination with hospital scenes and the film-within-the-film motif (actually re-enacting scenes from one of his previous films, *Mujeres al borde de un ataque de nervios*).[13] Along these lines, the presence of a number of Chanel outfits evokes *Tacones lejanos* and *Todo sobre mi madre*, but so does "the dressing room scene," which is central to all three films, as well as the ubiquitous and spectacular role of the colour red. What I am suggesting is that by including variations of the Chanel suit in three different films, Almodóvar is not merely paying homage to the timeless style of one of the couture houses and brands he most admires. Rather, I argue, the filmmaker is turning Chanel fashion into another crucial element of his own repertoire that reappears, in retroserial fashion, periodically in his films as a variation on a familiar theme. Chanel's eternal outfits, let us say it overtly, are already part and parcel of Almodóvar's own "eternal" visual style.

Chapter Three

Men in Underwear in Spanish Cinema

Scholarly accounts of men's dress and men's fashion are relatively scarce compared to the scholarship on women's wear, and are usually confined to the study of business attire. This comparative disinterest in men's clothing is closely associated with assumptions and beliefs about gender that developed during the nineteenth century (Reilly and Cosbey xii), as the result of the "Great Masculine Renunciation" that, as I explained in the introduction, supposedly imposed a universal austerity in men's sartorial styles. In this sense, Ted Polhemus sarcastically observes that modern men who aspired to succeed in the public sphere had to become invisible, and "the bland, ill-fitting suit" was their only option (47). These gender differences become even more pronounced when we narrow the discussion to underwear, given that men's underwear, until recently, has been routinely dismissed as irrelevant to fashion and cultural history (Jobling, *Man Appeal* 121).[1] For example, the editors of the 1985 *Esquire Guide to Style* – a special issue of the magazine *Esquire* devoted to men's fashion and released annually to much fanfare – surprisingly dedicated only a few paragraphs to underwear; they simply recommended that readers pick something comfortable. The alleged reason why they virtually overlooked an entire category of clothing was that a man's selection of intimate apparel was "strictly personal" and had no bearing on his public image or identity. The kind of underwear a man chooses, even if it is ridiculously unfashionable, would not hinder his career or "scandalize the community" (William Wilson 105). The clear message was that with underwear (or even without it), a man could never go wrong, as no one else will ever get to see or judge it.

To a contemporary reader, this sounds like a statement from a bygone era; today, underwear is widely seen as a form of social communication that "makes a potent statement about the wearer" (Delis Hill 8).

A man's underwear contributes significantly to his sense of self and identity. But this is a recent perception. For the longest time, men's underwear was considered primarily functional, "comforting to the body's shape, and made of sturdy, protective fabrics" (Benson and Esten 107). It was a practical article of clothing used for cleanliness and protection, not for communicating a sense of style and fashion, let alone for expressing sexiness or desirability – one of the primary functions of women's underclothes (Willett and Cunnington 15–16). Men's under-wear has also received scant critical attention due to its austerity com-pared to women's underclothes (Carter 9; Cole 7): it has mostly been a two-item affair (undershirt and underpants), while the inventory for women has also included articles like bras, corsets, girdles, and garter belts, to name but a few.

In 1951, a pioneering study of the history of underclothing gave an equal amount of space to both women's and men's varieties (Wil-lett and Cunnington). But the perception that men's undergarments were simple and had a merely utilitarian function explains why sub-sequent accounts have focused on women's underwear, often exclu-sively (Avellaneda, Caldwell, Ewing, Fontanel, Gavarrón, Martin and Koda, Wilson-Kovacs), with only brief mentions of men's styles and varieties (Carter, Fernández Flores). More recently, however, special-ized studies on men's underwear (Cole, Delis Hill), and the way it has been marketed to the public (Jobling, *Man Appeal* and *Advertising*), have begun to fill this gap, even if they concentrate almost entirely on the Anglo-American world. These studies have had to tackle a third hur-dle: representations of men's underwear in popular culture as a hu-morous subject. As Colin McDowell notes, "the sight of a man in his underwear – traditionally ludicrous – has been a staple of farce for generations. Baggy and all-concealing, such clothes robbed the male of dignity by making him comical" (14). As we shall see in my analysis of Spanish films, this convention is pervasive across national and gen-erational borders. From classics of the Francoist era such as *El verdugo* (Luis García Berlanga, 1963) to more recent popular films with a queer edge such as *Sobreviviré* (Alfonso Albacete and David Menkes, 1999), images of men in their underwear have ubiquitously produced a comic effect. Yet, this is not the only role male undergarments have played in Spanish cinema. Celluloid men in underwear have also frequently appeared in erotic contexts. Sometimes the focus on underwear was designed to keep the male genitals hidden from view (as in many of the soft-core pornographic films of the late 1970s and early 1980s); other times, the goal was to generate sex appeal by calling attention to male genitalia (such as in Bigas Luna's *Jamón, jamón* [1992]).

In this chapter, my goal is to scrutinize these representations. While my account is not fully comprehensive – I do not aim to offer a complete history of men's underwear in Spanish cinema – I draw some general conclusions from the wide variety of films discussed here. Representations have oscillated between the comical and the erotic, sometimes with an overlap between the two. Beyond the taxonomic impulse to catalogue examples in their appropriate category, my enquiry is driven by a conviction that the subject matter deserves critical attention because it is a fascinating indicator, even if not in a straightforward manner, of major social changes. One of the main lessons from Cecil Willett and Phillis Cunnington's work was the importance of better connecting our enquiries into both outerwear and underwear, since they have been traditionally approached as if they were two completely distinct spheres of cultural interest. Both of them respond to the same social forces and, as a matter of fact, "the influences responsible for the surface fashions have been responsible also for the changes beneath, though such changes may have taken longer to develop" (Willett and Cunnington 20). It is true that more ephemeral sartorial changes are less likely to influence the deeper layers, which are typically only affected by deep social turmoil. Indeed, a good marker of the intensity of a social upheaval is how profoundly it affects clothing. If it has any bearing on underwear, then it might be truly revolutionary.[2] In this sense, shifts in underwear patterns and styles may serve as an effective metric, though certainly not the only one, for measuring the dynamics of masculinity and its redefinition in relation to wider social transformations in Spanish society in the last few decades. In what follows, I show how Spanish cinema, through the hilarious and/or (un)erotic images of men in underwear, tells the story of evolving gender roles, developments in sexual politics, and changing trends in consumer society.

Laughable Underwear

Before the 1960s, it was not very common to see a man (or a woman, for that matter) in underwear in a Spanish film. The regime, which had a strict censorship code, expurgated any image that might have connoted eroticism. The image of a character in underwear inevitably implied the act of undressing, and the possibility of revealing intimate body parts that were meant to be kept out of sight. As is well known, during the 1960s, the processes that fuelled the modernization of Spain – economic development, industrialization, emigration, the surge of a vibrant consumer society, and the explosion of tourism – also exposed the country to new values and ideas. The opening of markets and borders stimulated the circulation of capital and people (European tourists coming to Spain, Spanish migrants moving to Europe), which in turn had a profound impact on the social fabric and on the relaxation of the hitherto rigid social mores. State censorship of cinema loosened up as well, especially after the new censorship law in 1964. Once the censors approved *Bahía de Palma* (Juan Bosch, 1962), in which spectators, for the first time, could see an actress clad in a bikini (the German actress Elke Sommer), the prohibition on bare skin in movies started to wane (Hopewell 64). While full nudity was still out of the question, images of characters in their underwear started to be increasingly common. However, these portrayals diverged dramatically along gender lines: images of women in underwear were usually meant to be arousing and erotic, while men in underwear almost always triggered hysterical laughter.

As a matter of fact, one of the most common visual correlations in Franco-era Spanish cinema was between a male character in his underwear and a humorous situation. The predictable nature of the visual image suggests that it was some sort of safety valve of masculinity under Franco. Spanish men were subjected to intense pressure to embody a virile ideal of masculinity; this same ideal underpinned Spanish society, with its patriarchal structure resting on male domination. The traits associated with this masculine ideal intertwined physical strength and sexual prowess (to be able to procreate and become the head of the family unit) with mental strength, self-assertiveness, and moral rectitude. In this sense, "[p]ositive male models reject self-indulgence in favor of self-renunciation and service," and seeking pleasure "was seen to interfere with the real work of 'being a man'" (Hartson 9). This ideal virile man was not supposed to be seen in sexual terms under almost any circumstances. Male attractiveness immediately elicited suspicions of effeminacy and, as a result, social disapproval. This was definitely not an exclusive feature of Iberian masculinity under Franco. As Valerie Steele notes, until recently, men who looked beautiful typically carried the stigma of effeminacy, "which is not only code for homosexual, but also appearing like a woman, which is being less than a man" ("Clothing" 60). Depicting men in underwear as amusing became a way for Spanish films to try to neutralize any unease about the potential effeminacy of their male characters. In addition to trying to offer Spanish men an alibi for their virility and providing a harmless form of comic relief, however, this derisive characterization of underwear was also frequently employed by filmmakers to speak to audiences about other issues – sometimes even involving social commentary or political messages. As I set out to explore in this section, the sight of Spanish men in underwear was frequently framed within debates on national identity, often as a visual representation of Spanish difference and the country's apparent backwardness in relation to Europe. Ridiculous-looking underwear became a cultural symbol of how Spaniards perceived their belated and uneven process of modernization, and their inferiority complex in regard to their European neighbours.

A cogent example of this comical rendition of men's underwear in a politically charged film can be found in *Fray Torero* (1966), directed by pro-regime filmmaker José Luis Sáenz de Heredia. A comedy, the film celebrates the renewal of the Catholic Church's pastoral mission after the Vatican II Council as much as it praises the development of a consumer society in Spain and the material prosperity enjoyed under the patronage of Franco in the 1960s. As I have examined elsewhere, the 1960s comedies that address the impact of Vatican II in Spain were complex works, extolling the country's economic development and certain aspects of cultural modernity while arguing that its shift to modernity should incorporate traditional values (*Confessional* 87). *Fray Torero* takes place in a small town in which eight friars live off alms in a fifteenth-century convent. The town's political and economic powers pressure the friars to sell the convent because it is the perfect location for a development project, which involves building a gas station on the side of a new highway. Threatened by the town's officials, most residents stop supporting the friars. One exception is Pascuala (Mercedes Barranco), a hard-working woman who sells wine. Midway through the film, Pascuala has to defend herself from a group of thugs hired by the officials to violently attack her – the thugs are known as "the untouchables," a comic intertextual reference to the 1959–63 American television series. When the "untouchable" played by Manuel Alexandre tries to intimidate Pascuala, his pants fall down, and he looks foolish in his white boxer shorts. The comical shot of this thug in his underwear mitigates the harshness of the situation. In particular, it serves to render the violent thugs as absurd figures whose manufactured virility is simply a pose. But the laughter also comes with a political dart. The laughable underwear is a vehicle with which to put down those who, just like these ridiculous thugs hired by the greedy officials, embrace rampant materialism and development without regard for the traditional religious backbone of Spanish national identity.

Perhaps no one has exploited the political potential of laughable underwear better than Luis García Berlanga. After a screening at the 1963 Venice Film Festival, his celebrated *El verdugo* garnered significant critical attention for putting forth an implicit critique of the Franco regime through its mockery of the death penalty. However, as Alberto Mira contends, the film offers much more than that. It tells a compelling story of how a subject gets interpellated by the tentacles of a social and political system by "gradually becoming trapped in a spider's web" of sex, marriage, and a new apartment ("*El verdugo*" 112). The subject being assimilated is Jose Luis (Nino Manfredi), who reluctantly agrees to become an executioner in exchange for access to subsidized housing. He is presented as a *calzonazos*, "the down-trodden, hen-picked man of much 1950s and 1960s cinema" (Marsh, *Popular* 142). This kind of man is a stock character in the history of Spanish cinema, and certainly a usual suspect in Berlanga's films; they evoke the archetype of the feeble men in Spanish culture. As their nickname indicates (*calzonazos* means "big underclothes" in Spanish), these men are ridiculously weak, and their girlfriends or wives wear the pants in the relationship.

Interestingly, in two key sequences, Berlanga uses the visual image of the *calzonazos* in his underwear to represent his progressive entrapment. The first instance – the eighth sequence –begins with a conversation between José Luis and Carmen (Emma Penella), in bed after sex. When Carmen's father, Amadeo (José Isbert), unexpectedly shows up, José Luis jumps out of the bed, still in his underwear, and tries in vain to hide in a corner of the room. Amadeo finds him and retreats to his bedroom in visible distress. To placate the disappointed father, José Luis stands in the doorway of his room and declares his intention to marry Amadeo's daughter. As he utters the word "hija" (daughter), José Luis's pants fall down. He looks pathetic in his boxer shorts in front of his future father-in-law. The rib-tickling dropping of the pants not only underscores the sexual nature of José Luis and Carmen's illicit encounter, but also makes a mockery of the sacred institution of marriage, one of the ideological pillars of the Franco regime.[3]

The second comical and poignant scene featuring men's underwear appears later in the film. José Luis and Carmen are breaking in their newly acquired spring mattress when the doorbell rings, interrupting their lovemaking session: he has been summoned to Palma de Mallorca for his first execution. Immediately, José Luis – still in his white boxer shorts and undershirt – sits down and starts writing a letter of resignation (see fig. 3.1). Amadeo gets up from bed and tries to convince him not to resign by promising that the prisoner will probably get pardoned. Interestingly, hanging on the wall behind them is a reproduction of *The Last Supper* (Leonardo da Vinci). This painting – a depiction of Jesus Christ's last meal with his disciples, when he announces that one of them will give him away the next day – suggests an impending moment of betrayal in the film. Once the family is in Palma de Mallorca and José Luis has to go to perform the execution, Amadeo suspects that he is going to escape and looks for a telephone to call the Guardia Civil

Fig. 3.1. José Luis (Nino Manfredi) writing a resignation letter in his underwear in *El verdugo*

(Civil Guard) and rat him out. The gravity of what is happening in the scene – both characters are negotiating whether or not José Luis will become the executioner of the brutal political regime – is curtailed, as in the scene with the marriage proposal, by the absurd image of the *calzonazos* in his underwear.

In both sequences, Emma Penella, clad in a sexy black nightgown with her hair down, is presented as a dark object of desire, embodying the male fantasy of the femme fatale who ensnares the male lead. In an interview with César Santos Fontela for the film magazine *Nuestro Cine*, Luis García Berlanga acknowledges that he cast Penella for this role precisely because she looked like "un animal erótico" (an erotic animal) (quoted in Antón Sánchez 213). He did not mention any kind of erotic intentions for the image of the male lead. While in the aforementioned scenes the camera definitely lingers more on the sight of Nino Manfredi in his underwear than on Penella, the male lead is visually presented as an absurd spectacle, prompting giggles rather than desire. Berlanga repeatedly uses the prospect of a man in his underwear as a prop for his signature dark humour, used here to comically connect sex with death. José Luis is faced with the ultimate penalty for committing a sexual act: being forced to become an executioner.

Berlanga also utilizes the image of a man stripped to his underwear, looking ridiculous, to connect marriage and death in *Vivan los novios* (1970). Leo Pozas (José Luis López Vázquez) is a middle-aged man who travels to a town on the Mediterranean with his elderly mother, Doña

Trinidad (Teresa Gisbert), to marry Loli (Lali Soldevila). The day before the wedding, Doña Trinidad unexpectedly dies, which sets in motion an absurd plan to hide her death until after the wedding. The situation reaches its ludicrous pinnacle in a scene in which Leo is wearing a suit jacket, a shirt, and a tie – sans pants. Loli is ironing his suit pants (he had comically fallen into a water fountain), leaving him in his underwear (standard white cotton boxer shorts). Meanwhile, his boss (played by Xavier Vivé), the attorney of the bank where Leo works, is writing a newspaper obituary for Doña Trinidad. This is one of Berlanga's famous long takes, a choral scene typical of the *sainete* tradition producing a "cacophonic effect," a dissonant upshot of the fluidity of relations among the characters in a comical situation (Marsh, *Popular* 128). The composition of the shot includes the absurd combination of the silly-looking Leo in white boxer shorts and a suit jacket; Loli dressed in sombre black to comply with the cultural convention of the *luto* (mourning); and the attorney writing a very formal and sombre obituary, even though we know that he has been frantically chasing attractive foreign ladies. At the same time, the tourists staying on the top floor of the building are being rowdy; through the depth of field of the shot, we can see Loli in the background, walking towards the hallway and hitting the ceiling with a broom while expressing her disgust with the tourists' lack of respect for their moment of (faked) grief. As in *El verdugo*, men's underwear is the trigger of the "dark laughter" that Berlanga generates to mock social institutions and cultural traditions sustaining the no-longer-so-robust ideological edifice of the Franco regime. This mockery draws on the grotesque and the absurd, elements of the tradition of *esperpento*, a paradigm of Spanish dark humour employed by Berlanga and other filmmakers in the 1960s to illustrate Spaniards' experience of "troubled modernity" in relation to Europe (Egea 27).

The ingredients that Berlanga blends in this clever sequence of *Vivan los novios* – the ridiculous sight of a sexually repressed Spaniard in his underwear against the backdrop of economic development, new consumerism, tourism, and incipient sexual liberation – is precisely the recipe employed by the *comedia sexy celtibérica* (Iberian sex comedy) of the late 1960s and the early 1970s. These comedies are most commonly known for the subgenre they spawned, called *landismo*: a series of films that propelled Alfredo Landa to national stardom for subordinating, like Barry Jordan and Mark Allinson observe, his acting skills "to the function of playing himself (personification)" (126). These sex comedies exploited for comical effects Landa's physical attributes: he was short, chubby, balding, and not particularly good-looking, almost the antithesis of a sex symbol. Landa was often "stripped down to his underwear" because "the sight of his bent legs always guaranteed a good laugh" (Fouz-Hernández and Martínez-Expósito 11). The formulaic narratives of these sex comedies highlighted the supposed appeal of the average Spaniard, who was "cast as the epitome of ordinary Spanish maleness" (Jordan and Allinson 126), for sexually liberated European ladies, almost always gorgeous, blonde, and tall – and intimidating to short Spanish men (Renard 114). These erotic encounters between what Annabel Martín cleverly calls *"don Juan turísticos* (tourist-industry Don Juans)"* (57) and European women were almost always a disaster, leading the male protagonist, whose virility is both reinforced and parodied, to realize that true sexual fulfilment comes through traditional marriage with a chaste Spanish lady.

The stakes for Spanish masculinity in these sex comedies were high. For a long time, these films were unanimously lambasted as unfortunate salutes to Spanish machismo and the submissive role of women as perfect wives and mothers (Vanaclocha 199–201). More recent enquiries, however, have complicated this one-dimensional account by pointing out that these Iberian sex comedies interrogate normative versions of masculinity (Epps, "Askance"; Pavlović, *Despotic* 73–86). Beneath the incessant stereotypes and vulgar jokes, *landismo* exposes the social anxiety over hegemonic masculinities in Spanish society, which are problematized "through the prism of inadequacy, be it sexual or economic" (Pavlović, *Despotic* 83). Take the film *Los días de Cabirio* (Fernando Merino, 1971), in which Alfredo migrates from his small village to the touristy town of Torremolinos, hoping to get work and escape from poverty. He does a casting session in front of a madam to work as a *palanquero* (male escort), only to feel ridiculous in his ill-fitting boxers, as they make the madam (and the spectators) laugh.

Perhaps the epitome of Spanish normative masculinity is exposed in Pedro Lazaga's *Vente a Alemania, Pepe* (1971). Pepe (Alfredo Landa) embodies the desires of many Spaniards who migrated to Germany in the 1960s and through the early 1970s in search of the "German dream," only to end up working as labour slaves. Pepe's clumsiness in the foreign setting represents the inferiority complex of Spain under Franco with respect to the modern Western European democracies. His physique literally typifies this inferiority complex, since one of his part-time jobs requires him to advertise a hair removal treatment in his underwear. Every evening, Pepe's hairy body is shown in the window display of a department store next to the smooth and muscular torso of a tall, blonde, and extremely attractive German man. Crowds gather to laugh at the body of the Spanish freak (humiliated as an animal-like specimen) and his unattractive long briefs. His German counterpart wears a sexy pair of briefs with a low waist and a fitted, more revealing design that emphasizes his muscular legs and his abdominal six-pack.

Iberian cultural inferiority is thus visualized in these sex comedies through Landa's physical attributes as well as through his underwear. As Diego Galán puts it, *landismo* is "un cine de calzoncillos antiguos y extranjeras pecadoras" (films full of old underwear and sinful foreign women) (quoted in Vanaclocha 265). The Spaniards' white boxer shorts contrast with the more innovative designs and fabrics available to men elsewhere. During the 1960s, in other Western countries, underwear options "underwent an explosion in colors and prints" and "the idea of sexy, colourful underwear for men was common" by the early 1970s (Delis Hill 58–9). Since outerwear styles for men had evolved during the 1960s to include brighter colours and "slimmer figure fitting garments" (Cole 90), underwear had to change as well. Young men started wearing underwear that exposed more flesh (which increased its erotic appeal) and was available in a variety of colours and patterns, but the average Spanish men of these popular Iberian sex comedies, and not just the ones starring Landa, continued to use regulation white boxer shorts that were, at best, made of cotton; sometimes they were made of stiffer and older-looking fabrics such as Dacron or *lienzo* (linen).[4] Compared to the delicate and enticing underwear used by the female characters – foreign or not – in the same films, these baggy white boxers made the male characters look anything but sexually desirable. Such is the case in *Cinco almohadas para una noche* (Pedro Lazaga, 1974). It is hard to believe that Sara Montiel, who appears with an arsenal of endearing lingerie, is truly interested in any of the five men with whom she has a sexual encounter over the course of a single night, all of them in bulky white boxers made of a stiff variety of Dacron.

As shown in this example, though Alfredo Landa seemed to have the patent for ill-fitting white boxers in Spanish cinema, plenty of other popular actors embodying the average (or even the above-average) Spaniard could have competed with him for that distinction. In *Lo verde empieza en los Pirineos* (Vicente Escrivá, 1973), Serafín (José Luis López Vázquez) is an antiquarian with an infantile fetish for bearded women. He goes to Biarritz, France, with two friends to cure his fetish by visiting cabarets and watching erotic films that were banned in Spain. In one of the most comical sequences of the film, he manages to get in bed with a prostitute but is so nervous and clumsy that he ends up running away in his white boxers, a white undershirt, and a ridiculous hat. In *Celos, amor y mercado común* (Alfonso Paso, 1973), Luis (José Sazatornil) is a married man who is cheating on his wife with a married woman. When her husband arrives home unexpectedly, Luis flees to the street, where he realizes that his car has been stolen. A long shot of Sazatornil in white boxers, a white undershirt, and long white socks in the middle of an empty street encapsulates the message that this film tries to convey: Spaniards always look absurd when they attempt to be unfaithful to their wives, because they are not as depraved as Europeans. This lack of sexual innovation – and of more enticing underwear varieties – might prevent them from entering the European Union, but who wants to be European when you can be morally superior? A third prominent example I want to mention is *El apartamento de la tentación* (Julio Buchs, 1971). Alberto (Juan Luis Galiardo) and Maximino (José Sacristán) are changing their clothes in the middle of the street to go to a costume party. All of a sudden, they are violently attacked by a group of construction workers who thought they were in the middle of a homosexual encounter; they have to escape in their underwear (routine white boxers and undershirt). This third example is especially relevant because in the 1970s, Juan Luis Galiardo was a well-known *galán* (hunky man) in Spanish cinema, and was therefore miles away from the image of the ordinary Spaniard that Landa and López Vázquez embodied. But he still wears shabby-looking underclothes that provoke intense laughter and even violence.

These three examples highlight that the image of a man in his underwear at the end of the Franco regime was visually disturbing, and often revealed cultural anxiety about the perceived backwardness of the country compared to an abstract vision of European modernity. But it was even more disturbing when the Iberian macho tried to bring his undergarments up to date. In *El puente* (1977), seasoned director Juan Antonio Bardem made a parody of the sex comedy and of the customary scene of Alfredo Landa in his underwear. In this film, Landa plays the role of Juan Gómez, an automobile mechanic who decides to hit the road for the weekend, hoping to have a fun time at the beach in the company of foreign women. At some point during his road trip, Juan and the camera, filming from his point of view, approach a road stop. A big crowd of older people (women dressed in black and men in formal suits) and a marching band playing solemn music are crossing the road in what appears to be a funeral procession. Close-ups of Juan's face are cross-cut with long shots of the outraged expressions of the multitude marching in the procession. The atmosphere of the sequence gets awfully tense, with the marchers pointing at Juan in severe irritation. In the reaction shots, Juan has a surprised expression on his face. Eventually the camera tracks backwards to the extreme long shot position to reveal the reason for the crowd's indignation: Juan is not wearing pants, only jungle-print briefs accompanied by long blue socks that match his blue motorcycle helmet. A cut to a high-angle shot shows the absurd contrast between the solemn funeral procession and Juan's ridiculous appearance. A few police officers pull Juan to the side of the road to give him a ticket for public scandal. This sequence implies that Spain is a backwards country whose progress is still bogged down (the flow of street traffic is literally halted in this case) by its cultural traditions (a Catholic ritual of mourning). In his goofy underwear, Juan represents the average Spaniard, foolishly trying to catch up with modernity by embracing cultural elements that do not suit him, which leads to social tensions. On a broader national scale, it stands for the uncritical adoption in the late-Franco years of developmental capitalism and rampant consumerism, and the country's attempts to attract tourism on a massive scale, without properly considering its repercussions for society at large.

Released in the previous year, *La trastienda* (Jorge Grau) provides a contrasting example of how innovative styles of underwear are visually indicative of emergent versions of Spanish masculinity at the end of Francoism. The male lead is Jaime (Frederick Stafford), a married doctor and a devoted member of Opus Dei, who has an affair with one of his nurses, Juana (María José Cantudo). When the affair becomes a public scandal, Jaime's priest and confessor pays him a visit at Juana's apartment to persuade him to go back to his wife. One of Juana's roommates goes to her bedroom to announce the visit, and in a long shot, the camera pans over Jaime lying in bed, nearly naked. Stafford's slender, toned body is only covered by a pair of stylish black briefs that highlight his long legs. This Czech actor was a global film star who played the lead in many prominent European spy movies – including Alfred Hitchcock's *Topaz* (1969). In another venue, I have noted that "his height (six feet three inches), his toned body and his chic underwear made him radically different from the male leads Spanish audiences were used to see in erotic comedies," especially Alfredo Landa ("Undressing" 100). Grau acknowledged that he received harsh criticism for this very reason (Gregori 504). For the film press, Stafford did not have the ethnic credibility to play a Spaniard. What Spanish film critics did not realize is that his "non-Spanish" looks exuded exactly the kind of masculinity he was meant to represent. He embodied the look of the accomplished Opus Dei professionals that infiltrated the upper economic and political spheres in Spain after Franco reshuffled his cabinet at the end of the 1950s. Spanish spectators could see in Jaime a personification of the elites who rationalized the economy and fashioned a more modern image of the country. A major component of this new image involved toning down Spanish cultural difference and presenting the country as more attuned to modern Western European democracies. Thus, Stafford's European looks, his tall and well-built body, and his trendy underwear serve to present a version of masculinity that diverges from the one typically seen in sex comedies of that era.

Hemingway's Underpants for Post-Franco Men

One might have presupposed that Spanish cinema after Franco would offer models of masculinity – and of male bodies and men's underwear – that were closer to Jaime in *La trastienda* than to the short and chubby Spaniards of the sex comedies, in their ill-fitting white boxers. But the reality, at least in the realm of comedy, was that aspiring young filmmakers continued to incorporate many of the representations of masculinity that were popular in earlier Iberian sex comedies. A prominent example of this surprising trend can be found in the so-called New Spanish Comedy, a series of urban comedies made by talented filmmakers such as Fernando Trueba and Fernando Colomo. These films focused on the emotional conflicts of young Spaniards post-Franco, a refreshing change in direction for the national industry. As Barry Jordan and Rikki Morgan-Tamosunas point out, these are low-budget films, shot with a preference for real locations over studio sets and direct sound over post-production dubbing; this lent the films a realistic aesthetic look that enabled them to connect with young audiences (69). While the male protagonists of these films are typically educated and progressive-minded young men who seem worlds apart from the boorish and provincial machos of the *landismo*, they nonetheless appear just as graceless as their predecessors during sexual encounters. More importantly for the purposes of my discussion, they look just as ridiculous in their underwear.

Fernando Trueba's debut film, *Ópera prima* (1980), might well be the best case in point of this astounding discrepancy. Recently divorced journalist and writer Matías (Oscar Ladoire) falls in love with Violeta (Paula Molina), and shortly thereafter moves into her apartment. In their first sexual encounter, Violeta invites Matías to join her in bed. A long shot shows Matías taking off his clothes while Violeta watches him intently. When Matías strips to his underwear – a pair of ugly white boxers made of a stiff, frayed fabric – Violeta bursts into laughter because his undies resemble her father's. In response, Matías utters a long speech, in which he claims those underpants are a conscious choice positioning himself alongside elegant masculine figures such as Cary Grant and Ernest Hemingway, and against "las bragas mariconas en Technicolor" (the queer-looking briefs of Technicolor films) that are becoming fashionable. He further argues that tight modern briefs – such as the ones worn by Jaime in *La Trastienda* – have supposedly been banned in the United States because they have been proven to cause impotency. Things (meaning the genitals) are supposed to hang naturally, without constraint. This sequence, which contains an example of the "witty dialogues" that critics praised in the film (Jordan and Morgan-Tamosunas 70), offers a comic reversal of the countless scenes of women taking off their clothes in the *cine de destape* (cinema of undressing) and the soft-core porn that followed the *landismo* fever. The object of the desiring gaze is now a skinny and nerdy-looking young man; the woman is the one watching the stripping spectacle, her naked body hidden under the covers. But the difference with regard to the *destape* films is that the male is not visually displayed as an erotic object of desire. Viewers contemplate his stripping exercise not from the lustful (at least initially) gaze of Violeta, but from a distant camera angle – a long shot from the rear part of the room. In addition, the poor artificial lighting of the scene (a bright bedside lamp situated right in the middle of the frame partially blinds the viewer instead of gracefully lighting Matías's body) contributes to de-eroticizing the male striptease.

Although this scene can be read as a clever intellectual pun, satirizing the *cine de destape*, and even as a humorous appropriation of the discourse of feminism (in its defence of non-constricting clothing choices), spectators of the early 1980s (like us today) would probably have linked this visual image of masculinity more to Alfredo Landa than to Hemingway. In addition to how ridiculous Matías looks in his underwear, he is clumsy in bed – he is unable to maintain an erection and they have to stop the lovemaking session. So rather than a visual representation of the new Spanish man, he seems like an anachronistic version of the unworldly Iberian macho. That is precisely the impression that the young Violeta, representative of a new generation of liberated, non-domestic women – she is a violin student, vegetarian, and lover of the hippie lifestyle – gets: "es que creía que ya no existían" (I thought that they no longer existed). Although she is referring to the ill-fitting white boxers, Violeta's words also seem to refer to an obsolete and absurd model of masculinity that does not seem to fade away in the democratic period.

Fernando Colomo also overloads his *comedias madrileñas* of the 1980s with funny scenes featuring male stars such as Antonio Resines (*La vida alegre*, 1987) and Antonio Banderas (*Bajarse al moro*, 1989) in their underwear. In the latter, Banderas is the target of a number of hilarious underwear scenes in which he is running towards or away from a danger. At the beginning of the film, his girlfriend Chusa (Verónica Forqué) runs to the balcony with his underwear. Alberto, naked, runs

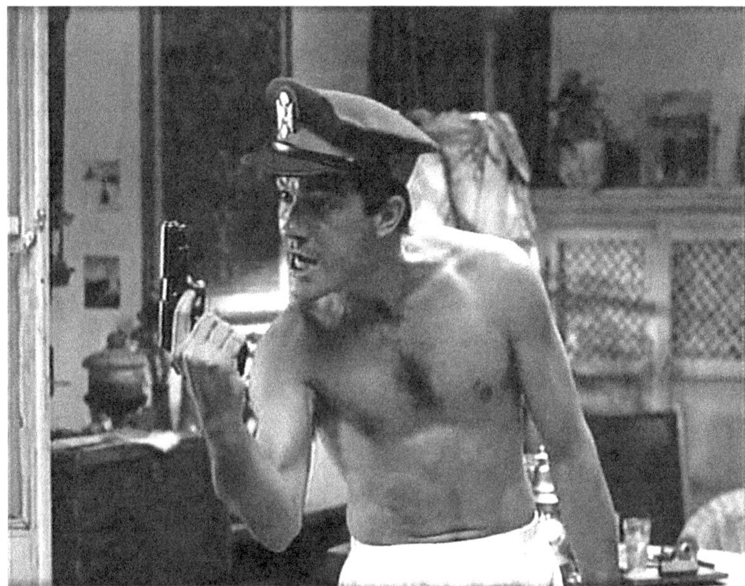

Fig. 3.2. Laughing at Antonio Banderas in his underwear in *Bajarse al moro*

after her and is ridiculed by the neighbours. Immediately thereafter, Jaimito (Juan Echanove) comes to report that Alberto, a police officer, is needed for an emergency situation. The potential eroticism of the long shot of Alberto wearing only tight-fitting cotton briefs, revealing a toned body, is mitigated by the amusing rush with which he has to dress up and run off. Later in the film, there is another comical scene of Banderas in underwear. A pair of drug addicts (one played by Carmelo Gómez) with withdrawal symptoms attack the group of friends in Chusa's apartment, wielding a knife. Jaimito manages to scare them off with Alberto's police gun. Once the drug addicts are gone, Alberto grabs his gun in visible distress (see fig. 3.2). He puts on his police hat and starts giving a demonstration of the danger of using a gun. With his polyester white boxers, police hat, and gun pointed at the amused Chusa and Jaimito, Alberto is mockingly portrayed as a symbol of male phallic power and legal authority. This example is particularly relevant because, as Chris Perriam notes, Antonio Banderas's stardom in the 1980s was heavily dependent upon his sex appeal and the constant display of his objectified body (*Stars* 8, 51–2). While Colomo obviously plays with Banderas's body (by then viewed as globally desirable, especially thanks to his collaborations with Almodóvar), every single underwear scene that

I have discussed is framed as humorous, not erotic. It is almost as if he wanted to make a mockery of Banderas's star image, or perhaps as a way of disavowing the homoerotic tension that a male body would create for the average male spectator at the time.

Beyond the *comedias madrileñas*, the sight of men in underwear has continued to incite laughter and sometimes social commentary in Spanish comedies. A number of popular comedies directed by Luis García Berlanga in the post-Franco period such as *Moros y Cristianos* (1987) and *París-Tombuctú* (1999) include sex scenes in which male characters look ridiculous in their saggy boxers. However, it is in *La vaquilla* (1985) where one can find Berlanga's signature scene, in which the humorous portrayal of men in underwear is used to put forth a pungent message. Set during the Civil War, the film narrates the mirthful journey of a group of Republican soldiers who cross the front line to try to steal a bull that the Nacionales are going to fight on a religious holiday. At some point during the eventful pilgrimage, soldiers from both sides coincide by a river and suspend the hostilities to take a peaceful bath without negotiating or even talking about it. Some of the soldiers jump into the water naked, but most are wearing rugged-looking boxers made of stiff linen. Berlanga uses the absurd and humorous sight of enemy soldiers calmly coexisting in a natural space and wearing ridiculous underwear to evoke the absurdity of the civil war, where siblings and neighbours fought on opposing sides. This scene visually suggests that, once stripped to the bones, all these men are created equal, and look equally ridiculous in their underwear.

Even provocative directors Alfonso Albacete and David Menkes, who have made a career out of eroticizing the male body and the image of men in underwear (more about that later), draw on the side-splitting effect of men's underwear to offer the audience a didactic message about the need to respect differences in *Sobreviviré* (1999). In this popular comedy (Albacete and Menkes's biggest commercial success, with over a million tickets sold), widow Marga (Emma Suárez) decides to come out of her shell to date Iñaki (Juan Diego Botto), who is not only gay but also ten years her junior. In their first sexual encounter, both are visibly nervous – it is Iñaki's first time with a woman and Marga's first time having sex in a long time – and Marga cannot help but start laughing when Iñaki takes off his jeans, revealing black leather briefs and a prominent erection. Marga proceeds to clarify that his underwear looks weird, as if he were wearing them for a gay S&M session in a porn film, which makes Iñaki laugh as well. At that point, Marga does not know about Iñaki's sexual preferences, but his stereotypical underwear comically outs him. Marga accepts the funny, gay-looking underpants just as she accepts Iñaki's full revelation of his sexual identity. The humorous role-play with men's underwear, which suggests an unprejudiced respect for sexual and gender fluidity, continues later in the film, once the couple is living together. Iñaki, just out of the shower, is desperately looking for a clean pair of underpants. Marga suddenly shows up wearing them, a pair of tight, white-cotton boxer briefs that are indeed flattering on her body and have the effect of turning him on. Marga is wearing Iñaki's underpants more as an erotic joke, to tease Iñaki than to make a serious gender-bending statement. Still, apart from a nod to the androgynous underwear styles that appeared in the 1990s,[5] the gesture draws attention to the open-mindedness about gender and sexual fluidity that drives this healthy romantic relationship.

Sexy Underwear

Apart from indicating social rank, men's underwear in the first half of the twentieth century had a predominantly utilitarian function.[6] It protected the body from cold weather and provided a sanitary layer that safeguarded the skin from outerwear, and vice versa, for clothes made of nice and delicate materials (Tobin 3; Willett and Cunnington 14–15). However, in the 1950s, underwear for men started to be advertised not only as utilitarian but also as erotic (McDowell 14).[7] The tempo of this shift was evidently different in Spain. The virile austerity expected of Spanish men and the overall disapproval and prohibition of erotic images during most of the Franco era meant that male body exposure in Spanish cinema, or in any other form of visual media, could only transpire in non-sexual situations, such as physical labour or sports. Only men branded as ultra-masculine could appear in underwear without raising suspicions of effeminacy or being derisively laughed at, as we saw in the previous sections. This was the case of the CIFESA production *¡A mí la legión!* (Juan de Orduña, 1942). In the first sequence, after establishing shots that locate the story of the film in a detachment of the Spanish *legión* in North Africa, there is a cut to the interior of a military barracks. As soldiers hear the morning bugle call and start getting dressed, there are some shots of soldiers in white boxers and others with bare torsos.

The visual treatment of this scene is somewhat eroticized. Although viewers are not afforded any close-ups – only long and medium-long shots in which the semi-naked men are shown as part of the larger group – some details of the framing and the lighting could be seen as erotic. As one soldier pushes himself up in bed, his head is framed at the level of another soldier's crotch; previously shown in white underwear, he is now getting dressed in front of the soldier in bed. The shot lingers, ostensibly due to the conversation between the soldier in bed – on the left side of the frame – and an officer reprimanding him for not being up yet – on the right side of the frame. Meanwhile, in the middle of the frame, the soldier getting dressed is buttoning his fly and, therefore, calling attention to his crotch. The officer yells "arriba, soldadito, que viene la manguera" (get up, little soldier, it's time for the hose), suggesting that he will get sprayed with a garden hose; but in this context, the sentence acquires phallic connotations – the "hose" that can emerge from the other soldier's crotch. The camera tracks forward to get closer to the soldiers, thus emphasizing the proximity of the beds and the male bodies. The soldier in bed stretches out his arms and yawns right in front of the other soldier's crotch, creating a naughty visual effect as if he were reaching out to touch his colleague's crotch/hose. An editing cut takes viewers to a different soldier getting out of bed with only his pants on, and his subsequent chat with another soldier in bed. The hard side lighting prominently illuminates his slim and naked torso, while the rest of the frame, including the other soldier, is poorly lit.

The sensual connotations of this initial sequence are underscored by the development of a homoerotic friendship between two heroic soldiers in the film, El Grajo (Alfredo Mayo) and Mauro (Luis Peña), which Spanish critic Félix Fanés regarded as an overt exaltation of male homosexuality (113). This film is part of the broader cycle of heroic films that were used "for the dissemination of the Falange's extreme nationalism of the early 1940s, its ideology of reevaluation of violence as creative and purifying, and the celebration of militarism and martial values" (Triana-Toribio, *Spanish National Cinema* 46). Viewers could detect the homoerotic tensions, especially because the film was almost a sequel to *¡Harka!* (Carlos Arévalo, 1941), another heroic film featuring the same two male actors, engaged in an even more homoerotic friendship/love story under the pretext of patriotic exaltation – *¡Harka!* generated serious reservations upon its commercial release (Mira, *De Sodoma* 336).[8] The homoerotic undertones and the sight of a man in underwear – both rather unusual images in a Spanish film of the early 1940s – were permitted only because they appeared within the context of military camaraderie and extreme virility.

In the 1960s, the processes of modernization went hand in hand with the introduction of new social values that transformed old mentalities, including new sexual mores and a more permissive attitude towards representing bodies in erotic terms. However, as Walter Bernecker argues, this transformation did not happen in a smooth, linear fashion. The new values did not suddenly supplant the old mentality, and they often triggered a reactionary movement to defend the old moral code (72). The laughable underwear of the Iberian sex comedies of the 1960s that I discussed earlier in the chapter was an indicator of the fear that social and cultural changes would affect Spanish masculinity: fear of feminization as well as anxiety about Iberian cultural inferiority compared to European modernity. While Spain underwent many of the same social and cultural transformations as other Western European countries, it remained far behind the curve on issues such as gender roles and relations (Buchanan 94). The "underwear underdevelopment" of the 1960s proved that Spain was still different when it came to gender and sexuality.

This contrast was even more conspicuous in the realm of undershirts. By the mid-1950s, film images had triggered an undershirt revolution. Marlon Brando and James Dean oozed sexuality by wearing their working-class white undershirts as T-shirts in *A Streetcar Named Desire* (1951), *The Wild One* (1953), and *Rebel without a Cause* (1955); they became popular, a dress code of sorts for a whole generation of rebellious youth (Benson and Esten 62; Bordo 138; Ferguson 82; Laver, *Costume* 260). The basic white, cotton-made undershirt had been an important gay signifier at least since the 1930s, but with Brando and Dean it became equally alluring for the heterosexual imagination (Steele, *Fetish* 128). Until then, undershirts had mostly been considered garments to be hidden underneath one's clothes, but Hollywood sparked this sartorial revolution by turning the undershirt into a regular piece of outerwear and a sex object for mainstream society.[9]

No such upheaval happened in Spanish cinema or society. White undershirts for men remained confined to the domain of underwear; Spanish men of all ages had to keep their undershirts hidden, or risk violating the rules of male dignity. A noteworthy, yet somewhat critically overlooked, example that illustrates the disruptive effects of transgressing this rigid social code can be found in *La tía Tula* (Miguel Picazo, 1963). Ramiro (Carlos Estrada) is a widower who is entrapped and infantilized by his sister-in-law Tula (Aurora Bautista). In her analysis of the film, Sally Faulkner has deemed the emphasis on Ramiro's body a sign of his infantilization, and his excessive sexual drive (he tries to rape Tula and later rapes a minor) a consequence of Tula's repression (117–18). There are two key scenes in which Ramiro appears in a white sleeveless undershirt (see fig. 3.3). In the first one, Ramiro walks down the hallway of the apartment he shares with Tula and his two small children, and Tula asks him to cover up, to put on a pajama top, because the sight of him in his undershirt makes her uncomfortable. The second scene takes place at night. Ramiro is having trouble falling asleep, as he

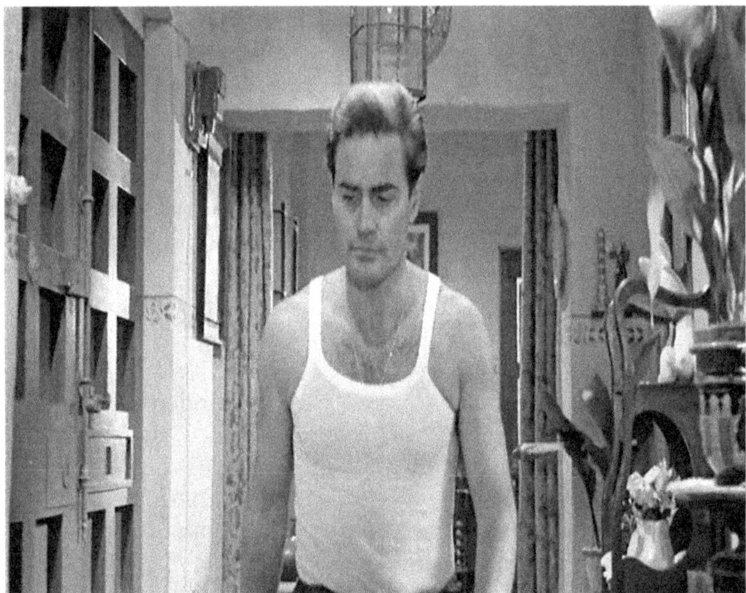

Fig. 3.3. Sleeveless undershirt and eroticism in *La tía Tula*

hears the off-screen sounds of a group of drunkards returning home. He gets up and sits on a chair. He is wearing a sleeveless white undershirt. A medium close-up shows him visibly excited and distressed, ruminating over something that he will do the next day: he will attempt to rape Tula. The room is fairly dark, but a beam of light coming in diagonally from above illuminates parts of his face and casts shadows on parts of his body. This low-key lighting creates a shadowy, gloomy atmosphere that the viewer is invited to interpret in moral terms, linked to Ramiro's predatory impulses (see fig 3.4). This is a conventional technique used on, for example, the sexy femme fatales of noir cinema, whose hidden impulses are revealed through the low-key lighting.

In the daytime scene, Tula is the one who calls attention to Ramiro's body. In the night-time scene, however, Ramiro is by himself, and he appears eroticized by the representational apparatus of the film – lighting, framing, and costume design – not by Tula's sexually repressed comments. Faulkner claims that Tula's attempts to desexualize Ramiro fail, but that his sexual drive remains linked to his infantilization: "even Ramiro the rapist remains infantilised as he is still defined exclusively in terms of his body. The need of an infant to be fed, clothed and nursed transfers to that of a man for sex" (117). Furthermore, she argues that

Fig. 3.4. Low-key lighting, gloomy atmosphere, and eroticized underwear in *La tía Tula*

male weakness and disempowerment is all the more highlighted by the fact that Ramiro is played by a fairly unknown Argentine actor (Carlos Estrada), while Franco-era star Aurora Bautista excels as Tula (115). It is true that the characterization here makes viewers focus on Bautista's masterful performance of Tula, but I differ on the point about how this makes Ramiro look weak and childlike, at least in terms of his physical appearance. Bautista unquestionably steals the show through her outstanding performance, but Estrada is visually depicted as a sexy man with a desirable body. With or without Tula, both scenes present a well-built male body in a form-fitting sleeveless shirt that emphasizes his muscular arms and shoulders, and reveals his hairy chest.

Critical approaches to this film might have unintentionally internalized or confirmed the views of the film's official censors, who were wary of any scene that might eroticize Bautista's body, but had no problem with the many scenes in which Ramiro appears in underwear or swimwear. The censors, for example, cut a scene "where Tula is shot in black lacy underwear, adjusting the suspender on her provocatively arched right leg" (Faulkner 111). For John Hopewell, the censors' elimination of some of Tula's scenes makes the film lose "much of its polemical force" (66). Yet, there is no commentary about the film's portrayal of an eroticized male body, which was truly radical for a mainstream commercial film in Spain. This is because men's underwear was not perceived as having the same erotic connotations. However, Ramiro's tight sleeveless undershirts, which partially reveal and partially conceal his fit body, do make him look quite attractive. Stella Bruzzi asserts that in the context of 1950s Hollywood cinema, "the white T-shirt telegraphs the male star's eroticism and his availability as an object of desire" (Bruzzi, "Gregory" 48). Although showcasing male eroticism was not as common in Spanish cinema, Ramiro's undershirts are fairly tight and show more chest than, for example, the white T-shirt that was used to create the quintessential eroticized male torso in Hollywood: that of Marlon Brando's Stanley Kowalski. The slim straps also allow for a full view of Estrada's muscular shoulders and expose more of his chest hair (one of the most conventional physical signs of virility). Estrada's white undershirt certainly does not have the connotations of youth rebellion that viewers would commonly associate with the "oppositional look" of Marlon Brando and James Dean (Church Gibson, "Brad Pitt" 69). Still, Estrada's undershirts more closely evoke the violent virility epitomized by Stanley Kowalski's dirty and sweaty T-shirt than the frumpy-looking undershirt covering Nino Manfredi's skinny body in *El verdugo*. Even if Tula's efforts to infantilize Ramiro have an influence on the representation of his body, he is still sexually desirable.

The climax of the openly erotic display of men's underwear in Spanish cinema came in the late 1970s with Eloy de la Iglesia's gay-themed realist dramas (*Los placeres ocultos* [1977] and *El diputado* [1978]), and his subsequent "cine quinqui" (*quinqui* films), which focused on social disaffection, drug addiction, and juvenile delinquency on the outskirts of the city at the beginning of the transition to democracy.[10] Spanish film critics unanimously considered *Los placeres ocultos* and *El diputado* groundbreaking because of their explicit representation of male homosexuality in Spanish cinema and, in particular, their erotic portrayal of the male body (Smith, *Laws of Desire* 129–51; Ballesteros, *Cine* 91–127; Melero Salvador 219–50). As Santiago Fouz-Hernández and Alfredo Martínez-Expósito note, these films follow the Greek-love model (116), with an asymmetrical relationship between a mature gay man and a younger boy of a lower social stratum. In this model, the "gap between the subject and the object affects the representation of the gay body in so far as the elder subject tends to remain clothed and act as the vehicle of the audience's desire for the object" (133). In the very first sequence of *Los placeres ocultos*, which was the last film that suffered the consequences of Francoist censorship, Eduardo (Simón Andreu), a wealthy middle-aged bank manager, stares at the rear end of a naked hustler who is getting dressed after a post-sex shower. After an editing cut, a POV shot from Eduardo's perspective shows the hustler in white cotton briefs and a tight T-shirt advertising the Los Angeles Rams, an NFL team. The same pattern appears in *El diputado*, with plenty of shots of the naked or semi-naked body of Juanito (José Luis Alonso) from the desiring gaze of the always fully clad Roberto (José Sacristán), a high-profile (married) politician.

De la Iglesia's five *quinqui* films maintained the same focus on the exhibition of the young male body. Interestingly, as Tom Whittaker has argued, the erotic display of the male body in these *quinqui* films goes beyond the traditional film gaze, inviting the audience to have "a more sensorial engagement with its subject matter" (158). The raw eroticism proposed by de la Iglesia "elicits a particularly tactile structure of spectatorship, one that appears to encourage an erotic fascination with surface and skin" (159). In so doing, de la Iglesia offers the audience what Laura Marks called "haptic visuality," which refers to the tactile sensorial experience of the film, since "the vision itself can be tactile, as though one were touching a film with one's eyes" (xi). In this tactile eroticism, the distance between the observer and the observed is reduced, and the audience participates "in the embodied nature of cinematic viewing experience," which entails an erotic encounter with the cinematic body (Marks 145). In effect, de la Iglesia does not treat the power of the gaze (of the mature gay men or of the audience) as a domineering tool, as in the traditional paradigm of visual representation; instead, the gaze prompts the viewer to feel the story through the teenagers' flesh. De la Iglesia adopts several haptic techniques to allow viewers to experience the embodied and tragic humanity of the teenage bodies. Close-ups and extreme close-ups of their bodies show the damage of their precarious and hazardous lifestyles: their arms are perforated by heroin needles (*El pico* [1983] and *El pico II* [1984]), their stomachs and legs are covered in tattoos (*Colegas* [1982]), and they have wounds from violent attacks (for example, the images of blood after the rape scenes in *Navajeros* [1980] and *El pico II*). In addition, he presents an array of images that suggest contact, such as shots of hands touching skin, and recurring images of the main characters hugging and kissing each other.

De la Iglesia also draws the viewer into an erotic mode of looking and feeling with recurrent images of José Luis Manzano – the main lead in all of his *quinqui* films – and other young actors (for example, Lola Flores's son, Antonio Flores, in *Colegas*) either completely naked or only wearing underwear. This emphasis on images of actors in their underwear created a distinctive visual style that Manuel Hidalgo termed "estética de calzoncillo" (underwear aesthetics) (38). I would like to add to the critical conversation about the phenomenological pleasure in these films by examining the eroticism of the underwear itself. That is, we need to take into consideration the way the underwear looks, its shape and colour against the fragile beauty of the teenagers' skin, as well as the way it feels, for the viewers also partake in the sensual experience of the fabric touching their skin.

This is substantially different from the incessant exhibition of men in underwear in the profitable soft-core pornographic films that inundated Spanish screens during those years (1977–82). Consider *La caliente niña Julieta* (1981) and *Esas chicas tan putas* (1982), two films by seasoned director Ignacio Iquino that offer a panoply of sexual scenes with female nudity – including graphic close-ups of vaginas – with a focus on the body of Andrea Albani, Iquino's erotic muse. Meanwhile, men's underwear, along with lighting tricks, consistently and often comically serves only to keep the male genitals hidden. Let us remember that filmic representations of the male body in commercial cinema have traditionally kept much of it invisible because they were designed to maintain the patriarchy. As Peter Lehman examines, cinematic portrayals of patriarchal masculinity typically hinge on avoiding explicit images of the male body and, especially, "on perpetuating the mystique of the penis-phallus" (5). Commercial cinema has conveniently kept the penis out of sight or has carefully controlled how it is represented, because "to show, write, or talk about the penis creates the potential to demystify it and thus decenter it" (30).[11] Patriarchal culture is centred and fortified when the penis is not seen. Curiously, though, the penis in these soft-core pornographic films is not hidden as a form of strategic concealment, to aggrandize male domination by preserving the mysticism of the phallus. Rather, male characters are frequently laughed at and humiliated in the films' sex scenes; the women tease them and immediately dispose of them – leaving them alone in their underwear – to engage in same-sex encounters. *La caliente niña* (1981) features an especially comical scene, in which Mario (Joaquín Gómez) is abandoned by two women in the middle of a sexual encounter in a barn and, surrounded by cows, has to finish himself off by masturbating.

In contrast, underwear serves to eroticize the male body in *quinqui* films. Since they also include many scenes with full frontal nudity (mostly starring José Luis Manzano), we cannot interpret the films' repeated use of men's underwear as a visual barrier to keep the genitals out of sight. It is noteworthy, I would add, that the films feature not just any type of underwear, but almost invariably white cotton briefs. Tony Fuentes and José Luis Manzano lead an entourage of juvenile delinquents who wear some version of the Jockey's classic Y-front brief, which prompted "a seismic revolution in underwear design" in the mid-1930s due to the style of the cut and the support it provided (Delis Hill 45). By the late 1970s, however, white cotton briefs were not the epitome of innovative or erotic underwear. Things changed drastically in 1982, of course, when Calvin Klein launched his men's underwear line with an aggressive marketing campaign: Bruce Weber's photographs of divine-looking men, including Olympic Pole-vaulter Tom Hintnaus, in their underpants on a huge billboard in New York City's Times Square (Bordo 181–2; Cole 101; Delis Hill 163–4; McDowell 14; Steele, *Fetish* 128). Although this was not the first time that eroticism was used to promote innovative underwear for men, as Paul Jobling has amply shown ("Underexposed," *Man Appeal*), Calvin Klein's underwear line did transform the industry. And the most astonishing part was that the design of these underpants "was almost identical to the Jockey's classic Y-front brief, except closer fitting in the behind" and that "the name Calvin Klein was woven into the waistband" (Cole 101).[12] Underwear historians agree that this campaign was the pinnacle of advertising for openly erotic men's underwear, to the extent that by the end of the decade, "'Calvins' had become the generic term for sexy" (Jobling, "Underexposed" 147). From that moment on, underwear was never again seen as an instrument to cover male genitalia, but instead as a seductive tool to suggest it and enhance it in an overall effort to showcase the male body as a site of sexual desire (Craik 133).

Granted, the "underwear aesthetic" introduced by de la Iglesia in Spanish cinema predated Calvin Klein's reinvention of the white brief, and was in no way associated with the classic, ancient Greek model of male beauty promoted by the ensuing advertising campaign. Rather, it displayed a raw – in the sense of unpolished – erotic masculinity embodied by men from low social and economic strata. It was a rough look that eroticized the bodies of disenfranchised male youth, including all the bodily scars and wounds associated with their lifestyle on the fringes of society. This lumpen eroticism is not necessarily tied to sexual encounters between two characters (though there are plenty of examples of that); it appears more frequently in scenes depicting homosocial rituals of communal dressing and undressing among brothers (in *Los placeres ocultos* and *Colegas*), friends in a public setting, in a locker room (*Colegas*), and in prison cells (*El pico II*). While this homosocial bonding is not initially of a romantic or sexual nature, it nonetheless leads to homoerotic scenes, such as when brothers masturbate in front of each other (*Colegas*) or when young characters are sexually attacked in prison (*El pico II*).

One sequence in *El pico II*, in particular, encapsulates all the undertones of this raw eroticism expressed through underwear. Paco (José Luis Manzano) and his prison friend Pirri (José Luis Fernández) are desperate to get their heroin fix. Paco visits El Tejas (Valentín Paredes), the leader of the prison's rival gang, knowing that getting the heroin will probably require him to perform some kind of sexual favour in return. The price for heroin turns out to be higher than agreeing to be gay for pay: Paco is robbed and raped by El Tejas and his three friends. El Tejas aggressively pulls down Paco's sweatpants and kneels to inspect his crotch area. A close-up shows El Tejas caressing Paco's inner thighs and bulky crotch, gently feeling the fabric of the white brief against the skin. El Tejas pulls down the back of the white brief, inserts his right hand, and starts rubbing Paco's underpants and legs gently while being cheered on by his friends, who are about to take turns penetrating Paco. The whole scene offers a disturbing type of haptic visuality, since it forces the viewer to participate in the massage, to feel the softness of the cotton underpants and the smoothness of Paco's body.

Editing and framing devices come to rescue the viewer, if only partially, for participating in the erotic perversity of this scene, since they are strategically used to establish a clear hierarchy in moral terms. High-angle shots of El Tejas are deployed to depict him as evil, while the reverse shots of Paco with low angulation somehow redeem his character by emphasizing his moral stature, visually signposting his superlative camaraderie, since he is sacrificing his body to get the heroin not only for himself, but also for Pirri. The pristine whiteness of his underwear – probably unrealistic in the context of an inmate with severe withdrawal symptoms – and the softness of the fabric also contribute to this sense of moral redemption. The colour and texture of the ever-present white cotton underpants suggest vulnerability and purity. It almost seems as if de la Iglesia were exonerating Paco, along with his other prison friends, who all invariably wear white cotton briefs – extensively on display in a wide array of homoerotic scenes – with one prominent exception: the black briefs worn by the one member of the group, who cowardly retreats and ruins their plan to escape from prison.

What is particularly noteworthy is de la Iglesia's systematic and cross-referential use of underwear as an important symbol not only throughout *El pico II*, but in the whole series of *quinqui* films. It gives audiences automatic insight into characters' qualities and moral conflicts – and allows them to differentiate good from evil. Underwear in *quinqui* films has a directive function to impel viewers towards a particular interpretation of the characters' moral stature, to help them discern who has a certain dignity and nobleness in an otherwise miserable existence.[13] Before Calvin Klein reinvented the white cotton Y-front brief to sell sophisticated classic masculinity, de la Iglesia's *quinqui* films deployed a modest version of it (without the fitted shape or the fancy brand name on the waistband) to exude a lumpen eroticism that proved alluring to a fairly large audience who enjoyed the type of embodied cinematic viewing experience enabled by the haptic images of these films.

Advertising Sexy Masculinity

By the early 1990s, it was apparent that men were showing more and more interest in their underwear, not only in terms of what felt comfortable and right, but also in terms of the repercussions that their choices had for their image and identity. However, Shaun Cole has exposed data gathered by underwear manufacturers and retailers demonstrating that about 70 per cent of men's underwear was still purchased by women at the time (148). While the data that Cole offers is limited to the Anglo-American world, the point is probably no less valid in the Spanish context. A noteworthy case in point appears in one of the most iconic Spanish films of this period, Bigas Luna's *Jamón, jamón* (1992), winner of a Silver Lion at the Venice Film Festival and the subject of a significant body of critical work. In that film, Conchita (Stefania Sandrelli) is an elegant middle-aged woman who runs an underwear factory along with her husband (played by Juan Diego). In the first few minutes of the film, Conchita makes a blunt statement to some business consultants regarding what they should strive to advertise: "No debes olvidar que son las mujeres las que compran los calzoncillos a los hombres, y un buen paquete vende" (Don't forget that women are the ones who buy underpants for men, and a good package sells). An editing cut takes us to a close-up of the kind of prominent male bulge that Conchita has in mind for the ad campaign. Shortly thereafter, the camera shows that the bulge belongs to Raúl (Javier Bardem), a delivery guy for a ham factory. Subsequent shots focus on the crotches of other participants in the casting session, which are cross-cut with images of their faces and torsos; by showing these male bodies fragmented into pieces, Bigas Luna consciously objectifies them in the same way that female bodies are conventionally objectified in mainstream cinema. The inclusion of the female gaze complements the reversal of this bodily objectification, for Conchita is the target audience for the casting video of the male "packages," which she watches with a mixture of business interest and libidinal desire. Predictably, Raúl gets the job, since his bulge is indeed the biggest of the cohort, and photos of his assets will be shown on highway billboards.

Conchita's statement encapsulates the shift that underwear companies had to make from the mid-1980s onward to secure their niche in the market: they had to make underwear look sensual by featuring a sexy male body and, most innovatively, the penis. As Susan Bordo has noted, "fashion ads today routinely feature men in underwear who are amazingly endowed," thus overtly drawing attention to their crotches (25). While sex appeal has been part of the advertising equation for men's underwear for quite some time, this overt focus on the penis was rarely seen prior to the Calvin Klein revolution in the early 1980s – at least in Spain. The motto chosen for the campaign advertising Raúl's package, "En tu interior hay un Sansón" (There is a Samson inside of you), evokes an ancient type of masculinity that promises to endow buyers with irresistible phallic energy and animal strength.[14] As Wolfgang Fritz Haug points out in his study of commodity aesthetics in modern advertising, "the commodity's illusion promises its being" (85). In this case, any man would buy the Samson underpants in order to become a strong man – metonymically signposted by the bulge those underpants would reveal – and not just to look like one. Of course, this particular commodity would only equip him with the illusion of strength, thus at best serving "merely as an imaginary satisfaction of omnipotent phallic fantasies" and "as a prop for heroic fantasies" (85), and not a real materialization of them.

Interestingly, Spanish film critics have neglected to point out that the underpants that Raúl is wearing during the casting session are Y-front white briefs. By the early 1990s, these underpants definitely carried connotations of a return to an archaic and phallic type of masculinity. Even the Calvin Klein campaigns for Y-front briefs veered away from selling sophisticated classic (and corporate) masculinity – in their 1980s campaigns mentioned previously – and began to market a "hyper-masculine masquerade" epitomized by the rough and robust virility of the rapper Marky Mark (now actor Mark Wahlberg) (Simpson 158). The fetishistic correlation between the underpants and the man wearing them (Marky Mark in Calvin Klein's campaigns, Raúl in Bigas Luna's film) assured the potential buyer that this particular piece of underclothing would keep him on the front lines of phallic masculinity. What is being sold is not Raúl's (or Bardem's) penis in itself, but rather the conflation of this penis with the underwear. His penis – supposedly huge, though it remains unseen – becomes as fetishized as the product itself.

For any spectator conversant in the history of Spanish cinema, this underwear choice may also evoke the lumpen eroticism of de la Iglesia's *quinqui* films, including the homoerotic implications associated with it. With or without this bonus overtone, the commodification of Raúl's crotch illustrates the ambivalent outlook that results from putting the male body on display in advertising campaigns as much as on cinema screens, since it portrays the men represented "as solipsistic narcissists, while also offering up their bodies for the spectatorial pleasures of others" (Jobling, "Underexposed" 153). The exhibition of Raúl's body in underwear is not merely an objectification of a corporeal commodity for sale; it is also "a narcissistic exercise – and indeed he will later use the impressively dimensioned poster as a way to demonstrate his worthiness to Silvia" (Fouz-Hernández and Martínez-Expósito 24–5), when he proudly conflates his persona with the advertised male crotch: "Ese soy yo" (That's me). Just like the underwear in advertisements, the representation of Javier Bardem's sexualized body in *Jamón, jamón* somewhat distorts the lines between the subject and object of desire – especially, given the evidence that Bardem himself manipulated that sexualized image by using a great deal of cotton to exaggerate his crotch (Fouz-Hernández, *Cuerpos de cine* 56). Equally unclear is whether men or women, heterosexual or not, are the target audience, which is exactly the point.

Furthermore, this iconic sexualized image of the male body promotes the fetishistic contemplation of the hefty, if artificially enlarged, contents of Raúl's briefs – and thus the consumption of a phallic form of masculinity – as much as it highlights the crisis of this very form of traditional gender identity in a changing Spain. The label of the briefs (Sansón) conjures up the Biblical hero whose superhuman powers originated from his long hair. Raúl enjoys the association with this mythical form of masculine strength, but, as Peter William Evans has noted, he misses the irony of this allusion, since he will also end up being emasculated by a woman (Bigas 83). Just as Samson was seduced and then betrayed by his lover Delilah, who had his hair cut off and thereby all his strength curtailed while he was sleeping before turning him over to his Philistine enemies, Raúl will be betrayed and metaphorically castrated by Conchita. Since Raúl is (self-)conflated with his underpants in the visual economy of the film, the implication is that Conchita, the owner of the underwear that he showcases and wears, also owns him. In fact, Raúl dies in Conchita's arms (she is a maternal figure, "la madre-puta"), not in the arms of Silvia, his much younger lover. Although the film offers viewers a pleasurable spectacle of phallic masculinity that is metonymically flaunted by Raúl's briefs and his huge package, it ultimately exposes the decline of that traditional masculinity. The "macho ibérico" might still sell a large number of briefs, but he no longer represents an exemplary form of adult masculine identity. Like the traditional Y-front white briefs, he is merely a relic.

Spanish cinema substantially diversified its underwear choices for men in the early twenty-first century, beyond the outmoded Y-front white briefs.[15] A new cohort of young stars was given plenty of opportunities to showcase their semi-naked bodies in stylish underpants. Many of them had already paraded their assets on popular television sitcoms and shows, and expediently dragged their followers to the big screen. Following the trend initiated in the late 1980s and 1990s, the display of the eroticized male body became crucial to becoming a male star in Spanish cinema (Perriam, *Stars* 11). Prior to the advent of Antonio Banderas and Javier Bardem, "these bodily values [male bodies as an object of desire] were invested almost exclusively in foreign actors in imported (mostly Hollywood) films" (Fouz-Hernández and Martínez-Expósito 67). In what seems like an indispensable precondition for male stardom, the new cohorts of young Spanish leads must have slim but muscular bodies; they also must be clean shaven (and increasingly so, all over), virile (though not necessarily rugged or rough-looking anymore), and definitely sexy.

In contrast to Banderas and Bardem's generation, these new stars have, and are indeed expected to have, gym-trained bodies. As Chris Perriam notes, although Antonio Banderas's star image was dependent on his physicality and, more specifically, on his ability to be displayed as an object of desire, "Banderas had to wait for the gyms in America" to attain a fully muscled body (*Stars* 11). Twenty-first-century stars such as Miguel Ángel Silvestre and Álex González moulded their bodies into a certain type prior to making the professional jump to Hollywood. González became known worldwide for playing the mutant Riptide in *X-Men: First Class* (Matthew Vaughn, 2011), but audiences (in Spain and elsewhere) were already familiar with his muscular torso and six-pack at least since *Segundo asalto* (Daniel Cebrián, 2005), a boxing film which was distributed internationally. Similarly, though Silvestre became well-known globally when he appeared in the high-profile Netflix series *Sense8* (2015–18) and *Narcos* (2015–17), his body had already been thoroughly commodified in the Spanish boxing film *La distancia* (Iñaki Dorronsoro, 2006), as well as in *Zhao* (Susi Gozalvo, 2008), *Lo mejor de Eva* (Mariano Barroso, 2011) and, of course, in the television series *Velvet* (2013–16), where he had a leading role as Alberto Márquez. In summary, these men were propelled to stardom precisely because they were able to acquire perfect bodies that are exhibited as neither natural nor normal. Theirs is a cultivated look, a sexy virility that does not try to pass itself off as spontaneous or effortless. On the contrary, especially in their boxing roles, we see both of them sculpting their physiques almost to exhaustion. No pain, no gain; that is the new motto of Spanish male stardom – the new method acting, if you will.

With this new cohort of male stars, masculinity is denaturalized and its (self-)objectification no longer needs to be disavowed. This is a response to changes in the film industry as well as in society at large. Their bodies are not only objectified with a female gaze in mind; they are also objectified for the male gaze, and not just for sexual purposes. It is now more commonly accepted that male spectators can enjoy gazing at the exhibition of another male body, and film producers take this into consideration. But it is also accepted that the fashionable image – in this case, of men in underwear – is not ineludibly created for sexual titillation, but in some cases as part of a complex process that involves the pleasure of looking at how others of the same sex dress. There is a component of male narcissism associated with consumption, of looking "at themselves and other men as objects of desire to be bought and sold or imitated and copied" (Edwards, *Men* 73). This is why, apart from their perfectly sculpted bodies, these young Spanish actors have also mastered the art of grooming, both for their acting roles as well as for their real-life personas.

This is where stylish underwear (as much as outerwear) comes into play to complete their cultivated look, and not just because underwear disclosure is the nearest one can get to male nudity in mainstream cinema. A meta-reflection on this subject appears in *Zhao*, where Martín (played by Miguel Ángel Silvestre) comically states: "No sé para qué me he traído tanta ropa, si siempre voy desnudo" (I don't know why I've brought so many clothes, since I always go around naked). Martín is never shot fully nude, but he does spend most of his time on screen in his underpants – a varied assortment of boxers and boxer briefs. What these actors are exhibiting is the advent of men's underwear as fashion. As historian Valerie Steele has observed, "fashion has become increasingly body-conscious, and underwear implies the body more closely than does any other garment" (*Fetish* 129). Young male actors' recurrent underwear scenes are thus crucial to selling a fashionable, sexy masculinity for male and female viewers regardless of sexual preferences. In *Combustión* (Daniel Calparsoro, 2013), the criminal Ari (Adriana Ugarte) seduces former car racer Míkel (Álex González) during his bachelor party (he is about to marry the rich heir of an elegant jewellery store) and their affair puts an end to the marriage engagement. During their first sexual encounter, shot in soft-core fashion with clichéd "sexy" music and shallow-focus photography, a medium close-up of his black Calvin Klein boxer briefs reveals what we could initially interpret as an aspirational look. The Calvin Klein boxer briefs exude an aura of casual yet sophisticated masculinity, perhaps exposing Míkel's futile desire to belong to a higher social class and display a powerful corporate look. Later on, once Míkel's girlfriend has kicked him out and he is living by himself in a downtown apartment, we get a series of long and medium shots of his muscular body in modish grey briefs with a white rubber band, although we don't see a brand name this time. The stylish briefs sell a cultivated virility (a prominent bulge accompanies the muscular torso and marked six-pack abdomen) for erotic contemplation as much as for narcissistic admiration and/or identification: it is a global image of chic rebellion for metrosexuals with interests in "masculine" activities like car racing.

What I am suggesting is that contemporary young stars' underwear scenes have appeal for male consumers interested in images of masculinity, with or without homoerotic undertones. *Mentiras y gordas* (Alfonso Albacete and David Menkes, 2009) offers an even more salient example of this. This popular film (more than seven hundred thousand tickets sold) is about a group of twenty-somethings during one hedonistic summer in a coastal town in Spain. The endless scenes of sex, drug use, and clubbing seem almost like an excuse to display the fit bodies of the rising female and male film stars (Mario Casas, Alejo Sauras, Hugo Silva, Maxi Iglesias, Ana de Armas, and Ana Polvorosa) either in underwear or naked (including a full-frontal nudity shot of Yon González). One underwear scene is particularly striking. After spending the night with Sonia (Marieta Orozco), Pablo (Maxi Iglesias) sneaks out of her apartment before she wakes up, taking Sonia's savings with him. While he searches for the hidden money, the viewer gets several shots of him in his underwear. Once he finds the money, a close-up of his crotch while he straps the cash onto the elastic band of his underwear reveals the brand name aussieBum. This choice of underwear is anything but accidental. Pablo is wearing a pair of "Wonderjock" briefs that the Australian brand launched in 2007 to enhance the appearance of the wearer's genitals. Amidst a number of brands' crotch-enhancement fever in the mid-2000s, aussieBum replaced the more traditional use of a strap with "seams around the pouch and an additional pocket within the pouch front to 'push up' the genitals." The goal was to craft pouches that would "reflect the genitals and their position rather than pressing them close to the body as in traditional brief underwear" (Cole, *Story* 137).[16] The close-up of Pablo's crotch with the cash clipped to its elastic band is a meta-reflection on what it takes to become a male film star nowadays: Maxi Iglesias looks like a stripper, whose sexy virility is sold through chic underwear that makes his genitals look bigger.

It is important to reiterate that this image sells much more than Maxi Iglesias's body (and his crotch as a synecdoche of it) as an object of (homo)sexual desire. The aussieBum "Wonderjocks" that he rocks should not be seen as merely indicative of advances in sexual politics or of a crisis in traditional models of masculinity, as in the case of Javier Bardem's Y-front briefs in *Jamón, jamón*, which signposted the decline of phallic masculinity. They highlight, and therefore advertise, a model of fashionable global virile masculinity to be desired and imitated by present-day men, whatever their sexual preferences.[17] Admiring them as viewers provides other men a means of participation in contemporary fashion cultures in which the fashionable image does not have to be inextricably associated with sexual display. But if it is, it no longer provokes laughter or disavowal.

We are far from the Franco-era anxiety over the sight of masculine undergarments. In this chapter, I have analysed a variety of filmic representations of men in underwear through which normative patterns of masculinity and virility in Spanish society are sometimes strengthened, sometimes challenged, and are eventually made obsolescent. These representations also reveal a great deal about prevailing notions of male sexuality and sexual pleasure. The ill-fitting boxers of the 1960s and early 1970s sex comedies downplayed, and even ridiculed, the male body as a site of sexual desire – thereby exposing the fear of feminization and the homophobia associated with the eroticized masculine subject. In the late 1970s, the *cine quinqui* of Eloy de la Iglesia introduced a major change with its "estética del calzoncillo," as for the first time in Spanish cinema male underwear appeared overtly sexualized, and so did the bodies of the young protagonists. Since then, barring occasional nods to the comic portrayal of men in underwear to make a humorous point about the decline of outdated models of masculinity, especially the *macho ibérico*, Spanish films have flaunted the underwear of male stars as a sexual prop. In fact, the purpose of this underwear exhibition has been to stimulate all sorts of spectatorial pleasures and identifications. By exposing how the male body is now up for grabs, it highlights developments in sexual politics in Spanish society. But it also draws attention to the marketing of male underwear as part of global consumerist trends. In this sense, in the last section of the chapter, I have discussed how images of young stars – such as Miguel Ángel Silvestre, Álex González, and Maxi Iglesias – exhibit the manufacturing and advertising of masculine images in underwear that spectators (heterosexual or otherwise) would want to emulate. They make apparent

the globalization and, to a certain extent, the democratization of underwear styles, but also the new tyranny of certain male body types, both
on and off the screens.

In the next chapter, I will continue to examine how Spanish films
have deployed clothing (or the lack thereof) as a key element of their
mise en scène to visualize cinematic male identities. In this case, the emphasis will be on the recurrent racialized stereotyping and objectification of the semi-nude male (and at times also female) bodies of migrant
characters in a variety of immigration films. This will entail a twofold
shift in focus. First, I will turn to costume design as a noteworthy signifying element within the visual narratives of immigration films that
is detached – unlike the films analysed in the first three chapters – from
fashion trends outside of the film texts. Second, the analytical lens will
veer from gender and sexuality to race and ethnicity, particularly in
terms of how the latter two are enacted as difference.

Chapter Four

Dressing the Immigrant Other

Clothes and fashion have always played an important role in the politics of difference. As Tim Edwards reminds us, these entail those "which effect, reinforce or even invent difference within groups and societies whether according to class, age, gender, race, sexual orientation or, more simply, the politics of bodily regulation" (*Fashion in Focus* 104). With this in mind, I turn my attention to how Spanish immigration films place a heavy weight on costume as an important signifier in producing racialized images of migrants, who are visualized in opposition to the exaggeratedly dissimilar clothing choices of native Spaniards. I concentrate on three specific migrant groups (sub-Saharan men, Caribbean women, and Central and Eastern Europeans), because their cinematic portrayals make these racialized patterns even more perceptible. In these films, costume becomes a mechanism of representation that fabricates what Stuart Hall calls "a form of racialized knowledge of the Other" (260), one profoundly associated with operations of power such as the attempt to condense, homogenize, naturalize, and resolve cultural differences. This visual discourse reduces the racial other to a few essentials through stereotypes and creates a hierarchy among migrant subjects according to ethnic origin, with white European migrants being the demographic least racially marked by sartorial codes.

Costume patterns in immigration films illustrate the blending of immigration and race in the Spanish popular imagination. As Steve Garber notes, this is a widespread phenomenon across the European Union, making "the conditions of entry and settlement more difficult for those people not racialized as 'white'" (62). Anyone of a non-white racial background is immediately supposed to be an (illegal) immigrant subject, regardless of national origin or how long he or she may have been in the country. The analysis of this immigration-racializing process entails tackling those discursive mechanisms that use racial phenotypes – biological markers – not only to classify human difference, but also to do so with tangible ideological effects, given that race is "a set of socially constructed boundaries, practices, and commonly held meanings mapped onto a population whose members themselves represent wide physical and social diversity" (Craig 9). Moreover, as a signifier of alterity, racialized costume patterns express how Spaniards perceive and construct themselves and their own identity as much as that of the newcomers. It is well known that, starting in the late stages of Francoism, Spain's European aspirations centred on a foundational utopia as a means of boarding the train to modernity – inextricably associated with Europe – and of shedding the perceived backwardness posed by its historical connections with Africa (Delgado 211). In this process of reinventing its identity, the "whitening" and therefore constructed homogenization of the national complexion went hand in hand with the disavowal and racialized othering of any non-white European heritage. Ironically enough, as Rosalía Cornejo Parriego notes (18), this symbolic whitening coincided with the actual darkening of the European population, as well as with the escalating presence of non-white postcolonial subjects that effectively challenged the viability of that foundational utopia.

"Spanish immigration films" is the umbrella term employed by scholars to describe a range of productions that portray the experiences of first-generation migrants as they relocate to Spain from countries of the global South. Spain had historically been a country of emigration, but membership in the European Union and the modernization of the country's political, economic, and social structures made it an attractive destination for migrants. While not as quickly as other forms of cultural production – such as popular music, which by the 1980s had already begun to address the new social landscape (Bermúdez, *Rocking* 5) – Spanish filmmakers first turned their lenses on this subject in the early 1990s. They started to produce a diverse corpus of films out of a genuine impulse towards fostering an ethics of solidarity and generating social awareness.[1] Immigration films are typically successful at denouncing the strict policies and surveillance mechanisms instated by European governments to prevent migratory flows, as well as the racist and xenophobic attitudes of some European citizens towards the newly arrived individuals and communities. However, as other scholars have duly noted, Spanish immigration cinema has proved to be an ambivalent form of social cinema, because its representational practices do not escape the stereotypical treatment of immigrants in public discourse (Flesler, "New Racism"; Nair 110; Peralta 61–2). Such treatment includes the "'invasion psychosis' and other psycho-social dysfunctions associated with xenophobia" (Fouz-Hernández and Martínez Expósito 171), which often underpins stereotypical assessments of the other. Films, especially those made in the 1990s and early 2000s, often depict migrants as an unknown, homogenized, and feared "other" whose integration is virtually impossible, above all in the case of North Africans. The few successful "integration stories" come about through an assimilation – typically of Latin American migrants – that entails erasing cultural differences, and, even more problematically, reinstating hierarchies evocative of colonial scenarios throughout history (Corbalán, "Questioning"; Flesler, *The Return*; Song). These films prove that "the visual field is not neutral to the question of race; it is itself a racial formation, an episteme, hegemonic and forceful" (Butler 17). Spanish immigration cinema is not an impartial medium; indeed, it is a visual technology of representation that produces images of migrants, including the power asymmetries at work in racialized portrayals.[2]

When we study cinema's role in the racialization of immigration, we should seriously consider a pertinent recommendation made by Ella Shohat and Robert Stam. As these authors remind us, it does not suffice to identify and catalogue the types of ethnic images that films offer and simply differentiate between "good" and "bad" ones. Nor should we reduce our analysis to determining whether characters are depicted realistically (199–210). The debate over positive versus negative images often presupposes the idea that meaning precedes filmic representations – and, therefore, that films merely reflect or reproduce the pre-existent reality of, in this case, the migrant subjects. In this way, representations "are seen not as constructs but as if they were real flesh-and-blood people," leading to futile debates that succumb to moralism (Shohat and Stam 201). This is why it is not enough to merely analyse the content of immigration films. We must go beyond the taxonomy of images and examine the mechanisms of visual production – the formal aspects of the films – that are active elements in the production of racialized images. To do so, we must scrutinize how textual practices become racial constructs that transform images of ethnic difference into racialized "otherness," and, by the same token, how depictions of white Spaniards are rendered transparent and unmarked.

In his pioneering study *White*, Richard Dyer argues that white hegemony plays a crucial role in certain elements of cinematographic representations. Dyer studies how the choices of film stock, make-up, and lighting are technical and technological devices used to convey tacitly racialized values. Following this line of enquiry, I aim to show how costume patterns in Spanish immigration films furnish an over-exposition of non-white characters (flashy colours, cheap fabrics, and body-revealing designs that hypervisualize them as exotic and sexualized) as "projections of white imaginings" (14). Conversely, Spanish characters are dressed understatedly, with restraint (muted colours, loose-fitting shapes, and discreet styles), in a way that presents them as occupying a neutral position: as the general norm according to which all divergences should be evaluated. Proving the existence of racialized dynamics in these representations through costume, Caucasian-featured migrants from Central and Eastern European countries are portrayed with similar sartorial subtlety as Spaniards are, even though the films enact other mechanisms to visualize them as inadequately white. As I will show, the pattern is so ubiquitous that it reveals what Maxime Cervulle calls "the hyper(in)visibility of whiteness" referring to the regime of representation in mainstream cinema that insists on "the unremarkable – and unremarked – invisibility of white people" (xviii). Clothes thus adopt a key function in the production and sustainability of white dominance in cinematographic representations of race relations, because, borrowing again from Richard Dyer, "as long as race is something only applied to non-white peoples, as long as white people are not racially seen and named, they/we function as a human norm. Other people are raced, we are just people" (1).

By insisting, through costume, on the invisibility of whiteness as a racial position, Spanish immigration cinema fabricates a scopic regime of representation. The notion of "scopic regime" was first coined by film theorist Christian Metz to distinguish cinema from other arts, especially the theatre. The cinematic scopic regime is defined by "the absence of the object seen," by detachment and independence from its "real" referent (61). As Nicole Fleetwood proposes, Metz's notion may be productively adopted to theorize, in broader terms, "the use of vision and visual technologies in a given historical and cultural context to maintain power relations," such as depicting the racial other as a visual aberration or deviation from the white norm (17). In my view, it is helpful to consider Spanish immigration films through this conceptual framework, in the sense that their scopic regime of representation engineers an all-encompassing visual discourse about the immigrant as an "other" that leaves no room for that other to contest it. I argue that costume is a fundamental part of this scopic regime that subjugates migrants through visual coding while Spaniards go unnoticed.[3] At the same time, I will also demonstrate that immigration films such as *El traje* (Alberto Rodríguez, 2002), *Los novios búlgaros* (Eloy de la Iglesia, 2003), *Princesas* (Fernando León de Aranoa, 2005), and *Agua con sal* (Pedro Pérez Rosado, 2005) use costume to unsettle the very scopic regime that defines the migrant other as such. These films effectively revise the function and boundaries of sartorial codes in racial marking by visualizing the possibility that unequal power dynamics between natives and immigrants become refashioned – pun intended. Significantly, this revision takes place in films that engage the topic of immigration with greater nuance by exploring how race and ethnicity intersect with other subject positions, such as class, gender, and sexuality.

In critiquing costume patterns in Spanish immigration films, my intention is not to deny that clothing differences may exist among people of diverse ethnic and national origins, and even among people of the same social group. That is not my point. Rather, I aim to study how films may overstate such differences through a racialized visual discourse with patterns that are pervasive across films, and which operates according to binary oppositions (self/other, civilization/nature, reason/ instinct) – oppositions that tend to reinforce hierarchies and sometimes redraw them in an effort to complicate or even undermine such binaries. Moreover, I certainly do not intend to imply that my book is the first to examine costume in this context. Several Spanish film scholars have focused their critical acumen on this element of specific films' mise en scène. However, at least to my knowledge, I am the first to offer a sustained analysis of costume's crucial role in immigration films as a whole. One more necessary disclaimer concerns the corpus of films under critical scrutiny: my enquiry is based on an extensive though not exhaustive archive of films. While I believe that I offer sufficient evidence for my ideas, my goal is not to claim that the same costume patterns appear in every Spanish immigration film.

(Un)Dressing African Male Blackness

The most prominent Spanish immigration films in the 1990s, *Las cartas de Alou* (Montxo Armendáriz, 1990) and *Bwana* (Imanol Uribe, 1996), centred on the representation of sub-Saharan black males. The focus of these films did not reflect migratory patterns to the Iberian Peninsula at the time (Solé and Parella 61), but media discourses and the film industry paid a disproportionate amount of attention to sub-Saharan immigrants (Burkhart 154). Such scrutiny corresponded to a broader trend that was also apparent in other forms of cultural production, such as literature and popular music: Spanish society ascribed a "black face" to immigration that was articulated – and, in the case of cinema, visualized – "as a racial category threatening Spain's materialization as a 'true' European nation" (Bermúdez 99). It is noteworthy that *Las cartas de Alou*, the pioneering Spanish immigration film, won the Golden Seashell at the prestigious San Sebastian International Film Festival.

In addition, the film was nominated for eight Goya Awards (and won two for Best Screenplay and Best Cinematography), also winning prizes at the Spanish Cinema Writers Circle Awards. Spanish film scholars generally agree that, in composing the character of Alou (Mulie Jarju), Armendáriz successfully eschews the tendency towards stereotyping that marks portrayals of African migrants in European cinema. Isolina Ballesteros credits Armendáriz for conferring agency on the Senegalese migrant not only through the narrative voice and the gaze, but also through Alou's ability to learn Spanish quickly and through his writing: for instance, he writes numerous letters to his parents and his friend Mulay, reflecting on his journey and experiences (*Cine* 221). Although I agree with Ballesteros that *Las cartas* effectively undercuts the stereotype of the illiterate migrant, the visual treatment of Alou's character does not always avoid typecasting. In fact, much like subsequent immigration films, this film performs a visual fetishization of the black migrant's body – and, therefore, the association of blackness with physicality, with nature, as opposed to reason and the intellect.

This fetishization is manifested early in the narrative (minute 11), in a scene in which Alou and his co-worker Kassim (Mamadou Lamine) are bathing in a tide pool by the seashore. Medium shots of both characters draw attention to their athletic bodies, especially Alou's muscular torso and arms. The camera lingers on his torso and flat belly in the water, creating a radiant effect that further emphasizes the exoticism of his black body against the backdrop of the brightly lit blue water at sunset. There are no shots of his genital area, which Isabel Santaolalla interprets as a way to avoid excessively sexualizing the character, even if the film visualizes him in relation to the colonial tradition that links blackness to pre-civilized primitivism. Santaolalla praises the film for incorporating this tradition into its visual discourse in order to counter it by tempering the sexual component – and, above all, for endowing Alou with emotional, psychological, and cognitive complexity (*Los "Otros"* 122). My own interpretation is less enthusiastic. Alou's body still receives a fetishistic treatment through fragmentation; specific parts of his body are substituted for the whole. The desire for the forbidden absent element (genitalia) is transferred to other parts of his body – in this case, his spectacularly visualized muscular torso and belly. This displaced form of visual representation through disavowal is key, as Stuart Hall notes, to the functioning of fetishism, where "a powerful fascination or desire is both *indulged* and at the same time denied" (267, emphasis in the original). The eroticization of Alou's naked body accompanies the eroticization of the gaze, allowing viewers to embrace an illicit or ambivalent desire disguised in ethnographic voyeurism.

We are encouraged to keep looking while disavowing the erotic nature of our gaze.

Narratively, the scene is superfluous, because the bond between Alou and Kassim is more effectively conveyed through costume. When Alou is about to relocate, Kassim gives Alou a shirt as a token of his friendship. Alou decides to wear the shirt, which has a checkered pattern (in several tones of red, blue, and grey), on his bus trip to Barcelona, as well as in several significant scenes in the second part of the film. Once in Catalonia, as Alou struggles to find a job and settle down, he comes across Moncef (Ahmed El-Maaroufi), a Maghrebi migrant who had crossed the strait in the same boat as Alou. Moncef teaches him to play checkers, a strategy game that allegorizes race relations (Tobin Stanley 6): a game between white and black checker pieces in which, as Moncef jokingly puts it, white always wins. Simplice Boyogueno reminds us that checkers is a modern version of a medieval Arabic game called *al-qirq*. It was brought to the Iberian Peninsula by the Moors and became known as *alquerque*, its derivative name in Spanish (179). By granting narrative importance to the game of checkers, which becomes a key motif for the rest of the film, Armendáriz cleverly emphasizes the preservation of Arabic culture in contemporary Spain. Simultaneously, he calls attention to the historical tensions between Spain and its North African neighbours: tensions updated with the growing presence of Moroccan immigrants, which forces Spaniards to confront the non-European elements of their national identity and culture (see Daniela Flesler's *The Return* for a lengthy discussion of this phenomenon). During a game at the local bar, the bar owner – who is also Alou's potential father-in-law (played by Albert Vidal) – forbids him from returning to the bar and dating his daughter. Alou's multicoloured shirt acquires symbolic meaning by providing a bright visual contrast to the black-and-white checkerboard, just as his friendships and alliances with fellow migrants of diverse ethnic and religious origins symbolically oppose the rigid and binary-bound relationships between native Europeans and foreign Africans.

The fetishistic presentation of Alou's body in the seashore scene betrays the effective work achieved by costume designer Maiki Marín in conveying a message of multicultural solidarity. It almost seems like a commercial concession to the audience, as if feeling pressure to uphold the sexualized portrayal of blackness that Spanish audiences might expect, especially after the release of *El rey del mambo* (Carles Mira, 1989). In this comedy, Alí (Kelvin Garvanne), a black Jamaican who works fixing television antennas, becomes a sex toy for a plethora of wealthy middle-aged housewives. Mira seems to be referencing *Angst essen*

Seele auf/ (*Ali: Fear Eats the Soul*) (1974), Rainer Werner Fassbinder's first international hit, in which the main character, also named Ali, is subjected to the middle-aged, female, heterosexual objectifying gaze. In Mira's film, Alí's first onscreen appearance sets the tone for his role in the rest of the film: a full-frontal nude in a medium-long shot, accompanied by a comment by Don Martín (José Luis López Vázquez), Alí's boss and the owner of the house, about the size of his penis. We do get to see Alí with his clothes on, but only in scenes where various parts of his body are fetishized for sexual titillation; for example, the close-ups of his buttocks in tight blue jeans before the desiring gaze of Carmen (Charo López), one of his wealthy customers, who will subsequently hire him to star in a domestic porn video. The film never explores Alí's personality traits or origins: he is wholly reduced to his sex appeal and the mythology of the black man's sexual organ. Although the diegetic space of the film presents this image as a positive one, a portrayal meant to combat racist attitudes towards black people, it is – at best – a white fantasy of exotic desire. These associations of blackness with virility and physical and sexual superiority do not obliterate the existing negative images of blackness, but rather reinforce them, because "exceptions confirm the rule, they illustrate the norm, and function to demarcate the extra-ordinary. The effect of white exoticism is thus to outline and underline the extraordinariness of blackness" (Hondius 46).

Subsequent Spanish immigration films offered audiences plenty of exoticizing images of undressed black African male migrants. *Bwana* is the best known in terms of its critical reception. In addition to receiving the Golden Shell Award in San Sebastián and three Goya nominations, *Bwana* was Spain's Best Foreign Language Film entry at the sixty-ninth Academy Awards. Film critics have noted how *Bwana* compares negatively to *Las cartas* in its controversial portrayal of sub-Saharan immigration. Notably, Isolina Ballesteros contends that Imanol Uribe draws on many stereotypes of the colonial imaginary (primitivism, animalization, exoticism, and an emphasis on sexual and physical prowess that negates intellectual skill) to construct the character of Ombasi (Emilio Buale) (*Cine* 223). Even if Uribe's intention was to display and ridicule the racist attitudes of an average middle-class Spanish family – Rob Stone describes this film as an "anti-racist parable" (*Spanish Cinema* 152) – the visual treatment of the black African migrant is extremely problematic. For example, when drug smugglers are about to attack the family, Ombasi scares off the culprits, screaming and carrying two torches as he emerges from the shadows. Although his brave deed earns him some trust from the family – the wife, Dori (María Barranco), praises him for acting like a real man – he is depicted as a primitive savage and valued only for his primal masculinity, which is nonetheless exoticized as deviating from the "civilized" virility of European men.

This portrayal invokes a colonial tradition of representing indigenous "savages" as either excessively virile or not virile enough – "which is a convenient way to delegitimize them as 'normal' men," because they diverged from the "'just right' virility" of European colonizers and their manners were coded in the realm of barbarity, bestiality, and primitivism (Taraud 339). In effect, during the night, Dori has an erotic dream in which Ombasi crawls up to her like an animal and starts caressing her legs. Back in reality, Dori lustfully contemplates Ombasi's naked silhouette when he climbs a hill to greet the morning sun and when he jumps into the ocean for a swim. Visually, he is identified with natural elements that affix him, along with the sounds of African drums that accompany his screen presence, in a wild, prelinguistic state (Santaolalla, *Los "Otros"* 165) – and, I would add, in a pre-sartorial primitivism detached from emblems of civilization like clothes. Stripped down, Ombasi turns from sexual object to vulnerable target in the final sequence: tracking shots show him running naked like an animal fleeing capture by a group of skinheads (Ballesteros, *Cine* 228; Deveny 37; Santaolalla, *Los "Otros"* 165). The end of the film finally grants him the narrative gaze, with a POV shot followed by an extreme close-up in which Ombasi sees the Spanish family driving away in the comfort of their car: a symbol for the civilized modernity denied to him.

Symbols of modernization and costume are also pivotal in the racialized portrayal of the migrant we find in *El dios de madera* (Vicente Molina Foix, 2010). The film opens with undocumented Senegalese Yao (Madi Diocou) completing his journey to Spain by hiding behind some solar panels in the countryside near Valencia. As clean sources of renewable, eco-friendly energy – they use natural sunlight to generate electricity and produce no greenhouse gas emissions into the atmosphere – solar panels are deployed here as symbols of Spain's technological and entrepreneurial innovation. The visual contrast between the dark tones of his skin and the pale brightness of the panels invites viewers to behold his figure in relation to the hackneyed binary of nature versus civilization – and, more specifically, the contrast between a primal form of African masculinity and European modernity. Once he settles in Valencia, Yao's attire provisionally undoes these initial spectatorial expectations. He survives by selling pirated DVDs, wanders around in loneliness, and silently observes the rhythm of urban life from the balcony of his motel room. Yao's muted personality is highlighted by the clothes he wears: outfits in grey, brown, and khaki tones that make his figure blend into his surroundings. Through costume, this film seems to be engaging what Steffen Köhn calls "the dialectics of in/visibility," to reference the dual process of concealment and exposure inscribed in the visual discourse on migration. The racialized visibility that migrants tend to receive in the mass media corresponds to their social invisibility, their negation as subjects with political and legal rights (30). Yao's "invisible," neutral-hued outfits effectively evoke both visual regimes – while still containing the potential to modify their terms of correlation. His clothes express his social exclusion and marginalization, his withdrawal from the gaze of society, without sartorially overexposing him as an exotic other. Not yet, anyway.

When he meets María Luisa (Marisa Paredes), a fifty-seven-year-old widow, Yao is wearing a white polo shirt, which suggests a sense of purity and innocence that catches her attention. To express his gratitude for her kindness, he brings her some tamarind, a pod-like fruit with an edible pulp inside. With its antioxidant powers that enrich cardiac health by lowering blood cholesterol, the tamarind, which is native to his country of origin, signifies the positive effects and renewal that Yao brings to her life. María Luisa's irritable personality starts to change under the soothing influence of his presence, visually flagged by his pristine white shirts. She even takes interest in learning about his country and why he moved to Spain, thus indicating that she starts to see him as an individual with a story to tell. Nevertheless, matters take a turn for the worse: Yao accidentally gets his shirt wet when using María Luisa's bathroom, a trite narrative pretext for him to take it off. Her desire instantly awakens at the sight of his muscular chest: "¡Qué negro eres, Yao! … Tienes un negro bonito, natural" (You're so black! Your skin is such a lovely black, all natural). Instinctively, she starts caressing his torso. Although she quickly stops herself and apologizes, the scene undermines the hitherto effective work by costume designer Cristina Rodríguez in challenging the dominant cinematic regime of migrant representation. By undressing Yao, *El dios de madera* reverts to the conventional depictions of black male bodies in mainstream media, stereotypically cast in such a sexual light that audiences struggle to picture them as anything beyond the generic migrant body that is objectified in the Spanish social imagination.

Yao's reply authorizes her conduct by stating, with his limited fluency in Spanish, "Yo veinticinco años y soy botarate" (I am twenty-five and a fool). In this way, he implicitly condones the practice of paternalism. Indeed, he begs for María Luisa's guidance, as he perceives her as possessing knowledge and experience; for one thing, she taught him the colloquial word "botarate." Given that she has already subjected his body to racialized exoticization, this sequence conjures the notion of paternalism that, according to Dienke Hondius, has played an important role in European racial discourses. Paternalist behaviour can comprise "ruling as well as protecting, caring as well as controlling" (19). When power imbalances are at work, such conduct may be deployed to justify domination, to "maintain the status quo," and to ensure "the continuity of unequal relations without confrontations" (26). In the context of this film, it naturalizes a patronizing attitude by the European woman who has the linguistic and sexual knowledge, the legal rights, and the financial means to mould Yao's behaviour in and out of bed. She teaches him table manners as much as she takes the lead in their sexual encounters – with a plethora of flatteringly lit shots of Yao's naked torso and rear body along the way.

This program of refinement of the African black male culminates with María Luisa dressing Yao in one of her ex-husband's suits for a formal dinner with her son Róber (Nao Albet). It marks the completion of the rite of passage from his (self-)infantilized state as a "botarate" to becoming a real man; after all, the suit is a quintessential symbol of mature masculinity. As a uniform of respectability, this suit suggests Yao's integration into this middle-class Spanish family, indicating a literal continuity with the previous patriarch by wearing his pants. It also signifies an evolution out of his premodern African origins through his assimilation into Western modernity, since the suit "is also a predominantly, though not exclusively, western phenomenon" (Edwards, *Fashion* 53).[4] Yet this externally imposed, racialized identity – in the sense that María Luisa is trying to "whiten" him – fails to provide him with any sort of secure status. Róber, jealous of Yao supplanting his dad, reports him to the police and Yao is detained. Once released, he goes to María Luisa's clothing store and falls asleep on the floor while waiting for her. Dressed in a white shirt, Yao is once again portrayed as infantilized subject in need of María Luisa's help, resources, and guidance.

Aided by symbolic enactments of costume, *El dios de madera* thus rehearses the possible integration of black African migrants. This prospect proves futile: the film returns the black migrant to a position of helplessness and marginalization in the host society. As in both *Bwana* and *Las cartas de Alou*, he is reduced to a precarious lifestyle that Giorgio Agamben calls "bare life," in reference to "the simple fact of living" that is common to plants, animals, and humans: a purely biological existence devoid of legal rights or political meaning (1, 2, 6). The bareness of the African black male migrant is quite literal in all three films. The protagonists are stripped of their clothes, their bodies visually fetishized as exotic objects for sexual titillation, just as they are stripped of legal status and excluded from Spanish society. While these films sought to raise awareness against racism and xenophobia, they ultimately reinforce one-dimensional media images of the black African male. Visualized through costume as a primitive savage like Ombasi or as an infantilized young man like Yao, they are portrayed, in both cases, as vulnerable subjects at the mercy of paternalistic Spaniards and their charity.

The similarities found in these examples from the archive of racialized representations raise a valid question: is there any room in Spanish immigration cinema for alternative ways of portraying the black African male migrant through costume? I will now turn to Alberto Rodríguez's *El traje* (2002) for an affirmative answer. This film delivers a more complex and multilayered depiction of racial difference by exploring the intersections of race, masculinity, and class. Patricio (Jimmy Roca) is a migrant from Equatorial Guinea who works as a guard in a parking lot. One day he receives a bag with a suit, a white shirt, a tie, and a pair of shoes as a gift for helping a man – we learn later that he is a basketball player who wears the same suit in promotional photographs – change a flat tire. When Patricio wears the suit, he immediately notices a difference in how other people perceive him. Before that, he had endured constant racist episodes: a young woman steps off the sidewalk as he approaches, a grumpy newsstand owner pressures him to buy a magazine he's been leafing through. Wearing the suit, though, clerks treat him with reverence when he walks into high-end stores. Patricio realizes that clothing is a major tool in the social construction of a personal image. Dressing properly – or dressing to impress, as Patricio does here – enables access to a socially prestigious position.

The suit in question is grey pinstripe, a style usually associated with bankers and executives; it is definitely the sartorial choice of a finance professional. Clearly, this particular suit signifies class, success, and affluence. As Diana Crane notes, "In the late twentieth century, the business suit is the epitome of a style that expresses social class distinctions" (173). Like director Vicente Molina Foix in *El dios de madera*, Alberto Rodríguez engages the dialectics of in/visibility. He shows how an external symbol of accomplishment draws Patricio out of the social invisibility that typically constrains migrants and allows him to "become a free urban *flâneur* without being constantly scrutinised due to his race and underprivileged status" (Ballesteros, "Foreign" 177–8). A series of tracking shots visually conveys this transformation: Patricio walks past store windows, pauses to look at his reflection in the glass, and compares his appearance to the stylish mannequins showcased there. Before leaving his apartment, a meticulously planned sequence plays with the conventions – discussed above – of how the black male

African body is represented. A close-up of Patricio buttoning his white shirt and tying his tie replaces the customary close-up of the muscular torso. After an editing cut and a close-up of his elegant black shoes, a tilting camera movement gradually shows Patricio's body parts to spectators until we get a full view of his figure. This is the type of visual fragmentation found in fetishistic treatments of the black male body in immigration cinema. The difference here is that the film is fetishizing the clothes, not the body. Although there are several scenes of Patricio in the bathroom or getting ready for his day, no shot visualizes his body without clothes. In several shots, we see him clad only in underwear and an undershirt when he gets out of bed in the morning, but the film's representational apparatus does not eroticize these scenes. Patricio wears loose-fitting white undershirts and boxers shown in long shots and without flattering lighting or camera angles that would entice viewers to fantasize about the body parts concealed by these garments.

Granted, Patricio's new-found status is both superficial and temporary, a mere façade of social significance achieved through an external symbol of respectability – the suit – that does not ultimately provide him with any valid options for improving his marginalized position in society. Various images of confinement express this precariousness. Multiple scenes frame Patricio behind the iron gate of a private home, the wire fence of a park, and the metal structure of a bus stop. All such images suggest imprisonment, underscoring the sense that the protagonist is trapped in a fake identity that will not lead him to social advancement (see fig. 4.1). On several occasions, Patricio almost gets the suit stained: near-accidents that further punctuate the fragility of his image. While he manages to keep the suit stain-free for days, these situations constantly remind him – and the viewers – that his manufactured image of respectability is one blemish away from being blotted out altogether. In fact, Patricio is evicted from his apartment due to his roommate's criminal activity; he gets fired from his job for being late; and María (Vanesa Cabeza), a shop clerk he tries to date, quickly figures out his invented identity.

The improved self-image only helps him when he decides to join a picaresque character nicknamed "Pan con Queso" (Bread and Cheese, played by Manuel Morón) in performing fraudulent tricks and petty crimes to survive on the streets of Seville. Pan had previously stolen Patricio's money in a shelter, so he starts shadowing the thief to reclaim what was his. A friendship develops between them – to the extent that, as Isolina Ballesteros argues, "*El traje* may indeed be read as a successful parable of race relations that optimistically proposes that Otherness and difference may be shared," especially among disenfranchised social groups ("Foreign" 180). In the final sequence, Patricio buries the

Fig. 4.1. Suit and confinement in *El traje*

suit jacket and Pan throws rocks at a billboard of the basketball player who had given Patricio an identical suit. As they walk away with Roland (Mulie Jarju), another sub-Saharan migrant, they have to climb a wire fence: a visual signal that they are leaving their symbolic imprisonment behind – the imprisonment of fake identities – and will start living life as their true selves from that moment on.

The open ending suggests a hopeful future for the characters, visualized by the eye-catching panoramic shot of the city on the horizon. This openness locates the film in the orbit of what Arjun Appadurai calls "an ethics of possibility," as it addresses the topic of migration as an opportunity for transnational alliances rather than as a conflict. The latter position is the one held by the dominant "ethics of probability": concerned only with perfecting the "modern regimes of diagnosis, counting, and accounting" (i.e., exclusionary immigration policies, surveillance mechanisms, and media coverage of migratory displacements) that govern the lives of citizens and non-citizens alike (295). By promoting an ethics of possibility, *El traje* increases our "horizons of hope" and "expand[s] the field of imagination" (295), so that viewers can dream of a society that might transform the prevalent structures of inequality into something better. This ending is not naïvely utopian, though. The characters' future is full of obstacles and precarious conditions, but we get the sense that they will manage to make it work.

In *El traje*, non-sexual interracial male bonding offers the possibility of racial integration into Spanish society beyond the compulsory heterosexual romantic situations of previous immigration films. Tellingly, the character who constitutes the third wheel of the characters' transnational alliance is played by Mulie Jarju, the leading actor in *Las cartas de Alou*. Any viewer conversant in Spanish cinema would notice this detail. Alberto Rodríguez is inviting us to view his film in conjunction with previous attempts to promote a politics of hope. As we have examined in this section, those earlier attempts ultimately reinforce dominant scopic regimes of representation by eroticizing black African migrants, whose naked bodies are fetishized. Such portrayals visually suggest that the migrants' lives are reduced to their literal skin and bones, "bare lives" without any political or legal representation. In *El traje*, misleading dress codes are also important, because the black African migrant must dispose of his mask of social rank and "Europeanness" – the suit itself – before he can truly build a future in Spanish society, albeit among the unprivileged social groups. Strikingly for a Spanish immigration film, Patricio is not stripped of all his clothes; in this way, he is never eroticized as an exotic other.

Fashioning Caribbean Women: Colonialism, Assimilation, and Cross-Cultural Alliances

As "the familiar other," Latin American migrants share linguistic, cultural, and religious ties, as well as blood kinship, with Spaniards. For this reason, they are perceived as a less threatening presence than other foreigners are, and they tend to fit more neatly into film narratives that address issues of national identity (Santaolalla, *Los "Otros"* 169–71). This perception explains why Latin Americans had a high degree of visibility in Spanish films in the late 1990s and 2000s. With the upturn in the process of "feminization" of immigration cinema (Ballesteros, "Embracing" 5), Caribbean women, especially those of Cuban origin, came to occupy a prominent place in those films.[5] The trend was somewhat surprising, given that Cuban women encompassed a small percentage of Latin American migrants at the time (Guarinos 4). Female migration from the Dominican Republic was more abundant, with a female-dominated migratory flow (59 per cent). However, data from the Instituto Nacional de Estadística informs us that their numbers were considerably lower than those of immigrants from countries such as Ecuador, Colombia, and Argentina by the early 2000s (Oso 210). Caribbean women populated Spanish screens at a much higher rate than they did Spanish cities.

A number of scholars have argued that the portrayal of Caribbean migrants in Spanish cinema can only be properly evaluated in relation to the recurrence of racial, gender, and sexual discourses harking back to the colonial cultural tradition (Corbalán, "Questioning" 78; Del Río Gabiola; Flesler, "New Racism"; Martí-Olivella; Martín Cabrera, "Postcolonial" 43; Murray, *Home Away* 32–3; Song 44–7; Vernon, "Imperio" 198). Caribbean women do not emerge in a "geopolitical neutral space," but in "a space of power relations that is always already informed and constituted by coloniality" (Grosfoguel, Cervántes-Rodríguez, and Mielants 8). The discrimination and even racial and gender violence endured by these characters remind us that contemporary Spain is a postcolonial society that still operates according to power structures and beliefs linked to its colonial history: what Peruvian sociologist Aníbal Quijano calls "the coloniality of power" (533). Above all, with their incessant use of the porno-tropical tradition that underlies sexualized and racialized depictions of black and mixed-race Caribbean women, Spanish films exhibit the return of a colonial mindset. Anne McClintock shows that this tradition developed from European travel narratives during the Renaissance, and, later, during the Victorian period, in which women from African, South American, and Caribbean countries "figured as the epitome of sexual aberration and excess," equally feared and desired (22). The hypersexualized Cuban women of colour in films such as *Los hijos del viento* (Fernando Merinero, 1995), *Flores de otro mundo* (Icíar Bollaín, 1999), and *Adiós con el corazón* (José Luis García Sánchez, 2000) exemplify the persistence of these deep-rooted notions, inherited from Spain's colonial past. They also illustrate Jerome Branche's point that Luso-Hispanic culture continues to operate according to colonial racial narratives that inscribe "blackness as negative difference" (2). My contribution to the existing bibliography on films featuring female migrants of Caribbean origin will centre on highlighting the role of costume in visualizing these women's ethnic, gendered, and sexual otherness.

Most of the films in question display a blatant and strategic visualization of difference by oversignifying attire. The construction of the Caribbean migrant as distinct reveals the fears and anxieties of Spaniards, who perceive the (postcolonial) non-white presence as disruptive to the ideal of a racially homogeneous national community. Spanish immigration films exhibit two divergent responses to or means of engagement with this clothes-related differentiation. In some films, clothing mismatches are used to demonstrate the presumed cultural incompatibility of lifestyles – a demonstration used, in turn, to justify attitudes of rejection and exclusion towards Caribbean women of colour. Only those women who adapt their dress code to the colours, fabrics, and shapes of the host society are able to successfully integrate.

Interestingly, they tend to be women who get involved in a heterosexual romance that results in the formation of a nuclear family sanctioned by a traditional marriage, thus implying that integration entails both acculturation and reinforcement of the heteronormative order. Other films explore alternative options for the incorporation of the female Latin American migrant into Spanish society. In *Sobreviviré*, *Princesas*, and *Agua con sal*, difference in attire plays a crucial, positive role in the bonds forged between Caribbean and Spanish women. The exchange of fashion and beauty secrets allows these women to develop non-sexual matrilineal connections, showing that heterosexual romance and miscegenation are not the only paths to transnational and interracial affinities. Other forms of kinship are possible, and they do not necessarily involve acculturation.

Flores de otro mundo is the most widely discussed film of the first group. Several scholars have noted that its mise en scène overstates incompatibilities in clothing, hairstyles, and culinary customs between Caribbean migrant subjects and Spanish natives (Martín Cabrera, "Postcolonial" 49; Martin-Márquez, "World" 265; Martínez-Carazo, "*Flores*" 378–9). The film also reactivates the colonial memory through the hypersexualized presentation of Milady (Marylin Torres), a black Cuban migrant who hopes to leave behind her past as a *jinetera* (sex worker). Upon her arrival in a small Castilian village, she steps out of her Spanish boyfriend's car wearing a tight halter top; Lycra leggings adorned with an American flag design; and platform tennis shoes that accentuate her height (see fig. 4.2). María del Carmen Rodríguez claims that the Stars and Stripes leggings epitomize Milady's opposition to the Cuban regime and her desire for democratic freedom (73). Other critics maintain that Milady's costume conjures the porno-tropical tradition that makes the body of the black Caribbean woman available to the objectifying male gaze and to the invasion and violence of the new colonizers (Del Río Gabiola 90; Song 53). Her costume seems to suggest that "Milady's body, as well as her sexuality, are trapped between American imperialism and European patriarchy" (Martín Cabrera, "Postcolonial" 46). However, as Isolina Ballesteros has observed, the follow-up sequence deploys the same outfit to subvert viewers' expectations ("Embracing" 9). As soon as they get home, Carmelo (José Sáncho) tries to exercise his claim on her body. Milady takes the initiative, gets on top of him, and provokes his orgasm without taking her clothes off, thus denying both Carmelo and the spectator a peek at her naked body. Icíar Bollaín could have continued to employ costume to challenge the stereotype of the sexualized black Caribbean woman, thus enabling the construction of new significations for this figure. Ultimately, she did not.

Fig. 4.2. Hypersexualized presentation of the Caribbean migrant in *Flores de otro mundo*

Later in the film, Milady wears a Lycra miniskirt and a form-fitting knock-off cashmere sweater, both in gaudy yellow, to tend the local bar. Her outfit, and her very presence in a traditionally male-dominated space, elicits objectifying looks and even the verbal attacks of several young troublemakers, who get into a fight with Carmelo. He covers her body with a jacket and takes her home, literally removing her from view. Milady temporarily tempers the colours and shapes of her clothes, her wardrobe transitioning to grey sweatpants and loose, long-sleeved white T-shirts. Although she is trying to fit in, this gesture only reinforces her alienation and the feeling that she is "out of place in this environment" (Santaolalla, *Cinema* 131, 125). Eventually, she understands that there is no room for her (or her outfits) in this rural community, so she leaves. Through her flashy clothes, the body of the black Cuban woman is visualized as an excess that cannot be contained or domesticated.

In comparison, this clothing unsuitability is even more apparent in the case of Patricia (Lissete Mejía), a Dominican immigrant in the same film. Patricia assimilates into her new rural life by drastically altering her clothing choices. When she first arrives in the village, Patricia is wearing a tangerine-coloured sleeveless dress; her hair is down, her face made up. Once she marries Damián (Luis Tosar), the colour palette of her costumes changes to "los colores del pueblo, tonos terrosos y verdes" (the colours of the village, earthy and green tones) (Masterson

173), and they take the form of loose-fitting garments such as heavy wool sweaters, sweatpants, and a knit cap to cover her hair. Patricia's attire conversion overlaps with the solidification of her marriage and her becoming a traditional housewife – new pregnancy and all – that gets rewarded with integration into a Spanish rural community. Tellingly, Patricia had formal training as a beautician in the Dominican Republic. Yet she only applies her expertise when she volunteers to give Milady a makeover – never herself. Patricia thus becomes not only Milady's close friend, but also her potential fashion and lifestyle mentor. Upon meeting Milady, the first thing she does is to cover the Cuban woman's upper body with a jacket to protect her from the cold (and the desiring male gaze). Patricia is the poster child of assimilation through miscegenation (and acculturation by forsaking her clothing habits), but she is ultimately an unattainable model for Milady, fashion-related or otherwise.

Costume is wielded once again as a strategic way to visualize a happy ending for the Dominican-Spanish family. The first communion ceremony for Patricia's daughter, Janai (Isabel de los Santos), is a symbolic ritual in which the members of this multicultural family dress up to celebrate the girl's reception of the Holy Sacrament. In the overall context of the film, though, the ceremony is even more significant. Etymologically, "communion" means "fellowship, mutual participation, or sharing." The photo taken by Lorna (Ángela Herrera) captures this sense of a multi-ethnic family composed of diverse constituents who adapt their customs to coexist in harmony – through mutual participation – while retaining some of their cultural idiosyncrasies. Damián and his mother are dressed in sober grey tones matching their personalities. Patricia regains her fashion sense by donning an elegant red dress, adorned with a shawl in the same colour, although she keeps her hair up – a style in line with the formality of the religious ritual. Her Dominican friend Graciela (Ada Mercedes) wears a muted white suit; muted in comparison with her previous outfits, that is, especially the bright yellow jumpsuit she donned for the singles party at the beginning of the film. However, her platform shoes and shiny plastic handbag, stamped with the word "TAXI" in gigantic capital letters, indicate that she is still imprinting her sassy personality and cultural tastes on the ceremonial decorum of the religious ceremony. Above all, the puff sleeves and ruffles of Janay's dress noticeably diverge from the minimalist austerity of what the only other girl celebrating her communion is wearing. Evidently, Janai's dress serves to inscribe "integration alongside Christianity, the common cultural denominator (together with language) that makes Latin Americans good candidates for integration with Spain" (Flesler, "New

Racism" 113). At the same time, it introduces a touch of hope that Janai will grow up embracing some ethnic markers of her roots. In this way, although *Flores de otro mundo* promotes a conservative assimilationist agenda for the Caribbean woman (Martínez-Carazo, "*Flores*" 387; Kim 184, 187–8), it ultimately challenges Manichean treatments of identity and difference, including its own sexualized sartorial presentation of Milady, thus offering a glance of what a multiracial Spanish family might look like.

I Love You, Baby also suggests that the integration of mixed-race or black Caribbean women into Spanish society is only possible through miscegenation and dress renunciation. The Dominican Marisol (played by Mexican actress Tiaré Scanda) and her Caribbean roommates and friends, such as Kenia (Marylin Torres) and Kati (Laura Ramos), both Cuban, are predictably visualized through racial stereotypes: they "appear as loud, physically large, colorfully or skimpily dressed" (Song 51). Moreover, they frequently come into view in spaces and settings that are prone to their "ethnification," such as the club "El Hollo," where migrants dance to Caribbean rhythms. Frances Aparicio argues that "to be ethnified" means "to be constructed and displaced as Other" by what is fundamentally "an imperial, colonizing gaze." Here, then, ethnification emerges in the fetishizing re-enactment of the exotic mixed-race or black woman dancer as an iconic figure: a transnational cultural signifier that "reveals the tensions, contradictions, and inner workings of patriarchy in (post)colonial, intercultural contexts" (95–6). The sexualized pattern of racial representation is even more exaggerated in the presentation of Luis, a mixed-race Dominican airhead (played by the Cuban actor Joel Angelino) who is obsessed with sex and always going out to dance in search of new conquests. One could argue that *I Love You, Baby* delivers a gendered, colonizing image of the mulatto in the terms set forth by Aparicio: indeed, Luis adheres to the sartorial presentation of the Caribbean women by perpetually wearing tight sleeveless Lycra shirts that help fetishize his body in motion. Marisol ignores Luis's repeated advances by claiming she is only interested in Spanish men. The implication is that she is looking for a "real man" – and that, consequently, she has internalized the colonizing gaze that "ethnifies" (and feminizes) the racial other. Her target is Marcos (Jorge Sanz), a gay man turned straight by accident – by a blow to the head while singing in a karaoke bar – and visualized as the sartorial opposite of Luis: he always wears multiple layers of clothes, including turtleneck sweaters and bulky jackets in grey and dark colours. Marisol eventually lands her Spanish husband. In the final sequence, the family runs into Marcos's ex-boyfriend at the airport, offering a clear picture of what it takes for a Caribbean woman to achieve integration in Spain. Pregnant with her fourth child, she wears a maternity dress and an off-white cardigan that conceals her curves and visually matches the light brown and grey hues of Marcos's clothes.

The interconnectedness of ethnicity, gender, and nation as subject positions, visualized through a racialized and gendered pattern of sartorial presentation, is especially patent in *Forasters* (Ventura Pons, 2008): an epic drama about the traumatic events affecting a dysfunctional Catalan family portrayed in two different periods, forty years apart. In coping with the imminent death of a cancer-afflicted mother in the 1960s and her daughter in the 2000s (both played by Anna Lizarán), a number of vicious family conflicts come to the surface. The arrival of newcomers to the upstairs apartment (Andalusian migrants in the twentieth century, Moroccan migrants in the twenty-first) contributes to aggravate family tensions. Based on Sergi Belbel's 2004 play, *Forasters* frames the concepts of family and home as predictable metaphors for the nation. The unknown neighbours, who become involved in the family dynamic while being regarded as an external threat, serve to address issues of belonging, exclusion, and xenophobia that are highly topical in today's multicultural European societies. Both families of newcomers are stereotypically presented by means of sonic cues (the Andalusians start dancing flamenco as soon as they move in; the Moroccans are always playing music while drinking tea, as if they had no other occupation), which highlight why the family/nation perceives them as a destabilizing presence, literally a nuisance. The tensions between the familiar and the unknown are punctuated by another foreign presence: a mixed-race domestic worker of Dominican origin, Patricia (played by Afro-Cuban actress Marieta Sánchez), who turns out to be married to Francesc (Joan Pera), the elder of the family in the 2000s, and is thus a legal resident. In return, she has to cope with Francesc's racist remarks – he calls the upstairs neighbours "moros de mierda" (fucking Moors) – and a paternalistic attitude towards her. He constantly calls attention to her differences from his family and nation; when she ignores his sexual advances, he declares that she would be dying of starvation in her country of origin if it weren't for him.

Notably, and unlike the situation of the foreign neighbours upstairs, her status as an "other" within the space of the home/nation is rendered not through sonic features, but through costume. The first time she appears onscreen, Patricia is wearing a strapless white-and-orange tank top with a low neckline and a pair of see-through white leggings that reveal a thong underneath. The second time we see her, her attire is even flashier: fluorescent pink leggings, a tracksuit jacket, and a gaudy green, red, and yellow top. Compared to the costumes of the Catalan characters – all dressed in discreet greys, browns, and mauves – Patricia's wardrobe choices reveal a deliberate strategy of visualization of racial difference. With its exaggerated, almost gimmicky pattern of construing the ethnic other as sartorially distinct – one of the Maghrebi neighbours pays a visit the Catalan family wearing an equally lurid neon pink and red shirt – *Forasters*, like *Flores* and *I Love You, Baby*, exploits visible features of the clothed body to categorize characters and create social differences across diverse subject positions such as race, class, and gender. Spanish-born characters remain visually unmarked; in all three films, they are customarily dressed in "invisible" (neutral- or discreet-hued) outfits. What I am proposing is that the scopic regime of these films uses dress codes to deploy "Spanishness" as whiteness: as a racial construction of the post-Franco ideal of European belonging. Attire that goes unnoticed is a cultural signifier of autochtonous superiority. Caribbean women of colour are granted integration as long as they tone down the colours of their outfits, substitute skimpy Lycra garments for loose-fitting wools, and become perfect wives and mothers.

Earlier in this section, I suggested the existence of another group of Spanish immigration films that adopt costume as a way to negotiate cultural differences and form interracial bonds between Caribbean women and Spanish natives. The most notable one is perhaps *Princesas*. Initially, though, this film seems to introduce costume differences as a form of enacting power asymmetries. Through the window of a hair salon where they frequently gather, a group of Spanish sex workers observes and passes judgment on migrant sex workers who are trying to earn a living in the plaza of a Madrid neighbourhood. The migrant women appear in the public space as a homogeneous group, devoid of individuality, even though they are of diverse origin (some are Caribbean, others are from Africa). The camera assumes the perspectives of Caren (Violeta Pérez) and Ángela (Mónica Van Campen): ironically, these women objectify the foreign sex workers by focusing on their bodies, especially on their prominent buttocks, thus evoking the porno-tropical tradition that eroticizes black women. Caren and Ángela's remarks concoct an all-encompassing discourse on otherness. The construction of racist stereotypes that homogenize cultural difference is a defensive strategy, one that proves itself anxious to disavow difference. Throughout the film, the dynamics of exclusion/inclusion of racial difference – much like "the dialectics of in/visibility" theorized by Steffen Köhn – are denoted in spatial terms. Furthermore – and crucially for the purposes of my discussion here – they are indicated in dress code terms, too. The migrant sex workers wear tight shorts and tank tops in bright colours such as gaudy pink, red, and purple. By contrast, the Spanish sex workers tend to dress in less conspicuous styles, typically in more neutral or sober colours like brown, cream, black, and pale blue. From a spatial perspective, the migrants have no choice but to occupy unprotected public areas; they are exposed to universal scrutiny and particularly vulnerable to the police cars always patrolling the plaza. The Spanish sex workers, however, have a safe space where they can gather, as well as civil institutions at their disposal: to defend themselves from the "invasion" of the foreign migrants, they call the police to perform a raid. The hair salon thus becomes a symbolic frontier, illustrating how borders as a concept are not necessarily linked to literal geographical boundaries (Sampedro and Doubleday 2). The hair salon is resemanticized as a protective space for a falsely uniform national identity, and as a fortress from which affiliates can reject the menace of otherness.

Borders are multifaceted constructs – not only geographic in nature, but also political, economic, cultural, religious, and so on – that are subjected to reconfigurations throughout the ongoing negotiation of their limits. Borders, too, are porous entities that can be crossed, transgressed, and even eliminated (Sampedro and Doubleday 3). *Princesas* explores the permeability of borders as sites that can be both negotiated and contested. Zulema (a Dominican sex worker played by Micaela Nevárez) overcomes these symbolic spatial barriers when she is admitted into the space of the hair salon: Caye (a Spanish sex worker played by Candela Peña) invites her to teach the Spanish-born hairdressers how to do African braids. The hair salon becomes a space of transnational cultural negotiation: while still governed by power relations, it nonetheless allows its inhabitants to articulate strategies that question its own hierarchies. It is crucial that Zulema gain access to a hitherto banned space by demonstrating her skill. In this way, *Princesas* shows how migrant subjects, typically demonized in public discourse as contaminating threats, bring about benefits and knowledge that may elicit positive changes in the host society. Furthermore, *Princesas* emphasizes that the porosity of transnational contact is reciprocal: Caye also gains access to the cultural and social spaces of her Dominican friend. Zulema takes Caye to a flea market, and then to a Dominican restaurant. Caye discovers new areas of her own city and comes into contact with what Carmen Gregorio Gil calls "una red social étnica" (an ethnic social network); that is, a cluster of relationships formed among migrant groups in a host society (179). These links can be economic, cultural, social, and/or family related, and they are essential to the development of transnational communities. Through these networks, diasporic subjects create their own consumerist styles and commercial relationships that do not automatically overlap with those of the host society.

Interestingly, cultural borders are transgressed through the development of intercultural bonds based on the same premises that fuel the exoticization of the Caribbean other: physical appearance and self-image as expressed through clothes. Caye deepens her friendship with Zulema because she is fascinated by her clothing, her hair, and her breasts – to such an extent that Zulema becomes the mirror in which Caye wants to look at herself (Zecchi, "Veinte" 174). Besides taking her to the flea market and doing her hair in braids – a physical marker of blackness that Caye embraces – Zulema lends Caye a black shirt with the text "Sexy Girl 69" printed on the back. While Zulema is doing her braids, Caye offers her skills as a make-up artist: "Si quieres, yo te pinto luego. Hice un curso, del INEM, de maquillaje para películas" (If you want, I can do your make-up. I did an INEM training course on makeup for movies). By sharing clothes and fashion secrets, Caye and Zulema forge a kind of transnational female solidarity based on non-sexual matrilineal kinship. Camerawork and editing highlight this bond: many of Caye and Zulema's shared sequences play with the visual conventions of romantic scenes in mainstream cinema. Their conversations in coffee shops, restaurants, and at home are visualized with a shot/reverse-shot pattern that accentuates their feelings and the dramatic impact of the dialogue in their facial expressions. Particularly prominent in one scene, apart from the shot/reverse-shot pattern, is a close-up of Zulema's hand grabbing Caye's to console her in a moment of existential anguish.

This non-sexual kinship redefines several stereotypical elements and grants them positive connotations. Homi Bhabha stresses that, although the exoticizing stereotype hinges on the concept of "fixity," this concept can be replaced with ambivalence as its defining element. This ambivalence helps activate the differences that the stereotype sought to disavow; consequently, the other may acquire a destabilizing potential (67). If we follow Bhabha's recommendation and explore this ambivalent side of the stereotype, a type of escape valve opens up in hierarchical relations – making more room, perhaps, for the other to exercise agency (66). My argument regarding *Princesas* is that it interrogates the ambivalence of the stereotype that exoticizes the body of the (migrant) sex worker to offer options for reclaiming a dignified female identity.

On the one hand, these women undeniably dress up and adorn their bodies to attract the gaze of their male clients. For example, as Michelle Murray has noted, the abovementioned "Sexy Girl 69" shirt involves Zulema's visual fragmentation, "metonymically represented through this piece of clothing that underscores her sexiness and helps her to advertise her sexual services to the Spanish public" ("Politics" 245). Similarly, Caye explains to her hairstylist that her clients have doubled since she got braids. Here, physical adornment serves to eroticize the female body towards being looked at – and, what's more, to be consumed like an exotic delicacy. As bell hooks argues, race and ethnicity are frequently commodified as sources of pleasure for white consumers. While hooks's remark focuses on US culture, her point is no less valid in early twenty-first-century Spain, the context addressed by *Princesas*. Consuming the racialized other – what hooks describes as "eating the Other" – is a form of pleasure that legitimates the status quo. Commodifying the racial other, a desire that goes hand in hand with perceiving the other as a threat, strengthens the privilege of the hegemonic group (436). Power dynamics that marginalize these women are marked, symbolically and literally, on their bodies. Both characters endure abusive violence at the hands of some clients, though the body of the Dominican sex worker suffers the most. While the devastating physical impact of social marginalization is constantly educed throughout the film narrative, we can also trace a positive appropriation of this oppressive reality in the deep connection between Zulema and Caye; that is, clothes and corporal adornment facilitate a matrilineal kinship and interracial friendship that enriches their lives. This phenomenon illustrates an important point made by fashion scholar Elizabeth Wilson in *Adorned in Dreams*: fashion is a double-edged sword, in that it can be either a liberating or a subjugating weapon (13). Therefore, fashion must always be evaluated in its concrete context of enunciation and reception, not as a social practice with a fixed or innate signification. Wilson's argument resonates in *Princesas*, in the sense that Zulema's and Caye's physical adornment is indisputably linked to the commodification of their bodies for consumption. Simultaneously, it is both an empowering mechanism and a survival strategy that helps them cross symbolic and physical frontiers, forge emotional bonds, and combat their loneliness.

The closing sequence recaps the importance of costume in the film's ethical conversation. After saying goodbye to Zulema at the Barajas airport (the Dominican woman has decided to return home to be with her family), Caye approaches two policemen in the vicinity and astonishes them with a speech that could be addressed to any Spaniard with xenophobic beliefs: "Mi amiga. Que se va porque quiere. No la echa nadie. Se va ella porque quiere estar con su hijo" (My friend. She's leaving because she wants to. Nobody's kicking her out. She wants to be with her son). Caye is wearing the "Sexy Girl 69" shirt that Zulema has left her as a parting gift. By dressing Caye in the very garment that signifies the network of female solidarity built in this film, Fernando León de Aranoa effectively reaffirms his commitment to an "ethics of possibility," to borrow again from Arjun Appadurai. In order to practise an active form of cultural critique, one capable of envisioning a future that is not built on the same structures of inequality as our contemporary societies are, Appadurai suggests that we seek out and explore "the zones and practices through which the ethics of possibility come into contact with the ethics of probability" (298). This scene of *Princesas* offers the audience an encounter between the world as we know it – underpinned by injustices and disparities, by mechanisms of surveillance, by the "modern regimes of diagnosis, counting, and accounting" (Appadurai 295), here represented by the police order – and a world of transnational alliances and interracial kinship that could usher in a better future, epitomized by the affective meaning of her shirt and her words.

Princesas joined other films about female characters of Caribbean origin that started to circumvent heterosexual romance as the only possible means of forging deep connections with Spanish natives and even of integrating into Spanish society. For instance, in *Sobreviviré*, Rosa (Mirtha Ibarra), a middle-aged undocumented Cuban migrant, and Marga (Emma Suárez), a Spanish single mother, meet by chance and reach a symbiotic agreement: Rosa lives in Marga's apartment rent-free in exchange for helping to take care of Marga's child. Beyond this financial accord, they become close friends and form a non-traditional family without a male figure. As in *Princesas*, costume and physical appearance play an important role: Rosa brightens Marga's life by compelling her to dress up and go out. At the beginning of the film, Marga wears bulky sweaters and tracksuits in invisible colours (greys and dark blues) that reflect her negative attitude and dull life. Rosa convinces her to go with her to a play at the theatre. As Isabel Santaolalla argues, as the women get ready for the outing, there is a glowing contrast between Rosa's sophisticated outfit (a leather pencil skirt and a tight, bright red top with a plunging neckline) and Marga's understated shapeless light brown dress (*Los "Otros"* 187). Rosa, a former Tropicana dancer and *jinetera*, embodies the stereotype of the joyful and exotic Caribbean woman. However, these predictable character elements are enacted to forge the non-sexual transnational kinship at the core of this film. Rosa's colourful clothing patterns serve as the inspiration for Marga to revamp her image and her life. She begins to dress more age-appropriately, just as she starts dating and having a social life.

The exchange of fashion tips and corporal adornment is also instrumental in the creation of transnational affective bonds in *Agua con sal*.

Olga (Yoima Valdés) leaves Cuba and moves to Spain, but she ends up working illegally in a furniture factory, where she meets Spanish-born Mari Jo (Leire Berrocal), who also works as a sex worker on the side. Despite Mari Jo's initial hostility, they become close friends after Olga teaches Mari Jo a home remedy to soothe her hands, abraded by the harshness of factory work: washing them with warm water and plenty of salt. From that point on, their exchange of fashion tips (such as hair and clothing styles) correlates to their sharing of personal experiences, resulting in a deep connection that helps both of them weather their arduous circumstances. Mari Jo transforms her self-image (she buys new clothes and dyes her hair the same colour as Olga's) not just to appeal to her clients, but for her own satisfaction. These dress and image changes help her improve her self-esteem and sense of personal dignity – the most important lesson she learns from her Cuban friend. As was also the case for Zulema in *Princesas*, this transnational friendship is not enough to convince Olga to stay in Spain. Lonely and disillusioned with her paltry job prospects, she chooses to return to Cuba. One could argue that both films ultimately endorse the patriarchy-affirming happy ending that dominates Spanish immigration films about Caribbean women (Rosales Herrera 99). Indeed, only those who engage in a traditional relationship with a Spanish man, and adapt their habits accordingly, attain integration into the host society. Nevertheless, I want to end this section with a more positive interpretation, revisiting Caye's speech to the police officers in *Princesas*. Elaborating on her words: these Caribbean women do not leave because they face deportation, but rather because they choose to go back. This is a considerably different outcome from what we saw in earlier immigration films like *Las cartas de Alou*. In addition, the women do not go back empty-handed. They take with them the affective ties and experiences – including clothes and fashion secrets exchanged – they have shared with their Spanish friends. Compared to the previously discussed racialized representations that make use of costume only to eroticize female migrants, this resolution is no small feat. These films envision the possibility that encounters with Caribbean migrants do not inevitably revitalize power asymmetries – or work to uphold the racial and sexual construction of colonial subjects in the Spanish imagination.

Costuming Inadequate Whiteness: Central and Eastern Europeans

The downfall of the communist system and the subsequent break-up of the Soviet bloc drastically altered the mobility patterns of Central and Eastern European populations across Europe. Northern European countries absorbed the majority of these migratory flows in the 1990s, but Spain and Italy became increasingly popular destinations in the 2000s. This was especially true for Bulgarians and Romanians, who constituted the largest source of immigration in Europe by the late 2000s. Social analysts attribute this geographical shift to the fact that both Spain and Italy had a sizeable informal economy, inadequate labour inspections, and less restrictive immigration policies as compared to other sought-after destinations, such as Germany, France, and Austria (Igor Prieto-Arranz and Iacob 1731–2; Stanek 1629; Viruela Martínez 35). Poles and Ukrainians were at the top of the region's migration to Spain in the 1990s, but Romanians and Bulgarians upended the trend in the early 2000s. By 2009, there were approximately eight hundred thousand Romanians in Spain – which made them the most numerous foreign group in the country (around 14 per cent of the foreign population), surpassing Moroccans – and around 155,000 Bulgarians (Viruela Martínez 34; Stanek 1632). While Central and Eastern Europeans by no means constitute a uniform ethnic group, Spaniards tend to perceive them as such (Santaolalla, *Los "Otros"* 153). To a certain extent, they are also better regarded (at least initially) than other migrant groups who do not speak Spanish as their native language, because they are European, white, and mostly Christian (Viruela Martínez 35). Despite the linguistic barriers, they have a moderately easier time blending into the host society as a familiar-yet-different type of European subject, still enigmatic and largely unknown. This status has not spared them xenophobic prejudice or media depictions that demonize them as criminals and threats to the social structure of Spain, especially in the case of Romanians. Interestingly, as Central and Eastern European countries joined the European Union in the expansions of 2004 and 2007, these negative perceptions did not cease. In fact, they escalated (Igor Prieto-Arranz and Iacob 1735), exposing a sense of social anxiety in Spanish society over losing their new-found Western European privilege to Europeans from underdeveloped regions.

Depictions of Central and Eastern European migrants in Spanish cinema echoed these societal perceptions. In Icíar Bollaín's directorial debut, *Hola, ¿estás sola?* (1995), the Russian character Olaf (Arcadi Levin) fits the initial view of Eastern Europeans as mysterious yet non-threatening foreigners. Niña (Silke), a twenty-something Spaniard, picks him up on the dance floor of a Madrid club. For a few days, he lives with Niña and her friend Trini (Candela Peña), who treat him as an exotic object of their sexual desires (Martínez-Carazo, *"Hola"* 80). He appears and disappears from the narrative without the female protagonists gaining any insight about his subjectivity. He barely speaks

Fig. 4.3. Eastern Europeans' sartorial restraint in *Hola, ¿estás sola?*

any Spanish, so he can engage in little meaningful communication with Niña and Trini, and his long speeches in Russian are not subtitled. All we know is that he works in the construction business. Trini christens him "Olaf," and, in line with Western constructions of "inhabitants of 'Oriental' countries as timeless, Biblical-like figures," she views him "as a Saint Joseph, straight out of a nativity scene" (Martin-Márquez, "World" 259–60). Olaf is objectified, though his visual presentation is significantly different from the racialized exotization of sub-Saharan and Caribbean migrants. Costume is key here. When Niña spots him in the club, he is wearing black jeans and a loose-fitting white linen shirt that, if anything, contributes to his ethereal aura. In subsequent scenes, he wears baggy T-shirts and a business casual look – chino pants, a long-sleeved plaid shirt, and leather shoes, all in discreet browns – to lunch at Niña's mother's house (see fig. 4.3). The film makes no sartorial distinction between Olaf and any twenty-something Spanish male at the time. Furthermore, although he appears shirtless in several scenes that lend themselves to his eroticization – coming out of the shower, lying in bed with Niña – these are all long or medium-long shots that do not particularly eroticize his thin, non-muscular torso.

Menos que cero (Ernesto Tellería, 1996) also sexually reifies the migrant without deploying exotic apparel. By chance, Zarco (Roman Luknár), an undocumented Romanian trying to make a living in Bilbao, meets Inés (Irene Bau), a street photographer who spots him doing graffiti. Inés shows the photograph to her friend Amaya (played by none other than Icíar Bollaín), who responds enthusiastically to the photo, and even more so to Zarco's physical appearance: "Este hasta tiene un polvo" (This one's a good fuck). Zarco works as a domestic employee for a wealthy couple, Salva (José Manuel Cervino) and Maite (Carme Elías), who are involved in criminal activities and will eventually cause his tragic end. The sight of Zarco on his knees, cleaning the floors, arouses Maite's sadistic desires; she starts to sexually harass him and humiliate him with power games. Like Olaf in *Hola*, Zarco is treated as a sexual object, yet he is not visually presented as such. Costume designer Carlos Díez does an effective job of constructing the character with subtlety and restraint. When he is not wearing his work uniform (blue coveralls), Zarco wears comfortable, casual, loose-fitting clothes, such as khaki pants, jeans, and long-sleeved shirts in neutral colours (greys and blues), always under a large dark coat. His attire does not distinguish him from any other Spaniard walking the cold streets of Bilbao, even if this does not mitigate the difficulties he must face.

Costume designer Carlos Díez also plays a major role dressing a Romanian character in *El sudor de los ruiseñores* (José Manuel Cotelo, 1998). Mihai (Alexandru Agarici) is a cello player who moves to Spain in hopes of landing a job in a philharmonic orchestra. As soon as he leaves the Atocha train station, a low-angle shot shows Mihai contemplating the bustling city of Madrid from a lookout point. The camera angle both aggrandizes his figure and, in combination with his attire (khaki pants, dark polo shirt, and a light blue blazer), gives him the respectable appearance of an affluent tourist. Once settled, Mihai puts on a nice suit to look for work as a musician, but reality strikes back. He is unable to get hired, finds himself the target of xenophobic insults, and even comes close to being arrested for a robbery he did not commit. He survives for a while by associating with Tote (Carlos Ysbert), a puppeteer who proposes that Mihai play his cello in the streets and subway stations. Once again, costume operates in tandem with camerawork to convey the initial distance that characterizes this unlikely alliance. Sitting on the stairs of a subway station, Tote and Mihai negotiate the terms of their business partnership. Individual close-ups and medium close-ups are connected by tracking camera movements. Yet the two men never appear together in the same frame: a visual expression of the distance between their points of view, as well as their cultural differences. Their opposing outfits reinforce this divide, as Mihai's formal suit drastically diverges from Tote's Hawaiian-style shirt.

Here – unlike in *El traje*, in which a well-tailored suit grants a sub-Saharan migrant temporary access to greater social repute – Mihai's fine-looking suit is a futile signifier of status. The outrageously dressed Tote – some of whose clothing choices border on the ridiculous, with flamboyant colour combinations like green and bright orange – reminds Mihai that his own clothes, like his musical education and good manners, are worthless in a context completely governed by his legal situation as an undocumented migrant. The scene in which Mihai manages to secure an interview with an orchestra conductor draws special attention to this thwartedness. The men meet at a performing arts theatre, both nicely dressed in formal suits. They look alike, and both belong to the high-art realm of classical music. And yet they are physically separated during their conversation by a balcony railing – a visual indication of the world between them. The conductor puts him off with an excuse, breaking the promise he had made to Mihai. No matter how proper his attire and manners may be, Mihai is still treated like an outcast in Spain. In fact, another xenophobic attack by a group of skinheads is the final catalyst that sends him back home. Both *Menos que cero* and *El ruido de los ruiseñores* dress the Romanian migrants in subdued colours and styles; this mutedness gives them an air of respectability and makes them indistinguishable from Spaniards. Even so, Zarco and Mihai are both subjected to prejudices that ultimately prevent them from integrating into Spanish society. These films show that the whiteness of Eastern European migrants is perceived as threatening to the structural stability of the community: it reveals an anxiety and reactionary attitude towards demographic changes and newly arrived immigrants, no matter how similar they might look.

Although public discourse and media outlets have principally targeted Romanians to make the erroneous – in the sense that it is unsupported by data (Corkill 54) – association between Eastern European immigration and crime, Spanish cinema has shone a spotlight on Bulgarians. All migrants and refugees depicted in *Los novios búlgaros* (Eloy de la Iglesia, 2003) are involved in criminal activities, whether prostitution or the illegal trafficking of radioactive materials from former Soviet countries. Their presence disrupts the existence of a group of wealthy, middle-aged gay men, especially Daniel (Fernando Guillén), a successful financial consultant from a traditional Spanish family who becomes sexually infatuated with Kyril (Dritan Biba), a Bulgarian in his early twenties. Kyril turns the older man's life upside down: Daniel not only funds Kyril's expensive lifestyle and wedding with his Bulgarian girlfriend Kalina (Anita Sinkovic), but also covers his criminal activities and becomes actively involved in illegal trafficking. Costume designer Pedro Moreno emphasizes the Bulgarians' unlawful existence by dressing them in stark contrast to Spanish characters: tight tank tops in flashy colours (such as vivid reds and oranges) accentuate their muscled arms and pecs, much unlike the neutral colours and loose-fitting shapes of the clothes worn by their gay Spanish benefactors.

With *Los novios búlgaros*, however, Eloy de la Iglesia goes far beyond a simplistic presentation of foreigners as a menace to the stability of the Spanish-born population. Reading the film in critical dialogue with Anglo-American antisocial queer theory, especially Lee Edelman's anti-futurist thought, Gema Pérez-Sánchez argues that de la Iglesia portrays the Bulgarians as a negative, antisocial body ("sinthohomosexual" in Edelman's terminology) that disrupts society's efforts to contain trans-gressive queer forces and to imagine the future as a totalizing fantasy of heteronormative coherence.[6] Their subversiveness is not necessarily sexual (although Kyril's sexual preferences remain rather ambiguous), but it is certainly related to their ethnic and racial difference, as well to as their status as migrants. As the narrative progresses, "by associating himself with the Bulgarian couple, by aiding them in their schemes, by paying Kyril to have sex with him, Daniel gradually comes to occupy the same disruptive anti-social position as Kyril and Kalina" (79). In fact, he starts becoming "Bulgarianized" by adopting certain cultural markers, such as the ringtone on his cell phone and "his use of the in-verted Bulgarian nods: yes for no, no for yes" (84). Most crucial for our discussion here, Daniel also starts dressing like the sinthomosexual Kyril. On Kyril's birthday, Daniel gives him a special gift as a symbol of their bond: a golden chain with the dollar sign, signposting Kyril's love for capitalist affluence. As the Bulgarian disassembles the chain to use the dollar-sign segments as earrings (redisrupting the normative arrangement of things), a two-shot frames the two men in equivalent outfits. Both are wearing blue pants and tight tank tops: black for Dan-iel and white for Kyril, as if teasingly inverting the colour symbolism to visualize Kyril as an innocent subject receiving a gift from his naughty lover.

The film ends with Daniel picking up Kyril's cousin – or the other way around, since the young Bulgarian is the one who makes the first move – in the dark room of the same gay club that appeared at the beginning of the film. This turn of events indicates that Daniel will continue to embrace the death-driven queer desire, the self-gratifying temporality of jouissance that sidesteps the heteronormative politics of reproductive futurism. Kyril's cousin is fittingly dressed in a tight black tank top – an outfit we would probably see Daniel emulate, if the film narrative were to continue. In the previous chapter, I discussed how Eloy de la Iglesia deployed underwear – white cotton briefs – as a cross-referential emblem to suggest a certain moral stature in the other-wise marginalized existence of the male characters in his late 1970s and early 1980s *quinqui* films. In his directorial comeback sixteen years later with *Los novios búlgaros*, the body-revealing and cruising-appropriate tank top emerges as the cogent symbol of sinthomosexuality, of the antisocial queer kinship between Spaniards and Eastern European migrants, veering away from any aspiration to assimilate into the heteronormative societal structures that had previously marginalized both migrants and queers.

With its endorsement of the antisocial space of the death drive, *Los novios búlgaros* is worlds apart from *A mi madre le gustan las mujeres* (Inés París and Daniela Fejerman, 2002), another film that introduces a non-heterosexual relationship between a Spaniard, a famous pianist played by Rosa María Sardá, and her Czech lover Eliska (Eliska Sirova). As Gema Pérez-Sánchez has noted, this film puts the transnational lesbian relationship at the service of perpetuating traditional family structures, and, thereby, "the fantasy of reproductive futurism" as theorized by Lee Edelman (77). A monogamous and completely desexualized lesbian couple, comprising two affectionate companions with no sexual chemistry at all, is used to add a seemingly progressive touch to what is ultimately a cinematic affirmation of traditional gender roles, as well as the integration of the migrant through a heterosexual marriage. Accordingly, the Central European migrant is (in)visibly dressed in discreet and elegant outfits – ample sweaters and abundantly layered garments – that have no bearing on the clothing excess with which *Los novios búlgaros* presents and celebrates transnational queer connections.

The excessive costuming of Bulgarian migrants who are perceived as a social threat returns in *Los veraneantes* (Jorge Viroga, 2008). In this film, a Bulgarian family of Roma ethnicity arrives at a small village in Cádiz where several Spanish families are enjoying their summer vacation. The Bulgarians' arrival immediately provokes xenophobic and racist attitudes – including violent attacks – among some of the Spaniards. The film plays with the hackneyed image of Roma people as itinerant, loud, involved in crime, and unable to assimilate into the social fabric. Costume reinforces this stereotypical (and Orientalist) presentation by having the mother wear a colourful and exotically overaccessorized outfit: a ruffled red-and-grey skirt, a red-and-black bodice that does not cover her stomach, a red bandana, and abundant sequins and *pailletes* decorating all three garments. Both the father and one of the daughters are always dressed in red shirts. The purpose of dressing the Bulgarian family in red is to provide a visual contrast with the blue polo shirts worn by Mr. Pombo (Carlos Manuel Díaz), the leader of the racist Spaniards. In the Spanish social imagination, these two colours have ideological significance. The blue of the traditional Catholic, racist, wife-beating husband suggests an association with the Franco era; the colour blue was among the symbols of the regime. Red is associated with leftist supporters, those defeated in war, or any kind of marginalized population during the Francoist dictatorship. These included the gypsies, "the foreigners within" (Corkill 52) or "insider others" (Santaolalla, "Ethnic" 58), who were severely persecuted due to their ethnic difference – and are still subjected to pervasive stereotyping and discrimination in contemporary Spain.

Spanish immigration films had thus far used Caucasian features to depict Romanians and Bulgarians, even if members of these groups were presented as "second-rate" or inadequately white. It is noteworthy that *Los veraneantes* visualizes them as ethnically Roma, precisely at the time when the 2007 enlargement had officially brought both Romania and Bulgaria into the European Union political structures (although the moratorium of the Spanish government limited their access to the labour market until the start of 2009). It seems, then, that this film expresses a newfangled social anxiety about portraying Eastern Europeans as ethnically different; as non-white; and, following the pattern we have discussed throughout this chapter, as hypervisible, all to stress the idea that Eastern Europeans occupy a dependent role as citizens of a less-developed Europe. Even though the integrity of the Bulgarians in *Los veraneantes* is restored at the end of the film, the Roma family still decides to leave the community and continue their nomadic existence, thus reinforcing the stereotype that they are unable to integrate into society. We should also mention that this was no ordinary film. Produced by Antonio Pérez for Maestranza Films, it was written and directed by teenage students at the school Orson the Kid, a summer camp that trains future filmmakers, supervised at the time by Jorge Viroga. The film was made with a clear intent to raise awareness against racism and xenophobia. However, the fact that younger generations ultimately framed people of Eastern European origins and Roma ethnicity as a threat to the still-operative ideal of a racially homogeneous country was hardly a promising sign that Spanish cinema and media would modify or tone down racialized representations of immigration.[7]

Disrupting the Cinematic Scopic Regime

These racialized patterns have remained widespread in Spanish cinema because the racial other has generally lacked access to the conduits of representation. Migrants, or their descendants, have been the object – not the creators – of their own film narratives. Drawing attention to the absence of what he calls "Afropean cinema" in Spain, José María Persánch argues that "not a single black filmmaker has, to my knowledge, directed a Spanish film production. If one exists, she or he is so marginal that no one knows about it (not even the internet search engines are able to find any independent 'Afro-Spanish' filmmakers!)." This explains why films "remain white, and extremely so" (131). Persánch has a point, although his conclusion is based on limited research. A more extensive investigation than a basic Internet search would reveal the existence of few but noteworthy filmmakers of colour. One of them is Omer Oke, who migrated to Spain from his native Benin and became the first Director of Immigration of the Basque Government, serving from 2001 to 2006. After stepping down from his political role, he directed two immigration films within the Spanish cinema industry: *Querida Bamako* (with Txarli Llorente, 2007) and *La causa de Kripan* (2009). These two films lead what many critics have identified as a second phase of Spanish immigration films from the mid- to late 2000s onward – along with *Retorno a Hansala* (Chus Gutiérrez, 2008), *Un novio para Yasmina* (Irene Cardona, 2008), and *Princesa de África* (Juan Laguna, 2008) – that provide a corrective to the clichéd representations of previous immigration films. They focus on the positive outcomes of intercultural encounters between Africans and Europeans and anticipate the possibility of successful coexistence and cultural hybridization in the Mediterranean regions (Ballesteros, *Immigration* 177–203; Corbalán, "Searching"; Deveny 69–79; Martin-Márquez, "Constructing"; Peralta; Rabanal; Zecchi, "Veinte años" 176, among others). These films also more fully contextualize migratory flows, setting parts of the films in the African countries of origin, so that viewers can understand the circumstances that move the characters to leave. Above all, they portray the migrants as subjects rather than as conventional objects of the Spaniards' stereotyping gaze (Peralta 68–9).[8]

Costume in these films also deviates from the previous sexualized treatments of black sub-Saharan male characters. In *La causa de Kripan*, Alassane (Gorsy Edú) is a migrant from Burkina Faso who decides to return home to prevent his daughter from undergoing genital mutilation. The entire population of Kripan, a small town in the Basque Country, fundraises to expedite the renewal of his expired passport and enable his trip. Like most young male residents of small Basque towns during the winter, Alassane dresses in casual jeans, abundant wool and turtleneck sweaters, coats in dark colours (blues, greys), and comfy sneakers. Back in his hometown, costume draws attention to his separation from Amina, his wife. In their first conversation at night, they sit quite far apart from each other, the distance indicating a gendered stratification of space in the local community. Their clothes separate them further. On the left side of the frame, Amina wears a traditional green dress with yellow patterning that covers her entire body. On the right side, Alassane wears blue jeans and a blue sweater. Amina's verdant colours visually portray her as a telluric character, someone deeply connected to the earth. Both green and yellow are particularly symbolic colours here, as they are part of the national flag of Burkina Faso: green symbolizes the country's natural agricultural resources, and yellow the guiding light of the country's independence from France. These warm, earthy colours contrast with the cold colour palette of Alassane's clothes, which signpost his integration into European society. The film efficiently (if predictably, one could argue) portrays the differences between traditional rural attire in a Burkina Faso village and clothes found in a European city – without exoticizing or passing value judgments on either one. Dress differences contribute to the documentary-like verisimilitude that Oke seeks for his socially committed story, but they are not deployed as a pretext to produce a spectacle of the other.

A second salient filmmaker is Santiago Zannou, born and raised in Madrid to a Beninese father and a Spanish mother. This director is known for his realist stories about urban working-class environments that include nuanced depictions of non-white Spaniards (first or second generation, black or mixed race), evading the processes of stereotyping (including clothing hypervisibility) that are prevalent in the industry. His debut feature-length film, *El truco del manco* (2008), received three Goya Awards (Best New Director, Best New Actor, and Best Original Song). Zannou also garnered the critical acclaim and public relevance he needed to fund and make another film, *Alacrán enamorado* (2013), where he could cast A-list stars such as Javier Bardem, Miguel Ángel Silvestre, and Álex González. Between the two films, he made the documentary *La puerta de no retorno* (2011), in which he accompanies his father back to his native Benin to take care of some unfinished family business. This documentary is Zannou's own tribute to his father and to the figure and experiences of the African migrant. But what is remarkable about his fiction films is that people of colour feature prominently in the narratives without necessarily being identified as immigrants – or, if they are, without the film calling attention to their status.[9] Zannou's films make cultural historian Paul Gilroy's wish come true, when he adamantly exhorted us "to conjure up a future in which black Europeans stop being seen as migrants" (xxi). Zannou's case suggests that, as second and third generations gain access to the means of cultural production, they will craft stories that creatively refashion visual discourses, and – hopefully – trouble the scopic regime that continues to produce racialized portrayals of ethnic identities in Spanish cinema through costume.

Chapter Five

Self-Fashioning Stardom: The Red Carpet Matters

Throughout most of this book, I have analysed clothes and accessories as costumes in films, with occasional nods to the impact of those costumes on street styles and fashion trends. In this chapter, I take my enquiry beyond the cinematic text to examine how Spanish actors of various generations and categories of stardom – Victoria Abril, Penélope Cruz, Eduardo Casanova, and Brays Efe – actively employ their sense of fashion and style off screen to shape their star images and the reception of their on-screen roles. Fashion, in its reductive association with frivolity and consumerism, has typically been considered the ultimate means of manipulating film stars. However, even when a star's stylish image is overtly affiliated with advertising, stars still exercise agency in how they present themselves to the public. Contemporary actors are entrepreneurs who take the reins of their own branding, including creating or revising their star personae – which is why Barry King describes stardom as "autographic" ("Embodying" 49). By constructing their own "style narratives" (Tulloch 276), film stars manage to renegotiate their position within the industry, as well as their relationships with fans, beyond simply complying with box-office imperatives. My goal is to stress that these processes are not mere duties dictated by endorsements and advertising deals (although stardom does obviously involve some of that), but, rather, that they entail radical interventions into their own images through styles that have a decisive impact on their careers and their reputations as actors.

My interest in extratextual fashion is motivated by the conspicuous shift in what makes a star fascinating to fans today. As I have discussed at some length in the introductory chapter, audiences and journalists are paying more attention to the styles of stars off screen – not to mention to stars' social media activity, involvement with humanitarian causes, and participation in philanthropic events. Accordingly, a common thread in contemporary approaches to film stardom – a subfield experiencing re-vitalized significance within film studies – is the need to consider stars beyond the sphere of textuality. In his supplementary chapter to a new edition of Richard Dyer's *Stars*, Paul McDonald criticizes the fact that stardom is conventionally regarded "as the effect of text and discourse, but not practice." To counter this state of affairs, he urges us to start posing different questions, and thus to explore what stars actually do instead of merely what they mean ("Reconceptualising" 200). To be fair, Dyer's pioneering work already acknowledged that the meaning of stars was not defined solely by their films. He maintained that films have a privileged role in the stars' image, but he also recognized the importance of: a) the promotion of those films and their respective stars through a range of media texts such as magazine ads, studio portraits, interviews, and public appearances; b) star-focused publicity that does not appear to be controlled by the studios or celebrity agents, e.g., any form of press coverage or gossip columns on stars and their private lives, including what stars themselves reveal to the media; and c) criticism and commentaries on stars in academic and journalistic accounts (*Stars* 60–3). In short, star images are multimedia and intertextual constructions manufactured by an array of media industries, but this manufacturing involves both the audience and the stars themselves in their transformation into commodities to be desired, imitated, and sold (*Heavenly* 3–5).

Scholarly interest in stardom has been rekindled by star studies' cross-pollination with other fields, such as the growing areas of celebrity studies and fashion studies, particularly spurred by the launch of the journals *Celebrity Studies* in 2010 and *Film, Fashion and Consumption* in 2011. Some scholars set great store by these synergies and even advocate for a conflation of fields, perceiving contemporary stars as a subgroup within the broader category of celebrity (Marshall). Others, viewing such intersections with suspicion, maintain that film stars should be understood as a "distinctive category, paralleled with celebrity," but not interchangeable. From this perspective, scholarly approaches to film stars should not be combined with celebrity studies: each poses unique "research questions and priorities" that "might or might not apply to other types of stardom" (Quiong Yu 14). While I certainly support calls to examine the specifics of film stardom, I feel it would be misguided to build a conceptual citadel around film stars as discrete entities, belonging only to the realm of film and unadulterated by other media. As Pamela Church Gibson contends, we need "to look sideways" and employ an interdisciplinary approach to understand the full relevance of contemporary visual cultures. Images, and star images among them, "bleed" across media, "from cinema to television to fashion shoot and advertising" (*Fashion* 11). The boundaries that previously separated "the different media institutions and strands within the media" have collapsed, "partly through the new power of the Internet" (*Fashion* 125). The world wide web offers an array of electronic communication conduits such as fan websites, YouTube, and online databases (for example, IMDb and Wikipedia) that have augmented the amount of information on stars and enabled more direct access to that material. This new scenario allows for the possibility of "unauthorized interaction with the process of constructing celebrity stardom" and opportunities for "alternative versions of official star narratives" (Cook, "Revisiting" 27). Sophisticated methods of image construction, publicity management, and media handling of film stars are still operative in the post-studio era – that is, stars continue to be manufactured, especially in Hollywood – but are not as conclusive in carving out a single definitive image of the star.

As cinema fans gain influence in the production of stardom, the "dispersal of authorship in star discourse" is undoubtedly intensifying (McDonald, *The Star System* 15). One might argue that this intensification makes stars more vulnerable, in the sense that their agents, stylists, and publicists can no longer produce a fixed, exclusive narrative about them. While media technologies make contemporary stars more exposed to the public eye, and therefore more susceptible to manipulation of their personae, they also offer stars new options for agency. Take social media outlets, for instance. Platforms such as Instagram, Twitter, and Facebook are of paramount importance to the construction of today's star images. For one thing, these platforms expedite the dissemination of information and messages; they also give stars the opportunity to craft new visions of selfhood, thus providing them with what Russell Meeuf calls "a new frontier in self-making and self-promotion" (23). In fact, the profitability of stars is increasingly measured less in terms of their box-office figures than in the number of followers they have on social media, which can translate into lucrative commercial endorsements.[1] Consequently, social media outlets should be taken seriously as influential channels of promotion and publicity. Many stars use social media to share news about their current and future acting projects, to express support for humanitarian causes and social advocacy, and even to divulge updates about their family, social, and romantic lives. There are at least two tangible benefits of film stars' active participation in social media. By supplying professional and personal information, they neutralize the potential damage that gossip writers and paparazzi can inflict on their image. Likewise, they help control the public narrative by anticipating or denying false rumors. At the same time, social media activity helps them close "the gap between their persona and personality" (Shingler 144), thus appearing more approachable to their fans. This engagement extends what Barry King calls "the molecular circulation of star and celebrity images" (*Taking* 196): the lines between their public and private selves continue to blur, and their star persona melts into aspects of their everyday lives.

While publicists and assistants may counsel stars on how to present themselves on social media, it would be simplistic to reduce their significance to the "manipulation thesis" that Richard Dyer aptly challenged: the star phenomenon misleadingly theorized as a simple story of "sheer manipulation" by the publicity apparatuses of the film industry (*Stars* 12–14). Film stars are active creators and editors of their star personae that circulate in secondary texts. Following an assortment of Spanish actors like Miguel Ángel Silvestre, Álex González, Paula Echevarría, Jon Kortajarena, and Eduardo Casanova on Instagram, it becomes clear that the stars themselves are authors of their content. They post material in circumstances under which external mediation is unlikely: for example, when they chime in with spontaneous comments on the posts of other colleagues and friends in the profession. Miguel Ángel Silvestre and Jon Kortajarena frequently upload stories with videos and photos conveying their physical fatigue at the end of a long shooting day. Late at night, as they finally get to eat dinner in the well-deserved peace of their hotel rooms, they appear to be as human as their fans. This glimpse of humanity further solidifies their star image, as they personify the crucial paradox of stardom (Ellis 92): they might have extraordinary jobs and careers, but they are also ordinary people working hard for their money. In another evident example, in a post on 25 January 2019, Miguel Ángel Silvestre elaborated on this image of ordinariness by uploading an impromptu video from a crowded bus in Madrid. Not only does he work hard for his money, the video suggests; he also takes public transportation like everyone else.

Fashion content is central to this self-telling via social media and other online channels (blogs and personal websites). Stars share all sorts of fashion-focused material with their fans: photo shoots, red carpet looks, interviews with the press and fashion magazines, stories about attending fundraising events, and even images of flattering outfits for daily wear. With the growth of what Nick Rees-Roberts calls "an increasingly fashion-literate public culture" (78), proficient self-presentation is part of the "portfolio of performance expertise" of contemporary stars and is as important as their acting prowess (Cook, "Revisiting" 27). In this way, fashion sense and style are, along with photogenic looks, essential prerequisites for stardom; in certain cases, they can even compensate for a lack of acting skills (Shingler 66). The red carpet event plays a prominent role among the many extra-cinematic activities in which stars are now expected to present themselves adequately in order to promote their persona as a brand. Nowadays, there is so much expectation, pressure, money, and reputation at stake for all participants in a red carpet event that it is no exaggeration to describe it as the new dividing line between the A-list (of stars, designers, and stylists) and everyone else. Getting dressed by a big fashion house (especially if paid to do so, as is now customary) can propel an emerging actor into a higher bracket of movie stars. A red carpet deal with Chanel, Armani, or Dior is as great a measure of stars' clout in the industry as their awards and box-office returns are. This scenario also means that stars can treat the red carpet strategically, approaching it as a platform to steer their image and careers in a certain direction. That is precisely the subject of the current chapter.

Below, I will concentrate on four Spanish stars who have successfully employed their red carpet looks, as well as other fashion performances, as tools to articulate – and sometimes to modify previous versions of – their star personae. I will show how their fashion sense can be seen as a form of performed agency, by which they display considerable control over the image that circulates in secondary texts. In doing so, they challenge the assumption that film stars are mere products of corporate control. I analyse a variety of fashion-related materials about these stars that have appeared in entertainment and fashion journalism (magazine articles, interviews, fashion blogs), as well as stars' personal websites and content from their social media accounts. I want to clarify that I do not intend to portray fashion as the only or even a definitive explanation for the professional success and popularity of these actors. Evidently, they have access to other performative tools that exceed the scope of my enquiry, and they use these tools to demonstrate their star authorship as well. Furthermore, it is indispensable to acknowledge from the outset that my goal is not to offer a fully comprehensive account of each star's image throughout their entire acting career. This disclaimer is especially pertinent to my first case study, Victoria Abril, whose career has spanned over four decades. Rather, I zoom in on a particular phase of each actor's trajectory in which fashion became exceptionally relevant to the discursive reformulation of their star persona.

Victoria Abril: Manufacturing Eccentricity

Determining Victoria Abril's star agency is no simple task. One clear difficulty involves her sheer professional longevity, as certain elements of her image prevail over others depending on the period in question.

Moreover, while she is recognized as a "pan-European" star – she has made films in Spain, France, Iceland, Italy, and Macedonia – her stardom is still largely defined in relation to national identity and what is regarded as a prototypical notion of "Spanishness." In his study of Abril's trajectory up to the early 2000s, Peter Williams Evans comments on yet another element that complicates her case: throughout her career, she has alternated appearances in popular films and roles in what are conventionally considered art-house or auteurist films. For that reason, applying Richard Dyer's semiotic/sociological methodology to Abril is particularly challenging. Instead of embodying the resolution of ideological contradictions – a central feature of stardom in Dyer's model – she has mostly acted in films in which "the exposure, not the resolution, of contradiction is the text's primary ideological justification" ("Victoria" 128). A key facet of her on-screen roles – supported by the star persona that has circulated in a variety of secondary texts, especially early in her career – is a provocative, sometimes aggressive, form of sexuality that does little to reconcile contradictory ideological discourses. On the contrary, in fact, by playing roles "that invariably courted sexual excess, ambiguity and scandal" (Stone, "¡Victoria?" 168), her star image has been closely associated with the transgression of traditional discourses of sexuality.

Initially, the sexualization of her girlish body on screen posed certain problems for her reputation: she had to counteract the image of an eroticized star with no acting talent. In this section of the chapter, my contribution to existing academic studies on her star image (by Peter William Evans, Chris Perriam, and Rob Stone) will consist of showing how Victoria Abril overcame this early pigeonholing by actively participating in the redesign of her star image. As Sabrina Quiong Yu argues, "stardom is like a masquerade, easily put on, changed and manipulated by the industry, but also by stars and audiences" (3). Throughout her career, Abril has cleverly employed not only her superb acting skills but also her appearance as a masquerade to influence perceptions about her persona. However, she has not done so by cultivating an image of conventional glamour and desirability, which is the most popular masquerade of stardom that audiences expect. Rather, she has manufactured an eccentric persona through her extravagant sense of style and fashion both on and off the screen. Although this performance of eccentricity has projected a disturbing image at times, possibly alienating fans and thus jeopardizing her overall economic value and earning potential, I argue that it has helped her carve out a distinctive niche in the transnational circuits of European art cinema.

Before becoming an international star, Abril's persona in Spain was forged through a mix of "residual processes of objectification" and a "new assertiveness" that corresponds to the representation of a post-dictatorship Spanish woman: sexually liberated, nonconformist, and transgressive of social norms (Evans, "Victoria" 130). Although she did an admirable job in her first roles – in Vicente Aranda's *Cambio de sexo* (1976) and *La muchacha de las bragas de oro* (1979), complex assignments dealing with issues such as transsexuality, auto-eroticism, lesbianism, and even incest – the image that circulated in secondary texts regrettably focused only on her body and sex appeal. In one of her first cover photos for a mainstream publication, the film magazine *Fotogramas*, on 12 September 1975, Abril wore a pair of unbuttoned jeans shorts, drawing the eye towards her crotch area, and a tank top that showed her flat abdominals and barely veiled her breasts. On the cover of the May 1979 issue of *Playboy*, Abril was photographed at a desk, wearing a schoolgirl uniform that showed her underwear, a pencil flirtatiously poised between her teeth. The cover was the hook for a story titled "Las colegialas" (the schoolgirls), written by Juan Marsé, which served as a promotional preview for the imminent release of *La muchacha de las bragas de oro* (based on Marsé's own novel).

Complicating this overtly sexualized image was an arduous mission for Abril, because Spanish audiences also associated her with her two-year tenure as one of the sexy *azafatas* (secretaries) on the hugely popular television game show *Un, dos, tres … responda otra vez* (1972–2004), created by Narciso Ibáñez Serrador. Some of her fellow *azafatas*, such as Ágata Lys and Blanca Estrada, went on to become stars of the *destape* subgenre in the late 1970s, a phenomenon intrinsic to the history of Spanish cinema that was characterized by the oversupply of sexual images without any apparent narrative intention. As Abril has expressed on multiple occasions, the popularity she gained though this television show proved to be more of a career block than a blessing: for a long time, no one took her seriously as an actor (Alvares and Frías 287). The complexity of her roles in other Vicente Aranda films, such as *Tiempo de silencio* (1986), *Si te dicen que caí* (1989), and *Amantes* (1991, for which she received the Berlin Film Festival Award for Best Actress), cemented her reputation as a strong performer while simultaneously reinforcing the pivotal role of provocative sexuality in her persona (see fig. 5.1). This nuance is especially conspicuous in *Tiempo de silencio* and *Si te dicen que caí*: she skilfully plays three different roles in each film, all powerfully sexual women, including two prostitutes. Unquestionably, her celebrated roles in Pedro Almodóvar's films *Átame* (1989) and

Fig. 5.1. Victoria Abril in *Amantes*

Tacones lejanos (1991) further solidified her versatility as an actor and the link between her stardom and sexual transgression.

Abril's sustained collaboration with internationally acclaimed film auteurs, especially Almodóvar, associated her star persona with Spain's refurbished aura in the 1980s and 1990s: that of a modern country that had left behind its oppressive past. As others have noted, Almodóvar became the poster child of that renewed image: "the embodiment of post-Franco Spain, the representation of the new nation" (Smith, *Desire* 2). For international audiences, the Almodóvar brand, including all contributors to and participants in it, became identified with the cultural values of a country that had successfully reinvented itself. Only later, with the success of *Todo sobre mi madre*, did his work become an icon of "global art cinema" (Rodríguez Ortega 44–5). As Alfredo Martínez Expósito has explored in depth, the seismic shift in the *marca-España* (Spain as a brand) was made possible by a consensus among many political and social stakeholders, including a coalition between cultural entrepreneurs and the government that was supported by most of the population (66). This was the cultural period that Cristina Moreiras Menor calls "re-encanto" (re-enchantment) (63), because it somewhat obliterated the feeling of disappointment with the unmet expectations of the transition to democracy, as well as the certain cultural and social agents' dissatisfaction with what was perceived as a failure to make a significant break with Francoist structures and values.

Victoria Abril undoubtedly benefitted from her iconic status as an international symbol of this hyperliberal image of post-Franco Spain. The scene in *Átame* in which her character uses a toy to masturbate in the bathtub (one of the reasons behind the film's X rating in the United States, opening a wider debate about film ratings), as well as the sex scene with drag queen Letal in the dressing room in *Tacones lejanos*, are just two examples of how Abril's international stardom and subversive image were positively shaped by roles charged with irreverent attitudes towards sexuality. While *Átame* and *Tacones* had more of an impact on her acting cachet, I want to highlight the importance of her last role for Almodóvar in *Kika* (1993), where she plays Andrea Caracortada, an exploitative reporter/reality TV host. This movie was a step back in Almodóvar's ascendant trajectory, but it added a crucial element to Abril's star image that she has cleverly embraced to redefine her transnational profile: fashion eccentricity, famously attained through the four bizarre couture costumes that Jean Paul Gaultier designed for her. The most provocative is a militaristic outfit that Andrea uses in her filming trips: "overlaid with militaristic and technological trimmings such as multiple zips, epaulettes studded with video controls, flip up shades, heavy-duty boots and a moulded helmet onto which her video camera is mounted" (Bruzzi, *Undressing* 11). Andrea rotates this robotic look – which Paul Julian Smith describes as attiring "less a woman than a cyborg," because she is a hybrid between a machine and a living organism (*Vision* 50) – with the glamorous air of a futuristic vamp when she dons a gown with prosthetic breasts and plastic blood for a show filmed live. These are superlative examples of intrusive costumes that are not necessarily intended to serve the narrative or characterization. They also create a distancing effect by diverting attention from Abril's body, so that the viewer focuses on the eccentricity of the styles themselves.

The tripartite partnership between Jean Paul Gaultier, Pedro Almodóvar, and Victoria Abril continued off screen. For the Paris premiere of *Kika*, Gaultier designed her an outfit that playfully fused epochs and styles, the old and the new. The lower part was a Victorian-era skirt made with scraps of blue denim fabric and fitted around a crinoline. For the upper part, Abril wore a white transparent chiffon blouse, adorned with an elegant fur stole and accessorized with costume jewellery and an aluminium bag shaped like a cooking pot. This eclectic blend of high fashion and street wear further enhanced Abril's image as linked to irreverent couture. Although she never worked with Almodóvar again, a fact she has publicly regretted,[2] she has continued her collaboration with Gaultier, which has oscillated between the professional and the personal. In addition to her periodically wearing his designs, they have also sustained a much-publicized friendship. They frequently appear together at public events, such as the 2004 Cannes Film Festival opening ceremony dinner. A 2011 photo shoot at the House of Gaultier in Paris for *S Moda*, the monthly fashion magazine distributed with the newspaper *El País*, appeared as the cover story, titled "Victoria Abril y Jean Paul Gaultier: Quien tiene un amigo (diseñador) tiene un tesoro" (Victoria Abril and Jean Paul Gaultier: She who has a [designer] friend, has a treasure), thus showcasing the longevity of this professional/ personal relationship. In fact, I would even argue that the publicity ensuing from her close affiliation with the enfant terrible of French fashion – along with her former connection to the enfant terrible of Spanish cinema – was a turning point in her career.

Victoria Abril was already notorious for her off-screen idiosyncrasies; her brusque behaviour towards paparazzi, who feared her; and "her outspokenness and sometimes outrageous demotic interviewee's prose" (Evans, "Victoria" 129). But the "*Kika* effect" continued long after the promotion of the film was over, as she took her unconventional image to a whole other level. From the mid-1990s on, Abril made her offbeat fashion sense a signature element of her stardom. This was especially conspicuous in the series of outrageous red carpet looks she has worn at the Cannes Film Festival. In 1996, she showed up wearing an Anna Karenina–inspired coat, opened up in the lower front to reveal leather boots extending all the way up to her waist. The bizarre combination of traditional woman and dominatrix was adorned with a pillbox hat sporting two Donald Duck–inspired ears made of wool fabric. Believe it or not, she amped up the quirkiness even higher in subsequent years. In 1997, she wore two scandalous looks that made the headlines. One was a translucent black tulle dress that exposed her breasts. The other one was a male suit jacket, seemingly conventional in front, complete with shirt and tie – but with an opening in the back that revealed she was only wearing a pair of boys' briefs overlaid with a thong design, all in full display.

It is striking that Abril's red carpet looks beyond Cannes have been far more sedate – with the possible exception of some indescribable outfits she donned for the César Awards ceremony. If one takes a careful look at her official website (www.victoria-abril.com), the link "Galerie Photos" contains a selection of red carpet photos. The subsection dedicated to Cannes encapsulates the most shocking combinations (including some of the ones mentioned above). By contrast, her choices for the Berlinale, Seville, Marrakech, Sarajevo, and other international film festivals have been much less unconventional; in fact, many fall within the parameters of a traditionally glamorous red carpet look. Clearly, Victoria Abril reserves her most flamboyant options for Cannes, the biggest film event in the world, representing the whole spectrum of the film industry – from mainstream celebrities to independent film crews and everything in between – and covered every year by more than four thousand journalists. This calculated performance of eccentricity has served her well in constructing a unique image of a versatile actress who, as noted by Alastair Phillips and Ginette Vincendeau, is resistant to typecasting in her European roles (153). While stars like Abril might circulate throughout the Continent's film industries with relative freedom, they are still expected to embody certain assumed national qualities or deviations thereof; for example, personifying the "other" of that alleged national type (Soila 9). Even when it comes to a well-established transnational icon, a deep-seated impulse still seeks her affiliation with a national identity and works to mould her persona through cultural and historical stereotyping. Instead of struggling against this somewhat inevitable national categorizing, however, Victoria Abril has developed mechanisms to appropriate it. As Chris Perriam claims, it is important that we pay attention to how Abril works "with and within stereotypes": how she denaturalizes them and can even turn them inside out, given that the crossing of geographical and conceptual spaces is by definition a crucial aspect of studying transnational cinema ("Victoria" 28). Abril has been prone to underscoring her ties to the post-Franco Spanish woman who is not afraid of transgressing social norms. Persistently, too, she has linked this identity to the self-manufactured image of eccentricity that has become a hallmark of her transnational profile.

Her biggest box-office hit in French cinema, the subversive comedy *Gazon maudit* (Josiane Balasko, 1995), was a salient example of this complex self-presentation. Abril had already played roles in France that were well received, receiving two César Award nominations for Best Supporting Actress as Bella in *La lune dans le caniveau* (Jean-Jacques Beineix, 1983) and as Patty in *L'Addition* (Denis Amar, 1984), respectively. But it was *Gazon maudit* that put her in the spotlight: the film was both a huge commercial success ($75 million in the box office with a $7 million budget) and critically praised (it was France's submission to the Sixty-eighth Academy Awards for Best Foreign Film). Abril plays Loli, a Spanish housewife who gets involved in a three-way relationship with her husband, Laurent (Alain Chabat), and a butch lesbian, Marijo (Josiane Balasko), who moves in with them. At the beginning of the film, Loli wears a variety of dull grey dresses. Once she starts her same-sex affair, her wardrobe changes, focusing now on bright red dresses adorned with a red *mantón de Manila* (Manila shawl) that she buys to celebrate her new life. It is clear that the film invites viewers to equate her stereotypically "Spanish" costume choices with a liberated eroticism that defies compulsory heterosexuality, although it does not enact this shift in a simple or straightforward way. Chris Perriam has rightly noted that the red shawl is indeed deployed to accommodate versatile meanings within the film. After having sex with Marijo, Loli uses it to cover her naked body when she tries "to comfort Laurent, banished to the sofa; it is used in a farcical moment to cover Laurent's own nakedness in a row between him and Marijo. It is a figure of lesbian sexuality, heterosexual reconciliation, emasculation, two cultures, several sexual possibilities" ("Victoria" 33). Here, by not ascribing the red shawl a monolithic value, but instead allowing it to suggest a multiplicity of (not necessarily incompatible) options, costume destabilizes rigid identity categories – quite a queer gesture indeed – through, and not against, clichéd "Spanish" traits.

A similar costume pattern, although it lacks the sexual subversiveness of what she wore in *Gazon maudit*, appears in Barry Levinson's *Jimmy Hollywood* (1994). This is her only role in the United States apart from the US/Spain co-production *On the Line* (1984), directed by Spanish filmmaker José Luis Borau, which was a resounding flop. In multiple interviews, Abril reported that she did not enjoy the experience, so she closed the door on Hollywood for the rest of her career. *Jimmy Hollywood* was a failed product from both a commercial and a critical perspective, but her role was more complex than its stereotypical façade might imply. Better put, by explicitly portraying her with conventional markers of her Spanish ethnicity, she bypassed the fate of Spanish transplants into Hollywood who came both before (Conchita Montenegro, Sara Montiel, and Antonio Banderas) and after (Penélope Cruz): the stereotype of the "generic Hispanic" or the beautiful, exotic Latina.[3] This is conveyed through both culinary touches – in one scene, her character, Lorraine de la Peña, makes a paella and a *tortilla de patatas* (Spanish omelette) – and costume. Throughout the film, Lorraine alternates hippie-style clothes and costume props signposting "Spanishness": a red fan, a hairclip with a red rose, and, above all, a red dress she wears with a *mantón de Manila* to go out one evening. These costume choices appear clichéd, even absurd in their contradictions, but at least she is not forced to hide her European identity.

The Spanish-inspired costumes, in tandem with transgressive sexual behaviour, are also central to *101 Reykjavík* (Baltasar Kormákur, 2000). In this Icelandic production, Abril is Lola Milagros, a Spanish flamenco teacher who combines the traditional flamenco dance dress she wears for work with extravagant outfits when she goes out at night. The latter include a garish 1970s-style jumpsuit with stripes in three different colours (black, white, and red) that she accessorizes with an enormous fur hat. On another night, she wears a net bodice over a gaudy orange top, her head adorned with a colourful butterfly hat. These outrageous outfits correspond to Lola's free-spirited lifestyle: she gets involved with one of her female students, Berglind (Hanna María Karlsdóttir), and moves in with her for the duration of the Christmas holidays. Then, while Berglind is out of town, Lola has a fling with Berglind's son, Hlynur (Hilmir Snær Guðnason). The similarities with her character in *Gazon maudit* are blatant: a stereotypically Spanish name (Lola/Loli), flamenco clothes, and nonchalant participation in a three-way sexual relationship that challenges heteronormative conventions. Clearly, *101 Reykjavík* relies on Victoria Abril as a star vehicle to sell the film as a European art cinema product to an international audience.[4] Here, interestingly, and in a shift from her roles in *Gazon maudit* and *Jimmy Hollywood*, Abril's European star persona already encapsulates the eccentric image she concocted in the late 1990s.

In the 2000s, Abril elaborated on this pan-European profile that strategically meshed Spanish ethnic markers with stylistic eccentricity. Her choice for the 2008 Cannes red carpet summarized this tactic: a red cocktail dress in which the lower part imitated the classic flamenco dress with a vast, ruffled *bata de cola* (tailed gown), complemented by a hairstyle with the traditional *peineta* (ornamental comb) adorned with two roses (although it omitted the traditional flamenco earrings). Eccentricity and typical "Spanishness" has helped Abril optimize her solid presence in European cinema: she became practically a staple in popular French comedies and television shows, and she was offered starring roles in the Italian production *Mari del Sud* (Marcello Cesena, 2001) and the multilingual Macedonia/Germany/Belgium/Turkey co-production *The Woman Who Brushed Off Her Tears* (Teona Strugar Mitevska, 2012). Although she periodically returned to Spain to work with prominent auteurs such as Agustín Díaz Yanes in *Sin noticias de Dios* (2001) and *Solo quiero caminar* (2009), Carlos Saura in *El séptimo día* (2004), and Vicente Aranda in *Tirant lo Blanc* (2006), her presence in Spanish productions has considerably diminished over the years, especially in the last decade.

Ironically, the more "quintessentially Spanish" her European star image became, the less popular she has turned out to be among Spanish audiences. For Rob Stone, the attenuation of her relevance in Spain was caused by multiple factors, such as her living in France since the early

1980s, twice marrying and divorcing foreigners, and the fact that she "has done her best work for directors (Aranda and Almodóvar) commonly associated with the seedier side of sexuality" ("¡Victoria?" 171). Victoria Abril has successfully exercised her fashion agency to manufacture a distinctively eccentric style narrative (including by co-opting dress stereotypes of national identity to her advantage), which has helped her navigate the intricate channels of Europe's transnational film industries. In the process, however, her relevance has faded in the domestic market, especially for younger spectators who might not know much about her. I now turn to a quite different example, Penélope Cruz, who has also relied on her fashion sense to build a globally recognized star persona, though hers has drawn on a more traditionally glamorous look. In her case, the strategy has paid off both in Spain and abroad.

Penélope Cruz: The Discreet Charm of Old Hollywood Glamour

More than that of any other actor in Spanish cinema, the case of Penélope Cruz prompts fundamental questions, ideological concerns, and production and consumption issues that are central to star theory. At certain stages of her career, her work has exemplified the collapse of the distinction between performer and star persona that characterizes, according to Richard Dyer, the star phenomenon itself. With her emphasis on glamour, she also epitomizes the image of the classical movie star. Relatedly, she has elicited discussions rooted in the perennial tensions between fashion and feminism. Some see "a post-feminist icon" for Spanish women in her dazzling star image (Stone, *Spanish Cinema* 200). To others, she is a mere member of the glitterati who has exploited her desirable looks (Jordan and Allinson 125), and whose acting is irrelevant to her image. Cruz is not the first Spanish actor to have attained an ongoing Hollywood career, nor is she the first to be recognized for her talent with an Academy Award (her husband, Javier Bardem, won Best Supporting Actor for his role in *No Country for Old Men* in 2008). However, she is very much the first to have developed a globally recognized profile based on an image of glamour and style while simultaneously – or better yet, eventually – achieving recognition for her accomplishments as an actor. No other Spanish star has shone like Cruz when the camera lights turn on for the red carpet, promotional events, and awards ceremonies. No other Spanish star has been compared to old Hollywood icons on a par with Audrey Hepburn and Grace Kelly (more about this later). And no other Spaniard has her own star on the Hollywood Walk of Fame (she received hers in 2011). Need we say more? We are dealing with a distinctive kind of stardom here – the glitziest of them all.

For all her success, Cruz's credibility as an active agent in advancing her career has frequently been up for debate. For one thing, her constant tabloid presence during her first years in Hollywood was initially detrimental to her image. She was often subject to gossip for her (real or alleged) romantic involvement with co-stars such as Tom Cruise, Matt Damon, Nicholas Cage, and her husband, Javier Bardem. To Barry Jordan and Mark Allinson, Cruz is the quintessential example of the star as a celebrity (125). Christine Geraghty defines celebrity as a type of stardom that relies more on a star's personal life and romantic attachments than on her or his acting talent. This is someone "who is famous for being famous" and whose status is "constructed through gossip, press and television reports, magazine articles and public relations" (99). Geraghty coined the term "star-as-celebrity" to differentiate celebrity stars from "professionals" and "performers," who are defined by their acting work, while their personal lives remain hidden (99–100). The "star-as-professional" is best understood in relation to a particular genre, as he or she maintains a consistent screen persona (Alfredo Landa would be a good example in Spanish cinema). By contrast, the "star-as-performer" is known for being able to impersonate many different types of roles, thus avoiding the potential conflation between star and role that can easily befall the star-as-professional type (e.g., Victoria Abril and Javier Bardem).

It would be futile to deny that Cruz fits Geraghty's category of star-as-celebrity. She has habitually occupied the media spotlight, her celebrity credentials have been shaped in part through her romantic involvement with other famous actors, and her image regularly graces the covers of glossy lifestyle and fashion magazines like *Vogue*, *Vanity Fair*, and *Marie Claire*. However, Cruz's case also illustrates an important point made by Martin Shingler: such clear-cut divisions between celebrity, professional, and performer are often hard to draw (57). As Ann Davies has studied, Cruz has committed to working as a performer, and her films are crucial texts towards understanding her star persona, even if they are not the *only* texts (*Penélope* 10). Davies's monograph gives due credit to Cruz's skill as an actor and values her work beyond "her slick physical appearance" (11). Cruz is indeed an accomplished performer who, besides her Best Supporting Actress Oscar for *Vicky Cristina Barcelona* (Woody Allen, 2008), has won numerous awards, including three Goya Awards, a European Film Award, a BAFTA award, a Best Actress Award at Cannes, the César Honorary Award, and the Donosti Honorary Award in San Sebastián. It is also important to note that Cruz had already made important films in Italy, Denmark, France, and the UK before going to Hollywood. In Spain, she had played roles "in several of the few Spanish films to garner international art-house distribution," such as *Jamón, jamón* (1992), *Carne trémula* (1997), and *Abre los ojos* (1997), as well as in "the two Spanish films of the decade to win the Best Foreign Film Academy Award," *Belle Epoque* (1993) and *Todo sobre mi madre* (1999) (Phillips and Vincendeau 220).

My contribution to these discussions of Cruz's persona will focus on recognizing that what makes her unique among Spanish actors is, precisely, her long-established ability to construct and sustain her stardom by drawing on both celebrity and performance. As her career has developed, attention has gradually (if not exclusively) shifted towards the latter. After 2007, once she started dating Javier Bardem, she ceased to be a regular in the romantic gossip columns. The couple married in 2010; since then, they have largely protected their discreet family from the media. Nevertheless, Cruz has not withdrawn from other dimensions of her celebrity persona, such as her status as a fashion icon. In fact, one could argue that she has even enhanced this aspect of her brand, which has helped her build a net worth currently estimated at $55 million. Her red carpet looks always make the headlines and are typically described as oozing glamour. At the time of this writing, Cruz is the official ambassador for Chanel, representing the fashion house's 2018–19 collection. She even made an appearance as a model (the second time in her career, after modelling for Victorio & Lucchino in 1998) for Chanel's Fall 2019 Collection; she participated in the last runway show to feature designs by Karl Lagerfeld, an event that also served as a tribute to the legendary designer (Okwodu). Previously, she had been the face and spokesperson for L'Oréal and Lancôme, and she is currently the face of John Hardy's latest jewellery collection. Furthermore, her presence on the covers of fashion magazines (for example, on the February 2019 issue of *Marie Claire*, and the April 2019 issue of *Vogue España*, for which she also served as guest editor) has only increased.

Cruz's performances on the red carpet, in fashion photo shoots, and at other promotional events should not be viewed as subsidiary to her film roles. Indeed, they are equally important to her enactment of stardom, part and parcel of her professional portfolio. On a theoretical level, they compel us to consider what Pam Cook, analysing the similar case of Nicole Kidman, calls "a broad understanding of performance that extends beyond acting in film" ("Revisiting" 41). The significance of Cruz's fashion performances as feeding her star image helps us problematize conventional theories of stardom that neglect the importance of these extra-cinematic paratexts, mentioning them only as means of interference in a star's artistic credentials. On the contrary, such performances should be valued as a form of expertise produced by creative effort and determination. As a matter of fact, my argument here is that they are visible ways in which Cruz has exercised active agency over her star persona – and that they have truly heightened her acting credibility by granting her a sophisticated aura that harks back to old Hollywood glamour. To develop the public profile of someone of Penélope Cruz's global stature obviously requires a complex collaboration among numerous people from the multidimensional publicity industries in orbit around cinema. Even if she is not the sole creator of her star persona, she is more than a mere figurine manipulated by third parties such as her agents, publicists, and the media. When assessing Cruz's stardom, we should no longer have to choose between ascribing it to either passive beauty or active performance (Davies, *Penélope* 125). Within such an obsolete and gendered framework – because male performers are not measured by the same standards – a female performer is forced to pick between talent or beauty; she cannot have it all.

Cruz had already established her fashion credentials on the global stage with her first appearances at the Academy Awards. In 2001, she presented the Oscar for Best Costume Design. There, she stood out less for the shimmering lace Ralph Lauren gown with its flirtatious off-the-shoulder neckline – she had a contract to wear this designer's clothes at that point – than for her whimsically wavy hairstyle, a semi-updo with face-framing curls that was commended for adding a personal, "Spanish-like" touch to her look. In a year when she had received harsh reviews for all her acting roles – including three Golden Raspberry Award nominations as Worst Actress for her work in *Blow*, *Captain Corelli's Mandolin*, and *Vanilla Sky* – this was no small success. Earning accolades for her creative sense of style was a way of saying, "Bear with me – I do have something special." In her return to the Oscars in 2005, she confirmed her fashion qualifications. She wore a stunning yellow gown – a tricky colour to pull off on a red carpet – in a sparkly silk taffeta fabric designed by Oscar de la Renta. In addition to the risky colour, the strapless dress had an enormous bow at the back that playfully complemented her slender silhouette. The oversized add-on could have appeared gimmicky, but was met with praise. Moreover, the Dominican designer publicly admitted that Cruz herself had proposed he create this look, which stressed her active agency in crafting her own glamorous image.

Apart from the much-praised Versace gown she donned for the 2007 Academy Awards, Cruz's talent for self-presentation was on full display in 2009, both in her red carpet look and in her acceptance speech as Best Supporting Actress. She stole the show by wearing a vintage white Pierre Balmain gown, strapless and delicately embroidered; it had a silhouette that evoked Victorian-era gowns, including a sweeping train that made her look like a fairy-tale princess. Cruz accessorized the magnificent gown with minimalist touches (a simple choker-type Chopard collar, her hair pulled back in a simple low bun, a youthful fringe, and discreet make-up), harking back to a form of old Hollywood glamour that some fashion commentators associated with Audrey Hepburn's iconic 1950s looks. Even in its calculated classical simplicity, however, this look was hardly risk free. First, her decision to wear vintage couture could have come across as trying too hard to follow in the footsteps of Julia Roberts – whose style Cruz has admitted emulating in her teenage years (McCarthy) – or hewing too close to the vintage Valentino worn by Roberts the year of her Oscar win. Also, the use of lace and the ruching technique employed to increase the garment's surface interest did look a bit bridal for a red carpet look, which could have undermined the overall effect by making her appear generically matrimonial. Ultimately, none of these negative outcomes materialized. Cruz added a dreamlike air to the look, with a dreamy story to match: she claimed that she had first seen this 1950s gown in 2001 at Lily and Cie, the famous Los Angeles store that is a premier destination for anyone looking for vintage couture clothes. She swore she would wear it one day. Luckily, years later, it was still available for her appearance at the Academy Awards. Clearly, we are not dealing with a passive object who merely follows the advice of a well-chosen team of publicists, but rather with someone who treats her red carpet performance as a painstakingly considered process and acts with purpose in shaping her own star image through fashion.

As if this story were not inspiring enough as a showstopper, Cruz completed her fairy-tale Oscar performance with an emotional acceptance speech. Fighting back tears, she proudly shared her humble origins with the world: "I grew up in a place called Alcobendas, where this was not a very realistic dream." The daughter of a car mechanic and a neighbourhood beautician, Cruz grew up in a working-class suburb of outer Madrid; her rise to stardom is a truly romantic "rags to riches" tale of commitment and hard work. It is also a testament to the transformational potential of glamour. Historians have shown that glamour holds the promise of social mobility and is therefore coupled with a fantasy of transformation, a desire to become a better or more appealing version of oneself (Dyhouse 3; Gundle 7). Cruz's image is all the more alluring precisely because audiences can imagine and dream of undergoing a similar metamorphosis. Her story offers the possibility, however far-fetched, of escaping ordinary living conditions. It may be unlikely (and glamour conceals all the hurdles she had to overcome), but it is not unimaginable.

Cruz's speech revealed other ways in which she discursively positions herself as auteur of her star image. She expressed her gratitude to a number of filmmakers who have been crucial to her career path: Woody Allen, the director who gave her the award-winning role; Pedro Almodóvar, the director who made her a global star; and Bigas Luna and Fernando Trueba, the two directors who discovered her in Spain. Apart from showing humility and consideration – one good turn deserves another – this was also another pertinent performance of star agency. In interviews, too, Cruz frequently praises the work of the film auteurs who direct her, speaking reverently about each one.[5] In deliberately implicating herself in these directors' artistic projects, she accentuates the mutually beneficial nature of their collaboration. As a matter of fact, Richard Dyer had already noted that the "notion of the star and the director mutually bringing something out in each other informs much auteurist criticism" (*Stars* 155). Cruz's exceptional synergy with Pedro Almodóvar is especially striking. She has said repeatedly that she decided to become an actor after seeing Almodóvar's *Átame* as a teenager. And both have spoken at length about how they feel they are a perfect fit for each other. Almodóvar has taken Cruz to places – in terms of the physical and psychological complexity of her roles – no other director ever has (i.e., an HIV-positive nun impregnated by a transsexual, a sex worker who gives birth in a public bus), and has made her a global star. Conversely, "Cruz has brought Almodóvar mainstream adulation and bigger box office"; to many, his "best films have starred Cruz" (France).

Cruz's red carpet magnetism continued in the post-Oscar festivities, when she traded the vintage Balmain for a white, one-shoulder Versace gown with a thigh-baring hemline that emphasized her most sensuous side. In many ways, her performance that evening signified the maturity of her brand: the global recognition of her professional work both on screen and off, her admittance into the select category of film goddesses who can captivate with their acting roles while simultaneously personifying classic glamour. The timing could not have been better. Only a few weeks later, Almodóvar released *Los abrazos rotos*, a film in which he idolizes Cruz as a movie star, portraying her with "larger-than-life old-Hollywood regality" (Schager). Dressed in a number of stunning Chanel outfits (see chapter 2 for a detailed analysis), Cruz frequently evokes Audrey Hepburn, Marilyn Monroe, and Sophia Loren. In this way, Cruz achieved the pinnacle of a certain stardom that had seemed like a thing of the past, with her on-screen role almost seamlessly matching, even completing, her off-screen image.

Cruz's strategic plan for embodying Golden Age glam reached new heights at the 2012 Academy Awards. She stepped onto the red carpet in an Armani Privé gown that stood out for its original blend of blue and grey, described by fashion commentators as a "stormy sky" and "dusty blue." From the waist up, the dramatic off-the-shoulder straps and fitted bodice enhanced her slim silhouette. From the waist down, the light, translucent chiffon fabric had a flowy effect that was reminiscent of classical screen sirens. But what drove home the reference to Hollywood's Golden Age was her retro-inspired faux bob hairstyle combined with a simple Chopard necklace. At once, she was glowingly deemed the "Spanish Grace Kelly." This was another tricky ensemble, because it made her look significantly older than she was; even more crucially, she ran the risk of looking too referential. Yet Cruz hit yet another bullseye by presenting her look as effortlessly intentional. This is a key feature of the glamour that audiences associate with her: making the difficult seem easy, hiding the hard work so that the girl from Alcobendas does not look like she is even trying. Glamour, as Virginia Postrel notes, "requires a kind of theatrical performance," like a special effect that hides "the pain, difficulty, flaws, and entropy" (81). When Cruz is described as oozing old Hollywood glamour, it means that she succeeds at creating an illusion of timeless elegance – one that looks "natural" and temporarily real, even if it remains a fabricated illusion.

Cruz's mastery of the red carpet performance is not just a matter of wielding control over possible garments, accessories, and hairstyles. It is a full performance, the total presentation of an entire look, complete with catwalk, posing, and answering questions. When Cruz walks on a red carpet, she owns it. Instead of merely standing in front of the cameras, she looks around, allowing photographers to catch multiple angles of her. In this way, when fashion editors have to make decisions about which looks to cover from a red carpet event, Cruz never fails to make the showcase selection. Her highly professional demeanour demonstrates that one is not simply born photogenic, but rather becomes so. Granted, winning the genetic lottery helps, but the point is that there is also talent, skill, and diligence involved. Consider her most iconic red carpet moment beyond the Oscars: her much-commented appearance at the 2010 Golden Globes, the year she was nominated as Best Supporting Actress for *Nine*. She appeared on the red carpet wearing another Giorgio Armani Privé mermaid gown, this time in solid black. The dress had plenty of eye-catching technical details – the horizontal ribbon stripes and fitted sleeves accentuating the mermaid silhouette, the embroidered lace that some commentators saw as evoking the Spanish *mantilla* – that were perfectly complemented by striking Chopard diamonds, Cruz's usual choice in jewellery. But what attracted the most attention was Cruz's self-assured walk down the wet carpet of the Beverly Hilton Hotel, holding an umbrella with great flair on an unexpectedly rainy evening. While some stars enlisted personal umbrella holders to protect them from the inclement weather (Sigourney Weaver, for example, who arrived right around the same time as Cruz), and others looked ostensibly flustered, their hairdos tousled, Cruz smiled radiantly, as if she had been rehearsing this wet carpet moment her entire life. And she might have – but her mastery of the theatrical performance of glamour made it all look graceful, unforced. When asked about it during an on-site interview with Ryan Seacrest for *E!*, she gave what became an insta-classic awards punch line: "I'm not like Puff Daddy, I hold my own umbrella." Talk about red carpet agency.

Few people may remember Cruz's Armani gown or Chopard jewels (as memorable as they were), but this red carpet performance is still described as one of her most glamorous moments. After all, glamour does not depend on a dress, accessories, or any other object. It is not "something you possess but something you perceive, not something you have but something you feel"; in other words, one may work hard to fabricate a glamorous effect through style, fashion, or sexual appeal, but "success depends on the perceiver's receptive imagination" (Postrel 12). Penélope Cruz has become synonymous with glamour because she has been able to secure a desiring audience, a loyal public seduced by her many attributes. She epitomizes some of what Stephen Gundle and Clino Castelli call glamour's "oxymoronic qualities," such as the "accessible exclusivity" predicated on the potential of glamour to offer "anyone the chance to use artifice to transform themselves" (13–14). Ultimately, she is known as a glamorous star because she embodies many of her audience's aspirational wishes (for beauty, sex appeal, elegance, luxury, celebrity, the capacity to personify different complex roles, and so on). Because they seem at least somewhat attainable, these desires incite audiences to some kind of action, striving for life-changing positive accomplishments and, above all, consumption.

Although her success depends on the subjective response of the audience, Cruz has done her part by performing deftly both on and off the screen and thus encouraging the imaginative desires projected onto her persona. Such performances do not only entail the visual pleasures I have been analysing (her on-screen image, red carpet looks, photo shoots, and other promotional materials), but also what she conceals from those desiring audiences. As her career has developed, Cruz has become more and more elusive and selective with the media in terms of what she discloses about her personal life. Moreover, in professional interviews, she sticks to a well-rehearsed script; never says anything negative about the actors, directors, or crews of her projects; and takes care to avoid making controversial remarks. Her social media accounts are managed by her publicity team, and one never sees the kind of impromptu posts that many other stars offer to their fans. This careful administration of her public image, and her elegant discretion, denotes for Ann Davies "a good deal of self-control" and "a deliberate career strategy in terms of publicity" (*Penélope* 123). I would add that it also reveals a superb understanding of another crucial component of glamour: mystery. Glamour only works if it entails the proper balance of approachability and distance. Much like the case of Conchita Montenegro that I analyse in chapter 1, Penélope Cruz has successfully stimulated a distanced identification with the audiences of her films and fashion performances. She is approachable enough to engage the audiences' imagination as projected onto her persona while maintaining enough distance to keep from breaking the spell.

Cruz's sustained involvement in the fashion industry outside of her film work, and beyond serving as a model for fashion and beauty brands, has greatly contributed to her aura as a creative author of her own glamorous image. In 2005, she started a fruitful collaboration with her sister Mónica to design jewels and handbags for Samantha Thavasa, a luxury fashion house in Japan. Then, beginning in 2007, the two sisters created four successful collections for the Barcelona-based fashion brand Mango. The generally positive reviews and commercial returns of their work with Mango led to subsequent collaborations with other brands, such as Loewe, Charles Vögele, and Agent Provocateur. Their work for the British lingerie retailer is especially noteworthy because it included the shooting of two fashion films written and directed by Cruz herself and used to launch the 2013 and 2014 collections of the high-end line L'Agent. The first film is a visually polished six-minute piece in which an elegantly dressed man (played by Spanish actor Miguel Ángel Silvestre) finds himself in a luxurious home, surrounded and seduced by a group of gorgeous lingerie-clad women. When the leading seductress (played by the Russian model Irina Shayk) is just about to kiss him, Silvestre is woken up by a construction worker – played by none other than Javier Bardem. The second film, which is significantly shorter (3:28), is set in a desert: a stranded, desperately thirsty traveller (played by Spanish model and actor Jon Kortajarena) crawls towards a group of women who show up in an old Cadillac (driven by Penélope Cruz) and start doing a sexy dance in their lingerie. The traveller reaches his oasis of female flesh and things get steamy, but he wakes up with the realization that it was all a mirage: he is left high and dry. These two fashion films tease the male protagonists (and the audience), luring them with objects of desire that vanish right when they seem within reach. In doing so, both films demonstrate how well Cruz understands the narrative and visual logic of persuading audiences into consuming a product – meaning both her lingerie and, more broadly, her star persona itself.

Writing and directing these films brings substantial benefits to Cruz's star image. Indeed, it reinforces her active agency in her fashion performances: she is not a mere mannequin for clothes, a face for a brand, or a name for a celebrity fragrance. By being the co-designer of the lingerie while also influencing how it is packaged and commercialized, Cruz proves herself as a legit player in the "brave new world" of fashion, "where the lines between celebrity and fashion designer have become blurred" (Agins xv). Such agency also adds another layer to her image as a "glamour girl." As we have seen, this image is not necessarily defined by the kinds of desires she elicits, but rather by her ability to invite audiences to project those desires onto her star persona – and, above all, by the key elements of her persona that trigger that yearning to begin with. She embodies the promise of self-transformation and escape from ordinary life; an effortless elegance that conceals the hard work behind it; and the careful balance between accessibility and mystery. Developing a star brand associated with old Hollywood glamour and vintage fashion has undoubtedly helped her on-screen image and her credibility as a film performer. Beyond her credentials and critical acclaim, Cruz can now be more selective with the parts she accepts. No longer typecast as an exotic Latina, she can play complex roles in international productions, including those directed by celebrated auteurs such as Fernando León de Aranoa (*Loving Pablo*, 2017), Asghar Farhadi (*Todos lo saben*, 2018), and Pedro Almodóvar (*Dolor y gloria*, 2019). She can also choose to appear in smaller European productions, such as *Venuto al mondo* (Sergio Castellito, 2012), and even become a co-producer of the risky *Ma ma* (Julio Medem, 2015). But she can also surprise audiences by switching to television (for the first time since the early 1990s) for a masterful performance as Donatella Versace in *The Assassination of Gianni Versace: American Crime Story* (2018). The casting of Cruz could not be more appropriate. She has elegantly donned many Versace gowns throughout her career, and her credentials as a designer of clothes and accessories, as well as a director of fashion films, make her perfectly credible in another fashion designer's shoes – so much so that the lines between the star persona and the character start to blur again. This very overlap is part of the Penélope Cruz brand: a "star text" where the allure of two glamour industries (fashion and cinema) gracefully converge.

Eduardo Casanova and Brays Efe: Fashioning Cult Stardom

At the 2017 Goya Awards Gala, host Dani Rovira notoriously put on a pair of red high-heeled shoes for a speech in favour of women in the film industry and society. Rovira's gesture had a perverse effect: he was blasted for trivializing feminist concerns by reducing them to the shoes women are expected to wear instead of offering self-criticism about the film industry's own culpability in objectifying them (Sota). The following year, however, men in heels made a surprising and well-received comeback when actor and director Eduardo Casanova showed up on the red carpet in a pair of black heels: a complement to a provocative three-piece suit without an undershirt. When the media asked him about the shoes, Casanova nonchalantly replied, "Yo no creo en el género" (I don't believe in gender). His casual gesture, although evidently not as inconsequential as he acted, sprang from an under-standing of gender as a culturally constructed category rather than as a natural or essential feature of any given person. Accordingly, he was able to stress that gendered dressing styles, in addition to the notion of gender itself, are social and cultural constructs. Unlike the oppor-tunistic born-again feminist Rovira, Casanova was not trying to jump on the #MeToo bandwagon. Rather, his gesture was part of his unique performance of stardom, a compelling genderqueer self-presentation that fans can enjoy in his red carpet appearances as well as in his pro-motion and publicity material; it also provides the perfect foil for the queer messages and the cult status of the films he has directed. In fact, I contend that his fashion performances have been instrumental to his perception as a cult queer auteur, as they resonate with millennial and postmillennial generations' social tolerance with respect to questions of gender fluidity and sexual identity.

The 2018 Gala was indeed a big night for Eduardo Casanova. His de-but feature-length film as a director, *Pieles* (2017), had three Goya nom-inations (Best New Actress, Best New Actor, and Best Make-up and Hairstyling). Even before its commercial release, it had become a cult film after being praised at the Berlinale and the Málaga Film Festival, among other venues. Yet Casanova was not automatically associated with cult cinema as we know it; in fact, he was known as a mainstream star. By the time Casanova started to make his own films, he had al-ready become a media celebrity for playing one of the first openly gay teenage characters on Spanish television, Fidel Martínez in the sitcom *Aída* (2005–14), the longest-running sitcom in Spain (238 episodes in total).[6] Casanova's role made him the poster child of gay visibility in society, which, for better or for worse, linked his film acting career to the role of the gay son, as in *Del lado del verano* (Antonia San Juan, 2012) and *Señor, dame paciencia* (Álvaro Díaz Lorenzo, 2017).

In parallel to his acting roles in mainstream television and film productions, Casanova started to acquire a reputation in the art-house cinema circuits by making short films like *Ansiedad* (2009), *Amor de madre* (2013), and *Eat My Shit* (2015). With their provocative content, dark humour, and a unique visual style marked by saturated colours and symmetrical compositions, his short films drew comparisons with auteurs on a par with John Waters, Wes Anderson, Luis Buñuel, and Pedro Almodóvar. The third of these shorts, which tells the story of Samantha (Ana Polvorosa), a young woman who is bullied and marginalized because she was born with her anus in her mouth – and vice versa – planted the seed for his first long film. *Pieles* features a group of people with physical or psychological deformities whom society would catalogue as freaks or monsters. Besides Samantha, the group features a pedophile, a young man who wants to cut off his legs to become a mermaid, a sex worker with skin for eyes, an obese woman with same-sex desires, and a preppy-looking man who is sexually drawn to women with physical abnormalities. All of these characters suffer from loneliness, rejection, social exclusion, and even violent bullying. In their search for acceptance, they realize that they must first learn to accept themselves in their own skin. The grotesque characters and situations – scatological humour, vomiting, and abundant full-frontal nudity, including that of an elderly woman who procures children for pedophiles – were photographed in highly saturated pink and lavender colours and framed within perfectly symmetrical compositions that provided a stylistically radical contrast with the disturbing images (see fig. 5.2).

Far from superfluous, this polished aesthetic look is fully integrated into the critical conversation of the film. By surrounding dark souls with pastel colours, Casanova literally paints grim realities through rose-coloured lenses. At first, and to a certain extent, the pastel hues and stylized compositions seem to mitigate the alienating effect of the bizarre scenarios; the visual style is immediately mesmerizing. Its purpose, though, is to make us question various social constructions, such as the boundaries between what society considers beautiful or ugly, appealing or repulsive, acceptable or unacceptable. Pink and lavender are two colours conventionally associated with women and the LGBTQ

Fig. 5.2. Symmetrical compositions and pink colours in *Pieles*

community, as well as with softness, daintiness, and femininity. Here, however, they are visually associated with situations of violence, destruction, and loneliness. Casanova has revealed in interviews that his obsession with affiliating the colour pink with dark subject matter comes from a disturbingly iconic image: the photo of Jackie Kennedy in her Chanel suit, spattered with JFK's blood (Bas).[7] It is in this sense that co-producer Álex de la Iglesia described the movie as "un cuchillo dentro de una tarta de cumpleaños" (a knife inside a birthday cake) (A. Delgado). The unexpected affinities between pink, loneliness, and violence in *Pieles* help problematize the gendered significance of different colours. Today's gendered cultural logic insists that blue is for boys and pink is for girls. While this logic has become utterly naturalized, it is, in reality, a construction. As Valerie Steele notes, "until about the 1920s most Americans tended to regard red and its pastel derivative pink more masculine, and blue as more feminine" ("Appearance" 15). The gender coding system did not shift into our current configuration until at least the Baby Boom generation (1946–64), the first to be born with colour codes (see Jo Paoletti for a complete social history of this colour coding). Although these historians refer specifically to the United States, the point is no less valid for other national contexts, such as the Spanish one portrayed in this film.

The aesthetics of pastel colours in *Pieles* is a cogent visual strategy intended to complicate gender as a social construct. Furthermore, it also enriches the contextual framework of Casanova's red carpet performance at the 2018 Goya Awards. In fact, this was one of many public appearances in which he deployed fashion and style to convey the message that masculinity and femininity are unstable signifiers, not fixed or natural features. For every promotional event or interview about this film – for example, on the Movistar+ television shows *Late motiv* and *Likes* – he wore some kind of pink-based outfit. So did the rest of the cast and crew. In the pre-shooting presentation for the press, Casanova convinced the entire cast, even the producers of the film (Álex de la Iglesia and Carolina Bang), to dress in pink. A similar pink party took place for the Berlinale screening in February 2017, as well as for the premiere in Madrid's Cine Capitol in July 2017.

Interestingly, Casanova has said on numerous occasions that he is not interested in fashion. For instance, in an "Encuentro Digital" for Europa Press right before the presentation of *Pieles*, he stated that he only cares about clothes as a tool for expressing his point of view in public events.[8] And yet, as soon he admits that clothes are an effective vehicle for us to tell our story and shape our image, his supposedly anti-fashion statement, repeated almost verbatim in other interviews, sounds rather oxymoronic. As a matter of fact, in his post-*Pieles* public appearances, Casanova has continued to surprise audiences with dramatic outfit choices that play with gendered expectations. In a highly publicized event to celebrate the thirtieth anniversary of *Vogue Spain* in July 2018, Casanova donned a total look by Palomo Spain: a Renaissance-inspired, two-piece white garment accompanied by patent leather clogs and a dazzling hair and make-up job, emphasizing small barrel curls on his forehead and fake tears on his cheeks. A few months later, he attended the launch of the television series *Arde Madrid* in an eclectic outfit inspired by the traditional *traje de luces* (bullfighter costume), combined with unconventional elements such as bright patent leather boots, a tank top underneath the bullfighting jacket, and a multicoloured pendant.

Given that Casanova has become a celebrated fixture in fashion discourse about red carpet events in Spain, one may wonder why he tries so hard to disavow his involvement with the fashion universe. At times, this disavowal even borders on fashion bashing, especially when he describes it as frivolous and superficial.[9] One reason behind this refutation is probably to discourage viewers from reading incongruous messages in his work. Both his short films and *Pieles* invite us to reflect on how normative notions of physical appearance have a negative impact on people's lives, leading to feelings of loneliness, social exclusion, and even violent destruction. Seen as an industry that determines beauty standards in society, fashion is thus regarded as a key component of the systemic problem that Casanova's films decry. Besides, *Pieles* ends with a somewhat uplifting message that seems to contradict the logic of fashion – a logic that provides people with recipes for becoming better versions of themselves through makeovers and physical transformations. In *Pieles*, the depressed characters realize that the only path to fulfilment entails accepting themselves with all their deformities and depravities rather than trying to discipline their bodies, appearances, and behaviours into conforming with dominant notions of identity.

Casanova's position seems to emerge from a common perception of fashion as a form of oppression associated with essentialist visions of identity (for instance, by linking acceptable forms of femininity and masculinity to certain external markers of beauty and choices in clothes, make-up, and hairstyles) and with rampant consumerism that only a privileged minority can indulge. However, his fashion performances say otherwise. These non-verbal forms of communication convey an empowering message that challenges gendered assumptions about appearance. In his red carpet looks, Casanova playfully mixes conventional markers of masculinity and femininity to advocate against the constraints that the gender binary imposes on us. He deploys a form of agency through fashion consumption and formulates a genderqueer discourse that signals the limitations of binary thinking and circumvents identity-based politics, including gay and lesbian issues. In short, Casanova is caught between two conflicting discourses about the role of fashion in society. On the one hand, he criticizes it for reinforcing gender essentialism; on the other, he appropriates it as a discursive weapon against binary social constructions of gender.

This tension leads us to another tangible outcome of Casanova's fashion performances: they have helped him reshape his own star image. Once a mainstream icon of inclusivity in a popular TV show that was heralded for promoting gay visibility (and thereby tied to identity politics), Casanova has become a cult figure who embodies messages on the importance of the transgressive, the deviant, the excessive, and even the extreme. Of course, describing Casanova as a "cult star" requires some unpacking, especially with respect to the question of agency in the process of cultification. The label "cult," typically viewed as something that audiences create, is inevitably associated with the discourse of reception studies. Most discussions of cult cinema emphasize that it has to do with consumption, with a "subcultural ideology" professed by cult fans in order "to produce a sense of distinction between themselves and the mainstream" (Jancovich et al. 1–2). Positioned at the margins of the mainstream, cult audiences "display reception tactics that have become a synonym for an attitude of minority resistance and niche celebration within mass culture" (Mathijs and Sexton 8). The problem with these established views of cult cinema is, as Justin Smith contends, that they have overemphasized "cult appreciation as a subcultural practice" at the cost of overshadowing "the necessary examination of texts (films, directors, actors)" (109). Any nuanced discussion of cult film or cult stardom thus requires a thorough consideration of audience activity, as well as of production strategies and textual properties.

Pieles illustrates this point because it became a cult film (as Casanova became a cult auteur) even before it was commercially released. As a matter of fact, its poor box-office returns (only 15,081 admissions) tell us that the film's real impact was felt beyond the theatres. Shortly after its commercial release, Netflix made it available internationally via its streaming platform (and in some territories, such as in the United Kingdom, even before its theatrical release), which significantly expanded its potential audience. But its cult reputation preceded the Netflix affiliation, cohering so instantaneously that it cannot be considered a merely audience-based phenomenon. Its cult status also involved journalistic discourse, certain textual properties of the film itself, and the strategies deployed by the agents behind it (director, producers, cast, and crew members). Upon its presentation at film festivals, film critics and journalists quickly spread the word about *Pieles*'s extreme subject matter and the impossibility of classifying it within any established genre or category. Every press release and every interview focused, excessively and often morbidly, on asking Casanova to define his film and to justify the use of what was perceived as disturbing content. The film's promotional materials also exacerbated such reactions. Both the previews and the initial poster were polemically censored for containing full-frontal nudity. In this sense, the swiftly assigned "cult status" label had much to do with judgments regarding its textual qualities and issues of cultural taste. Various journalists and critics admitted to Casanova that they could not stomach watching it (for example, Risto Mejide on the popular TV show *Chester* in February 2018). Indeed, the film contains a key feature of cult cinema that Matt Hills calls "moments of ontological shock" provoked by instances of "extreme visceral disgust" ("Question" 444). Its producers and members of the cast and the technical crew directly contributed to this cult discourse with their emphatic words to the press. Cast members such as Carmen Machi and Candela Peña repeatedly told the media that *Pieles* marked a turning point in Spanish cinema because of its subversive content and Casanova's unique directorial perspective.

Decisively, Casanova's own agency also affected this process. Instead of being offended by critics' and journalists' visceral disgust in response to the film, he almost perversely encouraged it. Here, his fashion and style performances proved expedient. Besides contesting gender expectations and cultural constructs, his garish pink outfits at red carpet events, public presentations, and television interviews visually associated him with the aberrant characters in *Pieles*. He reinforced this affinity by revealing in interviews that everything in his house was also pink (walls, furniture, decorative ornaments), and that his goal was not to scandalize but simply to express himself freely. Thus, he essentially presented himself as exhibit A in the freak show that his film displays, spurring curiosity and even morbid fascination with his persona. Evidently, the goal was to promote himself as a cult figure associated with transgression, excess, and abnormality. In doing so, Casanova fits the profile of what Ernest Mathijs calls an "active auteur": a director who intervenes in the public discourse about his films "in order to press certain receptions and interpretations of his films (and resist others)" ("Cronenberg" 147). For Casanova, this intervention was crucial in pre-empting knee-jerk associations between his films and his popular TV role – especially because he has not completely done away with that mainstream image. While heavily promoting *Pieles* as a subversive film, he took on an acting role as the gay son in the commercially successful comedy *Señor, dame paciencia* (more than 1.1 million admissions). Casanova has gained dual status as both a mainstream and a cult figure. He remains a widely known actor in popular films, but he has also attracted cult status, and his red carpet performances and involvement with the fashion industry have significantly contributed to his fabrication of a cult aura around his directorial persona.

These variable relationships between mainstream and cult stardom are also found at the heart of the last case I want to discuss, if briefly: Brays Efe. This multimedia star seemed destined to play any iteration of the gay best friend – as he did in *Cómo sobrevivir a una despedida* (Manuela Burló Moreno, 2015), *Unboxing* (Inés de León, 2016), and *¿Qué te juegas?* (Inés de León, 2019) – or the tech nerd, as in his supporting role as a freaky blogger in *Faraday* (Norberto Ramos del Val, 2013). But his career took a drastic turn with the web television series *Paquita Salas* (Javier Ambrossi and Javier Calvo, 2016), initially broadcast on the online platform Flooxer and attaining unexpected success. Netflix acquired the rights to air the second and subsequent seasons, which has made the show available beyond Spain. Brays Efe plays the protagonist, Paquita Salas, a talent manager with outdated professional methods who gets abandoned by her most important clients and must strike out in search of new actors. This role posed a major challenge to Efe, since he had to play a cis woman twenty years his senior. The complexity of his undertaking did not go unnoticed by critics, who named him Best Lead Actor in a TV Series in the 2017 Feroz Awards, an awards ceremony held by the Asociación de Informadores Cinematográficos de España that is gaining traction as a build-up to the Goyas.

Thanks to this role, Efe became what Matt Hills defines as a "subcultural celebrity," which corresponds to a type of stardom that is not widespread or pervasive, but rather restricted to the fanbases for the specific cult show in question ("Subcultural" 234). The cult appreciation for his role is so strong that actor and character have become closely intertwined – to the point that fans seem to want to see the character, not the actor. For instance, his IMDb profile displays a picture of Paquita Salas instead of himself. At the 2018 Goya Awards Gala, Efe introduced the Best New Actress award as Paquita Salas, and his performance was widely touted as the best part of the ceremony. There was even pre-ceremony speculation that he would show up to the red carpet dressed as Paquita Salas – although he ultimately appeared as Brays Efe in a suit and later changed his wardrobe to impersonate Paquita. As a cult performer, Efe is celebrated for his unrealistic work: full of excess, frequently transgressing performance norms. Paquita is extravagant in her physical gestures; in her vocalizations, delaying the pronunciation of the first syllable of everybody's first name; in her foul-mouthed comebacks when she gets angry; and, above all, in how she devours junk food. With Paquita Salas, Efe has developed what Steven Rawle calls an acting "idiolect," that is, "an identifiable collection of physical and vocal performance traits that are defined, and, perhaps most importantly for the cult star, appropriable, imitable, ironic or excessive" (127). Efe's idiolect is campy, outlandish, and rich in intertextual references, such as the acknowledged homage to TV celebrity Terelu Campus through Paquita's voluminous hairstyle. His celebrated cameo at the 2018 Goyas suggests that this idiolect could become so excessive and self-reflexive, as his career advances, that it may be difficult to restrict to his performance in *Paquita Salas* alone. In other words, it may carry over into his work in other productions (whether mainstream or cult) and into his whole star persona.

One reason for this potential conflation is that Efe deploys similar antics to Paquita Salas's in his everyday contact with fans (for example, through the Instagram live videos in which he fields their questions) and in other mediated performances, promotional/publicity events, and materials such as interviews, red carpet appearances, and catwalk shows for the fashion industry. Of course, these similarities boost his cult status by enhancing his image of authenticity – a key feature of cult stardom (Jancovich) – and closeness to his fans. The most important feature that spills over from the character to the actor's persona (and vice versa) is that both Paquita Salas and Brays Efe trumpet a body-acceptance discourse. In an era when the entertainment industry (in Spain as much as elsewhere) tends to include overweight people only in weight-loss shows such as *En forma en 70 días* (Antena 3), *En tu talla o en la mía* (DKISS), *La báscula* (Canal Sur), and *Doctor Romero* (TVE), presenting them as specimens to prove feel-good narratives of individual self-transformation, Paquita embodies unconditional fat acceptance. Never happier than when eating highly processed pastries, she epitomizes a non-stigmatizing relationship with food. Her role self-reflexively mocks the stereotype of the overweight female with an out-of-control personality who constantly transgresses norms of decorum: Paquita is known for her vulgar language, hypersexual impulses, and the fact that she acts on every instinct that pops into her head without feeling any self-doubt or ensuing guilt. Efe's off-screen persona is equally untamed and excessive. His Instagram posts and live videos often involve food intake. For example, in a hilarious February 2019 post, he uploaded a video in which he wandered his Madrid neighbourhood, Malasaña, frustrated at his inability to find a bar or restaurant that would make him a *sandwich mixto* (ham and cheese sandwich), which he interpreted as a sign of urban decadence.

This image is quite different from the one presented by other icons of body positivity. For instance, Melissa McCarthy has mastered performing on-screen obese trashiness, but has carefully portrayed her "'authentic' self" as "humble, well spoken, lovable and classy," ensuring that entertainment journalism portrays her as "a down-to-earth Midwestern mom who upholds healthy bourgeois values" (Meeuf 36–7). In the end, McCarthy's on-screen persona does not challenge normative constructions of femininity, but rather serves as a comical, abject image of the stereotypical obese woman who needs control and discipline to improve (Meeuf 46). By contrast, the always over-the-top Brays Efe has employed his cult star status (without tempering his raunchy behaviour) as a platform against fat shaming and bullying of LGBTQ populations, not as a way to promote his example as an individual success story.

Significantly, Efe has used fashion and style as key instruments to convey this message. He has become a muse for the brand Outsiders Division, a Spanish fashion house founded in 2012 that has been making urban clothes for a variety of body types with a perspective that exceeds normatively gendered dress codes. Following up on the colourful suit with multicoloured patchwork that he wore to the 2018 Goyas, Efe modelled for this brand at the 2018 Mercedes Benz Fashion

Week, wearing a spectacular outfit that promoted body positivity (both the jacket and pants were several sizes bigger than his body type) and questioned binary gender codes. His look juxtaposed conventional markers of masculinity (beard and moustache) and femininity (two braids in his hair secured by two scrunchies, one pink and the other blue, as a statement against gendered colour coding). At the 2019 Goyas, Efe caused a sensation yet again: he donned another Outsiders Division outfit, a flashy multicoloured pinstripe suit accompanied by sport boots. Fashion journalists commented on the eclectic inspirations behind the suit (Mondrian paintings and techno culture), but not on its technical construction. A far cry from the body-hugging trends in male red carpet suits, designed to highlight the actors' gym-sculpted bodies, Efe's suit had a loose cut in the sleeves, shoulders, waist, and legs that suggested comfort and casualness. A few weeks earlier, he had sidestepped the red carpet dress code with another casual and comfortable outfit, this time at the 2019 Feroz Awards: a red kimono-style suit with sporty white boots that gave him a gender-neutral appearance. He preceded the award for Best Preview by presenting himself to the audience as "el gordo" (the fat guy) from the show *Tu cara me suena* – an interlude that addressed the lack of visibility of non-normative bodies on TV screens, not to mention the fat phobia and sizeism of society in general.

The language of fashion affords Efe the chance to defy essentialist notions of identity and to articulate his persona as an example of intersectionality – neither of which can be defined by a singular factor, such as his gender or sexual orientation, nor constrained by societal expectations about a star's appearance. It is a way of saying, "I am here, fat, and queer, so deal with it." Brays Efe's fashion performances, along with his bold statements in interviews and his involvement with fans on social media, have helped him shape a cult star persona – perhaps too transgressive and over-the-top to be mainstream, though it is still early in his career. This persona flaunts a non-normative and critically queer body that does not simply affirm the importance of inclusion and diversity in the film and fashion industries, but also interrogates the underlying values that create oppressive structures in society.

Conclusion: The Red Carpet Matters

Throughout this chapter, I have explored the meaningful intersections between film stardom and fashion beyond the role of costume design in films. The four case studies selected for scrutiny have shown that the clothes and accessories worn by stars off screen are just as important – if not more so – than on-screen looks in forging their image. As a compelling form of non-verbal communication, fashion allows stars to construct and present themselves as unique, and thus to negotiate their relationships with audiences. In the past, the field of star studies only addressed fashion in reference to a form of manipulation of star personae. Today, stars are actually expected to master their self-presentation in numerous industry-related performances, such as red carpet appearances, interviews, fashion shoots, and fundraising events, as well as in their social media activities. Therefore, personal agency is not only possible but indeed required in the process of self-fashioning stardom. Stylists should obviously receive a lot of the credit for stars' fashion accolades, but those stars who integrate their own point of view, sense of style, and personality into their looks stand out from the rest. When they manage to forge a distinctive style narrative that becomes recognizable as one of their star signatures, it can have a substantial impact on their careers. As we have seen, both Victoria Abril and Penélope Cruz have successfully adopted fashion as a persuasive tool to modify their star images, thereby boosting their international profiles. Abril concocted a risky, one-of-a-kind image of eccentricity (especially on the Cannes red carpet) that overflowed into her complex roles in European film productions, which helped her secure a solid status in the transnational circuits of European cinema without being subjected to typecasting. When Penélope Cruz reached Hollywood, she spent a number of years playing roles that limited her to the "hot exotic Latina" – and being crucified by the media as a celebrity digger more devoted to cashing in on her romantic connections with co-stars than to perfecting her craft. I have shown that her dexterous fashion performances (such as red carpet events and photo shoots for fashion and lifestyle magazines) and her active involvement with the fashion industry (including as a thriving designer of clothes, accessories, and jewellery) have allowed her to associate her star image with old Hollywood glamour. Interestingly, the acknowledgment of her fashion sense has run parallel to critical recognition of her acting skills, which suggests that both facets of her stardom are tightly interwoven and thus equally essential to the global appreciation of her brand.

By foregrounding their agency and authorship in the process of renegotiating their stardom, Abril and Cruz prove that fashion should not be seen merely as a form of decoration attached or imposed onto stars' images. Indeed, it is, at least in their cases, closer to the etymological meaning of the word: fashion, from the Latin *factio* ("making" or "doing") and the verb *facere* ("to make" or "to do"), originally designated an activity or something people did. Furthermore, as Malcolm Barnard aptly observes, the modern word "faction" derives from the same Latin root, thus suggesting a political tenor within the family of the term "fashion" (faction in a broader context of cultural conflict between social groups), which "may even have connotations of an avant-garde, a radical sub-cultural group who do not necessarily agree with the larger or mainstream culture and who struggle against it" (*Fashion as Communication* 40). Cult stars Eduardo Casanova and Brays Efe invoke this sense of the politics of fashion in relation to notions of identity and difference. Both of these cogent case studies prove that "fashion and appearance have always played a key part in the politics of difference" (Edwards, *Fashion in Focus* 103–4), even if they are in no way linked to the identity politics of any specific social group. Rather, they have both appropriated fashion as a communicative tool to express individuality. For Casanova, fashion has been a valuable instrument used to shake off his mainstream image as the symbol of gayness on Spanish television. His genderqueer red carpet looks have drawn attention for performing gender identity as non-binary, multiple, and fluid. This unconventional self-presentation has enhanced his reputation as a cult auteur of films that fall outside the mainstream cinema world. Fashion, in a nutshell, has helped Casanova acquire cult credibility. For Brays Efe, the red carpet has been a means for him to heighten a cult star image associated with excess and the non-observance of prescriptive gender-presentation codes. In addition, it has allowed him to perform body positivity and raise fraught questions about fat phobia in society, as well as about the lack of opportunities for non-normative bodies in the film, fashion, and entertainment industries. Both Casanova and Efe illustrate that the red carpet is not only a stage that offers audiences a view of new clothing styles and accessories and advances careers by fashioning star images in a positive way; the red carpet also matters because it is a platform used to convey cultural messages that may influence audiences in their everyday lives.

Fashioning Identity and Stardom

The objective of this project as a whole has been to spotlight a crucial but frequently overlooked aspect of a film's visual style – costume – and foster an appreciation for the diverse ways in which film and fashion enrich each other. As influential industries that offer representations of ideas, values, and beliefs, both film and fashion shape and construct cultural identities. Focusing on the context of Spanish cinema, but reaching conclusions that extend to other film industries, I have shown that clothes in films are not merely narrative elements to tell a story by dressing a character in a believable manner. Besides this central function, clothes appearing as costumes should be understood as tools for non-verbal communication that represent and create – and not merely reflect – cultural values as well as identities, whether these are individual or collective. For instance, the first analytical chapter of the book focused on Spanish films of the 1960s that deployed clothes of the house of Balenciaga to present age-related aspirational looks: Isabel Garcés wore sophisticated outfits for mature women (often a marginal group in cinema) in a variety of leading and secondary roles, while Rocío Dúrcal was dressed by Balenciaga to introduce a new youth look for Spanish teenagers in *Rocío de la Mancha*. Before them, clothes designed by the Basque couturier also served to adjust the sensual image of two of the biggest stars of Spanish cinema (Conchita Montenegro in the early 1940s and Sara Montiel in the early 1960s) to the moral strictures of Francoist Spain. Certain details and accessories of their costumes in these films brought to the fore a conscious strategy to style their celluloid images to match that of a stereotypically Spanish woman.

The role of clothes and fashion in the making and remaking of gender identity is at the core of much costuming work that this book has examined. Chapter 2 focused on the tensions between feminism and fashion that surface in the spectacular Chanel outfits that appear in three films directed by Pedro Almodóvar. With the knock-off suit that Agrado dons in *Todo sobre mi madre*, Almodóvar compels us to reflect upon the performative nature of gender and to question essentialist notions of identity while simultaneously evoking the complex relationship of Chanel with feminist views. The classic Chanel suit (*tailleur*) is ubiquitous in *Tacones lejanos* but in the shocking context of queer incestuous seduction and desire. In *Los abrazos rotos*, a series of Chanel garments signpost the progressive agency of the female lead until she unshackles herself from her domineering male partner. Contrary to what previous approaches to this film have pointed out, fashion is used here to signify subjective empowerment rather than a symbol of female oppression.

Fashion as a barometer of changes in gender roles was also central in chapter 3. A tour through filmic representations of men in underwear (from the early Franco period to contemporary films) revealed shifts in models of masculinity as well as in developments of male sexuality in Spanish society. To the best of my knowledge, this is a pioneering effort that could serve as a methodological template for scholars who work not only on Hollywood films but also on the context of other national cinemas.

Shifting the focus from gender identity to race and ethnicity, in chapter four I discussed how costume is central in the racialized representations of first-generation immigrants in Spanish cinema. I showed how there is a noticeable hierarchy in the restraint with which white, Central, and Eastern European migrants dress in Spanish films compared with the hypervisibility of non-white migrants. While sub-Saharan black male migrants are often stripped of their clothes, Caribbean women of colour tend to appear in tight-fitting and garish costumes that render them exotic and overtly sexualized. Spaniards consistently dress with garments in neutral colours and shapes, which further contributes to highlight the racial hierarchy at stake in the costume choices of these films. Spanish immigration cinema makes all the more conspicuous what Maxime Cervulle calls "the hyper(in)visibility of whiteness" (xviii) by keeping whiteness transparent, unmarked by sartorial codes. In the concluding section of that chapter, I briefly argued that when people of colour get access to the means of film production, there is a significant rupture with this racialized regime of representation. Although examples such as the filmmakers Omer Oke and Santiago Zannou that I discussed are still scarce, they do offer hope for a not-too-distant future in which Spanish cinema will cease to deploy costume design as an aesthetic device to depict racialized subjects as exotic migrants who need to be presented drastically different from autochthonous people.

An interesting line of research for scholars interested in the representations of race relations and racial subjectivities in film will be to assess, using costume analysis as a methodological tool, the degree to which Spanish cinema can steadily portray racialized subjects as citizens, not necessarily as immigrants. Equally fascinating from a costuming point of view would be to explore how Spanish cinema has constructed what David Corkill calls "the foreigners within" (52): the Romani community. Although they have lived in the Iberian Peninsula since the early fifteenth century, the Romani still endure "virulent social and representational discrimination," often linked to exoticism and criminality (Santaolalla, "Ethnic" 58). Beyond their fairly uniform depiction in the folkloric musicals that Eva Woods Peiró studied in *White Gypsies*, and in subsequent Franco-era (musical) dramas such as *Los Tarantos* (Francisco Rovira Beleta, 1963), *Con el viento solano* (Mario Camus, 1966), and *El amor brujo* (Francisco Rovira Beleta, 1967), the image of gypsies in Spanish cinema has become more complex, varied, yet at times still stereotypically problematic in post-Franco films. These include Carlos Saura's flamenco trilogy (*Bodas de sangre* [1981], *Carmen* [1983], and *El amor brujo* [1986]), *Colegas* (Eloy de la Iglesia, 1982), *Calé* (Carlos Serrano, 1988), *Alma gitana* (Chus Gutiérrrez, 1996), *La leyenda del tiempo* (Isaki Lacuesta, 2006), and *Carmen y Lola* (Arantxa Echevarría, 2018), to name a few significant films. Although I make some brief comments about this in chapter 4 apropos the representation of Bulgarian gypsies in the film *Los veraneantes*, the topic is multifaceted and deserves more in-depth attention; its appropriate consideration is outside the scope of this book.

Throughout the book, I have paid sustained attention to the relevance of costume and fashion in the construction and transformation of star images from the 1940s until today. This laser focus on fashion makes an original contribution to star studies by complementing, and at times completely revamping, existing understandings of key Spanish cinema stars such as Conchita Montenegro, Sarah Montiel, Rocío Dúrcal, Victoria Abril, Penélope Cruz, and Javier Bardem, as well as of emerging stars Miguel Ángel Silvestre, Eduardo Casanova, and Brays Efe. In chapter 5, I specifically turned to the importance of stars' fashion performances off screen (red carpet events, photo shoots, magazine interviews and covers, as well as involvement with the fashion industry as runway models, designers, and even fashion film directors) as a way of wielding control over their star image. I showed how effective this fashion agency has been for Victoria Abril and Penélope Cruz to modify their transnational profile and avoid early-career typecasting by producing, with the help of stylists, a very different persona to the one performed on film, which eventually had a positive impact on their on-screen image. Towards the end of the chapter, I concentrated on two rising stars, Eduardo Casanova and Brays Efe, who have appropriated fashion to make subtle statements of defiance to the straightjacketed connotations about body shape, gender, age, and sexuality that are perpetuated in the fictional roles they have played in cinema and television.

Perhaps the main insight revealed in the final chapter is that fashion should not be considered an ancillary dimension in film stars' careers that is subordinate to their acting talent and controlled from the outside by publicists and stylists. Instead, the skills of effective self-presentation through fashion performances are part and parcel of an actor's craft nowadays, a new dividing line between the A-list and the rest. Inevitably, this scenario induces us to revise our conceptual frameworks to theorize film stardom, in the context of Spanish cinema and beyond. For instance, the boundaries between what Christine Geraghty defined as "star-as-celebrity" versus "star-as-performer" have become increasingly blurred. Emerging stars are particularly aware of this and no longer fear the potential disdain for embracing the celebrity side of their public persona, just as they are no longer afraid of losing prestige for crossing over to other media such as television and fashion. In fact, I have shown how they are quite savvy about the use of social media to enhance this celebrity and multimedia dimension of their stardom.

Understanding film stardom in relation to the fashion-celebrity node helps us part with former disciplinary confines and open up compelling avenues for future research. Rising stars such as Ester Expósito, Úrsula Corberó, Arón Piper, and María Pedraza, who have combined roles in cinema and television (in hugely successful series such as *La casa de papel* and *Élite*), are prime examples of "media convergence" (Jenkins 2–3), meaning that their stardom flows across multiple media platforms creating synergies that cannot be fully explained using only a traditional framework of analysis of one medium. All of them have recently become global stars with their prominent presence in television, cinema, social media platforms such as Instagram, and the fashion industry. Instagram celebrity status (25 million followers for Expósito; 20 for Corberó; and 12 for Pedraza and Piper at the time of writing) turns them into hot commodities sought by fashion brands for advertising and modelling deals. Images of these stars donning outfits increases their status as aspirational images of styles that are imitated globally, which also helps to generate even more interest in the films and television series in which they play roles. What I am suggesting is that we need new ways of theorizing how multiple media – in this case cinema, television, Instagram, and the fashion industry – participate in a transmedia ecology with symbiotic ties among them altering the conventional frameworks and relationships in the production and consumption of media.

I do not want to end with the impression that any and all thrilling opportunities for innovative enquiry can only be found off screen. I started this book lamenting that costume designers were not recognized enough for their work and delineating their especially precarious position within the Spanish film industry in relation to designers in other national cinemas such as the United Kingdom, Italy, and France, as well as Hollywood. However, not all prospects for the future are bleak. A number of Spanish costume designers have recently achieved international recognition by showcasing their work in major global productions. Consider the case of Sonia Grande. She had cemented a solid career in Spain working designing in films directed by Pedro Almodóvar, Alejandro Amenábar, and Fernando Trueba. But her pedigree reached new heights when she was commissioned by Hollywood to design the costume in Woody Allen's *Vicky Cristina Barcelona* (2008) and *Midnight in Paris* (2011) as well as the blockbuster romantic comedy *It's Complicated* (Nancy Meyers, 2009). Paco Delgado has followed a similar path. His work for Pedro Almodóvar and Álex de la Iglesia was noticed in the international stage, which translated into Oscar-nominated jobs for Tom Hooper's *Les Misérables* (2012) and *The Danish Girl* (2015). Are these isolated success stories or indicative of a larger trend of international recognition for the work of Spanish costume designers? Related to that, are these acclaimed designers creating a legacy in the form of new cohorts of Spanish designers who may follow their lead? Are these stellar costume designers contributing to the international visibility and pedigree of the Spanish film industry in general? These are only a few questions that can be raised and that bode well for the future of costume analysis within the overall structure of Spanish film studies.

Notes

Introduction

1 As the Castañer website explains, the French designer met the owners of the shoe atelier, Lorenzo Castañer and his wife Isabel Sauras, at a fair in Paris, and asked them to create this piece for him (www.castaner.com).

2 In 2017, as evidence of their canonization as a fashion classic, the Castañer wedge espadrilles were displayed (along with other iconic pieces, such as Chanel's "little black dress" and the Levi's 501) in the exhibit *"Is Fashion Modern?"* at MOMA in New York (Parga).

3 For example, Francisco Fernández de Alba and Marcela Garcés are publishing an edited volume, tentatively titled "Fashioning Spain" (forthcoming, Bloomsbury), which includes a collection of essays on diverse aspects of fashion in Spain and its impact on Spanish society and culture. The journal *Ciberletras* published a special issue in December 2017 entitled "Representations of Fashion and Clothing in Spanish and Latin American Literature," which ensued from an April 2017 symposium at CUNY Lehman College. A number of talks held at this symposium focused on the intersections of film costume and fashion.

4 Among her many accolades are an Academy Award, shared with Antonio Castillo, for *Nicholas and Alexandra* (Franklin Shaffner, 1971).

5 Lipovetsky further elaborates on this point: "Fashion is celebrated in museums, but among serious intellectual preoccupations it has marginal status. It turns up everywhere on the street, in industry, and in the media, but it has virtually no place in the theoretical inquiries of our thinkers. Seen as an ontological and socially inferior domain, it is unproblematic and undeserving of investigation; seen as a superficial issue, it discourages conceptual approaches" (3).

6 The application of Marxist views to fashion departs from the central distinction between "use value" (the practical function of a commodity) and

"exchange value" (its financial worth when traded). As an industry driven by making profit, fashion exemplifies exchange value and is therefore perceived as exploitative (Edwards, *Fashion* 13).

7 According to Flügel, the social upheaval caused by the French Revolution prompted this major shift. Elite men had previously used flamboyant styles as a way to distinguish themselves in terms of rank and wealth. The Revolution's democratic and egalitarian ideals promoted the abolition of these social distinctions, thus fostering greater sartorial uniformity and simplicity (112).

8 As evidence of the understated role played by men's styles in fashion history, Gilles Lipovetsky cites the absence of any institution comparable to that of the haute couture system to exhibit and promote innovations for men (56), as well as (until recently) the dearth of specialized press devoted to men's clothing (73).

9 These scholars have shown that the notion of the masculine renunciation must be revised, because "men did not renounce all colour and finery at this time" (Entwistle 160), and the use of the dark suit for corporate reasons did not become widespread until the late nineteenth century (Edwards, *Men* 19). As popular as it might have become by 1880, even then "it would have been worn *in addition* to other garments" (Entwistle 160, emphasis in the original).

10 The emergence of several volumes titled *The Men's Fashion Reader* is a good indication of progress in this regard. Within the context of Peninsular literary and cultural studies, in addition to Paul Julian Smith's insightful examination of Adolfo Domínguez's classic style and its status in the domestic and global fashion industry (*Contemporary* 34–60), several studies have turned their critical attention to the role of men's fashion in the construction of modern masculinity in Spain, with a particular focus on nineteenth-century and early twentieth-century literary representations (Díaz-Marcos; Heneghan; McKinney; Wolters).

11 Since at least the early twentieth century, several perspectives have developed in an attempt to explain the escalating importance of fashion in modern society. The most influential can be grouped into economic approaches, especially theories of emulation and consumption (Veblen, Simmel, Benjamin) and class distinction (Bourdieu); psychological approaches (Bergler, Flügel, Laver,); and semiological approaches, which view fashion as a language or a system of communication (Barnard, *Fashion as Communication*; Barthes, *Fashion System*; Calefato, *Clothed*; Danesi; Lurie). Space constraints prevent me from explaining them in detail here. See Tim Edwards (*Fashion in Focus* 11–39), Joanne Entwistle (40–77), and Ana María Díaz-Marcos (33–53) for three well-informed critical accounts of the strengths and limitations of these theoretical approaches to fashion.

12 In a recent major study, Nick Rees-Roberts problematizes this notion of the
fashion film "as a *new* form emerging both with the advent of digital technology and the corporate consolidation of global fashion brands"
(6, emphasis in the original). For him, the discussion should stop isolat-
ing contemporary forms of fashion film from earlier, pre-digital mani-
festations, as well as from fiction films. Instead, the fashion film "exists
as a hybrid genre," an umbrella term that encompasses both fiction and
non-fiction films, both big-budget and cheaper productions that "range
from the popular and mainstream to the more arty and experimental" (7).

13 As I discuss in chapter 5, none other than Penélope Cruz has written and
directed two fashion films that follow narrative film conventions for the
British underwear brand Agent Provocateur. Prominent Spanish actors
such as Javier Bardem, Miguel Ángel Silvestre, Jon Kortajarena, and Goya
Toledo have appeared in these two films.

14 In the week prior to the 2019 Gala, the pre-ceremony fashion buzz escalated. To give just one example, *El País* (via its *S Moda* magazine) revved
up the fashion engines for the Goya red carpet with daily articles such
as "Penélope Cruz: evolución y trucos de un estilo, pelo y maquillaje
de Goya" (26 January), "100 vestidos que ya son historia de los Premios
Goya" (27 January), and "Cómo prepara su 'look' una 'novata' en la al-
fombra roja de los Goya" (30 January). Fashion and film experts Clara
Ferrero and Carlos Megía even issued a thirty-minute podcast in which
they explained the process of selecting a red carpet look and interviewed
stylists in charge of dressing Gala attendees (30 January).

1. Fashioning National Stars: Balenciaga and Spanish Cinema

1 Curiously, the most infamous case was also one of the first instances of a
collaboration between film and fashion. In 1931, Metro-Goldwyn-Mayer
brought Coco Chanel to Hollywood with an exclusive contract (sources
say it was worth $1 million). However, this partnership barely lasted a
year because of Chanel's disagreements with the star, Gloria Swanson
(Charles-Roux 404–7; Leese 14). The designer did not want to compromise
her point of view for the sake of the films.

2 See Pedro Usabiaga's exhibit catalogue for a well-documented, descriptive
account of Balenciaga's costumes for different films and stars.

3 Apart from the strict censorship of the films, another difference with regard to the Hollywood studio system was that Spanish stars could not
limit themselves to a particular genre; they had to show their versatility in
a variety of genres, especially comedies and melodramas (Comas 34).

4 I must clarify that because of Montenegro's unique trajectory and relative
dearth of archival documentation about her career (Carmen Ro and Javier

Moro mention in their novels the legend that Montenegro had all personal documents of her acting years burned by her assistants), we can only speculate about the nature of her relationship with the house of Balenciaga or believe third-party testimonies about her alleged friendship with the couturier. I tried to get more information about her connection with the fashion house at the Museo Balenciaga that would help me explain why Montenegro was so often dressed by the Basque couturier in her late films, but the curators told me there is no record of Balenciaga's specific involvement with the films I analyse.

5 We know it is a Balenciaga dress because of the information provided by Pedro Usabiaga. The film credits, though, do not mention any involvement of Balenciaga in the film, only the work of the costume designer, Julio Laffitte. As I explain later, this leads me to believe that this was a costume choice by Montenegro herself (or perhaps even a piece from her own wardrobe) instead of a commissioned job.

6 In fact, this comment applies to the whole film. The only close-up of Montenegro in *Ídolos* is of her shoes, as she walks up and down the stairs of production companies in Paris, desperately trying to get a film role. We are not even afforded a close-up of her face during the romantic moments she shares with Juan Luis.

7 Later in the film, in the sequences that attempt to provide an "authentic" representation of Spanish folk culture, there are many examples of static visual compositions – full of geometrical patterns serving as framing devices – that resemble altarpieces. Examples include a shot of female weavers creating the mantle to cover a statue of the Virgin for an Easter procession; several shots of the audience at a bullfight; a saturated visual composition of a flamenco performance; and a shot of a literal altarpiece with a sculpture of an image from Holy Week.

8 There is scarce evidence of the commercial run of the film. Box-office figures were not systematically collected in Spain until 1965, as the result of the *Ley de Control en las Taquillas* (1964), which José María García Escudero implemented as part of his new *política cinematográfica*, to document the impact of the new policies on the Spanish industry. Until then, the only data on the films' commercial success was the number of days and weeks they were shown in commercial theatres. Any film shown for longer than six weeks in Madrid theatres was considered a "película de éxito" (box-office hit) (Camporesi 81). According to the *Catálogo del cine español*, *Ídolos* was shown for eleven days at the Cine Alcázar in Barcelona, and an unknown number of days at the Cine Capitol in Madrid. While there is not enough data to draw a definitive conclusion, judging by its poor showing in Barcelona, it does not seem like the film came anywhere near the status of a box-office hit.

9   In fact, the critics all praised this aspect of the film. For example, the re-
     viewer for *Cámara* (issue 27, December 1943) raved about the meticulously
     crafted setting and cinematography, even as he lamented the absence of
     an actual bullfight sequence, which he assumes is "por el temor a caer en
     la españolada" (to avoid falling into the españolada trope). Along those
     lines, the reviewer of *Radiocinema* (issue 94, November 1943) speculates
     that the film's flaws in psychological characterization are the result of the
     excessive focus on providing a counter-image of national folklore, which
     he deems successful.

10 That same year, a biography by Enrique Moreno, *Lola Montes, Reina de
     Reyes* (1944), had spurred interest in the figure of Lola Montes in Spain.
     Actually, as part of the promotional campaign for the film, *Primer Plano*
     included an interview with Moreno in its issue 212 (5 November 1944),
     in which the biographer attested to the historical rigour of the film adap-
     tation. This is a rather interesting promotional trick, given that the film
     contains plenty of historical inaccuracies. For example, in *Radiocinema* 98
     (March 1944), director Antonio Román admitted that the initial sequence
     of the film, which takes place in Seville, is not historically accurate – the
     real-life Lola Montes never went to Spain.

11 According to fashion historian Hamish Bowles, the timing of Balenciaga's
     Infanta dresses collection was perfect. That same year the new political
     regime approved an international exhibition of masterworks retrieved
     from Spanish art institutions, including iconic paintings by El Greco, Mu-
     rillo, Velázquez, and Goya. The exhibition was held in Geneva with great
     success: it "had a potent effect on the Parisian haute couture, and the press
     was quick to note the resonances in Balenciaga's work" (35).

12 It is important to point out that this was not a fashionable dress but rather
     a costume for a dress party around the theme of Louis XIV. The fashionable
     dresses dubbed *Infanta* were not nearly as close to the Velázquez paintings.
     I am indebted to one of the anonymous reviewers for this observation.

13 The film's censorship file reveals the censors were not convinced that
     Lola could atone for her sins. One of the censors claimed that she was a
     heartless woman unworthy of the love of a Spanish officer and, therefore,
     should die violently (Coira 89).

14 The novel by Darío Fernández-Flórez that inspired this film is even more
     explicit, as it openly states that the women cannot survive on what they
     make as models, so they have to prostitute their bodies for rich male cli-
     ents (18). As we saw in the analysis of *Ídolos*, the profession of mannequin
     was neither a lucrative nor a respected career choice in the 1940s and
     1950s. Fátima Gil Gascón explains that it was considered a last resort for
     attractive women who could not make it in better-regarded careers in the
     entertainment business (97–8).

15 Balenciaga, like Poiret, had disdain for the advertising side of the fashion
    business. He only gave one interview in his entire career, and there are
    very few photographs of the couturier (Irvine 9). Also like Poiret, he was
    worried about his identity as an artist. Unlike his predecessor, though,
    this concern was not tied to the Romantic notion of the artist. Poiret re-
    garded himself "not as a mere artisan or someone who had to hawk his
    own wares, but instead, as a creator and a dreamer who pursued inspi-
    ration without regard for commercial considerations" (Troy 216). Balen-
    ciaga was less preoccupied with his artistic persona than with protecting
    the quality of the clothes he created. His clothes, and not himself, were
    his legacy.

16 The name of Paco's building refers to Mariano Fortuny (1871–1949), an-
    other celebrated Spanish designer. Among other accomplishments, For-
    tuny was famous for the creation, along with his wife Henriette Negrin, of
    the "Delphos gown": an intricately pleated silk dress made using a com-
    plex method of pleating that remained a secret throughout their career.

17 While there is no reliable data on ticket sales for this film, we have enough
    evidence to conclude that its marketing potential did not translate into
    commercial success. *Alta costura* was screened for a total of eleven days
    (Pérez Perucha 8), which is far from the six-week benchmark for a box of-
    fice hit.

18 The name of this garment refers to the capital of the Philippines, Manila,
    which was a Spanish colony from 1565 until 1898. *Mantones* "are large
    squares of between 80 and 180 centimetres that envelop the female body
    when folded diagonally" (Miller 42). Although actually made in China,
    they were imported through the Philippines to Spain once the trimmings
    were added. As Hamish Bowles documents, Manila shawls were initially a
    luxury garment for upper-class ladies, but they "eventually became an es-
    sential feature of flamenco dance dress, and of Sevillana costume, crossing
    the otherwise clearly defined class divide" (144).

19 Hamish Bowles notes that this dress ended up being one of his most iconic
    garments, and a grandiose coda to his career, as it successfully evoked
    "the glories of fifteenth-century Spanish court dress in its linear purity and
    restrained medieval embellishment" (32).

20 Balenciaga was obsessed with creating the perfect sleeve. He believed
    that "a sleeve should adhere to the body, be its natural extension, and fall
    without the slightest flaw." This was as much a matter of comfort as an
    aesthetic and technical benchmark, "as if the construction of the garment
    crystallized entirely around the sleeves" (Golbin 19). For Balenciaga, the
    sleeve was the ultimate test of a couturier's value and the most reliable
    proof of her or his technical expertise, commitment to achieving perfec-
    tion, and forward-looking vision.

21 In this sense, the star image crafted for Rocío Dúrcal was different from the one that the French film industry concocted for Brigitte Bardot in the late 1950s. Like Dúrcal, Bardot embodied a new kind of French youth that was also exportable, and she performed roles that emphasized vitality, enthusiasm, and mobility. Unlike Dúrcal, though, Bardot's "clothes were ostentatiously sexualized, carefully designed to show off her figure," which offered young women "a powerful fantasy of sexual liberation" (Vincendeau, "Hot Couture" 140, 144).

22 This was part of a bigger promotional campaign that, as with her debut film, *Canción de juventud* (Luis Lucia, 1962), entailed the sale of an array of merchandise aimed at generating interest in the rising star – including sticker albums, pennants, books, and all kinds of paper cut-outs (Aguilar 55).

23 There is evidence that Balenciaga actually contemplated emulating his disciples Courrèges and Ungaro, who developed very successful ready-to-wear collections. However, Balenciaga "felt it was too late for him to learn what was essentially a new métier" (Bowles 32).

2. Almodóvar and Chanel: High Fashion, Desire, and Identity

1 Alberto Mira speculates about these two birthdates and posits that, given that his first feature film, *Pepi, Luci, Bom y otras chicas del montón*, was released in 1980, Almodóvar probably made up the later date so that he could fit into the category of "young genius," which is typically reserved for artists who emerged when they are under thirty ("Life" 96).

2 See also Cerdán and Fernández Labayen for a thorough analysis of the complex patterns of reception of Almodóvar's films in Spain.

3 Diverging from the prevailing interpretation of the rape scenes in Almodóvar films, Leora Lev invites us to examine them as beyond binary categorizations of aggressor and victim. Lev analyses how the over-the-top staging of the rape scenes with grotesque and camp elements works to undercut any sense of *jouissance* and to invite viewers to reflect upon how the exploitation of sexual violence is used in contemporary media to satisfy the audience's appetite. In other words, Lev suggests that these rape scenes, as hard to watch as they are, force "viewers to acknowledge their own complicity in perpetuating ideologies and practices that enable rape culture and rape itself" (222).

4 Chanel introduced the quilted handbag in February 1955, which is why she named it the 2.55. This bag, which later became known as "the Mademoiselle lock," was made of soft leather that was "stitched over padding to create a soft quilted effect and was given the trademark shoulder straps of leather plaited with gilt chain, the same chain used to weight the suit linings" (de la Haye 84). The soft leather straps made it easy to carry, thus

becoming another Chanel piece that encapsulated her signature mix of luxury and comfort.

5 In fact, Coco Chanel was openly critical of the dismal effect she felt the "New Look" was having on women's fashion by bringing back the artifice that oppressed women's bodies. When asked specifically about Dior, she was quoted saying: "Dior? He doesn't dress women, he upholsters them" (Garelick 370). She often admitted in public that she came back from retirement to redeem women's fashion from the bad taste spread by the likes of Dior in her absence (Urrea 136–7).

6 Chanel often ridiculed Courrèges for his adoption of the "mini" and the "maxi" skirt, but she was simultaneously mocked by him. He jeered: "I'm the Ferrari, Chanel the old Rolls, still in working order but inert" (Madsen 300).

7 "No mujer, cómo voy a gastarme yo medio millón en un Chanel con la de hambre que hay por el mundo. Yo lo único que tengo de verdad son los sentimientos y los litros de silicona que me pesan como quintales."

8 As Jérôme Gautier documents, John Redfern and Paul Poiret made some timid advances in popularizing unisex fashion before her, but it was Chanel who convinced mainstream women that androgyny was not the opposite of femininity (196).

9 This gender savviness was a major ingredient of the recipe of her success. Chanel dethroned her contemporaries because she was able to interpret the changing zeitgeist of her times regarding gender roles. Chanel made women feel modern and emancipated, while her rivals kept dressing them as trophy wives. For example, Paul Poiret made fun of the Chanel philosophy of including a luxurious detail on an otherwise austere outfit by calling it "misérabilisme de luxe" (Madsen 117). Ironically enough, Poiret had been a pioneer in the pre-war years by making timid attempts to popularize the tomboy look for upper-class women, but he failed to take it to the next level. He allowed women to flirt with some superficial "masculine" aesthetic traits, while Chanel, by creating a fantasy of the male dandy distinction through her brilliant use of the "hidden luxury," made them feel like they actually had access to male privilege.

10 See Triana-Toribio (*Spanish Film Cultures* 69) for an interesting discussion about the way Pedro Almodóvar's cinema shows that he learned valuable lessons from both the Nuevo Cine Español and the Viejo Cine Español. From the former, Triana-Toribio asserts that he learned the importance of creating a name for himself abroad as an auteur with a unique visual style that became revered in the most respected film festivals (similar to the pedigree of authorship that Carlos Saura and Víctor Erice were able to attain). From the latter, Almodóvar borrowed the use of melodrama, comedy, and elements of popular culture enjoyed by mainstream audiences.

11 Matthew Marr also offers a positive reading of the verbal dimension of this film from the perspective of disability studies. According to Marr, the plethora of monologues, voiceover, and speeches in *Los abrazos rotos*, considered by some critics to be a flaw of the film, "can be read as an inscription of the blind experience onto the texture of the film." This pertains not only to the process of perception of Mateo, the male lead, but perhaps also to "the sensory experience of actual visually impaired viewers of *Los abrazos rotos* at large" (136).

12 For a study that examines in great depth how throughout his career, Almodóvar borrows narrative and stylistic elements of Hitchcock's films, but revises and recreates them as he pleases, see Dona Kercher.

13 For Paul Julian Smith, *Los abrazos rotos* "reveals Almodóvar's nostalgia for his own back catalogue," which leads him to wonder if Almodóvar has "finally run out of new ideas" after three decades of restless creativity ("*Los abrazos rotos*").

3. Men in Underwear in Spanish Cinema

1 To be completely fair, scholarly attention to underclothes has been fraught, in general. Fashion and dress historians have pointed out that "underwear is a highly charged form of clothing" in Western culture (Craik 119). Issues of shame and morality have dictated even the language used to refer to it: euphemisms such as "underpinnings" and "unmentionables" have been frequently employed to refer to what was supposed to remain unnamed. This uncomfortable relationship with underwear is, of course, more conspicuous when dealing with men's varieties.

2 I say "might" because I do not mean to fall in the reductionist trap of linking every underwear style change – and its cinematic representation – to a specific major political event or social transformation. Spanish films serve as a visual record of changing fashions in men's underwear and, in so doing, enrich their narratives with meanings that pertain to social and cultural transformations taking place in Spain. But as I will show in my analysis, this is not a simple story of progression from traditional to modern styles, or from unflattering and merely functional to stylish and sexy.

3 As Laura Antón Sánchez documents, the censorship board had requested that this scene be eliminated due to its erotic connotations (57), but Berlanga and the producers decided to ignore that request. This daring gesture was rather felicitous, since this banned scene brilliantly encapsulates the dissident humour in this dark comedy.

4 A more recent film that captivatingly pays tribute to this "underwear underdevelopment" as a sign of Iberian cultural inferiority at the end of the Franco period is *Torremolinos 73* (Pablo Berger, 2003). The film

follows Alfredo (Javier Cámara), a struggling encyclopedia salesman, as
he transforms himself to adjust to the demands of the capitalist market:
he becomes an actor and director in self-made amateur adult films along
with his wife Carmen (Candela Peña). Alfredo's physique (short, chubby,
and hairy), his name, and his unfashionable white cotton Y-front briefs
are meant to evoke the figure of Alfredo Landa and the Iberian macho of
the Spanish sex comedies. By contrast, Magnus, a sexy, tall, and blonde
Danish actor (played by international star Mads Mikkelsen) – who is in a
film directed by Alfredo that ends up including a sex scene – appears in
sensual black bikini briefs. Carmen takes advantage of the sex scene with
Magnus to get pregnant (because Alfredo is sterile). Berger dwells on the
humorous contrast between the men's bodies and underwear choices to
pay homage to the Iberian cultural inferiority expressed in the *landismo*
and *destape* films of the 1970s.

5 In the 1990s, fashion houses such as Chanel and Calvin Klein launched
   campaigns betting strongly on female underwear inspired by men's styles,
   which included spectacular runway shows as well as fashion spreads with
   A-list Hollywood stars such as Julia Roberts and Sharon Stone showcasing
   these models (Muñoz 88–91).
6 Willett and Cunnington explained in detail how men, much more than
   women, have used underwear as a way of highlighting class distinctions.
   The quality of the fabric of a given undergarment separated the wealthy
   gentleman from the working-class man (17).
7 Paul Jobling actually claims that this shift started earlier in the century, at
   least in the context of Great Britain. He compiled evidence of erotic advertising of men's undergarments in the interwar period (*Man Appeal* 121);
   some of the images had homoerotic and queer undertones, displaying
   eroticized men in their underwear from behind, calling attention to anal
   sexuality (132).
8 The question of the homoeroticism in *¡A mí la legión!* and *¡Harka!* has
   spurred some further debate lately. Diana Jorza points out that the melodramatic "emotional excess" of the films has been misread as homoerotic (57), while Brad Epps, following up on Pavlović (35), admits that
   the films lend themselves for a queer take, since they have some "lapses
   and gaps," but these "cannot be paradoxically made good or stabilized
   through appeals to homosexual subtexts and homoerotic situations"
   ("Impressions" 50).
9 The shift from undershirts to T-shirts did not actually originate in the
   movies. Instead, as Shaun Cole documents, it can be "attributed to naval
   adoption and adaption" by the US Navy, and starting in the late 1930s,
   this trend was commercialized by underwear brands (61). But sex appeal
   was not used to advertise undershirts until Hollywood popularized it in

the 1950s. This is why Elaine Benson and John Esten note that the "under-shirt was first lost, then reborn, in the movies" (62). In the 1930s, under-shirt production went on a downward spiral after Clarke Gable appeared without an undershirt in the romantic comedy *It Happened One Night* (1934). Two decades later, another male star brought the undershirt back and made it what Michael Ferguson wittily calls "a take-home fetish" (81).

10 Eloy de la Iglesia's *quinqui* films included *Navajeros* (1980), *Colegas* (1982), *El pico* (1983), *El pico II* (1984), and *La estanquera de Vallecas* (1987). José Antonio de la Loma also directed his own series of *quinqui* films: *Perros callejeros* (1977), *Perros callejeros II* (1979), *Los últimos golpes del Torete* (1980), and *Yo, el Vaquilla* (1985).

11 See Fouz-Hernández and Martínez-Expósito (187–212) for a comprehensive account of the representation (or lack thereof) of the penis in Spanish cinema.

12 Besides the underpants, Calvin Klein also launched three types of under-shirts (crew and V-neck T-shirts as well as alluring tank tops) in traditional white, olive drab, and grey. For some underwear historians, this reinvention of the classic white brief may be related to a desire to return to a classic, "authentic" type of masculinity to counteract the effects of the sexual revolution of the 1960s and 1970s (Cole 105).

13 The crucial role of underwear in this series of *quinqui* films is all the more apparent if we compare it with the series directed by José Antonio de la Loma. Coetaneous films such as *Perros callejeros* (1977) and *Perros callejeros II* (1979) focus on similar themes – youth disaffection, juvenile delinquency, and drug addiction – and include several scenes of its young star, El Torete (Ángel Fernández Franco), in his underwear; however, there is no signifying logic (he wears a variety of briefs in red, yellow, and black), nor any suggestion of the type of erotic deployment of underwear. Recent examinations of de la Loma's films, which form part of a broader "revival quinqui" (Florido Berrocal et al. xiv), have focused on the problematic depiction of sexuality and the blatant machismo of their male characters (Torres 79), who are driven by excessive, animalistic sexual desires that need to be tamed and neutralized (Martín-Cabrera, "Los quinquis" 122–3). However, critics have overlooked the important question of how the male body is represented, and the role of the recurrent images of men in underwear in those representations, which is, in my view, crucial to understanding the significant difference between these films and de la Iglesia's *quinqui* films.

14 Several critics have already noticed this overt association of Raúl's masculinity with the animal world, which is displayed "visually through the various matching shots established between him and two animals closely related to Spanish culture and gastronomy, the bull and the pig" (Fouz-Hernández and Martínez-Expósito 21; also in Evans 83).

15 Pedro Almodóvar's *La mala educación* (2004) does offer a twenty-first-century example of Y-front white briefs in an erotic scene between Enrique (Fele Martínez) and Ángel/Juan (Gael García Bernal). Ángel begins to disrobe so he can swim in Enrique's swimming pool. As he notices Enrique's desiring gaze in anticipation of his nude body, he decides to leave his underpants on, "thus interrupting Enrique's (and the audience's) visual pleasure at such a 'spectacle'" (Fouz-Hernández and Martínez-Expósito 211). When Ángel comes out of the pool, close-ups of his wet briefs increase the erotic tension of the sequence. As Almodóvar expresses in the script of the film: "Los genitales se le adhieren al calzoncillo mojado provocando un efecto más obsceno que si anduviera desnudo" (His genitals stick to the wet briefs, causing a more obscene effect than if he were naked) (87). Y-front briefs, once again, are used in Spanish cinema both to suggest and conceal the male genitals; to sexualize the male body while maintaining the mysticism of the phallus, to borrow again from Peter Lehman. Of course, Almodóvar's use of Y-front briefs in this scene is not an act of underwear nostalgia, so to speak; the scene is supposed to take place at some point during the early post-Franco years.

16 Interestingly, these contemporary "push-up" briefs are a nod to the past. As historian Denis Bruna has documented, during the sixteenth century, men's clothing for all social classes (from nobles to peasants) included the codpiece, which was "a pouch, quite visible, often stuffed and sewn to the crotch, aimed at highlighting the penis and simulating an erection" (51). This protuberance was also decorated, sometimes quite creatively, which further made the penis into "the central point of male dress," until the codpiece disappeared towards the end of the century (54).

17 One noticeable exception to this contemporary trend is the romantic comedy, a genre that is enjoying a commercial boom among Spanish audiences. These films typically feature men in crisis because of shifting patterns in gender relations and/or because of the deleterious effects of the economic recession in their lives. Interestingly, these comedies recurrently include scenes with male actors in somewhat-dated models of boxers, as in the cases of Dani Rovira in Emilio Martínez Lazaro's *Ocho apellidos vascos* (2014) and *Ocho apellidos catalanes* (2015), Hugo Silva in *Tenemos que hablar* (David Serrano, 2016), and Fele Martínez in *Nuestros amantes* (Miguel Ángel Lamata, 2016). The underwear scenes are always associated with moments of intense laughter, in which the male leads appear ridiculous (Rovira escaping through a balcony, Silva practising autoerotic asphyxiation). The unflattering underwear choices contribute to the comical effect and, given that their characters stand for traditional forms of masculinity that strive to regain a central position in society, their underwear also connects them to cinematic models of masculinity that seemed

extinct. In the formulaic universe of the contemporary romantic comedy, the return of the sagging boxers visually indicates the return of the Iberian macho in post-crisis Spain.

4. Dressing the Immigrant Other

1 According to Isolina Ballesteros, the hybrid nature of immigration films makes them hard to pin down formally; she considers them almost "unmappable" (*Immigration* 3). The deliberate blending of filmic conventions from several genres (drama, realist documentary, road movie, and so on) parallels the experiences of crossing borders, both physical and metaphorical, as well as the transnational relationships that are so central to these stories ("Female" 144).

2 It is suitable to point out that Spaniards themselves have been racialized in foreign productions in ways that arguably mirror those in which migrants are depicted in Spanish cinema. In the next chapter, I examine the prominent cases of Victoria Abril and Penélope Cruz, who had to find ways of negotiating their international profile to avoid being typecast in stereotypical roles (the hot exotic Latina, the passionate flamenco dancer, and so on) when they have joined the cast of Hollywood or European productions. As I will discuss, both have effectively deployed fashion performances such as red carpet looks and photo shoots to counteract the stereotyping effect that their film roles (especially through clichéd costuming) had on their star image.

3 Without focusing on costume, Eva Woods Peiró has demonstrated that this inscription of race into film is part of a long-standing tradition in Spanish cinema that Spanish film critics have somewhat overlooked. The early to mid-twentieth-century folkloric musical comedy films she analyses show how "the story of self and racialized other is a key structural component of Spanish mass entertainment" (xi).

4 Tim Edwards observes that men in Eastern and Asian cultures wear garments such as the shift or kaftan, developed from "the earlier and more unisex development of the tunic or dress which still influences women's fashion," to appear respectable and proper (*Fashion* 53).

5 The list of Spanish films featuring Caribbean female migrant characters in the second half of the 1990s and the 2000s, most of them in a leading role, include *Los hijos del viento* (Fernando Merinero, 1995), *Cosas que dejé en La Habana* (Manuel Gutiérrez Aragón, 1997), *En la puta calle* (Enrique Gabriel, 1997), *Flores de otro mundo* (Icíar Bollaín, 1999), *Sobreviviré* (Alfonso Albacete and David Menkes, 1999), *Adiós con el corazón* (José Luis García Sánchez, 2000), *I Love You Baby* (Alfonso Albacete and David Menkes, 2001), *La novia de Lázaro* (Fernando Merinero, 2002), *Reinas* (Manuel

Gómez Pereira, 2005), *Agua con sal* (Pedro Pérez-Rosado, 2005), *Princesas* (Fernando León de Aranoa, 2005), *Volver* (Pedro Almodóvar, 2006), *Forasters* (Ventura Pons, 2008), and *Mentiras y gordas* (Alfonso Albacete and David Menkes, 2009).

6 Going against the mainstream view that links sexuality to a life force or Eros, and more specifically to reproduction and the assurance of an imagined future (that is, to "heterofuturity"), Edelman draws attention to the value of non-reproductive pleasure and to a view of the sexual instinct as primarily self-destructive, selfish, and death-driven. Queers, located as they are outside the logic of reproduction, take "the place of the social order's death drive" (3). This is why queers constitute, politically speaking, a threat to the heterosocial order. In Lacanian terms, Edelman views the disruptive place of queers as an embodiment of the Real that fractures the Symbolic order's fantasy of stability from within (22). The sinthomosexuals, like Kyril – and, increasingly, Daniel – are film characters who embody this queer antisocial force that seeks perpetual *jouissance*, and therefore troubles the fantasy of stability and progress.

7 In fact, the opposite has been the case. Spanish film and media narratives increasingly portray citizens of the former Soviet bloc as hazards to Western European values and social structures, often involved with or in charge of drug cartels and prostitution rings. For instance, Kathleen Connolly has analysed the negative portrayal of Russians and Romanians as criminals in the television show *Mar de plástico* (2015–16), stating that they possess a "deficient whiteness, which endangers Spaniards" (148–9). One may find similar depictions of Eastern Europeans as associated with criminality in prominent television shows such as *La casa de papel* (2017–) and *La zona* (2017–18).

8 Even the films from this second phase can be taken to task for the shortcomings of their representations. Elsewhere, I have argued that they do not fully delve into the root causes of migration and overlook, for example, "the past and present economic and political intrusions from the North" among the "push" factors that generate migratory displacements. In my view, these films fall short in their commitment by failing to pinpoint "the structural causes of migration beyond the demonization of African governments," thus showing a lack of self-critical evaluation that would also hold European powers – including Spain – accountable for part of the problem ("Reframing" 219, 226).

9 Notably, Santiago Zannou has recently published an op-ed article in *El País* ("Una España"), apropos the social debates surrounding the George Floyd case and the Black Lives Matter movement, in which he demanded that Afro-Spaniards be given more visibility within the Spanish society. His point is well taken: there are many Afro-Spanish musicians, writers,

actors, directors (like himself), college professors, and so on. It is of crucial importance that their achievements are highlighted so that they can help change social perceptions and also provide valuable referents for future generations.

5. Self-Fashioning Stardom: The Red Carpet Matters

1 A remarkable example of this phenomenon is the dramatic change experienced by the Spanish actors on the Netflix teen drama series *Élite* (2018) within weeks. Some of the actors had already played major big-screen roles, such as María Pedraza in *Amar* (Esteban Crespo, 2017) and especially Miguel Herrán, who won Best New Actor at the Goya Awards for his work in *A cambio de nada* (Daniel Guzmán, 2015), going on to appear in major films such as *1898: Los últimos de Filipinas* (Salvador Calvo, 2016) and *El guardián invisible* (Fernando González Molina, 2017). Just a few weeks after the October 2018 release of *Élite*, however, they had become global stars. By early 2019, both of them had over four million followers on Instagram, which for Pedraza has materialized in profitable deals with fashion brands such as Cacharel, Aristocracy, Bulgari, and Lancôme.
2 Abril has bluntly expressed her resentment at having become a forgotten "chica Almodóvar." See, for example, her interviews for mainstream publications such *Vanity Fair* (López), *S Moda / El País* (Guerra), and *La Otra Crónica / El Mundo* (Pascual).
3 See Vicente Sánchez-Biosca for a discussion of how, when Spanish stars cross over to Hollywood, they are almost invariably restricted to playing the exotic Latina/o, normally with a Caribbean type in mind. With the sole exception of the myth of Carmen, the representation of Spanish stereotypes has not sparked much interest in Hollywood ("Latin Masquerade" 133).
4 The strategy worked fairly well. Although the film was not a major commercial success beyond Iceland, it received accolades at numerous international film festivals, including awards and nominations in Toronto, Locarno, Bogotá, Buenos Aires, and the European Film Awards.
5 A recent example occurred on the red carpet of the 2019 Goya Awards, where Cruz took the opportunity to praise the Iranian filmmaker Asghar Farhadi, director of the film *Todos lo saben* (2018), for which Cruz received the Best Actress nomination.
6 Prior to Casanova, Alejo Sauras played the gay teenager Santi in the popular TV series *Al salir de clase* (1997–2001).
7 Eduardo Casanova's latest film, the short *Lo siento mi amor* (2018), features Sara Rivero as Jackie Kennedy in a pink suit, a knock-off of the famous Chanel suit worn by the First Lady on the day her husband was

assassinated. Only the teaser has been released at the time of this writing, and it contains some of Casanova's signature ingredients: a pink-hued mise en scène in the context of violence and physical abnormalities (Jackie K. is having doggie-style sex with an extraterrestrial; at one point she picks up a rifle to shoot).

8 Casanova's complete statement was: "No me interesan nada la ropa ni la moda … Cuido mi imagen porque soy un personaje público, y además creo que desde la imagen se puede mantener un discurso y contar cosas, y lo único que pretendo con la ropa que me pongo es corporativismo y tener un discurso" (I am not interested in clothes or fashion. I take care of my image because I'm a public figure, and also because I believe that you can have a coherent narrative and tell a story through your image, so the only intentions behind the clothes I wear are corporate interests and having a point of view).

9 For example, in an interview with Antonio Sánchez for the Valencia-based newspaper *Levante: El Mercantil Valenciano*, Casanova was asked to give his opinion about the world of fashion, and he boldly declared: "No me interesa en absoluto. Creo que el mundo que rodea la moda es frívolo, y a mí no me gusta nada la frivolidad. Creo que el arte que plantea la moda puede ser muy superficial" (It doesn't interest me at all. I think the fashion world is frivolous, and I don't like frivolity. I think the type of art that fashion offers can be very superficial).

Filmography

Los abrazos rotos, dir. Pedro Almodóvar, prod. El Deseo/Universal Pictures International/Canal+, 2009.

Abre los ojos, dir. Alejandro Amenábar, prod. Canal+/Las Producciones del Escorpión/Les Films Alain Sarde/Lucky Red/Sogetel, 1997.

A cambio de nada, dir. Daniel Guzmán, prod. A cambio de nada/Canal Sur/Televisión/Canal+/El Niño Producciones/ICAA/La Competencia/La Mirada Oblicua/Luis Pérez Gil/Telefónica Estudios/TVE/The Spanish Ratpack/Ulula Films/ZircoZine, 2015.

Acompáñame, dir. Luis César Amadori, prod. Cámara Producciones Cinematográficas, 1966.

L'Addition, dir. Denis Amar, prod, Swanie Productions/TF1 Films Production/Union Générale Cinématographique, 1984.

Adiós con el corazón, dir. José Luis García Sánchez, prod. Alta Films/Antena 3 Televisión/Canal+, 2000.

Agua con sal, dir. Pedro Pérez Rosado, prod. Canal 9 Televisió Valenciana/Pérez Rosado Producciones/Televisió de Catalunya, 2005.

Alacrán enamorado, dir. Santiago Zannou, prod. Buziana/El Monje La Película AIE/Morena Films, 2013.

All About Eve, dir. Joseph Mankiewicz, prod. Twentieth Century Fox, 1950.

Alma gitana, dir. Chus Gutiérrez, prod. Samarkanda Cine-Video, 1996.

Alta costura, dir. Luis Marquina, prod. CIFESA, 1954.

Amantes, dir. Vicente Aranda, prod. Pedro Costa Producciones Cinematográficas/Televisión Española, 1991.

Amar, dir. Esteban Crespo, prod. Amar/Avalon/FILMEU/Netflix/Televisión Española, 2017.

¡A mí la legión!, dir. Juan de Orduña, prod. CIFESA, 1942.

A mi madre le gustan las mujeres, dir. Inés París and Daniela Fejerman, prod. Fernando Colomo Producciones Cinematográficas, 2002.

El amor brujo, dir. Carlos Saura, prod. Emiliano Piedra, 1986.

El amor brujo, dir. Francisco Rovira Beleta, prod. Exclusvas Floralva Producción/Films Rovira Beleta, 1967.

Amor de madre, dir. Eduardo Casanova, prod. Fobia Social, 2013.

Anastasia, dir. Anatole Litvak, prod. Twentieth Century Fox, 1956.

The Angel Wore Red, dir. Nunnally Johnson, prod. Titanus/Metro-Goldwyn-Mayer/Spectator, 1960.

Angst essen Seele auf (*Ali: Fear Eats the Soul*), dir. Rainer Werner Fassbinder, prod. Filmverlag der Autoren/Tango Film, 1974.

Ansiedad, dir. Eduardo Casanova, prod. Factor 78, 2009.

El apartamento de la tentación, dir. Julio Buchs, prod. Ízaro Films, 1971.

The Assassination of Gianni Versace: American Crime Story, dir. Ryan Murphy, prod. Color
 Force/Ryan Murphy Productions/FX Productions, 2018.

¡Átame!, dir. Pedro Almodóvar, prod. El Deseo, 1989.

Aventura, dir. Jerónimo Mihura, prod. CEPICSA, 1944.

Bahía de Palma, dir. Juan Bosch, prod. Este Films, 1962.

Bajarse al moro, dir. Fernando Colomo, prod. Ion Films/Lola Films/Televisión Española, 1989.

Belle Epoque, dir. Fernando Trueba, prod. Animatógrafo/Euroimages/Fernando Trueba Producciones Cinematográficas/Lolafilms/Sogepaq, 1992.

Blow, dir. Ted Demme, prod. Apostle/Avery Pix/New Line Cinema/Spanky Pictures, 2001.

Boda en el infierno, dir. Antonio Román, prod. Hércules Films, 1942.

Bodas de sangre, dir. Carlos Saura, prod. Emiliano Piedra, 1981.

Bwana, dir. Imanol Uribe, prod. Aurum/Creativos Asociados de Radio y Televisión/Origen Producciones cinematográficas, 1996.

Calé, dir. Carlos Serrano, prod. Carlos Serrano Producciones Cinematográficas, 1988.

La caliente niña Julieta, dir. Ignacio Iquino, prod. IFI Producción, 1981.

Cambio de sexo, dir. Vicente Aranda, prod. Impala/Morgana Films, 1977.

Canción de juventud, dir. Luis Lucia, prod. Procusa/Época Films, 1962.

Captain Corelli's Mandolin, dir. John Madden, prod. Universal Pictures/StudioCanal/Miramax/Working Title Films/Free Range Films/Canal+, 2001.

Carmen, dir. Carlos Saura, prod. Emiliano Piedra/TVE, 1983.

Carmen la de Ronda, dir. Tulio Demichelli, prod. Producciones Benito Perojo, 1959.

Carmen y Lola, dir. Arantxa Echevarría, prod. Comunidad de Madrid/ICAA/Orange S.A./Tvtec servicios audiovisuales, 2018.

Carne trémula, dir. Pedro Almodóvar, prod. El deseo/Ciby 2000/France 3 Cinéma, 1997.

Las cartas de Alou, dir. Montxo Armendáriz, prod. Elías Querejeta Producciones Cinematográficas/Televisión Española, 1990.

La casa de la lluvia, dir. Antonio Román, prod. Hércules Films, 1943.

La causa de Kripan, dir. Omer Oke, prod. Omer Oke, 2009.

Celos, amor y mercado común, dir. Alfonso Paso, prod. José Frade Producciones Cinematográficas, 1973.

Cinco almohadas para una noche, dir. Pedro Lazaga, prod. Aldebarán Films, 1974.

Colegas, dir. Eloy de la Iglesia, prod. Ópalo Films, 1982.

Combustión, dir. Daniel Calparsoro, prod. Antena 3 Films/Canal+, 2013.

Como dos gotas de agua, dir. Luis César Amadori, prod. Producciones Benito Perojo, 1963.

Cómo sobrevivir a una despedida, dir. Manuela Burló Moreno, prod. Nostromo Pictures/Antena 3 Films, 2015.

Con el viento solano, dir. Mario Camus, prod. Pro Artis Ibérica, 1966.

Cosas que dejé en La Habana, dir. Manuel Gutiérrez Aragón, prod. Canal+/Sogetel/Sogepac, 1997.

The Danish Girl, dir. Tom Hooper, prod. Working Title Films/Pretty Pictures/ReVision Pictures/Senator Global Productions/Dentsu/Fuji TV, 2015.

Del lado del verano, dir. Antonia San Juan, prod. Trece Producciones, 2012.

Los días de Cabirio, dir. Fernando Merino, prod. José Frade Producciones Cinematográficas, 1971.

El Dios de madera, dir. Vicente Molina Foix, prod. Canal 9 Televisió Valenciana/DC Media/Generalitat de Catalunya-Institut Catalá de les Indústries Culturals, 2010.

El diputado, dir. Eloy de la Iglesia, prod. Fígaro Films/Ufesa/Prozesa, 1978.

La distancia, dir. Iñaki Dorronsoro, prod. Ábaco Movies/MadridSur Producciones, 2006.

Dolor y gloria, dir. Pedro Almodóvar, prod. El Deseo/Canal+/TVE, 2019.

Eat My Shit, dir. Eduardo Casanova, prod. The Other Side Films, 2015.

En la puta calle, dir. Enrique Gabriel, prod. A.T.P.I.P. Producciones/Trastorno Films, 1997.

Esas chicas tan putas, dir. Ignacio Iquino, prod. Ignacio Ferrés Iquino (IFISA), 1982.

La estanquera de Vallecas, dir. Eloy de la Iglesia, prod. Compañía Iberoamericana de TV/Ega Medios Audiovisuales/Ministerio de Cultura, 1987.

La estrella vacía, dir. Enrique Gómez Muriel, prod. Producciones Corsa, 1960.

The Fall, dir. Tarsem Singh, prod. Googly Films/Absolute Entertainment/Deep Films, 2006.

Faraday, dir. Norberto Ramos del Val, prod. Apaches Entertainment/Norber Films, 2013.

Le femme et le pantin, dir. Jacques de Baroncelli, prod. Société des Cinéromans, 1929.

La flor de mi secreto, dir. Pedro Almodóvar, prod. CiBy 2000/El Deseo, 1995.

Flores de otro mundo, dir. Icíar Bollaín, prod. Producciones La Iguana/Alta Films, 1999.

Forasters, dir. Ventura Pons, prod. Els Films de la Rambla/Televisió de Catalunya (TV3)/2008.

Fray Torero, dir. José Luis Sáenz de Heredia, prod. Cesáreo González Producciones Cinematográficas, 1966.

Gazon maudit, dir. Josiane Balasko, prod. Canal+/Les Films Flam/Renn Productions/TF1 Films Productions, 1995.

El guardián invisible, dir. Fernando González Molina, prod. Nostromo Pictures/Atresmedia Cine/Nadcon Film/ Zweites Deutsches Fernsehen/ ARTE, 2017.

¡Harka!, dir. Carlos Arévalo, prod. CIFESA, 1941.

Las hijas de Helena, dir. Mariano Ozores, prod. José Frade Producciones Cinematográficas, 1963.

Los hijos del viento, dir. Fernando Merinero, prod. El Mecanismo Encantado, 1995.

Hola, ¿estás sola?, dir. Icíar Bollaín, prod. Canal+/Fernando Colomo Producciones Cinematográficas, 1995.

Ídolos, dir. Florián Rey, prod. CIFESA/Sevilla Films, 1943.

I Love You, Baby, dir. Alfonso Albacete and David Menkes, prod. Alquimia Cinema/Twentieth Century Fox, 2001.

It Happened One Night, dir. Frank Capra, prod. Columbia Pictures, 1934.

It's Complicated, dir. Nancy Meyers, prod. Unversal Pictures/Relativity Media/Waverly Films/Scott Rudin Productions/Dentsu, 2009.

Jamón, jamón, dir. Bigas Luna, Lola Films/Ovídeo TV/Sogepaq, 1992.

Jimmy Hollywood, dir. Barry Levinson, prod. Baltimore Pictures, 1994.

Kika, dir. Pedro Almodóvar, prod. El Deseo/Ciby 2000, 1993.

La ley del deseo, dir. Pedro Almodóvar, prod. El Deseo/Laurenfilm, 1987.

La leyenda del tiempo, dir Isaki Lacuesta, prod. De Palacio Films/Jaleo Films/ Mallerich Audiovisuales, 2006.

Lobo, dir. Miguel Courtois, prod. Castelao Producciones/Mundo Ficción, 2004.

Lola Montes, dir. Antonio Román, prod. Alhambra Films/Andalucía Films/ Astoria Films, 1944.

Loving Pablo, dir. Fernando León de Aranoa, prod. Escobar Films/B2Y Productions, 2017.

La lune dans le caniveau, dir. Jean-Jacques Beineix, prod. Gaumont/TF1 Films Productions/S.F.P.C./Opera Films Produzione, 1983.

La mala educación, dir. Pedro Almodóvar, prod. Canal+/El Deseo/ICAA, 2004.

Lo siento mi amor, dir. Eduardo Casanova, prod. Elora Post House/The Other Side Films, 2018.

Ma ma, dir. Julio Medem, prod. Ad hoc studios/Backup Media/Instituto del Crédito Oficial/ICAA/Ma ma Películas/Mare Nostrum Productions/ Morena Films/Movistar+/Televisión Española, 2015.

Mari del sud, dir. Marcello Cesena, prod. Cattleya/Medusa Film/Creativos Asociados de Radio y Televisión/The Producers Films, 2001.

Más bonita que ninguna, dir. Luis César Amadori, prod. Cámara Producciones Cinematográficas, 1965.

Matador, dir. Pedro Almodóvar, prod. Compañía Iberoamericana de Televisión/TVE, 1986.

Lo mejor de Eva, dir. Mariano Barroso, prod. AXN/Audiovisual Aval SGR/ Canal+, 2011.

Menos que cero, dir. Ernesto Tellería, prod. Cartel S.L/ Ikusmen, 1996.

Mentiras y gordas, dir. Alfonso Albacete and David Menkes, prod. Agrupación de Cine 001 AIE/Castafiore Films/Tornasol Films, 2009.

Midnight in Paris, dir. Woody Allen, prod. Mediapro/Versátil Cinema/Gravier Productions/TV3/Catalan Films & TV, 2011.

1898: Los últimos de Filipinas, dir. Salvador Cano, prod. 13 TV/CIPI Cinematográfica/ ICAA/TVE, 2016.

Les Misérables, dir. Tom Hooper, prod. Universal Pictures/Working Title Films/Cameron Mackintosh Ltd./Relativity Media, 2012.

Mi último Tango, dir. Luis César Amadori, prod. Producciones Benito Perojo/ Suevia Films, 1960.

Moros y Cristianos, dir. Luis García Berlanga, prod. Anem Films/Anola Films/ Estela Films, 1987.

La muchacha de las bragas de oro, dir. Vicente Aranda, prod. Films Zodiaco Prozesa/Morgana Films/Proa Cinematográfica, 1980.

Mujeres al borde de un ataque de nervios, dir. Pedro Almodóvar, prod. Laurenfilm/El Deseo, 1988.

Navajeros, dir. Eloy de la Iglesia, prod. Acuarius Films/Fígaro Films/ Producciones Fenix, 1980.

Never the Twain Shall Meet, dir. W.S. Van Dyke, prod. Metro-Goldwyn-Mayer (MGM), 1931.

Nicholas and Alexandra, dir. Franklin Shaffner, prod. Horizon Pictures II, 1971.

No Country for Old Men, dir. Ethan Coen and Joel Coen, prod. Paramount Vantage/Miramax/Scott Rudin Productions/Mike Zoss Productions, 2007.

North by Northwest, dir. Alfred Hitchcock, prod. Metro-Goldwyn-Mayer, 1959.

La novia de Lázaro, dir. Fernando Merinero, prod. Amanda Films/Vendaval Producciones, 2002.

Un novio para Yasmina, dir. Irene Cardona, prod. Tangerine Cinema Services/ Tragaluz Estudio de Artes Escénicas, 2008.

Los novios búlgaros, dir. Eloy de la Iglesia, prod. Altube Filmeak/Conexión Sur/Creativos Asociados de Radio y Televisión, 2003.

Nuestros amantes, dir. Miguel Ángel Lamata, prod. Ad hoc studios/BemyBaby Films, 2016.

Ocho apellidos catalanes, dir. Emilio Martínez Lázaro, prod Lazonafilms/Mogambo/Telecinco Cinema, 2015.

Ocho apellidos vascos, dir. Emilio Martínez Lázaro, prod. Lazonafilms/Kowalski Films/Snow Films, 2014.

101 Reykjavík, dir. Baltasar Kormákur, prod. Blueeyes Productions/Filmhuset As/Liberator Productions/Troika Entertainment GmbH/Zentropa Entertainments, 2000.

On the Line, dir. José Luis Borau, prod. Amber Films/El Imán Cine y Televisión, 1984.

Ópera prima, dir. Fernando Trueba, prod. Les Films Molière/Salamandra Producciones Cinematográficas, 1980.

Paquita Salas, dir. Javier Ambrossi and Javier Calvo, prod. DMNTIA, 2016–.

París-Tombuctú, dir. Luis García Berlanga, prod. Anola Films/Calabuch Films/Freedonia, 1999.

Paris When It Sizzles, dir. Richard Quine, prod. Richard Quine Productions/George Axelrod Productions, 1964.

Pecado de amor, dir. Luis César Amadori, prod. Cesáreo González Producciones Cinematográficas/Producciones Benito Perojo/Transmonde Film, 1961.

La pelota vasca, dir. Julio Medem, prod. Alicia Produce, 2003.

Pepi, Luci, Bom y otras chicas del montón, dir. Pedro Almodóvar, prod. Fígaro Films, 1980.

Perros callejeros, José Antonio de la Loma, prod. Films Zodíaco/Profilmes, 1977.

Perros callejeros II, José Antonio de la Loma, prod. Films Zodiaco/Prozesa, 1979.

El pico, dir. Eloy de la Iglesia, prod. Ópalo Films, 1983.

El pico II, dir. Eloy de la Iglesia, prod. Ópalo Films, 1984.

Pièges, dir, Robert Siodmak, prod. Spéva Films, 1939.

Pieles, dir. Eduardo Casanova, prod. Nadie es Perfecto/Pokeepsie Films, 2017.

Los placeres ocultos, dir. Eloy de la Iglesia, prod. Alborada P.C., 1977.

Princesa de África, dir. Juan Laguna, prod. Producciones Bereberia, 2008.

Princesas, dir. Fernando León de Aranoa, prod. Reposado Producciones/Mediapro/Antena 3 Televisión, 2005.

Prohibido enamorarse, dir. José Antonio Nieves Conde, prod. Arturo González Producciones Cinematográficas, 1961.

El puente, dir. Juan Antonio Bardem, prod. Arte 7, 1977.

La puerta de no retorno, dir. Santiago Zannou, prod. Shankara Films, Dokia Films, Canal+ España, 2011.

¿Qué he hecho yo para merecer esto?, dir. Pedro Almodóvar, prod. Kaktus Producciones Cinematográficas/Tesauro, 1984.

Querida Bamako, dir. Omer Oke and Txarli Llorente, prod. Abra Producciones, 2007.

¿Qué te juegas?, dir. Inés de León, prod. Ajedrez Para Tres/Alwin Films/Bowfinger International Pictures/Macaronesia Films/Movistar+, 2019.

Ready to Wear (Prêt-à-Porter), dir. Robert Altman, prod. Etalon Film/Miramax, 1994.

Rear Window, dir. Alfred Hitchcock, prod. Alfred J. Hitchcock Productions, 1954.

Rebel without a Cause, dir. Nicholas Ray, prod. Warner Bros, 1955.

Reinas, dir. Manuel Gómez Pereira, prod. Warner Bros/Lucky Red/Fortissimo Films, 2005.

Retorno a Hansala, dir. Chus Gutiérrez, prod. Maestranza Films/Muac Films, 2008.

El rey del mambo, dir. Carles Mira, prod. José Esteban Alenda, 1989.

Roberta, dir. William Seiter, prod. RKO Radio Pictures, 1935.

Rocío de la Mancha, dir. Luis Lucia, prod. Época Films/Procusa, 1963.

Rojo y negro, dir. Carlos Arévalo, prod. CEPICSA, 1942.

Rosa de Madrid, dir. Eusebio Fernández Ardavín, prod. Producciones Ardavín, 1927.

Segundo asalto, dir. Daniel Cebrián, prod. Aiete-Ariane Films/Canal+ España/Sogecine, 2005.

Señor, dame paciencia, dir. Álvaro Díaz Lorenzo, prod. Atresmedia Cine/Canal Sur Televisión/DLO Producciones/Maestranza Films/Suroeste Films, 2017.

El séptimo día, dir. Carlos Saura, prod. Lolafilms/Artédis/Televisión Española/Canal+, 2004.

Sin noticias de Dios, dir. Agustín Díaz Yanes, prod. Flamenco Films/Tornasol Films/Cartel Films/Telemadrid/Ensueño Films/DMVB Films/Evescreen/Vía Digital/Antena 3 Televisión/France 2 Cinéma/TPS Cinéma/Euroimages/TF1 International/Altavista Films, 2001.

Si te dicen que caí, dir. Vicente Aranda, prod. Ideas y Producciones Cinematográficas/Televisió de Catalunya, 1989.

Sobreviviré, dir. Alberto Albacete and David Menkes, prod. Antena 3 Televisión/Aurum Producciones/El Paso Producciones Cinematográficas, 1999.

Solo quiero caminar, dir. Agustín Díaz Yanes, prod. Canana Films/Boomerang Cine, 2008.

Sortilegio, dir. Agustín de Figueroa, prod. Agustín de Figueroa, 1927.

Stolen Holiday, dir. Michael Curtiz, prod. Warner Bros, 1937.

A Streetcar Named Desire, dir. Elia Kazan, prod. Charles Feldman Group/Warner Bros, 1951.

El sudor de los ruiseñores, dir. Juan Manuel Cotelo, prod, ITP, 1998.

Tacones lejanos, dir. Pedro Almodóvar, prod. Canal+/CiBy 2000/El Deseo, 1991.

Los Tarantos, dir. Francisco Rovira Beleta, prod. Tecisa/Films Rovira Beleta, 1963.

Tenemos que hablar, dir. David Serrano, prod. Atresmedia/Atípica Films/Canal + España, 2016.

Tengo ganas de ti, dir. Fernando González Molina, prod. Antena 3 Films/Zeta Audiovisual, 2012.

Testament of Orpheus, dir. Jean Cocteau, prod. Cinédis/Les Editions Cinégraphiques, 1960.

La tía Tula, dir. Miguel Picazo, prod. Eco-Surco, 1963.

Tiempo de silencio, dir. Vicente Aranda, prod. Lolafilms/Morgana Films/Televisión Española, 1986.

Tirant lo Blanc, dir. Vicente Aranda, prod. Carolina Films/DeAPlaneta/Feelmax/Future Film Group/Future Film Production/Future Films/Mikade Films, 2006.

Todo sobre mi madre, dir. Pedro Almodóvar, prod. El Deseo/Renn Productions/France 2 Cinéma, 1999.

Todos los saben, dir. Asghar Farhadi, prod. Memento Films/Morena Films/Lucky Red/France 3 Cinéma/Untitled Films/Rai Cinema/Ledafilms/Cineart/Canal+/Movistar+, 2018.

Topaz, dir. Alfred Hitchcock, prod. Universal Pictures/Alfred Hitchcock Productions, 1969.

Torremolinos 73, dir. Pablo Berger, prod. Estudios Picasso/Mama Films/Nimbus Film Productions, 2003.

El traje, dir. Alberto Rodríguez, prod. Canal+/Televisión Española/Tesela Producciones Cinematográficas, 2002.

La trastienda, dir. Jorge Grau, prod. José Frade Producciones Cinematográficas, 1976.

Tres metros sobre el cielo, dir. Fernando González Molina, prod. Antena 3/Canal+/Cangrejo Films/Cattleya/Generalitat de Catalunya/Globomedia/Instituto de Crédito Oficial/ICAA/La Sexta/Zeta Audiovisual, 2010.

El truco del manco, dir. Santiago Zannou, prod. Media Films/Televisión Española (TVE)/ Instituto de Crédito Oficial (ICO), 2008.

El último cuplé, dir. Juan de Orduña, prod. CIFESA, 1957.

Los últimos golpes del Torete, José Antonio de la Loma, prod. Cam España /Camera Rent/Films Zodiaco/Prozesa, 1980.

Unboxing, dir. Inés de León, prod. Freckles Films, 2016.

Vanilla Sky, dir. Cameron Crowe, prod. Paramount Pictures/Cruise-Wagner Productions/Vinyl Films/Sogecine/Summit Entertainment/Artisan Entertainment, 2001.

La vaquilla, dir. Luis García Berlanga, prod. In-Cine Compañía Industrial Cinematográfica/Jet Films, 1985.

Vente a Alemania, Pepe, dir. Pedro Lazaga, prod. Aspa ProduccionesCinematográficas/ Filmayer, 1971.

Venuto al mondo, dir. Sergio Castellitto, prod. Medusa Film/Alien Produzione/ Mod Producciones/Picomedia./Telecinco/Sky Cinema/Mediaset, 2012.

Los veraneantes, dir. Jorge Viroga, prod. Jorge Viroga/Maestranza Films/Orson the Kid, 2008.

La verbena de la paloma, dir. Benito Perojo, prod. CIFESA, 1935.

Lo verde empieza en los Pirineos, dir. Vicente Escrivá, prod. Filmayer, 1973.

El verdugo, dir. Luis García Berlanga, prod. Naga Films/Zebra Films, 1963.

Vertigo, dir. Alfred Hitchcock, prod. Alfred Hitchcock Productions, 1958.

Vicky Cristina Barcelona, dir. Woody Allen, prod. The Weinstein Company/ Mediapro/Gravier Productions/Antena 3 Films/Antena 3 Televisión/ Televisió de Catalunya, 2008.

La vida alegre, dir. Fernando Colomo, prod. El Catalejo, 1987.

La violetera, dir. Luis César Amadori, prod. Producciones Benito Perojo/Trevi Cinematográfica/Vic Film, 1958.

Vivan los novios, dir. Luis García Berlanga, prod. Cesáreo González Producciones Cinematográficas, 1970.

Volver, dir. Pedro Almodóvar, prod. Canal+/El Deseo/Ministerio de Cultura/ Televisión Española, 2006.

The Wild One, dir. Laslo Benedek, prod. Stanley Kramer Productions, 1953.

The Woman Who Brushed Off Her Tears, dir. Teona Strugar Mitevska, prod. Sister and Brother Mitevski/ Ostlicht Filmproduktion/Vertigo/Entre Chien et Loup/Luminary Media, 2012.

The Women, dir. George Cukor, prod. Metro-Goldwyn-Mayer, 1939.

X-Men: First Class, dir. Matthew Vaughn, prod. Twentieth Century Fox/ Marvel Entertainment/Dune Entertainment/Bad Hat Harry Productions/ Donners' Company/Ingenious Media/Big Screen Productions, 2011.

Yo, el Vaquilla, José Antonio de la Loma, prod. Golden Sun/Jet Films/In-Cine Compañía Industrial Cinematográfica, 1985.

Zhao, dir. Susi Gozalvo, prod. La Penúltima Producciones, 2008.

Works Cited

Abril, Victoria. www.victoria-abril.com.

Acevedo-Muñoz, Ernesto. *Pedro Almodóvar*. British Film Institute, 2007.

Agamben, Giorgio. *Homo Sacer: Sovereign Power and Bare Life*. Stanford University Press, 1998.

Agins, Teri. *Hijacking the Runway: How Celebrities Are Stealing the Spotlight from Fashion Designers*. Gotham Books, 2014.

Aguilar, José. *Rocío Dúrcal, volver a verte*. Madrid, Nuevos Escritores, 2007.

Alameda, Marta. "Premios Goya: Calentando motores." *Elle España*, www.elle.com/es. Accessed on 15 January 2019.

Allinson, Mark. *A Spanish Labyrinth: The Films of Pedro Almodóvar*. I.B. Tauris, 2001.

Almodóvar, Pedro. *Los abrazos rotos*. 2008. Biblioteca Nacional de España.

– *La mala educación*. Madrid, Ocho y Medio, 2004.

Alvares, Rosa, and Belén Frías. *Vicente Aranda/Victoria Abril: El cine como pasión*. Valladolid, Semana Internacional de Cine, 1991.

Amago, Samuel. *Spanish Cinema in the Global Context: Film on Film*. Routledge, 2013.

Antón Sánchez, Laura. *Disfraz y pasión creativa: La modernidad de la escritura en* El verdugo *(Luis García Berlanga, 1963)*. Madrid, Editorial Universitas, 2008.

Aparicio, Frances. "Ethnifying Rhythms, Feminizing Cultures." *Music and the Racial Imagination*, edited by Ronald Radano and Philip Bohlman, University of Chicago Press, 2000, pp. 95–112.

Appadurai, Arjun. *The Future as Cultural Fact: Essays on the Global Condition*. Verso, 2013.

Armero, Álvaro. *Una aventura americana: Españoles en Hollywood*. Madrid, Compañía Literaria, 1995.

Arranz, David Felipe. *Cine y Moda: ¡Luces, cámara, pasarela!*. Madrid, Grupo Editorial Sial Pigmalión, 2015.

Arzalluz, Miren. *Cristóbal Balenciaga: The Making of a Master (1895–1936)*. V&A
  Publishing, 2011.

– "Iconoclastic Visions of the Silhouette: Cristóbal Balenciaga." *Fashion Game
  Changers: Reinventing the 20th-Century Silhouette*, edited by Karen Van
  Godtsenhoven, Miren Arzalluz and Kaat Debo, Bloomsbury, 2016, pp. 33–81.

Avellaneda, Diana. *Debajo del vestido y por encima de la piel ... Historia de la ropa
  interior femenina*. Buenos Aires, Nobuko, 2007.

Balda, Ana. "Two Views on the Popular Costume." *Coal and Velvet: Views
  on the Popular Costume*, edited by Ana Balda Arana, Guetaria, Fundación
  Cristóbal Balenciaga, 2016, pp. 53–72.

Ballesteros, Isolina. *Cine (ins)urgente: Textos fílmicos y contextos culturales de la
  España postfranquista*. Madrid, Editorial Fundamentos, 2001.

– "Embracing the Other: The Feminization of Spanish Immigration Cinema."
  Studies in Hispanic Cinemas vol. 2, no. 1, 2005, pp. 3–14.

– "Female Transnational Migrations and Diasporas in European
  "Immigration Cinema." *Exile through a Gendered Lens: Women's Displacement
  in Recent European History, Literature, and Cinema*, Palgrave, 2012, pp. 143–68.

– "Foreign and Racial Masculinities in Contemporary Spanish Film." *Studies
  in Hispanic Cinemas* vol. 3, no. 3, 2006, pp. 169–85.

– *Immigration Cinema in the New Europe*. Intellect, 2015.

– Performing Identities in the Cinema of Pedro Almodóvar." *All About
  Almodóvar: A Passion for Cinema*, edited by Brad Epps and Despina
  Kakoudaki, University of Minnesota Press, 2009, pp. 71–100.

Balmaceda, María José. *La moda femenina en el París de entreguerras:
  Las diseñadoras Coco Chanel y Elsa Schiaparelli*. Barcelona, Ediciones
  Internacionales Universitarias, 1996.

Barnard, Malcom. *Fashion as Communication*. Routledge, 1996.

– *Fashion Theory: An Introduction*. Routledge, 2014.

Barthes, Roland. *The Fashion System*. University of California Press, 1990.

– *The Language of Fashion*. Bloomsbury, 2013.

– *Mythologies*. Hill and Wang, 1972.

Bas, Borja. "Eduardo Casanova: Nunca nadie me ha parado." *El País* 8 June
  2017, www.elpais.com/elpais/2017/06/02/icon/1496413147_020893.html.

Baudot, François. *Chanel*. Universe Publishing, 1996.

Bayo, Juan, Álex Navarro, and Roberto Olcina. *Vestir los sueños: Figurinistas del
  cine español*. Valladolid, Semana Internacional de Cine de Valladolid, 2007.

Beauvoir, Simone de. *The Second Sex*. Vintage Books, 1974.

Belloir, Véronique. "The Choice of Black." *Balenciaga in Black*, edited by
  Véronique Belloir et al., Rizzoli Electa, 2018, pp. 12–17.

Bellos Caballero, Juan Antonio. "De la cantante pop a la gran dama. *Tacones
  lejanos 1991*." *Las películas de Almodóvar*, edited by Antonio Castro, Madrid,
  Ediciones JC, 2010, pp. 135–54.

Belluscio, Marta. *Vestir a las estrellas: La moda en el cine*. Barcelona, Ediciones B, 1999.

Benet, Vicente. *El cine español: Una historia cultural*. Barcelona, Paidós, 2012.

Benjamin, Walter. *The Arcades Project*. Harvard University Press, 2002.

Benson, Elaine, and John Esten. *A Brief History of Unmentionables*. Simon & Schuster, 1996.

Berg, Angelika, and Regine Engelmeier. "Design or No Design: Costume Designers and Couturiers in the Great Days of Hollywood." *Fashion in Film*, edited by Regine and Peter W. Engelmeir, Munich, Prestel, 1990, pp. 18–21.

Bergler, Edmund. *Fashion and the Unconscious*. International Universities Press, 1992.

Bermúdez, Silvia. *Rocking the Boat: Migration and Race in Contemporary Spanish Music*. University of Toronto Press, 2018.

Bernecker, Walter. "The Change in Mentalities during the Late Franco Regime." *Spain Transformed: The Late Franco Dictatorship, 1959–1975*, edited by Nigel Townson, Palgrave Macmillan, 2010, pp. 67–84.

Berry, Sarah. *Screen Style: Fashion and Femininity in the 1930s Hollywood*. University of Minnesota Press, 2000.

Bhabha, Homi. *The Location of Culture*. Routledge, 1994.

Blume, Mary. *The Master of Us All: Balenciaga, His Workrooms, His World*. Farrar, Straus and Giroux, 2013.

Bond, David. *Coco Chanel y Chanel*. Zaragoza, Edelvives, 1995.

Bordo, Susan. *The Male Body: A New Look at Men in Public and Private*. Farrar, Straus and Giroux, 1999.

Bou, Núria, and Xavier Pérez. "La destrucción de una sex symbol: Conchita Montenegro." *El cuerpo erótico de la actriz bajo los fascismos: España, Italia, Alemania (1939–1945)*, edited by Núria Bou and Xavier Pérez, Madrid, Cátedra, 2018, pp. 41–53.

Bourdieu, Pierre. *Distinction: A Social Critique of the Judgement of Taste*. Routledge, 1984.

Bowles, Hamish. *Balenciaga and Spain*. Skira Rizzoli/Fine Arts Museums of San Francisco, 2011.

Boyogueno, Simplice. "El proceso de construcción de la otredad en *Las voces del Estrecho* y *Las cartas de Alou*." *Memoria colonial e inmigración: La negritud en la España postfranquista*, edited by Rosalía Cornejo Parriego, Barcelona, Edicions Bellaterra, 2007, pp. 167–89.

Bradshaw, Peter. "Cannes Film Festival Review: Almodóvar's Broken Embraces Reels You In." *The Guardian*, 19 May 2009. www.guardian.co.uk. Accessed on 6 May 2010.

Branche, Jerome. *Colonialism and Race in Luso-Hispanic Literature*. University of Missouri Press, 2006.

Breward, Christopher. *The Hidden Consumer: Masculinities, Fashion and the City Life 1860–1914*. Manchester University Press, 1999.

Brownmiller, Susan. *Femininity*. Paladin, 1984.

Bruna, Denis. "Falsity and Pretense: Stuffed Codpieces." *Fashioning the Body: An Intimate History of the Silhouette*, edited by Denis Bruna, Bard Graduate Center/Yale University Press, 2015, pp. 51–5.

Bruzzi, Stella. "Gregory Peck: An Anti-Fashion Icon." *Fashioning Film Stars: Dress, Culture, Identity*, edited by Rachel Moseley, British Film Institute, 2005, pp. 39–49.

– "The Pink Suit." *Fashion Cultures Revisited*, edited by Stella Bruzzi and Pamela Church Gibson, Routledge, 2013, pp. 234–48.

– *Undressing Cinema: Clothing and Identity in the Movies*. Routledge, 1997.

Bruzzi, Stella, and Pamela Church Gibson, editors. *Fashion Cultures: Theories, Explorations and Analysis*. Routledge, 2000.

Buchanan, Tom. "How 'Different' Was Spain? The Later Franco Regime in International Context." *Spain Transformed: The Late Franco Dictatorship, 1959–1975*, edited by Nigel Townson, Palgrave Macmillan, 2010, pp. 85–96.

Burkhart, Diana. "The Disposable Immigrant: The Aesthetics of Waste in *Las cartas de Alou*." *Journal of Spanish Cultural Studies* vol. 11, no. 2, 2010, pp. 153–65.

Butchart, Amber. *The Fashion of Film: How Cinema Has Inspired Fashion*. Mitchell Beazley, 2016.

Butler, Judith. "Endangered/Endangering: Schematic Racism and White Paranoia." *Reading Rodney King, Reading Urban Uprising*, edited by Robert Gooding-Williams, Routledge, 1993, pp. 15–22.

Byrne, Barry. "Broken Embraces (*Los Abrazos Rotos*)." *Screen Daily* 19 May 2009. www.screendaily.com/features/broken-embraces-los-abrazos -rotos/4043655.article. Accessed on 6 May 2010.

Caldwell, Doreen. *And All Was Revealed: Ladies' Underwear 1907–1980*. St. Martin's Press, 1981.

Calefato, Patrizia. *The Clothed Body: Dress, Body, Culture*. Oxford: Berg, 2004.

– editor. *Moda y cine*. Valencia, Engloba, 2002.

Cámara. "El veraneo de Conchita Montenegro." 24, 1943, n.p.

Cámara. 27, 1943, n.p.

Camporesi, Valeria. *Para grandes y chicos: Un cine para todos los españoles (1940–1990)*. Madrid, Ediciones Turfan, 1993.

Carter, Alison. *Underwear: The Fashion History*. Dram Book Publishers, 1992.

Castillo, Silvia, and Xescu Prats. "100 prendas icono de la moda en el cine." *Cine y Moda: ¡Luces, cámara, pasarela!*, edited by David Felipe Arranz, Madrid, Grupo Editorial Sial Pigmalión, 2015, pp. 99–159.

Cerdán, Josetxo, and Miguel Fernández Labayen. "Almodóvar and Spanish Patterns of Film Reception." *A Companion to Pedro Almodóvar*, edited by Marvin D'Lugo and Kathleen Vernon, Wiley-Blackwell, 2013, pp. 129–52.

Cervulle, Maxime. "Looking into the Light: Whiteness, Racism and Regimes of Representation." Introductory essay to *White*, by Richard Dyer, Routledge, 2017, pp. xiii–xxxii.

Charles-Roux, Edmonde. *Descubriendo a Coco Chanel*. Barcelona, Lumen, 2009.

Church Gibson, Pamela. "Brad Pitt and George Clooney, the Rough and the Smooth: Male Costuming in Contemporary Hollywood." *Fashioning Film Stars: Dress, Culture, Identity*, edited by Rachel Moseley, British Film Institute, 2005, pp. 62–74.

– *Fashion and Celebrity Culture*. London: Berg, 2012.

– "Film Costume." *The Oxford Guide to Film Studies*, edited by John Hill and Pamela Church Gibson, Oxford University Press, 1998, pp. 36–42.

Cine Asesor. "Alta costura." 675, 1954.

Coira, Pepe. *Antonio Román: Un cineasta de la posguerra*. Madrid, Editorial Complutense, 2004.

Cole, Shaun. *The Story of Men's Underwear*. Parkstone International, 2010.

Collado Becerra, Noemí. *Cristóbal Balenciaga 1914–1968: La excelencia en la Alta Costura*. Madrid, Editorial Dykinson, 2015.

Comas, Ángel. *El star system del cine español de posguerra (1939–1945)*. Madrid, T&B Editores, 2004.

Connolly, Kathleen. "*Mar de plástico*: Masculinity, Whiteness, and Eastern European Migrants in Spanish Prime Time Television." *Transmodernity* vol. 8, no. 2, 2018, pp. 138–56.

Cook, Pam. *Fashioning the Nation: Costume and Identity in British Cinema*. British Film Institute, 1996.

– "Revisiting Performance: Nicole Kidman's Enactment of Stardom." *Revisiting Star Studies*, edited by Sabrina Quiong Yu and Guy Austin, Edinburgh University Press, 2017, pp. 25–44.

Corbalán, Ana. "Questioning Cultural Hybridity: Perceptions of Latin American Immigration in Contemporary Spanish Cinema." *Collapse, Catastrophe, and Rediscovery: Spain's Cultural Panorama in the Twenty First Century*, edited by Jennifer Brady, Ibón Izurieta, and Ana María Medina, Cambridge Scholars Publishing. 2014, pp. 75–93.

– "Searching for Justice in *Return to Hansala* by Chus Gutiérrez: Cultural Encounters between Africa and Europe." *African Immigrants in Contemporary Spanish Texts: Crossing the Straits*, edited by Debra Faszer McMahon and Victoria Ketz. Farham, Ashgate Publishing, 2015, pp. 99–113.

Corkill, David. "Race, Immigration and Multiculturalism in Spain." *Contemporary Spanish Cultural Studies*, edited by Barry Jordan and Rikki Morgan-Tamosunas, Arnold, 2000, pp. 48–57.

Cornejo Parriego, Rosalía. "Introducción: De la mirada colonial a las diferencias combinables." *Memoria colonial e inmigración: La negritud en la España postfranquista*, edited by Rosalía Cornejo Parriego, Barcelona, Edicions Bellaterra, 2007, pp. 17–35.

Craig, Maxine Leeds. *Ain't I a Beauty Queen? Black Women, Beauty, and the Politics of Race*. Oxford University Press, 2002.

Craik, Jennifer. *The Face of Fashion: Cultural Studies in Fashion*. Routledge, 1994.

Crane, Diana. *Fashion and Its Social Agendas: Class, Gender, and Identity in Clothing*. University of Chicago Press, 2000.

Danesi, Marcel. *Of Cigarettes, High Heels, and Other Interesting Things: An Introduction to Semiotics*. Palgrave, 2008.

Dapena, Gerard. "Making Spain Fashionable: Fashion and Design in Pedro Almodóvar's Cinema." *A Companion to Pedro Almodóvar*, edited by Marvin D'Lugo and Kathleen Vernon, Blackwell, 2013, pp. 495–523.

Davies, Ann. *Pedro Almodóvar*. Grant & Cutler, 2007.

– *Penélope Cruz*. British Film Institute/Palgrave Macmillan, 2014.

Debord, Guy. *The Society of the Spectacle*. Zone Books, 1995.

de la Haye, Amy. *Chanel: Couture and Industry*. V&A Publishing, 2011.

Delbourg-Delphis, Marylène. *Le chic et le look: Histoire de la mode fémenine et des mœurs de 1850 à nos jours*. Paris, Hachette, 1981.

Delgado, Alicia. "'Pieles': Eduardo Casanova habla de su primera película como director." *SensaCine.com* 7 July 2016. www.sensacine.com/noticias /cine/noticia-18543634/.

Delgado, Elena. "La nación deseada: Europeización, diferencia y la utopía de (las) España(s)." *From Stateless Nations to Postnational Spain/De naciones sin Estado a la España postnacional*, edited by Silvia Bermúdez, Antonio Cortijo, and Timothy McGovern, Society of Spanish and Spanish-American Studies, 2002, pp. 207–21.

Delis Hill, Daniel. *History of Men's Underwear and Swimwear*. DanielDelisHill .com, 2011.

Del Río Gabiola, Irune. "Re/Indagación al choteo: Sujetos cubanos en el cine español contemporáneo." *Cinema Paraíso: Representaciones e imágenes audiovisuales en el Caribe Hispano*, edited by Rosana Díaz-Zambrana and Patricia Tomé. San Juan, Editorial Isla Negra, 2010, pp. 86–103.

Deveny, Thomas. *Migration in Contemporary Hispanic Cinema*. Scarecrow Press, 2012.

Díaz-Marcos, Ana María. *La edad de seda: representaciones de la moda en la literatura española (1728–1926)*. Universidad de Cádiz, 2006.

D'Lugo, Marvin. "*Los abrazos rotos/Broken Embraces* (Pedro Almodóvar, 2009): Talking Cures." *Spanish Cinema 1973–2010: Auterism, Politics, Landscape and Memory*, edited by María Delgado and Robin Fiddian, Manchester University Press, 2013, pp. 212–25.

– *Pedro Almodóvar*. University of Illinois Press, 2006.

D'Lugo, Marvin, and Kathleen Vernon. "Introduction: The Skin He Lives in." *A Companion to Pedro Almodóvar*, Wiley-Blackwell, 2013, pp. 1–17.

Donapetry, María. "Cinematernidad." *La mujer en la España actual: ¿Evolución o involución?*, edited by Jacqueline Cruz and Barbara Zecchi, Barcelona, Icaria, 2004, pp. 373–94.

Dyer, Richard. *Heavenly Bodies: Film Stars and Society*. Routledge, 2004.

– *Stars*. British Film Institute, 1998.

– *White*. Routledge, 2017.

Dyhouse, Carol. *Glamour: Women, History, Feminism*. Zed Books, 2011.

Ebert, Roger. "Ready to Wear (Prêt-à-porter)." 25 December 1994. www .rogerebert.com/reviews/ready-to-wear-pr%C3%AAt-%C3%A0-porter-1994.

Edelman, Lee. *No Future: Queer Theory and the Death Drive*. Duke University Press, 2004.

Edwards, Tim. *Fashion in Focus: Concepts, Practices and Politics*. Routledge, 2011.

– *Men in the Mirror: Men's Fashion, Masculinity and Consumer Society*. Cassell, 1997.

Egea, Juan. *Dark Laughter: Spanish Film, Comedy, and the Nation*. University of Wisconsin Press, 2013.

Egginton, William. *The Theater of Truth: The Ideology of (Neo) Baroque Aesthetics*. Stanford University Press, 2010.

Ellis, John. "Stars as a Cinematic Phenomenon." *Stardom and Celebrity: A Reader*, edited by Sean Redmond and Su Holmes, Sage, 2007, pp. 90–7.

Engelmeier, Regine and Peter W. *Fashion in Film*. Munich: Prestel, 1990.

Entwistle, Joanne. *The Fashioned Body: Fashion, Dress and Modern Social Theory*. Polity, 2000.

Epps, Brad. "Askance, athwart, aside: the queer plays of actors, auteurs and machines." *Performance and Spanish Film*, edited by by Dean Allbritton, Alejandro Melero Salvador, and Tom Whittaker, Manchester University Press, 2016, pp. 122–41.

– "Impressions of Africa: Desire, Sublimation and Looking 'Otherwise' in Three Spanish Colonial Films." *Spanish Erotic Cinema*, edited by Santiago Fouz-Hernández, Edinburgh University Press, 2017, pp. 37–54.

Evans, Caroline. "The Walkies: Early French Fashion Shows as a Cinema of Attractions." *Fashion in Film*, edited by Adrienne Munich, Indiana University Press, 2011, pp. 110–34.

Evans, Caroline, and Minna Thornton. "Fashion, Representation and Femininity." *Feminist Review* 38, no. 1, 1991, pp. 48–66.

Evans, Peter William. *Bigas Luna: Jamón, jamón*. Barcelona, Paidós, 2004.

– "Victoria Abril: The Sex Which Is Not One." *Constructing Identity in Contemporary Spain: Theoretical Debates and Cultural Practices*, edited by Jo Labanyi, Oxford University Press, 2002, pp. 128–37.

Ewing, Elizabeth. *Dress and Undress: A History of Women's Underwear*. B.T. Batsford, 1978.

Faiers, Jonathan. *Dressing Dangerously: Dysfunctional Fashion in Film*. Yale University Press, 2013.

Fanés, Félix. *CIFESA, la antorcha de los éxitos*. Valencia: Institución Alfonso El Magnánimo, 1982.

Faulkner, Sally. *A Cinema of Contradiction: Spanish Film in the 1960s*. Edinburgh University Press, 2006.

Ferguson, Michael. *Idol Worship: A Shameless Celebration of Male Beauty in the Movies*. STARbooks Press, 2005.

Fernández Flores, Concepción. "Secretos de seda y encaje: la sensual sugerencia en el vestir interior." *Moda y sociedad: Estudios sobre: Educación, lenguaje e historia del vestido*, edited by Emilio García Wiedemann and María Isabel Montoya Ramírez, Universidad de Granada, 1998, pp. 261–71.

Fernández-Flórez, Darío. *Alta costura (Las máscaras de la moda)*. Esplugat de Llobregat, Ediciones G.P., 1975.

Figueras, Josefina. *Moda española: Una historia de sueños y realidades*. Madrid, Ediciones Internacionales Universitarias, 2011.

– *Protagonistas de la moda*. Madrid, Ediciones Internacionales Universitarias, 2005.

Fleetwood, Nicole. *Troubling Vision: Performance, Visuality, and Blackness*. University of Chicago Press, 2011.

Flesler, Daniela. "New Racism, Intercultural Romance, and the Immigration Question in Contemporary Spanish Cinema." *Studies in Hispanic Cinemas* vol. 1, no. 2, 2004, pp. 103–18.

– *The Return of the Moor: Spanish Responses to Contemporary Moroccan Immigration*. Purdue University Press, 2008.

Florido Berrocal, Joaquín et al, editors. *Fuera de la ley: asedios al fenómeno quinqui en la Transición española*. Granada, Editorial Comares, 2015.

Flügel, J.C. *The Psychology of Clothes*. Hogarth Press, 1950.

Fontanel, Béatrice. *Support and Seduction: The History of Corsets and Bras*. Harry N. Abrams, 1997.

Fouz-Hernández, Santiago. *Cuerpos de cine: Masculinidades carnales en el cine y la cultura popular contemporáneos*. Barcelona, Bellaterra, 2013.

Fouz-Hernández, Santiago, and Alfredo Martínez-Expósito. *Live Flesh: The Male Body in Contemporary Spanish Cinema*. I.B. Tauris, 2007.

France, Louise. "Interview: Pedro Almodóvar and Penélope Cruz ... the mentor and the muse." *The Guardian* 22 August 2009. www.theguardian.com/film/2009/aug/23/almodovar-cruz-film-interview.

Fritz Haug, Wolfgang. *Critique of Commodity Aesthetics: Appearance, Sexuality and Advertising in Capitalist Society*. Polity Press, 1986.

Gaines, Jane. "Costume and Narrative: How Dress Tells the Woman's Story." *Fabrications: Costume and the Female Body*, edited by Jane Gaines and Charlotte Herzog, Routledge, 1990, pp. 180–211.

Gaines, Jane, and Charlotte Herzog, editors. *Fabrications: Costume and the Female Body*. Routledge, 1990.

Ganeva, Mila. *Women in Weimar Fashion: Discourses and Displays in German Culture, 1918–1933*. Camden House, 2008.

Garber, Steve. "The European Union and the Racialization of Immigration, 1985–2006." *Race/Ethniticy: Multidisciplinary Global Contexts* vol. 1, no. 1, 2007, pp. 61–87.

Garcés, Marcela. "The Shortcomings of Simulacra: Fragments of the Past in Pedro Almodóvar's *Broken Embraces*." *Océanide* 5, 2013. www.oceanide.es /index.php/012020/article/view/10/59.

García Carrión, Marta. *Sin cinematografía no hay nación: Drama e identidad nacional española en la obra de Florián Rey*. Zaragoza, Colección de Letras, 2007.

García de Dueñas, Jesús. *¡Nos vamos a Hollywood!* Madrid, Nickel Odeón, 1993.

Garelick, Rhonda. *Madamemoiselle Coco Chanel and the Pulse of History*. Random House, 2014.

Garlinger, Patrick. "All about Agrado, or the Sincerity of Camp in Almodóvar's *Todo sobre mi madre*." *Journal of Spanish Cultural Studies* vol. 5, no. 1, 2004, pp. 117–34.

Garrudo, Roberto. "Conoce la historia de las zapatillas de esparto." www. robertogarrudo.com/blog/zapatillas-de-esparto.

Gautier, Jérôme. *Chanel: The Vocabulary of Style*. Yale University Press, 2011.

Gavarrón, Lola. *Piel de ángel: Historias de la ropa interior femenina*. Barcelona, Tusquets, 1982.

Geraghty, Christine. "Re-Examining Stardom: Questions of Texts, Bodies and Performance." *Stardom and Celebrity: A Reader*, edited by Sean Redmond and Su Holmes, Sage, 2007, pp. 98–110.

Gil Gascón, Fátima. *Españolas en un país de ficción: La mujer en el cine franquista (1939–1963)*. Sevilla, Comunicación Social, 2011.

Gilroy, Paul. "Migrancy, Culture and a New Map of Europe." *Blackening Europe: The African American Presence*, edited by Heike Raphael-Hernandez, Routledge, 2004, pp. xi–xxii.

Golbin, Pamela. *Balenciaga in Paris*. Thames & Hudson, 2006.

Gregori, Antoni. *El cine español según sus directores*. Madrid, Cátedra, 2009.

Gregorio Gil, Carmen. *Migración femenina: Su impacto en las relaciones de género*. Madrid, Narcea Ediciones, 1998.

Grosfoguel, Ramón, Margarita Cervantes-Rodríguez, and Eric Mielants. "Introduction." *Caribbean Migrations to Western Europe and the United States: Essays on Incorporation, Identity, and Citizenship*, edited by Margarita Cervantes-Rodríguez, Ramón Grosfoguel, and Eric Mielants, Temple University Press, 2009, pp. 1–17.

Guarinos, Virginia. "Un conflicto de género: La representación de la mujer americana en el cine español de hoy." *Actas del I Congreso Iberoamericano*

"El Futuro de la Comunicación," edited by Antonio Checa Godoy and Ana Fernández Lamas, Seville, Universidad de Sevilla-Fundación El Monte (CD ROM edition), 2004.

Guerra, María. "Victoria Abril: Almodóvar no me quiere desde hace 20 años." *S Moda*, 26 March 2016.

Gundle, Stephen. *Glamour: A History*. Oxford University Press, 2008.

Gundle, Stephen, and Clino T. Castelli. *The Glamour System*. Palgrave Macmillan, 2006.

Gutiérrez-Albilla, Julián Daniel. "Becoming a Queer (M)Other in/and /through Film: Transsexuality, Trans-subjectivity, and Maternal Relationality in Almodóvar's *Todo sobre mi madre*." *A Companion to Spanish Cinema*, edited by Jo Labanyi and Tatjana Pavlović, Wiley-Blackwell, 2013, pp. 563–80.

Hall, Stuart. "The Spectacle of the Other." *Representation: Cultural Representations and Signifying Practices*, edited by Stuart Hall, Sage, 1997, pp. 223–79.

Harper, Sue. *Picturing the Past: The Rise and Fall of the British Costume Film*. British Film Institute, 1994.

Hartson, Mary. *Casting Masculinity in Spanish Film: Negotiating Identity in a Consumer Age*. Lexington Books, 2017.

Harvey, John. *Men in Black*. University of Chicago Press, 1995.

Healy, Robyn. *Balenciaga: Masterpieces of Fashion Design*. National Gallery of Victoria, 1992.

Heneghan, Dorota. "What is a Man of Fashion? Manuel Pez and the Image of the Dandy in Galdós's *La de Bringas*." *Anales Galdosianos* no. 44–5, 2009, pp. 57–70.

Hepburn, Audrey. "The Costumes Make the Actors: A Personal View." *Fashion in Film*, edited by Regine and Peter W. Engelmeier, Munich, Prestel, 1990, pp. 9–11.

Herzog, Charlotte. "'Powder Puff' Promotion: The Fashion Show-in-the-Film." *Fabrications: Costume and the Female Body*, edited by Jane Gaines and Charlotte Herzog, Routledge, 1990, pp. 134–59.

Hidalgo, Manuel. "Arrojarse a los pies del caballo." *Diario 16*, 18 September 1983, p. 38.

Hills, Matt. "The Question of Genre in Cult Film and Fandom: Between Contract and Discourse." *The SAGE Handbook of Film Studies*, edited by James Donald and Michael Renov, SAGE, 2008, pp. 436–53.

– "Subcultural Celebrity." *The Cult TV Book*, edited by Stacey Abbott, I.B. Tauris, 2010, pp. 233–8.

Hondius, Dienke. *Blackness in Western Europe: Racial Patterns of Paternalism and Exclusion*. Transaction Publishers, 2014.

hooks, bell. "Eating the Other: Desire and Resistance." *Media and Cultural Studies: Keyworks*, edited by Meenakshi Gigi Dirham and Douglas M. Kellner, Blackwell, 2001, pp. 424–38.

Hopewell, John. *Out of the Past: Spanish Cinema after Franco*. British Film Institute, 1986.

Hueso, Ángel Luis. *Catálogo del cine español: Películas de ficción 1941–1950*. Madrid: Cátedra, 1998.

Igor Prieto-Arranz, José, and Mihai Iacob. "The Perception of Romanian Immigrants in Spain: The Case of the *Hola, soy rumano* Campaign." *Bulletin of Spanish Studies* vol. 94, no. 10, 2017, pp. 1729–49.

Irvine, Susan. *Vogue on Balenciaga*. Quadrille Publishing, 2013.

Jancovich, Marc. "Cult Fictions: Cult Movies, Subcultural Capital and the Production of Cultural Distinctions." *Cultural Studies* vol. 16, no. 2, 2002, pp. 306–22.

Jancovich, Marc, et al. "Introduction." *Defining Cult movies: The Cultural Politics of Oppositional Taste*, edited by Mark Jancovich, Antonio Lázaro Reboll, Julian Stringer and Andy Willis, Manchester University Press, 2003, pp. 1–13.

Jeffers McDonald, Tamar. *Hollywood Catwalk: Exploring Costume and Transformation in American Film*. I.B. Tauris, 2010.

Jeffreys, Sheila. *Beauty and Misogyny: Harmful Cultural Practices in the West*. Routledge, 2005.

Jenkins, Henry. *Convergence Culture: Where Old and New Media Collide*. NYU Press, 2006.

Jobling, Paul. *Advertising Menswear: Masculinity and Fashion in the British Media since 1945*. Bloomsbury, 2014.

– *Man Appeal: Advertising, Modernism and Menswear*. Oxford: Berg, 2005.

– "Underexposed: Spectatorship and Pleasure in Men's Underwear Advertising in the Twentieth Century." *Paragraph* 26, nos. 1–2, 2003, pp. 147–62.

Join-Diéterle, Catherine. "Dior and Balenciaga: A Different Approach to the Body." *The Golden Age of Couture. Paris and London 1947–1957*, edited by Claire Wilcox, V&A Publications, 2007, pp. 139–56.

Jordan, Barry, and Mark Allinson. *Spanish Cinema: a Student's Guide*. Hodder Arnold, 2005.

Jordan, Barry, and Rikki Morgan-Tamosunas. *Contemporary Spanish Cinema*. Manchester University Press, 1998.

Jorza, Diana Roxana. "Triunfalismo nacional y mística guerrera en ¡Harka! y ¡A mí la legión!" *Bulletin of Hispanic Studies* vol. 89, nos. 7–8, 2012, pp. 49–59.

Jouve, Marie-Andrée. *Balenciaga*. Thames and Hudson, 1997.

Kaplan, E. Ann. "Is the Gaze Male?" *Feminism and Film*, edited by E. Ann Kaplan, Oxford University Press, 2000, pp. 119–38.

Kercher, Dona. *Latin Hitchcock: How Almodóvar, Amenábar, De la Iglesia, Del Toro and Campanella Became Notorious*. Wallflower Press, 2015.

Khan, Natalie. "Stealing the Moment: The Non-Narrative Fashion Films of Ruth Hogben and Gareth Pugh." *Film, Fashion and Consumption* vol. 1, no. 3, 2012, pp. 251–62.

Kim, Yeon-Soo. *The Family Album: Histories, Subjectivities and Immigration in Contemporary Spanish Culture*. Bucknell University Press, 2005.

Kinder, Marsha. "All About Brothers: Retroseriality in Almodóvar's Cinema." *All About Almodóvar: A Passion for Cinema*, edited by Brad Epps and Despina Kakoudaki, University of Minnesota Press, 2009, pp. 267–94.

– *Blood Cinema: The Reconstruction of National Identity in Spain*. University of California Press, 1993.

– "Restoring Broken Embraces." *Film Quarterly* vol. 63, no. 3, 2010, pp. 28–34.

King, Barry. "Embodying an Elastic Self: The Parametrics of Contemporary Stardom." *Contemporary Hollywood Stardom*, edited by Thomas Austin and Martin Barker, Arnold, 2003, pp. 45–61.

– *Taking Fame to Market: On the Pre-History and Post-History of Hollywood Stardom*. Palgrave Macmillan, 2015.

Koda, Harold, and Andrew Bolton. *Chanel*. Metropolitan Museum of Art/Yale University Press, 2005.

Köhn, Steffen. *Mediating Mobility: Visual Anthropology in the Age of Migration*. Wallflower Press, 2016.

Lannes, Horace. *Moda y vestuario en el cine argentino*. Buenos Aires, Instituto Nacional de Cine y Artes Visuales, 2010.

Laurino, Maria. *Were You Always an Italian?: Ancestors and Other Icons of Italian America*. W.W. Norton & Company, 2000.

Laver, James. *Costume and Fashion: A Concise History*. Thames and Hudson, 2002.

– *Modesty in Dress: An Inquiry into the Fundamentals of Fashion*. Heinemann, 1969.

Laverty, Christopher. *Fashion in Film*. Lawrence King, 2016.

Leese, Elizabeth. *Costume Design in the Movies*. BCW Publishing, 1976.

Lehman, Peter. *Running Scared: Masculinities and the Representation of the Male Body*. Wayne State University Press, 2007.

Lev, Leora. "Our Rapists, Ourselves: Women and the Staging of Rape in the Cinema of Pedro Almodóvar." *A Companion to Pedro Almodóvar*, edited by Marvin D'Lugo and Kathleen Vernon, Wiley-Blackwell, 2013, pp. 204–24.

Leymarie, Jean. *Chanel*. Abrams, 2010.

Lipovetsky, Gilles. *The Empire of Fashion: Dressing Modern Democracy*. Princeton University Press, 1994.

Llinás, Francisco. *José Antonio Nieves Conde: El oficio del cineasta*. Valladolid, 40 Semana Internacional de Cine, 1995.

López, Ianko. "Victoria Abril: No entiendo por qué Julieta no la he hecho yo." *Vanity Fair*, 20 February 2017. www.revistavanityfair.es/cultura /entretenimiento/articulos/entrevista-victoria-abril-desfile-andres-sarda -relacion-pedro-almodvar/23538.

López de Hierro, Helena. "Spanish Black." *Balenciaga in Black*, edited by Véronique Belloir et al., Rizzoli Electa, 2018, pp. 19–23.

Lurie, Alison. *The Language of Clothes*. Heinemann, 1981.

Maddison, Stephen. "All about Women: Pedro Almodóvar and the Heterosocial Dynamic." *Textual Practice* vol. 14, no. 2, 2000, pp. 265–84.

Madsen, Axel. *Chanel: A Woman of Her Own*. Henry Holt, 1990.

Marks, Laura. *The Skin of the Film. Intercultural Cinema, Embodiment, and the Senses*. Duke University Press, 2000.

Marquand, Liliou. *Chanel en la intimidad*. Madrid, Espasa-Calpe, 1991.

Marr, Matthew. *The Politics of Age and Disability in Contemporary Spanish Film: Plus Ultra Pluralism*. Routledge, 2013.

Marsh, Steven. "Missing a Beat: Syncopated Rhythms and Subterranean Subjects in the Spectral Economy of *Volver*." *All About Almodóvar: A Passion for Cinema*, edited by Brad Epps and Despina Kakoudaki, University of Minnesota Press, 2009, pp. 339–56.

– *Popular Spanish Film under Franco: Comedy and the Weakening of the State*. Palgrave Macmillan, 2005.

Marshall, P. David. *Celebrity and Power: Fame in Contemporary Culture*. University of Minnesota Press, 1997.

Martí-Olivella, Jaume. "Cuba and Spanish Cinema's Transatlantic Gaze." *Arizona Journal of Hispanic Cultural Studies* 5, 2001, pp. 161–76.

Martín, Annabel. "The *Desarrollismo* Years: The Failures of Sexualised Nationhood in 1960s Spain." *Spanish Erotic Cinema*, edited by Santiago Fouz-Hernández, Edinburgh University Press, 2017, pp. 55–73.

Martin, Richard. "Preface." *A History of Men's Fashion*, editded by Farid Chenoune, Paris, Flammarion, 1993, pp. 3–5.

Martin, Richard, and Harold Koda. *Infra-Apparel*. Metropolitan Museum of Art, 1993.

Martín-Cabrera, Luis. "Postcolonial Memories and Racial Violence in *Flores de otro mundo*." *Journal of Spanish Cultural Studies* vol. 3, no. 1, 2002, pp. 43–55.

– "Los quinquis nunca fueron blancos: Infrarrealismo, interseccionalidad y postsoberanía en el cine de José Antonio de la Loma." *Fuera de la ley: asedios al fenómeno quinqui en la Transición española*, edited by Joaquín Florido Berrocal et al., Granada, Editorial Comares, 2015, pp. 109–27.

Martin-Márquez, Susan. "Constructing *Convivencia*: Miquel Barceló, José Luis Guerín, and Spanish-African Solidarity." *Border Interrogations: Questioning Spanish Frontiers*, edited by Benita Sampedro and Simon Doubleday, Berghahn Books, 2008, pp. 90–104.

– *Feminist Discourse and Spanish Cinema: Sight Unseen*. Oxford University Press, 1999.

– "Pedro Almodóvar's Maternal Transplants: From *Matador* to *All About My Mother*." *Bulletin of Hispanic Studies* vol. 81, no. 4, 2004, pp. 497–509.

– "A World of Difference in Home-Making: The Films of Icíar Bollaín." *Women's Narrative and Film in Twentieth-Century Spain*, edited by Ofelia Ferrán and Kathleeen Gleen, Routledge, 2002, pp. 256–72.

Martínez-Carazo, Cristina. "*Flores de otro mundo*: la pluralidad cultural como propuesta." *Letras Peninsulares* vol. 15, no. 2, 2002, pp. 377–90.

– "*Hola, ¿estás sola?* De Icíar Bollaín: Otro discurso, otra estética." *Letras femeninas* vol. 28, no. 2, 2002, pp. 77–94.

Martínez Expósito, Alfredo. *Cuestión de imagen: Cine y Marca España*. Vigo, Editorial Academia del Hispanismo, 2015.

Masterson, Araceli. "La genealogía femenina en *Flores de otro mundo* de Icíar Bollaín: vertebrando la nueva familia mestiza." *Arizona Journal of Hispanic Cultural Studies* 11, 2007, pp. 171–9.

Mathijs, Ernest. "Cronenberg Connected: Cameo Acting, Cult Stardom and Supertexts." *Cult Film Stardom: Offbeat Attractions and Processes of Cultification*, edited by Kate Egan and Sarah Thomas, Palgrave, 2013, pp. 144–62.

Mathijs, Ernest, and Jamie Sexton. "Introduction." *Cult Cinema: An Introduction*, edited by Ernest Mathijs and Jamie Sexton, Blackwell, 2011, pp. 1–9.

McCarthy, Lauren. "Penélope Cruz, New Face of John Hardy and Red Carpet Royalty, Has Come a Long Way from Her Self-Proclaimed 'Julia Roberts Wannabe' Days." *W Magazine*, 30 January 2019. www.wmagazine.com /story/penelope-cruz-john-hardy-red-carpet-fashion-tips/.

McClintock, Anne. *Imperial Leather: Race, Gender, and Sexuality in the Colonial Contest*. Routledge, 1995.

McDonald, Paul. "Reconceptualising Stardom." *Stars*, by Richard Dyer, British Film Institute, 1998, pp. 175–211.

– *The Star System: Hollywood's Production of Popular Identities*. Wallflower Press, 2000.

McDowell, Colin. *The Man of Fashion: Peacock Males and Perfect Gentlemen*. Thames and Hudson, 1997.

McKinney, Collin. "Men in Black: Fashioning Masculinity in Nineteenth-Century Spain." *Letras Hispanas* vol.8, no. 2, 2012, pp. 78–93.

McNeil, Peter, and Vicki Karaminas, editors. *The Men's Fashion Reader*. Oxford: Berg, 2009.

Mears, Patricia. "Balenciaga in the 1960s: Beyond Fashion." *Paris Refashioned 1957–1968*, edited by Colleen Hill, Yale University Press, 2017, pp. 182–205.

Medhurst, Andy. "Heart of Farce: Almodóvar's Comic Complexities." *All About Almodóvar: A Passion for Cinema*, edited by Brad Epps and Despina Kakoudaki, University of Minnesota Press, 2009, pp. 118–38.

Meeuf, Russell. *Rebellious Bodies: Stardom, Citizenship and the New Body Politics*. University of Texas Press, 2017.

Melero Salvador, Alejandro. *Placeres ocultos: Gays y lesbianas en el cine español de la transición*. Madrid, Notorious Ediciones, 2010.

Metz, Christian. *The Imaginary Signifier: Psychoanalysis and the Cinema*. Indiana University Press, 1982.

Miller, Lesley Ellis. *Balenciaga: Shaping Fashion*. V&A Publishing, 2007.

Mira, Alberto. *De Sodoma a Chueca: Una historia cultural de la homosexualidad en España en el siglo XX*. Barcelona, Egales, 2004.

– *Historical Dictionary of Spanish Cinema*. Scarecrow Press, 2010.

– "A Life, Imagined or Otherwise: The Limits and Uses of Autobiography in Almodóvar's Films." *A Companion to Pedro Almodóvar*, edited by Marvin D'Lugo and Kathleen Vernon, Wiley-Blackwell, 2013, pp. 88–104.

– *Miradas insumisas: Gays y lesbianas en el cine*. Barcelona, Egales, 2008.

– *Para entendernos: Diccionario de cultura homosexual, gay y lésbica*. Barcelona, Ediciones de la Tempestad, 1999.

– "*El verdugo*/The Executioner." *The Cinema of Spain and Portugal*, Wallflower, 2005, pp. 109–17.

Moreiras Menor, Cristina. *Cultura herida: Literatura y cine en la España democrática*. Madrid, Libertarias, 2002.

Moreno, Enrique. *Lola Montes, Reina de Reyes*. Madrid, Ediciones Morata, 1944.

Moro, Javier. *Mi pecado*. Madrid, Espasa, 2018.

Moseley, Rachel, editor. *Fashioning Film Stars: Dress, Culture, Identity*. British Film Institute, 2005.

Mulvey, Laura. "Visual Pleasure and Narrative Cinema." *Feminism and Film*, edited by E. Ann Kaplan, Oxford University Press, 2000, pp. 34–47.

Munich, Adrienne. "Introduction: Fashion Shows." *Fashion in Film*, edited by Adrienne Munich, Indiana University Press, 2011, pp. 1–12.

Muñoz, Paloma. "Las mujeres se adueñan también de los calzoncillos." *Revista Tiempo* 561, 1993, pp. 88–91.

Murray, Michelle. *Home Away from Home: Immigrant Narratives, Domesticity, and Coloniality in Contemporary Spanish Culture*. University of North Carolina Press, 2018.

– "The Politics of Looking in Fernando León de Aranoa's *Princesas* (2005)." *Studies in Spanish and Latin American Cinemas* vol. 11, no. 3, 2014, pp. 241–53.

Nadoolman Landis, Deborah. *Costume Design*. Amsterdam, Focal Press, 2003.

– *Costume Design*. Amsterdam, Focal Press, 2012.

– *Dressed: A Century of Hollywood Costume Design*. HarperCollins, 2007.

Nail, Thomas. *The Figure of the Migrant*. Stanford University Press, 2015.

Nair, Parvati. "Borderline Men: Gender, Place and Power in Representations of Moroccans in Recent Spanish Cinema." *Gender and Spanish Cinema*, edited by Steven Marsh and Parvati Nair, London: Berg, 2004, pp. 103–18.

Needham, Gary. "The Digital Fashion Film." *Fashion Cultures Revisited*, edited by Stella Bruzzi and Pamela Church Gibson, Routledge, 2013, pp. 103–11.

Okwodu, Janelle. "Penélope Cruz Leads a Parade of Chanel Muses in an Emotional Tribute to Karl Lagerfeld." *Vogue* 5 March 2019. www.vogue .com/article/penelope-cruz-chanel-muses-walk-karl-lagerfeld-final-show.

Oliva, Ignacio. "Inside Almodóvar." *All About Almodóvar: A Passion for Cinema*, edited by Brad Epps and Despina Kakoudaki, University of Minnesota Press, 2009, pp. 389–407.

Omi, Michael, and Howard Winant. *Racial Formation in the United States*. Routledge, 2015.

Oso Casas, Laura. "Dominican Women, Heads of Households in Spain." *Caribbean Migration to Western Europe and the United States: Essays on Incorporation, Identity, and Citizenship*, edited by Margarita Cervantes-Rodríguez, Ramón Grosfoguel, and Eric Mielants, Temple University Press, 2009, pp. 208–31.

Palencia, Isabel de. *El traje regional de España*. Madrid, Voluntad, 1926.

Paoletti, Jo. *The Pink and the Blue: Telling the Boys from the Girls in America*. Indiana University Press, 2012.

Parga, Mónica. "Las alpargatas de Castañer se convierten en obra de arte en el MOMA." *Vanity Fair*, 6 November 2017. www.revistavanityfair.es/lujo /articulos/museo-moma-nueva-york-alpargatas-castaner-yves-saint -laurent/27065.

Pascual, Luis Miguel. "Victoria Abril: Para Almodóvar yo estoy muerta." *El Mundo*, 14 January 2018. www.elmundo.es/loc/famosos/2018/02 /14/5a844998ca474109078b461e.html. Accessed on 30 January 2019.

Paulicelli, Eugenia. *Italian Style: Fashion and Film from Early Cinema to the Digital Age*. Bloomsbury, 2016.

Pavlović, Tatjana. *Despotic Bodies and Transgressive Bodies: Spanish Culture from Francisco Franco to Jesús Franco*. State University of New York Press, 2003.

Pavlović, Tatjana, Chris Perriam, and Nuria Triana Toribio. "Stars, Modernity, and Celebrity Culture." *A Companion to Spanish Cinema*, edited by Jo Labanyi and Tatjana Pavlovic, Wiley- Blackwell, 2013, pp. 319–42.

Peralta García, Lidia. *Los nuevos héroes del siglo XXI: Las migraciones subsaharianas vistas por el cine en España y África*. Barcelona, Editorial UOP, 2016.

Pérez, Jorge. *Confessional Cinema: Religion, Film, and Modernity in Spain's Development Years (1960–1975)*. University of Toronto Press, 2017.

– "Reframing Accountability in Spanish Immigration Cinema: Mediterranean Modernity in the Shortcomings of 'NGO Films'." *Journal of Mediterranean Studies* vol. 24, no. 2, 2015, pp. 215–29.

– "Significant Outfits: Almodóvar Wears Chanel." *Modern Language Notes* vol. 133, no. 2, 2018, pp. 336–56.

– "Undressing Opus Dei: Reframing the Political Currency of *Destape* Films." *Spanish Erotic Cinema*, edited by Santiago Fouz-Hernández, Edinburgh University Press, 2017, pp. 92–108.

– "Vestida para medrar: Rocío Dúrcal y la modernidad por debajo de las rodillas." *Un hispanismo para el siglo XXI: Ensayos de crítica cultural*, edited by Rosalía Cornejo-Parriego and Alberto Villamandos, Madrid, Biblioteca Nueva, 2011, pp. 81–101.

Pérez Perucha, Julio. *El cinema de Luis Marquina*. Valladolid, 28 Semana Internacional de Cine de Valladolid, 1983.

Pérez-Sánchez, Gema. "One Big Queer European Family? Immigration in Contemporary Spanish Gay and Lesbian Films." *21st-Century Gay Culture*, edited by David A. Powell, Newcastle-upon-Tyne, Cambridge Scholars Publishing. 2008, pp. 71–85.

Perriam, Chris. "Sara Montiel: entre dos mitos." *Archivos de la Filmoteca* 54, 2006, pp. 196–209.

– *Stars and Masculinities in Spanish Cinema*. Oxford University Press, 2003.

– "Victoria Abril in Transnational Context." *Hispanic Research Journal* vol. 8, no. 1, 2007, pp. 27–38.

Persánch, José María. "From Impurity of Thought toward the Glocalization of Whiteness in Spain." *Transmodernity* vol. 8, no. 2, 2018, pp. 110–37.

Phillips, Alastair, and Ginette Vincendeau, editors. *Journeys of Desire: European Actors in Hollywood*. British Film Institute, 2006.

Polan, Brenda, and Roger Tredre. *The Great Fashion Designers*. New York: Berg, 2009.

Polhemus, Ted. "The Invisible Man: Style and the Male Body." *Material Man: Masculinity, Sexuality, Style*, edited by Giannino Malossi, Harry Abrams, 2000, pp. 44–51.

Postrel, Virginia. *The Power of Glamour: Longing and the Art of Visual Persuasion*. Simon & Schuster, 2013.

Potvin, John. *Giorgio Armani: Empire of the Senses*. Ashgate, 2013.

Primer Plano. "Alerta contra la españolada," 137, 1943, n.p.

Primer Plano. "El biógrafo y el guionista de Lola Montes frente a frente." 212, 1944, n.p.

Primer Plano. "El estreno de la película *Idolos* a beneficio de la Asociación de la Prensa," 154, 1943, n.p.

Primer Plano. No. 160, 1943, n.p.

Primer Plano. "Ídolos." 161, 1943, n.p.

Primer Plano. "Lola Montes: ¡Sí, en España podemos hacer buen cine!" 186, 1944, n.p.

Quijano, Aníbal. "Coloniality of Power, Eurocentrism, and Latin America." *Nepantla* vol. 1, no. 3, 2000, pp. 533–80.

Quiong Yu, Sabrina. "Introduction: Performing Stardom: Star Studies in
    Transformation and Expansion." *Revisiting Star Studies*, edited by Sabrina
    Quiong Yu and Guy Austin, Edinburgh University Press, 2017, pp. 1–22.

Rabanal, Haley. "Rethinking Integration in Contemporary Spanish Film:
    Convivencia and the Cosmopolitan Outlook in Chus Gutiérrez's *Retorno a
    Hansala* (2008)." *Journal of Iberian and Latin American Studies* vol. 20, no. 2,
    2014, pp. 135–59.

Radcliffe Richards, Janet. *The Sceptical Feminist: A Philosophical Inquiry.*
    Penguin, 1982.

Radiocinema. 901943, n.p.

Radiocinema. "Ídolos." 94, 1943, n.p.

Radiocinema. 98, 1944, n.p.

Radiocinema. "Rápidos." 103, 1944, n.p.

Radner, Hilary, and Natalie Smith. "Fashion, Feminism and the Neo-Feminist
    Ideal: From Coco Chanel to Jennifer Lopez." *Fashion Cultures Revisited*,
    edited by Stella Bruzzi and Pamela Church Gibson, Routledge, 2013,
    pp. 275–86.

Rawle, Steven. "Hal Hartley's 'Look-out-Martin-Donovan's-in-the-house!'
    Shot: The Transformative Cult Indie Star-Director Relationship and
    Performance 'Idiolect'." *Cult Film Stardom: Offbeat Attractions and Processes of
    Cultification*, edited by Kate Egan and Sarah Thomas, Palgrave, 2013,
    pp. 126–43.

Rees-Roberts, Nick. *Fashion Film: Art and Advertising in the Digital Age.*
    Bloomsbury, 2018.

Reilly, Andrew and Sarah Cosbey, editors. *The Men's Fashion Reader.* Fairchild
    Books, 2008.

Renard, Santiago. "Las reinas Cristinas conquistan España. Cine, turismo,
    sexo e identidad." *Turistas de película: Sus representaciones en el cine hispánico*,
    edited by Antonia del Rey-Reguillo, Madrid, Biblioteca Nueva, 2013,
    pp. 107–27.

Rey-Ximena, José. *El vuelo del Ibis: Leslie Howard al servicio de Su Majestad
    Británica.* Madrid, Ediciones Facta, 2008.

Richards, Melissa. *Chanel: Key Collections.* Welcome Rain Publishers, 2000.

Rivière, Margarita. *Historia informal de la moda.* Barcelona, Plaza & Janés, 2013.

Ro, Carmen. *Mientras tú no estabas.* Madrid, La Esfera de los Libros, 2017.

Rodríguez Fernández, María del Carmen. "Relaciones de poder y de
    identidad en el cine hispano-caribeño contemporáneo: La madre tierra y el
    sujeto postcolonial." *Cinema Paraíso: Representaciones e imágenes audiovisuales
    en el Caribe Hispano*, edited by Rosana Díaz-Zambrana and Patricia Tomé,
    San Juan, Editorial Isla Negra, 2010, pp. 67–85.

Rodríguez Fuentes, Carmen. *Las actrices en el cine español de los cuarenta.*
    Benalmádena, Caligrama, 2002.

Rodríguez Ortega, Vicente. "Trailing the Spanish Auteur: Almodóvar's, Amenábar's and de la Iglesia's Generic Routes in the US Market." *Contemporary Spanish Cinema and Genre*, edited by Jay Beck and Vicente Rodríguez Ortega, Manchester University Press, 2009, pp. 44–64.

Rosales Herrera, Raúl. "El melodrama de la otredad: Mujeres afrocaribeñas en el cine español contemporáneo." *Fotogramas para la multiculturalidad: Migraciones y alteridad en el cine español contemporáneo*, edited by Mónica Cantero-Exojo, María Van Liew, and José Carlos Suárez, Valencia, Tirant Lo Blanch, 2012, pp. 95–113.

Sampedro, Benita, and Simon Doubleday. "Introduction." *Border Interrogations: Questioning Spanish Frontiers*. Berghahan Books, 2008, pp. 1–14.

Sánchez, Antonio. "Eduardo Casanova: No soporto la estética vacía, me da asco." *Levante: El Mercantil Valenciano*, 12 June 2017. www.urbanvlc.com /noticias/2017/06/12/eduardo-casanova-no-soporto-la-estetica-vacia -me-da-asco/.

Sánchez-Biosca, Vicente. "The Latin Masquerade: The Spanish in Disguise in Hollywood." *Journeys of Desire: European Actors in Hollywood*, edited by Alastair Phillips and Ginette Vincendeau, British Film Institute, 2006, pp. 133–9.

Sánchez Vidal, Agustín. *El cine de Florián Rey*. Zaragoza, Caja de Ahorros de la Inmaculada Aragón, 1991.

Sanderson, John. "To the Health of the Author: Art Direction in *Los abrazos rotos*." *A Companion to Pedro Almodóvar*, edited by Marvin D'Lugo and Kathleen Vernon, Wiley-Blackwell, 2013, pp. 471–94.

Santaolalla, Isabel. *The Cinema of Icíar Bollaín*. Manchester University Press, 2012.

– "Ethnic and Racial Configurations in Contemporary Spanish Culture." *Constructing Identity in Contemporary Spain: Theoretical Debates and Cultural Practices*, edited by Jo Labanyi, Oxford University Press, 2002, pp. 55–71.

– *Los "Otros": Etnicidad y "raza" en el cine español contemporáneo*. Zaragoza, Prensas Universitarias de Zaragoza, 2005.

Schager, Nick. "Broken Embraces." *Slant Magazine*, 21 September 2009. www.slantmagazine.com. Accessed on 6 May 2010.

Seguin Vergara, Jean-Claude. *Pedro Almodóvar, o la deriva de los cuerpos*. Murcia, Tres Fronteras Ediciones, 2009.

Shingler, Martin. *Star Studies: A Critical Guide*. Palgrave Macmillan, 2012.

Shohat, Ella, and Robert Stam. *Unthinking Eurocentrism: Multiculturalism and the Media*. Routledge, 2014.

Simmel, Georg. "Fashion." *American Journal of Sociology* vol. 62, no. 6, 1957, pp. 541–58.

Simpson, Mark. *Male Impersonators: Men Performing Masculinity*. Casell, 1994.

Smith, Justin. "Vincent Price and Cult Performance: The Case of Witchfinder
    General." *Cult Film Stardom: Offbeat Attractions and Processes of Cultification*,
    edited by Kate Egan and Sarah Thomas, Palgrave, 2013, pp. 109–25.
Smith, Paul Julian. *"Los abrazos rotos/Broken Embraces*. Lava Lovers
    and Celluloid Cocoons." June 2009. Blog: sites.google.com/site
    /pauljuliansmithfilmreviews/Home/los-abrazos-rotos-broken-embraces.
– "Almodóvar's Self-Fashioning: The Economics and Aesthetics of
    Deconstructive Autobiography." *A Companion to Pedro Almodóvar*, edited by
    Marvin D'Lugo and Kathleen Vernon, Wiley-Blackwell, 2013, pp. 21–38.
– *Contemporary Spanish Culture: TV, Fashion, Art and Film*. Polity Press, 2003.
– *Desire Unlimited: The Cinema of Pedro Almodóvar*. Verso, 2000.
– *Laws of Desire: Questions of Homosexuality in Spanish Writing and Film
    1960–1990*. Oxford University Press, 1992.
– *Vision Machines: Cinema, Literature and Sexuality in Spain and Cuba,
    1983–1993*. Verso, 1996.
– "Women, Windmills, and Wedge Heels." *Sight and Sound* vol. 16, no. 6, 2006,
    pp. 16.
S Moda. "Victoria Abril y Jean Paul Gaultier: Quien tiene un amigo
    (diseñador) tiene un tesoro." no. 14, 24 December 2011.
Soila, Tytti. "Introduction." *Stellar Encounters: Stardom in Popular European
    Cinema*, edited by Tytti Soila, Herts: John Libbey, 2009, pp. 1–18.
Solé, Carlota and Sònia Parella. "Migrant Women in Spain: Class, Gender, and
    Ethnicity." *Gender and Ethnicity in Contemporary Europe*, edited by Jacqueline
    Andall, Oxford: Berg, 2003, pp. 61–76.
Song, Rosi. "Migration, Gender, and Desire in Contemporary Spanish
    Cinema." *Border Interrogations: Questioning Spanish Frontiers*, edited by
    Benita Sampedro and Simon Doubleday, Berghahn Books, 2008, pp. 42–64.
Sota, Idoia. "Por qué los tacones de Dani Rovira consiguieron el efecto contrario
    al que buscaban." *La Vanguardia* 5 February 2017. www.lavanguardia.com
    /de-moda/20170205/414027364253/tacones-dani-rovira-feminismo.html.
Sotinel, Thomas. *Pedro Almodóvar*. Paris, Cahiers du cinéma, 2010.
Stacey, Jackie. *Star Gazing: Hollywood Cinema and Female Spectatorship*.
    Routledge, 1994.
Stanek, Mikołaj. "Patterns of Romanian and Bulgarian Migration to Spain."
    Europe-Asia Studies vol. 61, no. 9, 2009, pp. 1627–44.
Steele, Valerie. "Appearance and Identity." *Men and Women: Dressing the Part*,
    edited by Claudia Brush Kidwell and Valerie Steele, Smithsonian Institution
    Press, 1989, pp. 6–21.
– "Clothing and Sexuality." *Men and Women: Dressing the Part*, edited by
    Claudia Brush Kidwell and Valerie Steele, Smithsonian Institution Press,
    1989, pp. 42–63.
– *Fetish: Fashion, Sex and Power*. Oxford University Press, 1996.

– *Women of Fashion: Twentieth-Century Designers*. Rizzoli, 1991.

Stone, Rob. *Spanish Cinema*. Pearson, 2002.

– "¡Victoria? A Modern Magdalene." *Gender and Spanish Cinema*, edited by Steven Marsh and Parvati Nair, London, Berg, 2004, pp. 165–82.

Street, Sarah. *Costume and Cinema: Dress Codes in Popular Film*. Wallflower Press, 2001.

Svendsen, Lars. *Fashion: A Philosophy*. Reaktion Books, 2006.

Taraud, Christelle. "Virility in the Colonial Context: From the Late Eighteenth to the Twentieth Century." *A History of Virility*, edited by Alain Corbin, Jean-Jacques Courtine, and Georges Vigarello. Columbia University Press, 2016, pp. 325–45.

Tobin, Shelley. *Inside Out: A Brief History of Underwear*. The National Trust, 2000.

Tobin Stanley, Maureen. "Seeing (as) the Erotized and Exoticized Other in Spanish Im/migration Cinema: A Critical Look at the (De)Criminalization of Migrants and Impunity of Hegemonic Perpetrators." *Studies in 20th & 21st Century Literature* vol. 43, no. 2, 2019, pp. 1–26.

Torres, Steven. "Las contradicciones del cine quinqui en el seno de la reconfiguración del estado neoliberal." *Fuera de la ley: asedios al fenómeno quinqui en la Transición española*, edited by Joaquín Florido Berrocal et al., Granada, Editorial Comares, 2015, pp. 67–90.

Triana-Toribio, Nuria. *Spanish Film Cultures: The Making and Unmaking of Spanish Cinema*. British Film Institute, 2016.

– *Spanish National Cinema*. Routledge, 2003.

Troy, Nancy. *Couture Culture: A Study in Modern Art and Fashion*. MIT Press, 2003.

Tulloch, Carol. "Style-Fashion-Dress: From Black to Post-Black." *Fashion Theory* vol. 14, no. 3, 2010, pp. 273–304.

Uhlirova, Marketa. "One Hundred Years of the Fashion Film: Frameworks and Histories." *Fashion Theory* vol. 17, no. 2, 2013, pp. 137–58.

– "Preface: If Looks Could Kill." *If Looks Could Kill: Cinema's Images of Fashion, Crime and Violence*, edited by Marketa Uhlirova, Koenig Books, 2008, pp. 12–13.

Urrea, Inmaculada. *Coco Chanel: La revolución de un estilo*. Madrid, Ediciones Internacionales Universitarias, 1997.

Usabiaga, Pedro. *Un sueño de Balenciaga, el cine*. Getaria, Museo Cristóbal Balenciaga, 2013.

Vanaclocha, José. "El cine sexy celtibérico." *Cine español: cine de subgéneros*, edited by Equipo Cartelera Turia, Valencia, Fernando Torres, 1974, pp. 193–284.

Varderi, Alejandro. *Severo Sarduy y Pedro Almodóvar: Del barroco al kitsch en la narrativa y el cine postmodernos*. Madrid, Pliegos, 1996.

Vaughan, Hal. *Sleeping with the Enemy: Coco Chanel's Secret War*. Alfred Knopf, 2011.

Veblen, Thorstein. *The Theory of the Leisure Class*. Routledge, 2017.

Vernon, Kathleen. "Imperio, identidad y nostalgia: Cuba recuperada en el reciente cine español." *Cine, nación y nacionalidades en España*, edited by Nancy Berthier and Jean-Claude Seguín, Madrid, Casa Velázquez, 2007, pp. 185–202.

Vernon, Kathleen, and Eva Woods Peiró. "The Construction of the Star System." *A Companion to Spanish Cinema*, edited by Jo Labanyi and Tatjana Pavlovic, Wiley-Blackwell, 2013, pp. 293–318.

Vincendeau, Ginette. "Hot Couture: Brigitte Bardot's Fashion Revolution." *Fashioning Film Stars: Dress, Culture, Identity*, edited by Rachel Moseley, British Film Institute, 2005, pp. 134–46.

– *Stars and Stardom in French Cinema*. Continuum, 2000.

Vincenot, Emmanuel. "Superficialidad y mise en abyme: sobre dos tendencias de la imagen almodovariana." *Almodóvar: El cine como pasión. Actas del Congreso Internacional "Pedro Almodóvar,"* coordinated by Fran Zurián and Carmen Vázquez Varela, Cuenca, Ediciones de la Universidad de Castilla-La Mancha, 2005, pp. 243–53.

Viruela Martínez, Rafael. "The Romanian Migrants in Spain: An Exceptional Migratory Flow." *International Review of Social Research* vol. 1, no. 1, 2011, pp. 31–59.

Walker, Myra. *Balenciaga and His Legacy: Haute Couture from the Texas Fashion Collection*. Yale University Press, 2006.

Wallach, Janet. *Chanel: Her Style and Her Life*. Nan A. Talese/Doubleday, 1998.

Walsh, Anne. "Spanish Stars, Distant Dreams: The Role of Voice in Shaping Perception." *Stars in World Cinema: Screen Icons and Star Systems across Cultures*, edited by Andrea Bandhauer and Michelle Royer, I.B. Tauris, 2015, pp. 92–103.

Warner, Marina. *From the Beast to the Blonde*. Chatto & Windus, 1994.

Whittaker, Tom. "Sonorous Flesh: The Visual and Aural Erotics of Skin in Eloy de la Iglesia's *Quinqui* Films." *Spanish Erotic Cinema*, edited by Santiago Fouz-Hernández, Edinburgh University Press, 2017, pp. 154–68.

Willett, Cecil, and Phillis Cunnington. *The History of Underclothes*. Michael Joseph, 1951.

Williams, Linda. "Melancholy and Melodrama: Almodovarian Grief and Lost Homosexual Attachments." *All About Almodóvar: A Passion for Cinema*, edited by Brad Epps and Despina Kakoudaki, University of Minnesota Press, 2009, pp. 166–92.

Wilson, Elizabeth. *Adorned in Dreams: Fashion and Modernity*. University of California Press, 1987.

– "Introduction: Dressed to Kill: Notes on Dress and Costume in Crime Literature and Film." *If Looks Could Kill: Cinema's Images of Fashion, Crime and Violence*, edited by Marketa Uhlirova, Koenig Books, 2008, pp. 14–19.

Wilson, William. *Man at His Best: The Esquire Guide to Style*. Esquire Press, 1985.

Wilson-Kovacs, Dana. "The Fall and Rise of Erotic Lingerie." *Dressed to Impress: Looking the Part*, edited by Willliam Keenan, Oxford: Berg, 2001, pp. 159–77.

Wolf, Naomi. *The Beauty Myth: How Images of Beauty Are Used against Women*. Vintage, 1990.

Wolters, Nicholas. "Outfitting the Avant-Garde: Men's Fashion and Ramón Gómez de la Serna." *Hispanófila* 175, 2015, pp. 229–45.

Woods Peiró, Eva. *White Gypsies: Race and Stardom in Spanish Musicals*. University of Minnesota Press, 2012.

Yarza, Alejandro. *Un caníbal en Madrid: La sensibilidad camp y el reciclaje de la historia en el cine de Pedro Almodóvar*. Madrid, Libertarias, 1999.

Zannou, Santiago. "Una España sin referentes." *El País*, 5 July 2020.

Zecchi, Barbara. "All about Mothers: Pronatalist Discourses in Contemporary Spanish Cinema." *College Literature* vol. 32, no. 1, 2005, pp. 146–64.

– "Veinte años de inmigración en el imaginario fílmico español." *Imágenes del Otro. Identidad e inmigración en la literatura y el cine*, edited by Montserrat Iglesias, Madrid, Biblioteca Nueva, 2010, pp. 157–84.

Zecchi, Barbara, and Jacqueline Cruz. "Maternidad y violación: Dos caras del control sobre el cuerpo femenino." *La mujer en la España actual: ¿Evolución o involución?*, edited by Jacqueline Cruz and Barbara Zecchi, Barcelona, Icaria, 2004, pp. 147–74.

Index

Toronto Iberic